SCIENTIFIC REASONING FOR SOCIAL WORKERS
Bridging the Gap Between Research and Practice

LEONARD E. GIBBS

University of Wisconsin—Eau Claire

Merrill, an imprint of
Macmillan Publishing Company
New York

Collier Macmillan Canada, Inc.
Toronto

Maxwell Macmillan International Publishing Group
New York   Oxford   Singapore   Sydney

To Betsy and Martin

Cover Art: Brian Cook
Editor: Sally Berridge MacGregor
Developmental Editor: Linda James Scharp
Production Editor: Peg Connelly Gluntz
Art Coordinator: Raydelle M. Clement
Text Designer: Debra A. Fargo
Cover Designer: Russ Maselli

This book was set in Bookman.

Macmillan Publishing Company
866 Third Avenue, New York, New York 10022

Collier Macmillan Canada, Inc.

Library of Congress Catalog Card Number: 90–61327
International Standard Book Number: 0–675–21079–8

Printing: 1 2 3 4 5 6 7 8 9   Year: 1 2 3 4

FOREWORD

Professor Gibbs, who has worked as both a clinician and a researcher, has written a most timely book. Schools of social work have been teaching "research" for many years. But, historically, research and practice have been disconnected activities that often have run parallel to one another. Harkening back to the days of settlements and "scientific charity," when research strategies were very much a part of the social work repertoire, research-oriented social workers made futile arguments about the relevance and importance of research. Few practitioners listened. This text is intended to bridge that gap between research and practice.

Later, when science became relevant, it did so in a hostile way. As well-designed studies of social work practice were published in the late 1950s and into the decades of the '60s and '70s, the research findings did not support practice. In fact, the better studies found no difference between treated and untreated groups. It seemed as if we were wasting our time and money by doing social work.

All of that is changing. Practice has changed, partially as a result of those findings. Recent well-designed studies indicate positive results for many newer interventions, as well as some of the older ones. Practitioners are now incorporating research-based strategies to evaluate their own practice in the form of single system designs. More and more practitioners know how to evaluate an intervention by reviewing the literature, using computer databases, and collecting data from their own practice.

Professor Gibbs is the sole author of this text, which is unusual in this field. The book's practical focus is just one of many benefits from information being filtered through the lens of one person who has worked as both practitioner and researcher. He has produced an up-to-date guide to straight thinking and knowledge building specific to social work, not just sociology or social science in general. Amazingly, it contains over 600 references. The text reflects clinical reasoning literature and applies the most useful features of research methods for practical use. It guides and motivates the practitioner to take a question raised in practice and formulate it into a research question for which one can obtain specific answers.

Finally, the most common fallacies that clinicians fall prey to are discussed and laid to rest. This is a lucid guide to improving social work practice using scientific tools. Social work appears ready for this now. It has been a long time coming.

Fredrick W. Seidl, MSW, Ph.D.
Professor and Dean, School of Social Work
State University of New York at Buffalo

PREFACE

I vividly recall my first vital practice decision. I was 24 years old and a recent graduate of the Master of Science—Social Work (MSSW) Program at the University of Wisconsin—Madison. My first position was as an intake worker at a massive psychiatric facility. One of my first clients was a distraught woman who I thought might be in danger of committing suicide. Concerned about what she might do, yet reluctant to recommend that she be admitted to the hospital because of the stigma and stress that being an inpatient might cause her, I sought the advice of a warmhearted senior practitioner. He listened carefully as I described the client's situation, her history, and what I considered to be the most salient features of her mental status. Then he asked: "What is your gut feeling?"

For a moment I was baffled about how to reply. Feeling?! I empathized with the woman's pain. I wanted her to survive. At that moment, I did not realize that the kindly senior practitioner and I were mixing two questions: "How do you feel about that?" and "What is the probability of suicide in such a case?" We decided that she did not need to be admitted—neither of us was aware of the kind of evidence that will be evaluated in this text regarding risk assessment—and we were wrong. That night the woman attempted suicide and was admitted to the hospital. Fortunately, she lived, improved in the hospital setting, and continued to recover as an outpatient.

This example is not included to prove that had we just known the literature about suicide prediction we would have admitted this client at the outset, but to illustrate that there are two major dimensions in the helping process: (a) feelings that motivate us to empathize and to want to help our clients; and (b) reasoning about how best to help. This text acknowledges *both* dimensions of the helping process.

This research methods text and the exercises herein have one principal objective: to bridge the gap between practice and scientific thinking. This will be done through examples from practice, careful documentation from up-to-date sources, explanation of common errors in reasoning about practice that violate principles of good science, clear explanations of how basic research principles apply to practice, and even a modicum of humor. The text documents all major conclusions and is intended to demystify some of the greatest methodological advances of our times, including single-subject designs, explicitly stated heuristics (i.e., ways to understand cause), operational definitions of practice outcomes, meta-analysis (study synthesis), methods of formulating a specific research question, decision trees, principles of risk analysis, principles of survey design, and on-line computer searching to retrieve appropriate studies quickly enough to guide practice decision making.

This basic research methods text was class-tested for one quarter in a graduate course and over a two-year period in a class for advanced undergraduates. It is intended to be useful at the advanced undergraduate and beginning graduate levels.

Avoiding an emphasis on memorizing a survey of soon-to-be-forgotten research facts and procedures, this text focuses instead on a few basic research principles and how each one can be applied effectively in social work practice. It is not patterned after research texts in sociology, psychology, or medicine, but true to social work's eclectic approach, where a research advance in these disciplines can be modified for use, such advances are adapted with reference to a source.

Because the chapters follow a logical sequence and make frequent reference to prior chapters, they should be read in order. Research methods texts need a motivational chapter. If the reader encounters examples that effectively demonstrate why research principles are vital, half the battle is won; the rest is discovering exciting, new, and practical ways to reason about intervention. The first chapter's shocking historical examples from medicine, psychology, and social work are intended to motivate the reader to want to understand research principles for humane reasons. Each example illustrates lessons that demonstrate the importance of sound research methods. Chapters 2 and 3 define how scientific principles can be applied to thinking about practice situations, first through examples that illustrate weak, prescientific thinking, then by defining 10 characteristics of scientist-practitioners. (All names in examples given within this text are fictitious.) The case material presented in Chapter 4 illustrates how practitioners use rules of thumb as guidelines to judge whether a method is causing a client to change. These guidelines, because they concern basic principles of causality, form a preliminary intuitive base for principles of experimental design as defined and illustrated in Chapter 5. Midway through the book, Chapter 6 explains in step-by-step fashion how to formulate a clear, specific, testable question that implies a single-subject or a group study design. Chapter 7 underscores measurement's importance and outlines principles of good measurement for social workers. Chapter 8 details how to use on-line computer technology to locate studies to guide practice. Computer search logic can narrow a search to studies about effects of particular methods, for particular client types, against particular outcome criteria. Chapter 9 assumes that computer searches will create a new problem—information overload. To deal with this problem, the Quality of Study Rating Form was developed and pretested to rate study quality and treatment effect size reliably. Chapter 10 uses current examples from child-abuse research to illustrate how principles for risk assessment and decision trees can help practitioners make better decisions. Chapter 11 applies principles of survey design to show how case examples comprise extremely weak evidence in terms of what is generally true of clients or groups of clients. Chapter 12 assumes that the reader has resolved to incorporate this text's lessons into practice. It forewarns scientist-practitioners of potential difficulties, and suggests ways to over come them.

Acknowledgments

I wish to thank the following individuals for their help in the preparation and production of this book: All those affiliated with the Eau Claire Foundation, University Research and Creative Activities Grants Program, and the Office of Graduate Studies and University Research; Penny France, Barb Stevens, Carol Kane, and Richard Bell of the Reference Department, and Kay Henning of the Interlibrary Loan Department of the McIntire Library; Donna Raleigh of Academic Computing; Terry Fields of the Media Development Center; Wilbur Weder, program analyst, Family Support Administration; John Baker, Eau Claire Office of AFDC Quality Control; Susan J. Wells, Assistant Director, National Legal Resource Center for Child Advocacy and Protection, American Bar Association; Dorothy Whitcomb, Middleton Medical Library, University of Wisconsin—Madison; Bruce A. Thayer, School of Social Work, University of Georgia; Lynn Videka-Sherman, Dean of the School of Social Welfare, State University of New York at Albany; Joel Strayer, Social Worker, Eau Claire School District; Thomas Dow, M.D., Chippa Valley Eye Clinic; Cyndee Kaiser, cartoonist; Mary Bornac, Melissa Farrell, and Linda Reed, typists; Phil Groth, University of Wisconsin—Rock County; Michael Hakeem, Professor Emeritus, University of Wisconsin—Madison; Kathy Stahl, Department of Social Work, University of Wisconsin—Eau Claire; Pat Bennett, Poudre Valley Hospital, Fort Collins, Colorado; Brian Seemann, Rosemount Corporation; Linda James Scharp, Peg Gluntz, Gloria Jasperse, and Raydelle Clement, of Macmillan Publishing Company; the students in my Methods of Social Work Research class, who patiently and insightfully reacted to previous drafts of this text; and Betsy McDougall Gibbs for encouragement and editorial help.

Finally, I appreciate the comments and suggestions provided by the reviewers of my manuscript during the development of this text: Jack C. Finley, Portland State University; John W. Gibson, University of Washington; Morris D. Klass, Memphis State University; Nancy P. Kropf, Virginia Commonwealth University; Carol A. Heintzelman, Millersville University; Mona Schatz, Colorado State University; Dale L. Sultzbaugh, Bloomsburg University; and Victor L. Whiteman, Michigan State University.

CONTENTS

1

Motivation to Apply Scientific Thinking to Social Work

THE NEED TO MOTIVATE SOCIAL WORKERS AT THE BEGINNING OF THEIR RESEARCH COURSE

A most important prerequisite to the study of research methods is motivation. A text on the subject must cover this essential step—the reader needs to understand why it is vital to learn how principles of scientific thinking apply to social work practice. Indeed, motivation may be so important that if this chapter helps the reader feel the need to operate scientifically for humane reasons, half the battle may be won. The remaining half, learning the text's lessons about how to apply scientific principles to social work practice, should then be more purposeful and possibly easier. This chapter seeks to motivate using carefully chosen examples to illustrate how the need for scientific thinking applies universally to the helping professions. Each example illustrates at least one "lesson for practitioners" that underscores the need for a scientific approach to practice.

There are 12 lessons to be learned from the examples, each concerning a principle that can be applied to the helping process regardless of the professional's particular discipline. These principles are intended to motivate the reader to delve more deeply into the scientific maxims highlighted in the text.

AVOID DOING HARM

Good intentions do not necessarily yield good results. In spite of high hopes, empathic concern, and sincerely held beliefs, a practitioner's efforts may be ineffective or even harmful. In some instances, the damage may be traced directly to the intervention.

The history of the helping professions is fraught with examples of heroic efforts by well-intentioned practitioners who were harming or killing those they were supposedly "helping." This chapter begins by presenting two of medicine's more infamous instances of **iatrogenic effects,** that is, ailments induced by a treatment. The first example concerns the practice of bloodletting and the second, the use of mercury as a drug. The chapter then turns to questionable medical practices of more recent times: giving heavy concentrations of oxygen to premature babies, with resultant retrolental fibroplasia (a form of blindness), and the uncritical use of neuroleptic medications for the mentally ill, resulting in tardive dyskinesia (uncontrollable erratic movements). The chapter continues with a description of dubious procedures that have been administered and supported by human service workers—the Lifers' Program for delinquency prevention, encounter groups, and aggressive relocation of the aged.

By recognizing that some widely accepted procedures can be ineffective or worse, the practitioner may develop the questioning attitude essential to reasoning scientifically about practice. It is hoped that this first chapter will encourage practitioners to question and to be wary of a deadly fallacy: **well intentioned therefore effective.**

EXAMPLES OF DAMAGE CAUSED BY ANTIQUATED TREATMENT

Bloodletting: How They Bled the President

One of the most remarkable accounts of iatrogenic effects is that of President Washington's physicians, who used aggressive methods to treat him for what may have been a common cold. According to Washington's doctors (*Death of General George Washington,* 1799):

> Some time in the night of Friday, the 13th of December, having been exposed to a rain on the preceding day, GENERAL WASHINGTON was attacked with an inflammatory affection of the upper part of the wind pipe, called in technical language, Cynanche Trachealis. The disease commenced with a violent ague [fever with chills], accompanied with some pain in the upper and fore part of the throat, a sense of stricture in the deglutition [swallowing], which were soon succeeded by fever and a quick and laborious respiration. The necessity of blood-letting suggesting itself to the General, he procured a bleeder in the neighborhood, who took from his arm, in the night, twelve or fourteen ounces of blood. He could not be prevailed on by the family, to send for the attending physician till the following morning, who arrived at Mount Vernon at about eleven o'clock on Saturday. Discovering the case to be highly alarming, and foreseeing the fatal tendency of the disease, two consulting physicians were immediately sent for, who arrived, one at half after three, and the other at four o'clock in the afternoon; in the mean time were employed two copious bleedings, a blister was applied to the part affected, two moderate doses of calomel [mercury salts] were given, and an injection was administered, which operated on the lower intestines, but all without any perceptible advantage, the respiration becoming still more difficult and painful. On the arrival of the first consulting physician, it was agreed, as there were yet no signs of accumulation in the bronchial vessels of the lungs, to try the effect of another bleeding, when about thirty-

"I told you the treatment might produce harmful effects."

two ounces were drawn, without the least apparent alleviation of the disease. Vapours of vinegar and water were frequently inhaled, ten grains of calomel were given, succeeded by repeated doses of emetic tartar, amounting in all to five or six grains, with no other effect than a copious discharge from the bowels. The power of life seemed now manifestly yielding to the force of the disorder [perhaps to the force of the treatment]; blisters were applied to the extremities, together with a cataplasm of bran and vinegar to the throat. Speaking, which had been painful from the beginning, now became almost impracticable: respiration grew more and more contracted and imperfect, till half after eleven on Saturday night, when, retaining the full possession of his intellects, he expired without a struggle! (p. 475–476)

Lesson for Practitioners

1. Reverence for the client does not ensure the method's success.

Bleeding may well have caused Washington's untimely death at age 67.

Why on earth would those devoted to helping others practice such grisly procedures? Haller's (1981) history of bleeding suggests that one possible reason was pure speculation—ancient observers might have noticed that hemorrhages sometimes preceded critical periods of some diseases. These observers might have noticed the sedative effects of blood loss, or other changes in pulse and respiration.

Certain theories that sounded plausible in the 1790s no longer sound plausible today. Haller (1981) identified two dominant theoretical orientations among bleeders: revulsion and derivation. Revulsionists believed that disease was best treated by tapping a vein near the part of the body most affected by the disease. Thus, madness might be alleviated by coaxing the disorder out of the head with the affected blood. Derivationists, on the other hand, believed that one should tap a vein as far from the diseased part as possible, and by slow bleeding and gentleness, coax the disorder away from the affected part.

Lesson for Practitioners

2. Reasons for using a method that may sound sensible at the time are not always legitimate.

Another reason for bloodletting may have been tradition. Neither Hippocrates nor the early Greek physicians referred to bleeding as a new technique. It had been practiced for thousands of years before it was used by physicians in Europe and in the United States.

Lesson for Practitioners

3. Years of experience with a method do not necessarily prove its effectiveness.

Unlike many who died in the care of well-intentioned bleeders, the practice of bleeding died a slow and fitful death. Advocacy for the practice by the medical profession declined gradually from 1830 to 1890, with a mild resurgence in the 1870s (Bryan, 1964). Haller (1981) argues that bleeding ceased to make sense in light of advances in chemistry, pharmacology, physiology, and pathology, and that it was these advances that sounded the death knell for bleeding. However, concurrent with these advances was the advent of statistical record keeping and data analysis (see Table 1.1 for Bennett's tallies of mortality data).

Modern uses for the leech anticoagulant hirudin and use of leeches to remove blood from delicate tissues after microsurgery do not prove that, as a general rule, bloodletting was effective (Conniff, 1987). Such highly specific use in a limited number of cases bears no resemblance to the indiscriminate bleeding practices of the past.

Mercuric Chloride (Calomel) Used as a Drug

The use of the grainy white powder calomel often went hand in hand with bloodletting. Calomel, now called mercuric chloride, is now known to be a deadly poison. At one time calomel was used as a purgative to clean the bowels; it produced a green stool thought to be bile from the liver. It was taken by sprinkling it on food, by swallowing a capsule, by smearing an ointment on the body, or by breathing fumes given off by heated mercury compounds.

Mathias (1810), a physician whose titles included "Surgeon Extraordinary to the Queen and Her Majesty's Household," was one of the first to question the use of calomel to the extent of writing about its possibly damaging effects. While not altogether condemning it, he criticized its overzealous use, complaining that

TABLE 1.1
Bleeding practices and associated death rates

Method	Deaths
Heroic Bleeding	1 in 3
Bleeding and Tartar Emetic	1 in 4½
Moderate Bleeding	1 in 10
Expectant Medicine	1 in 7¼

Note: From *Clinical Lectures on the Principles and Practice of Medicine* (pp. 250–292) by J. H. Bennett, 1863 (2nd American edition from the last Edinburgh edition), New York: William Wood. Adapted by J. S. Haller (1981). *American Medicine in Transition 1840–1910.* Urbana: University of Illinois Press, p. 56.

(Mathias, 1810): "Even in more modern times, we find some practitioners who use this mineral in quantities [from 20 to 30 grains per day], and upon principles hardly credible" (p. viii). He then described ill effects that he himself had observed: "I have before observed that, during a mercurial course when the mouth is much affected, the dentes molares [teeth] by their pressure of their inflamed cheeks often occasion an ulceration and slough [fall out]" (p. 120).

Other questions about the efficacy of this treatment came to the fore. According to Brieger (1967), during the American Civil War the surgeon-general of the Union Army, Dr. William A. Hammond, issued an order banning calomel from the supply table and from all requisitions by army medical directors. Hammond was concerned about reports of excessive salivation and mercurial gangrene among soldiers treated with calomel. Violent criticism of Hammond's order erupted immediately. Editors of medical journals and leaders of medical societies called for his resignation, denouncing Hammond on the grounds that he was "a mere theorist who was not a practicing physician" (p. 220).

Hammond's critics won the struggle—he was forced to resign. We know now that Hammond's unpopular stand and Mathias's skepticism about the therapeutic value of large doses of calomel were well-founded. Seventeen grains of mercuric chloride can be fatal (Eau Claire Poison Control Center, personal communication, January 27, 1988). Those who had administered a dosage of 20 to 30 grains very likely were killing their patients.

Lesson for Practitioners

4. Heroic measures do not ensure heroic results.

SOME QUESTIONABLE MODERN MEDICAL PROCEDURES

Oxygen Therapy for Premature Infants

This account of the early history of retrolental fibroplasia (RLF) is based on the perceptive and candid comments of medical educator William A. Silverman, who warned those contemplating new and untested treatment methods that they are like those in a darkened fireworks factory: "It is better to curse the darkness, than to light the wrong candle" (Silverman, 1975, p. 2).

According to Silverman, Stewart Clifford of Boston was one of the first physicians to observe the RLF disorder when he went out on a call in Dorchester for a routine home visit on February 14, 1941, to examine an infant girl. Clifford was shocked to find during his examination that the well-developed infant, who had been born prematurely the previous November, was blind.

Just after arranging a consultation for this child, Dr. Clifford got an urgent call from a prominent Boston family to examine a 7-month-old twin who had been born on July 13, 1940 (the other twin had died). The family was concerned about the surviving child's unusual behavior. When Clifford arrived at the home, he found the same features as in the child he had seen earlier. Again, he had to tell the family their child was blind.

Clifford then called in a consulting physician, Theodore Terry, who at first thought the infants had congenital cataracts. After seeing still more cases of the disorder, however, Terry began to suspect a pattern. He noted "a grayish-white, opaque membrane behind each crystalline lens . . . [and] a jerky, irregular, and somewhat reaching nystagmus [involuntary, rapid movement of the eyeball]" (Terry, 1942, p. 203). (Figure 1.1 shows a normal retina compared with one typical of RLF.) He concluded: "In view of these findings [that the cases all involved prematurity] perhaps this complication should be expected in a certain percentage of premature infants. If so, some new factor has arisen in extreme prematurity to produce such a condition" (p. 204). Terry's observations turned out to be tragically correct. Later investigations confirmed that approximately 4% of extremely premature babies developed the eye symptoms and, in spite of all efforts, went blind (Owens & Owens, 1950).

Needless to say, pediatricians and ophthalmologists searched diligently for the cause or causes of the disorder. At first, oxygen therapy seemed an unlikely candidate. Premature infants most often died of respiratory problems, and oxygen seemed to make breathing much easier for ones so small. Initially, oxygen was administered by mask or by a tube inserted into the nostrils, but later the oxygen was piped into an air-tight incubator. Premature infants placed in these incubators sometimes received pure oxygen, fully in accordance with manuals describing accepted practice for treating premature infants during this period.

According to James and Lanman (1976), among the many hypotheses investigated for what caused the blindness were: use of artificial light (but an experiment where infants had one eye patched failed to determine a difference between patched and unpatched eyes); Vitamin E deficiency (but promising early results could not be reproduced); lack of the hormone ACTH (but a randomized trial found higher rates of blindness among infants treated with the ACTH); lack of supplemental vitamins (but those who received them fared no better than those who did not); insufficient Vitamin A (but trials found no protective effects of the vitamin); and drinking cow's milk (but results on kittens could not be replicated on children).

It was Australian physician Kate Campbell who noted that there had been few cases of RLF before a more efficient method for delivering oxygen had been

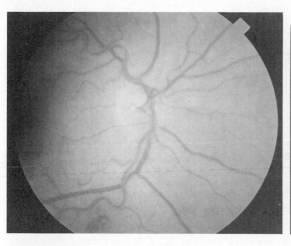 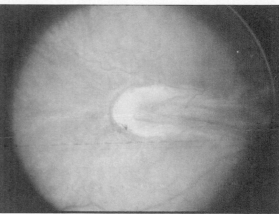

FIGURE 1.1

*Normal retina (left) and retina affected by RLF (right). (Source: C. Thomas Dow, M.D.,
Chippewa Valley Eye Clinic, Eau Claire, WI.)*

installed in her hospital's nursery (Campbell, 1951). Table 1.2 summarizes Campbell's experience with high and moderate oxygen levels during a 3-year period at two hospitals.

Though Campbell's numbers were small and her procedures for measuring oxygen levels were not clearly stated, the values given in Table 1.2 show that 23 of 123 infants receiving high amounts of oxygen contracted RLF (19%)—in the other two groups receiving moderate amounts, only 4 of 58 (7%).

With Campbell's promising evidence to draw on, doctors at an American hospital alternately assigned every other premature infant to high-oxygen groups and monitored the incidence of RLF. They found that among the 60 infants in the high-oxygen group, 12 became blind as a result of RLF, as contrasted with only 1 in the low-oxygen group—and that infant had been on supplemental oxygen for 10 days (Patz, Hoeck, & De La Cruz, 1952). Patz and his associates concluded that "the data suggest strongly that high oxygen administration is a factor in the pathogenesis of retrolental fibroplasia" (p. 1248). Subsequent carefully controlled studies, both on animals and on humans, have supported this conclusion (James & Lanman, 1976).

TABLE 1.2

*Retrolental fibroplasia (RLF) in
high and moderate oxygen
groups*

Oxygen Group	RLF	No RLF	Total
High	23 (19%)	100 (81%)	123 (100%)
Moderate	4 (7%)	54 (93%)	58 (100%)

Note: From "Intensive Oxygen Therapy As a Possible Cause of Retrolental Fibroplasia: A Clinical Approach" by Kate Campbell, 1951, *Medical Journal of Australia, 2,* p. 49. Copyright © 1951 by *The Medical Journal of Australia,* adapted by permission.

Consequently, texts in the field of pediatrics published prior to 1954 that had recommended liberal use of oxygen were replaced by texts that advised sparing use. Local history of the RLF epidemic reflects change in the literature. In California the number of RLF cases had risen steadily—from 1 in 1946 to approximately 90 in 1951. Then the number declined steadily to 1 case in 1958 (Silverman, 1975, slide 23).

Lesson for Practitioners
5. Before widespread use, a method should be carefully evaluated.

The case of the deleterious effects of administering high levels of oxygen is not yet closed, however. Although the preponderance of evidence still supports claims that high oxygen levels caused the epidemic of RLF, new evidence and a reanalysis of data from earlier studies indicate that RLF is most strongly associated with very low birth weight; so there may be many factors, compounded with the amount of oxygen administered, that can affect the oxygenation of the delicate tissues in a child's eye (Lucey & Dangman, 1984; Shapiro, 1986). There is a new name for retrolental fibroplasia—"retinopathy of prematurity" (National Library of Medicine, 1988, p. 409), but whatever the name, affected children are just as blind.

Neuroleptic Medication and Tardive Dyskinesia

Antipsychotic medications have had a profoundly positive effect on treatment for schizophrenia. In 1955 the census in U.S. mental hospitals had reached its apex at 559,000. The decline in the years that followed can be attributed largely to the advent of neuroleptic medications, for example, Thorazine, Prolixin, Haldol, Stelazine, Mellaril, Compazine, Quide, Trilafon, Serentil, and Moban. Still, in spite of their therapeutic value, neuroleptic medications may produce uncoordinated movements—tardive dyskinesia—which may or may not be reversible.

Chouinard and Bradwejn (1982) described the case of a 61-year-old Chinese woman who came to them for medical treatment. She had been a prostitute and had a history of alcohol abuse. At age 52, she developed a "paranoid psychosis with auditory hallucinations of an accusatory nature, paranoid delusions, and regressive behavior" (p. 360). After 3 months of neuroleptic injections, her physicians noted akathisia (severe muscle rigidity causing frequent changes in position in an attempt to find a comfortable position) and akinetic parkinsonian symptoms (impairment of voluntary movement). About 8 months after the injections of neuroleptic medications began, she developed "severe constant dyskinetic movements of her pelvis and her arms and legs, which resulted in her having an impaired gait" (p. 361). On her admission to a neurological institute, it was determined she had tardive dyskinesia induced by neuroleptic medication. Consequently, all antipsychotic medications were discontinued. Four months later her symptoms ceased. At age 56, when her symptoms returned, she began taking fluphenazine (more commonly known as Prolixin or Periril) orally. After 14 months of this medication, she developed mild peribuccal movements (cheek muscle spasms). Four months later, she experienced "full-blown dyskinesia with severe movements of the lips, tongue, arms and legs, and pelvis, and her respiration was irregular" (p. 361). While her earlier symptoms may have been the reversible type (Jeste, Jeste, & Wyatt, 1983), the patient's symptoms were now chronic—3 years after her neuroleptics were discontinued she still had the symptoms.

At best, the symptoms of tardive dyskinesia are troublesome; at worst, debilitating. As described by Krupp and Chatton (1982):

> *Tardive dyskinesia* is a syndrome [group of symptoms] of abnormal involuntary stereotyped movements of the face, mouth, tongue, and limbs occurring after months or (usually) years of treatment with neuroleptic agents. . . . Early manifestations include fine worm-like movements of the tongue at rest and facial tics [twitches] or jaw movements of recent onset. Later manifestations include bucco-linguo-masticatory movements [involving muscles of cheek, tongue, and jaw], lip smacking, chewing motions, mouth opening and closing, puffing of the cheeks, eye blinking, choreoathetoid [jerky, writhing] movements of the extremities. (p. 613)

Such involuntary movements can be deeply distressing to those afflicted. Rosen, Mukherjee, Olarte, Varia, and Cardenas (1982) found that among 70 patients who were diagnosed as having tardive dyskinesia, a third were fully aware of their irregular movements; this awareness increased with the severity of the irregular movements.

Although tardive dyskinesia does occur approximately three-and-one-half times as frequently among those treated with neuroleptics than among those not so treated, the fact that it occurs at times in the absence of neuroleptics makes it difficult to determine just how much of a contributing cause neuroleptics are (Jeste & Wyatt, 1981). In their review of 36 studies measuring the prevalence of tardive dyskinesia, Jeste and Wyatt (1981) reported that their sketchy evidence implied the syndrome was uncommon (possibly 0.5%) among mental patients before the advent of neuroleptics.

One possible problem with early studies is that clinicians might not have known what to watch for in diagnosing the syndrome. Jeste and Wyatt (1981) reported that in more recent studies, higher rates of dyskinesia were found among those who received the drugs. They also stated that among the 36 studies reviewed, the rate of tardive dyskinesia among chronically mentally ill patients was 13.6% before 1970. After 1970 it rose to 23.3%, and the most recent 5 studies place the rate at 25.7%.

Lesson for Practitioners

6. Although initial experience with a method may be positive, negative effects may become apparent in the long run.

Given such evidence regarding the prevalence of tardive dyskinesia, how to prevent iatrogenic effects of neuroleptics and still use them to the benefit of the chronically mentally ill may become an increasingly vital topic for mental health workers. In the opinion of Kalachnik (1985), systems to monitor patients for dyskinesia are "not only possible but mandatory for any facility using neuro-leptic drugs" (p. 133). He described several court cases in which patients and their families were awarded substantial settlements because prescribers had not warned their patients of the potential for tardive dyskinesia, nor watched for the first appearance of dyskinetic movements, and had prescribed excessive amounts of neuroleptics. Wettstein (1983) asserts that clients and their families should give informed consent before medications are used in long-term treatment.

DAMAGE CAUSED BY PSYCHOSOCIAL TREATMENT

Juvenile Awareness Project

In March 1977, I chanced to hear a radio interview with Judge George J. Nicola of the Juvenile and Domestic Relations Court, Middlesex County, New Bruns-wick, New Jersey. Judge Nicola described the Lifers' Program, which he consid-ered to be a remarkably effective and inexpensive program for preventing criminal acts among delinquency-prone youths. Also notable was the fact that the program was run almost exclusively by inmates of Rahway State Prison in New Jersey. Juveniles were brought to the prison to hear from members of the Lifers' Club—convicts serving life sentences. It was believed that the tragic testimonies of the inmates convinced the juveniles of the consequences of delinquent behav-ior—the road that they, themselves, now wish they had not taken.

In response to my request, Judge Nicola sent more information about the Juvenile Awareness Project run by the lifers. His packet included letters from the Lifers' Group outlining the purpose of the program, copies of laudatory newspa-per articles from communities scattered around the country, and supportive let-ters from local police, probation, and school officials.

Shortly after its inception, according to articles in Judge Nicola's packet, the Lifers' Program caught the imagination of members of the popular press. One newspaper article, "Inmates Detail Facts of Life" (Eastmond, 1976a), describes how young delinquents were warned: They were informed that if they were im-prisoned they would become victims of homosexual rape because of their youthful attractiveness, they were told that violence and murder were commonplace among inmates who preyed upon each other and killed over a pack of cigarettes, they were advised that prison food was terrible and that prison life was lonely without friends and family.

Another article (Golan, 1977) begins:

> The 11-year-old boy, shaking, faced the convicted murderer as he threatened the boy with an iron rod. "First, I'm gonna beat you," the murderer said, "and then I'm gonna rape you."
>
> In the distance a prison door clanged shut, reminding the boy—a Hoboken juvenile who had committed several minor offenses—that he was now in maxi-mum-security Rahway State. (p. 6)

The success rate of the Lifers' Program was touted by the press. According to an article titled, "It Is Like Hell," that appeared in the *Los Angeles Times* (p.

4), "In the six months that the program has been underway, three hundred youths have visited Rahway. Only four are known to have subsequently been arrested for a new crime." The *Asbury Park Press,* Neptune, New Jersey (Eastmond, 1976b), reported that "only four are known to have been subsequently arrested for a new crime" (p. A19).

The Scared Straight *Film*

Of all the accounts about the Lifers' Program, by far the most well-known is the powerfully sensational *Scared Straight* (Shapiro, 1978) television documentary (now available as a 35mm film). This one-hour program, narrated by actor Peter Falk, vividly describes the experiences of 17 youths with the Juvenile Awareness Project. After being aired first in Los Angeles, the sponsor, Signal Companies, Incorporated, showed it nationally in hundreds of major cities in spring of 1979.

The film begins with an opening narration:

> Over 8,000 juvenile delinquents have sat in fear on these hard wooden benches, and for the first time they really heard the brutal realities of crime and prisons. The results of this unique program arc astounding. Participating communities report that 80 to 90 percent of the kids that they sent to Rahway went straight after leaving this stage. That's an amazing success story, and it is unequalled by traditional rehabilitation methods. (Shapiro, 1978)

The film then shows the inmates taking turns yelling, often inches from the juveniles' faces, about the degradation, fear, and violent homosexual behavior that they consider to be commonplace in prison. The language is rough and brutally explicit.

This segment is followed by a statement by Falk that of the 17 juveniles shown in *Scared Straight*, 16 are "straight" 3 months after Rahway. The film ends with statements by prison officials, juvenile probation officers, guards, and judges affirming that the program is effective.

Lesson for Practitioners

7. Personal experience with a method does not guarantee desirable results.

The Formal Evaluation

In 1977, after approximately 2,000 juveniles had participated in the Lifers' Program, James Finckenauer, a professor at Rutgers University, was asked by the commissioner of the New Jersey Department of Corrections to conduct an evaluation study. Finckenauer's (1982) goals were to determine how the confrontation with the inmates was viewed by the subjects, whether the program had a constructive influence on future behavior of the subjects, and which subjects were most likely to benefit from participation.

Concerned that results might be biased if either severely delinquent or unusually "straight" subjects were admitted to the program from referring agencies, Finckenauer used a stratified random sampling procedure to select 100 participants. That is, from his list of 49 agencies that referred clients to the program, he selected 28 agencies at random (i.e., each agency had an equal chance of being chosen). Then he selected a number of subjects from each agency proportionate to the number of eligible subjects served at each agency.

Unfortunately, Finckenauer ran into problems collecting his data: Only 11 agencies provided the necessary names. Some were simply uncooperative; others could not provide transportation or could not obtain permission from parents of prospective participants. Also, there was an unwillingness to accept random assignment to the program or to a control (nontreated) group. Ultimately, 6 counseling agencies, 2 police departments, a high school, a neighborhood employment service, and a YMCA provided candidates.

Initially, Finckenauer's design called for random assignment of 100 juveniles to either a 50-member treatment program or a 50-member control (or nontreatment) group. Ultimately, due to attrition, assignment was random (as Finckenauer defined it) for only 5 of the 11 agencies; however, he still considered the design "sufficiently rigorous to protect against the effects of extraneous variables on the outcome measures" (p. 121).

In order to test the deterrent effect of the fear and intimidation experienced by the program's participants, Finckenauer and his assistant consulted the juvenile court records for each subject before beginning the experiment, and again 6 months later.

Pretreatment measures for participants and controls were almost identical; however, posttreatment differences favored *controls*. That is, 6 months after the program ended, fewer controls had committed a delinquent act than had program participants!

The data in Table 1.3 indicate that 81 juveniles of the original 100 were included in the experiment and were successfully followed up at posttest. Just under 59% of experimentals (program participants) did not display delinquent behavior in the 6 months following their exposure to the Lifers' Program. During the same period, almost 89% of controls (nonparticipants) avoided delinquent behavior. Thus the statistically significant difference of about 30% favors controls. Controls also committed statistically significant less-serious offenses. These differences favoring controls have held up in Finckenauer's subsequent analyses (1982, pp. 139–147).

Shortly after Finckenauer published his preliminary findings, journals for corrections professionals, such as *Corrections Digest* and *Law Enforcement News,* carried summaries of his study. A detailed pamphlet distributed by the National Center on Institutions and Alternatives (undated) concluded: "Thus, the remarkable public acclaim presently surrounding this program is for the most part groundless, a product of excessive hype, not of a reasoned strategy for solving a severely troubling problem" (p. 16).

Possibly in response to Finckenauer's negative findings, professionals began to warn against adopting the Lifers' Programs uncritically. In June 1979, after 30 states had started such programs locally, the Subcommittee on Human Resources of the Committee on Education and Labor met in the House of Representatives to hear testimony regarding the effectiveness of the program and to investigate claims that the makers of the *Scared Straight* documentary had biased the re-

TABLE 1.3
Comparison of experimentals versus controls by outcome

	Success	Failure	Total
Experimentals	27 (58.7%)	19 (41.3%)	46 (56.8%)
Controls	31 (88.6%)	4 (11.4%)	35 (43.2%)
Total	58	23	81

$\chi^2 = 8.87$; 1 *df*; $p < .01$; $c = .44$ (corrected).

Note: James O. Finckenauer, SCARED STRAIGHT! AND THE PANACEA PHENOMENON, © 1982, p.135. Reprinted by permission of Prentice-Hall, Inc., Englewood Cliffs, NJ.

sponses of the juveniles (Bunis, 1980). Members of the American Correctional Association's Delegate Assembly issued a policy statement ("Scared Straight," 1979, p. 40) urging that if such programs are to be started, they should include:

1. A "monitored" research design to evaluate the impact of such a program
2. Procedures that are sensitive to the participants and to the security needs of the institution
3. Careful selection of both the adult offenders and juvenile participants
4. A commitment from involved juvenile supervisory agencies to provide follow-up counseling services
5. Provisions for adult offenders to develop positive motivation and constructive behavior significant to their own habilitation

The statement concluded,

> We are greatly concerned about the accent placed upon a simplistic approach to such an extremely complex problem. Attack treatment and scare tactics are not new or innovative. They are rooted in ancient history as well as in many past treatment attempts in the United States. (p. 40)

Lesson for Practitioners

8. Simplistic cures for complex problems are not likely to be effective.

Encounter Groups

History

Encounter groups, sometimes called sensitivity groups, T-groups, basic encounter groups, growth laboratories, or communications labs, reached the height of their popularity in the early 1970s. The mecca of the encounter group movement was the breathtakingly beautiful 9-acre Esalen retreat, located in the Big Sur region of California. There, according to Maliver (1973), a unique combination of intellectual and far eastern religious thought combined to generate the encounter movement. During the early 1970s, thousands flocked to Esalen sessions conducted by renowned leaders of the encounter group movement including Fritz Pearls, Carl Rogers, and William Schutz.

Characteristics

Absence of a unifying theory underlying such groups, purposefully vague goals, and wide variation among techniques used for confrontation among members make it difficult to describe the essence of what went on in encounter groups. Still, there do seem to be some common themes in the writings of major theorists in the encounter movement.

Proponents of encounter groups believe that such groups emerged as a reaction to the alienation felt by members of a modern industrial society. According to Goldberg (1970):

> Self-help groups have attempted to help the hollow, stuffed individual buttress himself against the devastation of alienation and social deprivation through small groups of peers who share, support, and reinforce the individual's own striving, ambition, and quest for a viable and acceptable sense of identity. (p. 24)

By being open to any new experience, groups were supposed to give meaning to life. Mann (1970) illustrates vague goals and wrote of openness to confrontation:

> What is an encounter group? An encounter group consists of a group of people who want to encounter—themselves, each other, those aspects of their potentialities which they have overlooked, avoided, ignored. No one can predict beforehand just when and with whom a confrontation will occur. But it is recognized as inevitable when it occurs. (p. ix)

Freedom to express feelings in a confrontational manner, regardless of the nature of those feelings, is evident in this excerpt from a weekend encounter group (Mann, 1970):

ANN: I don't know what it is, but every time you open your mouth, I would just like to belt you one. And if I did, I think you would look at me with a tolerant sneer on your lips and a pitying expression. . . . You can't believe that anyone could possibly have that reaction to you, could you?

FRANK: I don't know what to think. Do we really have to go into this? Does it have anything to do with me?

RICHARD: There are several ways we could approach this situation . . . both get up, go to different ends of the room, look at one another and then slowly walk together.

ANN: Nothing more?

RICHARD [group leader]: If you try it, you will find that it can be quite a lot.

ANN: I'm game.

RICHARD: Well, if you both are, then get up and move to opposite corners of the room . . . that's right . . . and when you come together, then do whatever feels natural . . . but no words . . . (I am very tense. . . . Is she going wallop him? . . . I am afraid she might. . . . She looks angry and intent. . . . My right arm is clenching so

> tight, it hurts. . . . She really is making him sweat . . .
> walking around him . . . stalking him. . . . It's lucky
> he can't see how she looks. . . . It must be hard to
> have someone who is hostile standing behind your
> back . . . but he won't move. . . . What kind of an idiot
> is he? . . . maybe he thinks she won't touch him if he
> does that. . . . He doesn't know women. . . . Oh wow!
> Wow! . . . It's lucky she hit him in the shoulder . . .
> Boy, she really means it . . . he looks like it hurts. . . .
> Oh, that's better. He has stopped her. . . . Boy, now
> she is really angry). (pp. 21–25)

Although it is difficult to characterize encounter groups because of the wide variation among them, leaders of the movement seem to express a genuine concern for the individual's alienated feelings and need for connectedness with others. To achieve this connectedness, they advocate brutal honesty, complete candor about feelings, openness to whatever goals the group chooses, and various exercises for achieving these ends quickly.

Harmful Effects

Maliver (1973) began his review of effects of encounter groups after a close friend joined an encounter group and shortly thereafter committed suicide. Through interviews of former participants, he located examples of injuries—bruises, broken limbs, contusions, sprains, a punctured eardrum (occurred when a participant in a marathon session was encouraged to vent her anger and struck another group member)—to group members, divorce (traced to dissatisfaction with the member's life-style after exposure to that espoused at Esalen), and at least 6 suicides (pp. 92–97).

According to Maliver, the worst aspects of the encounter movement include the following: (a) Due to the vagueness of the groups' goals, people may enter groups not knowing what to expect (e.g., persons seeking the curative effects of psychotherapy may mistakenly enter encounter groups); (b) nonprofessionals often do not provide safeguards to prevent exploitation of members; (c) emotionally fragile members may fall victim to "psychological karate" (in which the object is to strip away one's customary emotional defenses); (d) encounter groups may not be as cost-effective as claimed; (e) some groups overcontrol the personal lives of their members; (f) nonprofessionals are not trained to recognize signs of serious psychiatric disorder early enough to take protective action; (g) many leaders in the encounter movement sexually exploit group members; and (h) by holding the participants responsible for the outcome of their treatment and by not keeping records of successes and failures, leaders of encounter groups evade the requirement that those who administer treatments should be accountable for the effects (pp. 191–192).

Whereas Maliver's evidence was largely anecdotal, Lieberman, Yalom, and Miles (1973) conducted a controlled study. Their study measured effects of various forms of encounter groups on students enrolled at Stanford University. Lieberman and his colleagues classified 206 student volunteers into homogeneous groups according to their prior participation in encounter groups. Then they randomly assigned students from these groups to 10 different types of groups: T-Group or Sensitivity Group, Gestalt Therapy, Transactional Analytic, Esalen Eclectic, Personal Growth (National Training Laboratory Groups, Western Style), Synanon, Psychodrama, Marathon, Psychoanalytically Oriented, and Encounter Tapes (leaderless groups). Led by prominent professionals the groups were carefully monitored for characteristic procedures, leadership style, and effects on group members, which were measured immediately following the termination of the group, and again 6 months later, using an Index of Change (a composite measure of the student's symptom discomfort, interpersonal functioning, and self-awareness).

Lieberman and colleagues (1973) defined a casualty as being

an individual who, as a direct result of his experience in the encounter group, became more psychologically distressed and/or employed more maladaptive mechanisms of defense. Furthermore, to be so defined, this negative change must not be transient, but enduring, as judged eight months after the group experience. (p. 171)

Of those who completed at least half of the meetings, about 9% suffered "significant psychological injury" (p. 173). The researchers also found that three times as many experimentals (13%) as those in the nontreated comparison group (4%) entered some other form of psychotherapy after the groups.

The authors concluded that high-risk groups were distinguished by "a leader whose style is characterized by high aggressive stimulation, high charisma, high individual focus, high support, and high confrontation" (Lieberman et al., 1973, p. 174). Those harmed by participation in such groups are more likely to be persons who have a higher level of psychopathology to begin with and who enter the group thinking they will experience a successful outcome without undergoing a painful growth period; or as the authors wrote, the casualties expected "pleasant magic to be worked on them" (p. 332).

Hartley, Roback, and Abramowitz (1976) reviewed 9 studies that evaluated effects of encounter groups. Casualty rates reported in these studies ranged from about 1% to 50%. Hartley and her fellow reviewers attributed this range to various definitions of "casualty" and how leaders and subjects were recruited for study. The review confirmed earlier findings that those who are psychologically more fragile are most likely to be casualties in encounter groups. Other indications of likely harm, according to the review, included lack of group structure, lack of task orientation, encouragement of confrontation and anger, coercion of participants, and frequent attacks by the group on the participants' defenses.

The authors of the review concluded that potential participants should be screened for psychopathology and should be warned of risks and told of group procedures before entering; group leaders should be trained to deal with the kinds of problems that can occur in such groups.

Lesson for Practitioners

9. Although a method becomes popular, it may not be based on sound research principles or even on common sense.

Aggressively Relocating the Aged

In the annals of scientific investigation, few will compare with the humane intentions, scientific rigor, fearless analysis, and tragic results of the study by Blenkner, Bloom, and Nielsen (1971). Deeply concerned about the plight of the "mentally impaired aged living within the communities outside of institutional walls" (p. 483) they designed an experiment to test the effects of intensive social casework on a sample of the aged in the Cleveland area.

To test effects of their special program, they randomly assigned 88 aged persons to a control group that was given no special community services, and randomly assigned 76 others to a special intensive social casework group.

The intensive service group was given aggressive intervention. Four carefully chosen experienced social workers with master's level training were instructed to: "Do, or get others to do, whatever is necessary to meet the needs of the situation" (p. 489). No effort was spared. Funds from the project were used to support: "financial assistance, medical evaluation, psychiatric consultation, legal consultation, fiduciary and guardianship services, home aide and other home help services, nursing consultation and evaluation, and placement in a protective setting" (p. 490). During the year of intensive intervention, the four caseworkers conducted 2,421 personal casework interviews with the 76 aged persons and their collaterals, an average of 31.8 interviews per participant. At the end of the year, on every service monitored, the intensive casework group received substantially more help.

During the year of the demonstration project, both the caseworkers and the researchers who conducted follow-up interviews were moved by the "full range of pathology, frustration, and pathos" (Blenkner et al., 1971, p. 488) in the lives of the aged with whom they worked. Imagine the authors' feelings when they wrote:

> In regard to death—the ultimate deterioration in competence—the rate at the end of the demonstration year was 25 percent for the service participants and only 18 percent for the control participants—a discouraging but not [statistically] significant difference. (p. 492)

Lesson for Practitioners

10. Genuine sympathy for troubled clients does not ensure that one is effectively helping them.

"The difference in institutionalization rates [placement in nursing homes] during the demonstration year—34 percent among the service participants and 20 percent among the controls—was consistent with other findings on protection" (pp. 492, 494). The authors, who carefully controlled for age in their analysis, were concerned that those getting the more intensive intervention were more likely to be relocated to institutions than were controls, and that this relocation may have inadvertently harmed clients. Their deep concern for clients is evident:

> These are discouraging facts that should not deter us from further attempts to help. We should, however, question our present prescriptions and strategies of treatment.

Is our dosage too strong, our intervention too overwhelming, our takeover too final? Some of the data pertaining to factors predictive of institutionalization on survival suggest that we are prone to introduce the greatest changes in lives least able to bear them. (p. 499)

The findings of Blenkner and her colleagues (1971) may be a special case. Relocation does not appear to affect the aged adversely in all contexts, with all individuals, in response to all procedures for relocation. Borup, Gallego, and Heffernan (1980) reviewed 6 studies reporting increased mortality, 13 studies reporting no effect, and 1 reporting lower mortality among relocated persons. Cohen (1986) also reported such inconsistencies across studies.

However, equivocal results do not exclude harmful effects of relocation. Relocation may have a differential effect. That is, some elderly persons, because of their age, constitutional factors, and personal resources, may respond favorably to relocation, while others may deteriorate. The way professionals handle the relocation may also be a factor in client survival. Thus, practitioners may be well advised to be aware of differential effects when making a relocation decision.

Lesson for Practitioners

11. The same procedure may help one client, harm another, and not affect another.

Damon (1982) summarized a number of research studies and identified the following predictors of death following relocation: "Patient is physically fragile. Patient is psychologically fragile. Pre-move preparation has been inadequate. Patient has severe brain dysfunction. Environment change is extreme" (p. 148). Others reported additional factors associated with higher mortality, including: low daily functioning (Borup et al., 1980); older, nonambulatory patients (Killian, 1970); and patients' refusal to make necessary life changes (Aldrich & Mendkoff, 1963). After an extensive literature review regarding such factors, Borup (1983) concludes: "We need now to direct our attention to possible adverse conditions that are causal to an individual's vulnerability to mortality when relocating" (p. 241).

Lesson for Practitioners

12. Iatrogenic effects may be much more common than one might expect.

A NOTE OF OPTIMISM

The preceding negative examples illustrate the need for scientific thinking to avoid harming clients, but after reading about so much negative evidence the reader may feel a bit discouraged. That this whole text teaches how to avoid the pitfalls just described is one call for optimism. That this chapter's 12 lessons for practitioners can be implemented to minimize risk to clients is another. Still another positive point concerns evidence of beneficial effects of social work interventions.

Sound studies have shown that particular social work interventions most likely *do* help people. The following studies were among the 12 that Rubin (1985) judged to be the most methodologically sound in his review of social work research: mentally retarded adults who participated in a social skills training group conducted by social workers improved their skills (as evidenced by fewer nonsense statements, fewer insults, more positive statements) more than did clients in a no treatment or traditional treatment group (Matson & Senatore, 1981); a study of orthopedic patients found that early and comprehensive social work intervention reduced the length of hospital stays (Boone, Coulton, & Keller, 1981); a study of a community-based residential treatment program for mentally ill individuals headed by a social worker with master's level training demonstrated better adjustment among program participants than among those randomly assigned to a control group (Velasquez & McCubbin, 1980); highly self-critical young women who participated in a social worker's group counseling were less fearful of negative evaluation and had a higher self-opinion after treatment than did similar nontreated women (Berlin, 1980).

Coulton's (1985) review has demonstrated how social work research has greatly affected practice in health settings. Such research has been partly responsible for shaping the following trends in health care: (a) development of more systematic ways to assess risk and psychosocial needs of patients, (b) greater involvement of patients in their own treatment, and (c) greater use of interventions that strengthen the patient's coping capacities and strategies for modifying the environment (p. 283). These studies represent only a few of those existing in the steadily increasing pool of excellent outcome studies in social work. Later chapters will define criteria for a study, including, in Chapter 5, a detailed analysis of a Stein and Test (1980) study that was included in Rubin's list.

SUMMARY

The physicians who probably killed George Washington revered and loved him, or so the tone of their recollections implies. The physicians who administered heroic doses of calomel sincerely believed it would help to heal. Those who prescribed liberal amounts of oxygen for premature infants were convinced it would help the children to survive without harming them. The humanity of those who treat the mentally ill, or try to prevent the tragedy of juvenile crime, or devote their lives to helping the aged, is not in question. *But good intentions, as this chapter documents, do not insure against negative outcomes.*

Learning how to reason scientifically about practice is our best insurance against repeating the mistakes of the past. Although there will always be uncertainties in social work practice, by resolving to question intelligently, practitioners will, it is hoped, be more likely to avoid the well-intentioned-therefore-effective fallacy. To be mo-

tivated to think scientifically in our field, we must appreciate the dangers of undisciplined or unsystematic thinking and aim toward the rewards of a scientific approach.

Lessons for Practitioners

1. Reverence for the client does not ensure the method's success.
2. Reasons for using a method that may sound sensible at the time are not always legitimate.
3. Years of experience with a method do not necessarily prove its effectiveness.
4. Heroic measures do not ensure heroic results.
5. Before widespread use, a method should be carefully evaluated.
6. Although initial experience with a method may be positive, negative effects may become apparent in the long run.

7. Personal experience with a method does not guarantee desirable results.
8. Simplistic cures for complex problems are not likely to be effective.
9. Although a method becomes popular, it may not be based on sound research principles or even on common sense.
10. Genuine sympathy for troubled clients does not ensure that one is effectively helping them.
11. The same procedure may help one client, harm another, and not affect another.
12. Iatrogenic effects may be much more common than one might expect.

Scientific practitioners will pose major questions whenever they consider an intervention:

1. Is the method effective?
2. Are there any harmful effects associated with a particular method?
3. Are there other, more effective methods?
4. Which method is most effective with which client type?
5. How credible is the supporting evidence?

The rest of this volume is intended to apply scientific thinking to social work's practical questions.

EXERCISES

1. Here are some thought-provoking questions for class discussion:
   a. Are there methods used by social workers that have not been proven effective?
   b. Are there methods used by social workers that have been proven to be harmful?
   c. How would one best determine the effectiveness of a method currently being used by social workers?
2. Obtain a copy of *Scared Straight* (Shapiro, 1978). View the film (a little over an hour in length) and allow at least a half-hour for discussion. Take notes during the film so that you may describe the following:

   a. What is the film's one major conclusion about the program?
   b. How does the film play on the emotions?
   c. What arguments are made in support of the Lifers' Program?
3. Compare your class's assessment of *Scared Straight* against that of a videotaped class of social workers who also viewed and reacted to the film: Gibbs, L. E. (Speaker), & Schleicher, D. (Director). *Scared Straight! Classroom discussion* (Cassette Recording No. 1065). University of Wisconsin–Eau Claire, Media Development Department.

REFERENCES

Aldrich, C. K., & Mendkoff, E. (1963). Relocation of the aged and disabled: A mortality study. *Journal of the American Geriatrics Society, 11*(3), 185–194.

Berlin, S. (1980). Cognitive-behavioral intervention for problems of self-criticism among women. *Social Work Research & Abstracts, 16,* 19–28.

Blenkner, M., Bloom, M., & Nielsen, M. (1971). A research and demonstration project of protective services. *Social Casework, 52*(8), 483–499.

Boone, C. R., Coulton, C. J., & Keller, S. M. (1981). The impact of early and comprehensive social work services on length of stay. *Social Work in Health Care, 7*(1), 1–9.

Borup, J. H. (1983). Relocation mortality research: Assessment, reply, and the need to refocus on the issues. *The Gerontologist, 23*(3), 235–242.

Borup, J. H., Gallego, D. T., & Heffernan, P. G. (1980). Relocation: Its effects on health, functioning and mortality. *The Gerontologist, 20*(4), 468–479.

Brieger, G. H. (1967). Therapeutic conflicts and the American medical profession in the 1860s. *Bulletin of the History of Medicine, 41*(1), 215–222.

Bryan, L. S. (1964). Bloodletting in American medicine, 1830–1892. *Bulletin of the History of Medicine, 38*(1), 516–529.

Bunis, L. (1980). Rahway Prison's Scared Straight Program: The medium or the message? *Enforcement Journal, 19*(4), 46.

Campbell, K. (1951). Intensive oxygen therapy as a possible cause of retrolental fibroplasia: A clinical approach. *Medical Journal of Australia, 2*(48), 48–50.

Chouinard, G., & Bradwejn, J. (1982). Reversible and irreversible tardive dyskinesia: A case report. *American Journal of Psychiatry, 139*(3), 360–362.

Cohen, E. S. (1986). Legislative and educational alternatives to a judicial remedy for the transfer trauma dilemma. *American Journal of Law and Medicine, 11*(4), 405–432.

Conniff, R. (1987). The little suckers have made a comeback. *Discover, 8*(8), 85–94.

Coulton, C. J. (1985). Research and practice: An ongoing relationship. *Health and Social Work, 10*(4), 282–291.

Damon, L. E. (1982). Effects of relocation on the elderly. *American Family Physician, 26*(5), 144–148.

Death of General George Washington. (1799). *The Monthly Magazine and American Review, 1*(6), 475–477.

Eastmond, W. (1976a, March 10). State prison lifers' group picks panel to advise, aid inmates. *Asbury Park Press,* p. A9.

Eastmond, W. (1976b, September 13). Inmates detail facts of "life." *Asbury Park Press,* p. A9.

Finckenauer, J. O. (1982). *Scared Straight! and the panacea phenomenon.* Englewood Cliffs, NJ: Rutgers University Press.

Golan, M. (1977, February 26). Inmates' tale of hell sobers kids. *The Weekend Dispatch,* p. 6.

Goldberg, C. (1970). *Encounter: Group sensitivity training experience.* New York: Science House.

Haller, J. S. (1981). *American medicine in transition 1840–1910.* Urbana, IL: University of Illinois Press.

Hartley, D., Roback, H. B., & Abramowitz, S. I. (1976). Deterioration effects in encounter groups. *American Psychologist, 31*(3), 247–255.

It is like hell. (1977, January 30). *Los Angeles Times,* p. 4.

James, L. S., & Lanman, J. T. (1976). History of oxygen therapy and retrolental fibroplasia. *Pediatrics, 57*(4), 589–642.

Jeste, D. V., Jeste, S. D., & Wyatt, R. J. (1983). Reversible tardive dyskinesia: Implications for therapeutic strategy and prevention of tardive dyskinesia. *Modern Problems of Pharmacopsychiatry, 21,* 34–48.

Jeste, D. V., & Wyatt, R. J. (1981). Changing epidemiology of tardive dyskinesia: An overview. *American Journal of Psychiatry, 138*(3), 297–309.

Kalachnik, J. E. (1985). Applied aspects of tardive dyskinesia monitoring: Over, under, sideways, down; backward, forward, square, and round. *Advances in Learning and Behavioral Disabilities, 4,* 133–180.

Killian, E. C. (1970). Effect of geriatric transfers on mortality rates. *Social Work, 15*(1), 19–26.

Krupp, M. A., & Chatton, M. J. (1982). Psychiatric disorders. In M. A. Krupp & M. J. Chatton (Eds.), *Current medical diagnosis and treatment.* Los Altos, CA: Lange Medical.

Lieberman, M. A., Yalom, I. D., & Miles, M. B. (1973). *Encounter groups: First facts.* New York: Basic Books.

Lucey, J. F., & Dangman, B. (1984). A reexamination of the role of oxygen in retrolental fibroplasia. *Pediatrics, 73*(1), 82–96.

Maliver, B. L. (1973). *The encounter game.* New York: Stein & Day.

Mann, J. (1970). *Encounter.* New York: Grossman.

Mathias, A. (1810). *The mercurial disease.* London: Becket and Porter.

Matson, J. L., & Senatore, V. (1981). A comparison of traditional psychotherapy and social skills training for improving interpersonal functioning of mentally retarded adults. *Behavior Therapy, 12,* 369–381.

National Center on Institutions and Alternatives. (undated). Scared straight: A second look. (Available from NCIA, 1337 22nd Street, NW, Washington, DC, 20037)

National Library of Medicine (1988). *Medical subject headings.* Bethesda, MD: U.S. Department of Health and Human Services, Public Health Service, National Institutes of Health, National Library of Medicine.

Owens, W. C., & Owens, E. U. (1950). Retrolental fibroplasia in premature infants. *Archives of Ophthalmology, 44,* 479–480.

Patz, A., Hoeck, L. E., & De La Cruz, E. (1952). Studies on the effect of high oxygen administration in retrolental fibroplasia: Nursery observations. *American Journal of Ophthalmology, 35,* 1248–1252.

Rosen, A. M., Mukherjee, S., Olarte, S., Varia, V., & Cardenas, C. (1982). Perception of tardive dyskinesia in outpatients receiving maintenance neuroleptics. *American Journal of Psychiatry, 139*(3), 372–373.

Rubin, A. (1985). Practice effectiveness: More grounds for optimism. *Social Work, 30*(6), 469–476.

"Scared Straight"? (1979). *Corrections Today, 41*(6), 40–41.

Shapiro, A. (Producer). (1978). *Scared straight* [film]. Santa Monica, CA: Pyramid Films.

Shapiro, C. (June 1986). Retrolental fibroplasia: What we know and what we don't know. *Neonatal Network,* 33–45.

Silverman, W. A. (1975, April). *Experimentation in children: American-style.* Paper presented at the first Richard L. Day Lectureship, College of Physicians and Surgeons, Columbia University, NY.

Stein, L. I., & Test M. A. (1980). Alternative to mental hospital treatment. *Archives of General Psychiatry, 37,* 392–412.

Terry, T. L. (1942). Extreme prematurity and fibroplastic outgrowth of persistent vascular sheath behind each crystalline lens. *American Journal of Ophthalmology, 25*(203), 203–204.

Velasquez, J. S., & McCubbin, H. I. (1980). Toward establishing the effectiveness of community-based residential treatment: Program evaluation by experimental research. *Journal of Social Service Research, 3*(4), 337–359.

Wettstein, R. M. (1983). Tardive dyskinesia and malpractice. *Behavioral Science and the Law, 1*(1), 85–107.

2

Unscientific Reasoning

Examples in Chapter 1 illustrated how those in the various helping professions, although motivated by benevolent intentions, were actually harming their clients, and in some cases, were going so far as to consign them to an early grave. Sadly, the helpers' good intentions were not sufficient to produce good results. So how can social workers avoid harmful effects and help successfully?

Scientific reasoning, although by its very nature providing tentative answers, can guide the social worker's decision making more surely than can reasoning based on less rigorous and unsystematic patterns of thought. To clarify what a scientific approach is not, this chapter defines nine common fallacies as they apply specifically to judging effects of social work practice:

- appealing to experience
- attacking the person rather than examining the person's argument
- appealing to authority
- accepting uncritical documentation
- appealing to numbers or popularity
- appealing to tradition or newness
- accepting testimonials
- acquiescing to the manner of a person presenting an idea
- assuming that practitioners who are soft-hearted must also be soft-headed.

Such fallacies can be deadly because they obscure the mission—determining which methods are effective and applying those methods competently. Characteristics of pseudoscientific reasoning are also described in order to further delineate what scientific thinking is not. Pay careful attention to the practitioners' fallacies presented: They are part of a learning quiz at the end of the chapter.

DEFINITIONS

One hallmark of social work is the incredible variety of clients, settings, and intervention methods encountered. For example, social workers may use reality orientation for confused elderly individuals, placement in sheltered workshops for adults with developmental disabilities, progressive relaxation for anxiety-prone clients in a mental health clinic, token rewards for improving children's school performance, assertiveness training for victims of abuse, group-counseling techniques for adolescents who are becoming sexually active, rapport-building techniques when beginning an interview, and goal-clarification exercises to direct the efforts of the helping professional. Because of this diversity, it would be impossible to define "*the* social work method." However, for our purposes, an **intervention method** is anything a social worker does to help a client achieve some goal. By this definition, all those methods are intervention methods.

Reasoning is the process by which people decide what to believe and what to do. Certainly, helping social workers reason more analytically and scientifically would be a worthy goal. In social work what could be a better tool than reasoning to decide which homes are suitable places for foster care or adoption? Where could reasoning for social workers be more important than in determining how best to prevent a child's reabuse, or in choosing a method that would most effectively help a mentally ill person live as a productive member outside the institution?

Learning to spot common fallacies is one way to improve reasoning. "A *fallacy* is an 'incorrect' argument, an argument in which the reasons advanced for a claim fail to warrant acceptance of the claim" (Moore & Parker, 1986, p. 104). One such fallacy affecting social work practice is the **testimonial.** Clients who give testimonials describe their participation in a treatment and tell others, often in sincere and emotional terms, how much they have been helped by a particular intervention or method.

We will call such common errors in reasoning about social work practice **practitioners' fallacies.** The nine fallacies defined in this chapter—which all violate basic principles of research methods—are those often committed by social work practitioners as they discuss clients with individual co-workers or in case conferences.

Practitioners' fallacies are rarely committed in pure form. Usually, practitioners' fallacies are combined with other fallacies, or appear along with stronger evidence. Thus, it takes a discerning ear to detect them. To sharpen your skills, as you read the examples and definitions of each fallacy, think of how the fallacy may have been committed in your agency, in writing about how best to help social work clients, or at the most recent workshop or conference regarding an intervention.

PRACTITIONERS' FALLACIES

Appealing to Experience

The fallacy of appealing to experience can often be detected by the way the argument begins. Those who commit the fallacy often say: "From my experience I have learned that" or "From my experience I know that" (Gula, 1979, p. 71). Although personal experience can be an invaluable teacher if based on systematic observation, careful record keeping and sound reasoning, personal experience may also be of the "seen everything and learned nothing" variety (Black, 1952, pp. 258–260). The untrained observer or the practitioner whose day-to-day involvement in intervention hinders objective analysis may base conclusions on vivid recollection of unrepresentative events, may misinterpret what really happened, and may care so deeply about clients that judgment is clouded.

For our purposes, the **appeal to experience** implies that: (a) an assertion is made that something is true about a client or that a method is effective, (b) the proponent's conclusion is based on personal experience with the method, and (c) no measures, records, or experimental evidence are offered to support the conclusion.

Of course, this is not to say that personal experience is useless in the reasoning process. In fact, the practitioner, counselor, or therapist may use personal experience effectively to generate questions for investigation. (How such questions can be formulated into specific research questions and hypotheses will be addressed in Chapter 6.)

The difficulty lies in using personal experience to judge an intervention's effectiveness. Remember how those who bled, purged, and blistered George Washington were experienced in their methods. Doctors who had years of experience administering high oxygen levels did not know of the possible iatrogenic effects. Likewise, the experienced social workers who relocated the aged in the Blenkner, Bloom, and Nielsen (1971) study thought that relocation was necessary. Without doubt, those who administered such methods to help clients used methods they believed would produce positive results. What caring practitioner knowingly uses an ineffective method?

Attacking the Person (*Ad Hominem*) Rather Than Examining the Person's Argument (*Ad Rem*)

Every day in social service agencies, nursing homes, hospitals, and other human service agencies, professionals meet to make decisions about clients. In case conferences or staff meetings, persons themselves are sometimes attacked, rather than their arguments. Following is an example of failure to make such a distinction in a case conference at a nursing home:

SOCIAL WORKER: I'm not sure we're handling Mrs. Davidsen well. According to the chart, she has an advanced stage of Parkinson's disease. I don't feel that our getting her up and walking her rapidly down the hall for exercise is appropriate. Also, it seems

NURSE: to me we're a little impatient with her when she spills her food and dribbles it on her gown.

NURSE: Mrs. Davidsen is walked briskly because the exercise won't do any good otherwise. Also, in my opinion, her dribbling is attention-seeking behavior.

SOCIAL WORKER: I don't think I agree with you; I recently read an article by Rosal (1978) that discusses proper management of people with Parkinson's disease. I understand from the article that our expectations may be too high for what Mrs. Davidsen can accomplish at this late stage of her disease.

NURSE: Mrs. Davidsen's level of performance is a medical problem. You'll recognize when you become a little more experienced with patients like Mrs. Davidsen that they tend to manipulate us a lot. But then (turning to other staff members), what would you expect of a social worker who is still wet behind the ears?

OTHERS: (Laughter)

The nurse's argument here is fallacious. She has ridiculed the social worker's level of experience and has derided the social work profession. According to Chase (1956, p. 61), when you try to state your case by diverting attention from the credibility of the argument and by discrediting the person who is presenting the argument, you argue at the person, or **ad hominem.** The nurse missed the chance to argue **ad rem**—at the thing—that is, against the social worker's argument. She missed the opportunity to learn something from the argument and to care more effectively for Mrs. Davidsen. Had the nurse argued *ad rem,* she would have discussed the contents of the article with the social worker and weighed the credibility of arguments in the article, along with the credibility of other arguments about Parkinson's patients that may have been offered by staff members. Similarly, if a social worker were to reject a nurse's argument simply because it came from a nurse, the same fallacy would be committed.

Another interesting case of *ad hominem* appeared in the letters to the editor column of *Social Work* after Joel Fischer (1973) published his review of research, titled "Is Casework Effective?: A Review." Fischer had concluded that research done prior to 1973 showed that social casework, then based on a largely psychoanalytic orientation, was ineffective. Responding to Fischer, one *ad hominem* letter to the editor included these statements: "As a marvelous client of mine would say: 'You in a *bag,* Mr.!' I'm afraid social casework *is* in a bag that's been closed up and tied shut" (Crumb, 1973, p. 124). The argument that Fischer was "in a bag" did not enlighten. However, others argued more effectively against Fischer's conclusions. These *ad rem* arguments included the fact that Fischer had not adequately defined social casework, had based his review on studies that used outmoded methods, and had included studies with serious methodological flaws (Starr, 1973).

Failure to draw the *ad hominem/ad rem* distinction can occur when others are examining credibility of someone's idea and in the process, the idea's presenter becomes angry. In such a case the idea's presenter thinks that those who are examining the idea's credibility are attacking the idea's proponent—the idea has become almost an extension of self. For example, a student questioned a professor's conclusion that the diagnostic related groups established by federal law were used to determine the amount of payment for Medicaid patients. The professor became red-faced and angry at the student, possibly assuming the student was attacking him as an instructor, rather than his argument.

Appealing to Authority (*Ad Verecundiam*)

Here is an example of an appeal to authority to support a conclusion about conjoint family therapy: "As far as I'm concerned, Dr. Cheng is one step below God when it comes to family therapy. I try to duplicate her methods, but I know I will never be as effective as she is."

The appeal to authority is a "classical fallacy" (Chase, 1956), meaning that it has been around for a long time. According to Chase, quoting a revered authority and pushing it too far "freezes mental activity" (p. 89). The appeal to authority is particularly damaging when social work professionals blindly follow gurus in the profession who advocate particular intervention methods. It is a fallacy to accept an argument *simply* because a famous person advocates it. The esteemed names in our discipline still need to submit their ideas to tests to determine the effectiveness of their intervention methods. Therefore, the definition of **appeal to authority** includes the following components: (a) there is an assertion that an intervention is effective, (b) this assertion is based purely on the authority's status, and (c) the authority does not refer to studies that both support and refute the method's effectiveness.

Those with status can be wrong—possibly dead wrong—about reality. A renowned, gray-haired, molecular biologist at the University of California at Berkeley—a member of the prestigious National Academy of Sciences, who was California's Scientist of the Year in 1971—Dr. Peter Duesberg stated as late as 1988 that AIDS is *not* caused by a virus. Furthermore, Dr. Duesberg declared that tests used to detect Human Immunodeficiency Virus (HIV) antibodies are a waste of time, and that, "If somebody told me today that I was antibody positive, I wouldn't worry one second" (Miller, 1988, p. 62). Those impressed by the appeal to authority might have been misled by Dr. Duesberg's high status, and might have accepted his conclusions based purely on that status. Such reasoning can be risky if translated into action.

Accepting Uncritical Documentation

No matter how absurd or farfetched an idea, it may be possible to document it somehow. Even prestigious sources sometimes document absurd ideas. For example, highly prestigious sources have reported that children have been raised by various kinds of beasts. Witness the fable that may be documented by the reference: Foley, J. P. (1940a). The "Baboon Boy" of South Africa. *Science, 91*(2360), 291–292.

Foley (1940b), who graciously acknowledged documentation provided by Dr. Raymond A. Dart, professor of anatomy at the University of Witwatersrand, Johannesberg, South Africa, offered this account of the "baboon boy":

> Coming across a troop of baboons playing in a clearing in a remote part of the South East Cape, they [troopers of the Cape Mounted Police] fired into the group, and were surprised to notice that one animal, not as fast as the others, was left behind. The laggard was caught and found to be a native boy between 12 and 14 years of age. The boy was taken to a mental hospital where he remained for a year, before being given over to a farmer, for whom he has subsequently worked. (p. 292)

The baboon boy's captors observed the boy's

> long arms and the abnormal development of the haunches . . . strong desire to walk on all fours . . . a constant jerking and nodding of the head, scratching of parts of his body with the index finger, and a peculiar and frightened-looking grin . . . chattered like an ape . . . was very mischievous and wild and "full of monkey tricks." (p. 292)

After Foley (1940a) published a more detailed account in the *American Journal of Psychology,* the story of the baboon boy unraveled. Robert Zingg (1940) of the University of Denver investigated the story to discover that the baboon boy, according to documented evidence, was found in a location other than that claimed by the police. Hospital records of the time made no mention of a baboon boy's existence, and George H. Smith, who promoted the story, apparently taking advantage of the boy's mental retardation, fabricated the baboon story for personal gain. Zingg (1941) concluded that the whole incident illustrates "how thorough investigation must be in matters of this kind, and how cautious and conservative scientists should be in accepting the evidence for feral man" (p. 462).

Dr. Zingg should have taken his own advice. Zingg, who chronicled (1941) India's "wolf children" (see Figure 2.1), met the same fate in Evans's (1958) critique. The following is an excerpt from Dr. Zingg's article, "India's Wolf Children: Two Human Infants Reared by Wolves," which appeared in the March 1941 issue of *Scientific American.*

> In 1929, when I first heard of wolf-children, my reaction, no doubt like that of everyone else, was that such stories were stuff and nonsense. However, when the study of other scientific problems brought me back to the subject of wolf-children, I found evidence of some respectability for about 30 cases on feral or wild man. . . . The best of these cases is that of the wolf-children of Midnapore, India. . . . The two wolf-children of India were first seen living as wolves among wolves . . . by an Anglican missionary, Rev. J. A. L. Singh. . . .

Rev. Singh writes [of his discovery]:

> "Then, all of a sudden, a grown-up wolf came out of one of the holes. This animal was followed by another of the same size and kind. The second was followed by a third, closely followed by two cubs, one after the other. Close after the cubs came the 'ghost'—a hideous-looking creature—hand, foot, and body like a human being. Close at its heels came another awful creature, exactly like the first, but smaller.

FIGURE 2.1
The two wolf-children soon after their rescue, sleeping wolf-puppy fashion, or curled-up in a "monkey-ball," with the younger one on top. (Source: "India's Wolf Children: Two Human Infants Reared by Wolves" by Robert Zingg, 1941, Scientific American 164(3), p. 137.)

Their eyes were bright and piercing, unlike human eyes. However, I at once came to the conclusion that they were human beings." (p. 135)

The fallacy of uncritical documentation is assuming that because something is documented it must be true. Readers taken in by the fallacy may think, "Who am I, just the reader, to question ideas of someone who has written a book or an article?" Those duped by the fallacy fail to recognize that an author is bound by the same rules of evidence that apply to everyone else.

Appealing to Numbers or Popularity

Group pressure can be incredibly persuasive, especially when that pressure comes from supervisors and co-workers. Consider such pressure in this hypothetical situation: You are working at a home for the developmentally disabled, and you think that a 14-year-old boy's frequent self-abusive behavior (banging his head against the wall and striking his face with his fist) might be better controlled by using positive practice (a form of overcorrection, based on learning theory, which involves the elimination of an undesired behavior through repeatedly performing a competing appropriate behavior). You advocate positive practice at a staff meeting and start to discuss the evidence of Foxx and Azrin (1973) to support your conclusions. However, your co-workers interrupt you and, without examining records of the method's success or citing literature to support their position, someone speaking for the group says to you, "Get with it. We are all using restraints in such cases."

The appeal to numbers or popularity is a commonly defined fallacy (Fearnside & Holther, 1959; Gula, 1979; Moore & Parker, 1986). The distinctive features of the **appeal to numbers or popularity** fallacy, when applied to social work practice, are: (a) a worker is pressured to adopt a method or accept a conclusion about clients, (b) such pressure is based on the number of people who use the method (implying that so many people cannot be wrong), and (c) no balanced evaluations of outcome or survey evidence are given.

Appealing to Tradition or Newness

Accepting or rejecting an intervention method simply because of the method's traditional use or newness invites disastrous decision making. One argument given by those who sold patent medicine was that their preparations had been on the market for a number of years, and thus had to be effective. Cramp (1921) investigated such claims during the heyday of patent medicine and concluded that such medicines, although ineffective, were widely advertised to be cures because the manufacturers took credit for situations in which the body healed itself.

Relating to social work, **appeal to tradition or appeal to newness** implies that: (a) the method is effective, (b) the method has been used for a long time (or is new), (c) because of the method's long-term use (or newness), the method is considered to be effective, and (d) no studies designed to test the method's effectiveness objectively are described.

The strange and tragic history of how fetal alcohol syndrome was discovered, forgotten, and rediscovered illustrates weaknesses of basing an idea's acceptance on the idea's newness or age. Fetal Alcohol Syndrome (FAS), found in children whose mothers drank alcohol while pregnant, is the third most frequently occurring birth defect, following spina bifida and Down's syndrome, according to the National Institute on Alcohol Abuse and Alcoholism (1978). Iber (1980) cited datum that "suggests that FAS occurs about as frequently as the trisomy 21 Down's syndrome," which, he continues, "given the fact that it most usually causes mental impairment. . . . may make [FAS] the most common birth defect of which we are currently aware" (p. 8).

Classical manifestations of FAS include a constellation of craniofacial defects (i.e., small head circumference, short palpebral fissure, epicanthic folds, short nose, small midface, indistinct philtrum, thin reddish upper lip, and jaw deformities), joint and heart abnormalities, retardation of physical growth, and slowed intellectual and motor development (Anderson & Grant, 1984; Iber, 1980). Infants born to drinking mothers may not have the full-blown syndrome but may still develop slowly and behave peculiarly (Coles, Smith, & Falek, 1987).

The history of FAS illustrates how relying on whether an idea is new or old is poor reasoning—ideas can go in and out of fashion regardless of the truth. Strangely, winds of intellectual fashion have discovered, forgotten, and rediscovered FAS over the past 250 years (Warner & Rosett, 1975). From the early 1700s to the mid 1800s, pharmacists, doctors, and community leaders described weak, feeble, distempered, sickly, and mentally defective children with arrested growth who were born shriveled and old-looking. In England the upsurge in the numbers of these children could be traced to the "gin epidemic," the sudden availability of inexpensive distilled alcohol. Later, the rum trade in New England in the 1800s was associated with similar descriptions. Studies done in the late 1800s and the early 1900s generally indicated that alcohol consumption by pregnant women was associated with birth defects, "idiocy," and high infant mortality. Subsequently, not long after Prohibition was repealed, researchers in the United States discounted and ridiculed pre-Prohibition literature. Many argued that alcohol had no effect whatsoever on offspring. Then in the 1960s literature about prenatal effects of alcohol reappeared and culminated in what was essentially a rediscovery of FAS (Jones, Smith, Ulleland, & Streisguth, 1973).

Obviously, relying on whether an idea is new or old is no assurance of the idea's truth. FAS is a grim reality, regardless of how new or old the ideas about its existence are.

The tendency for professionals in human services to embrace fads and then discard them is common enough that those dedicated to careful reasoning should beware. Mykel (1981) documented such fads, including primal scream therapy, hydrotherapy (placing the mentally ill in specially designed bathtubs to literally soak away their pathology), and frontal lobotomy (severing the nerve fibers of the frontal lobes of the brain to alter troubled personality and disordered thinking). Jurjevich (1978) believed that those who subscribe to psychotherapeutic fads have done harm by encouraging their clients to be less rational.

Accepting Testimonials

Testimonials are statements given by recipients of intervention to prove that a method works. See Figure 2.2 for a testimonial from a woman who took a patent medicine called Natex. A participant in a smoking cessation program (Eau Claire Stop Smoking Center, 1981) had this to say:

> For a point of reference, it may reassure you to know that I was a smoker for 27 years. The day before therapy began I counted 67 cigarettes I smoked (that was not unusual). I was convinced I could not stop without great anguish and agony. I was wrong, because the Stop Smoking Clinic helped me to stop, and I am able to continue working every day without any withdrawal problems. I commend their methods to you. It worked for me. I quit—you can too! (p. 5)

People give testimonials for other than products. Here is a testimonial that appeared in a social work journal in favor of a family life education group (Funt, 1962):

> I have found that our household runs more smoothly since we have attended these lectures. We give a little more thought to what we are doing with our children. (p. 134)

A **testimonial** occurs when: (a) an assertion is made that a given method works, (b) a client's own experience with a method is offered as proof that the method works, and (c) this experience is given not to illustrate how the method is applied, but to support the claim that it is effective.

"Junior used to be a terrible biter until he saw a social worker."

Testimonials are selected to support a bias. The testimonial in Figure 2.3 appeared in print 19 days *after* Mr. Sheckler's death notice appeared in the same newspaper (I wouldn't be without new Konjola, 1929).

Look again at the testimonial from Mary Deemer (Figure 2.2). Mary Deemer's testimonial appeared on the same newspaper page as her own death notice (Figure 2.4).

Mrs. Deemer probably was quite sincere when she gave her testimonial. Those who analyze them are convinced that testimonials are generally not faked or purchased, but are documentarily genuine and sincere (Cramp & Simmons, 1936, p. 197); so why are testimonials so subject to bias? It may be that most people are simply not competent to judge the effects of an intervention to which they themselves have been exposed. They are not trained and impartial observers. They have a vested interest in wanting a particular method to succeed. The power of suggestion and persuasion may convince people that they may have been helped somehow. Also, because there is a self-limiting nature to many human problems (that is, some problems become acute, improve, and may become acute again), if clients come in for help during an acute phase, they may assume that the improvement—a natural, cyclical phase—was brought about by the "help" they received. (Such cyclical patterns will be examined in Chapter 4.)

Acquiescing to Manner

Being able to disengage from the speaker's persuasive manner of presentation to detect the real substance of an argument is difficult for even experienced practi-

LOCAL LADY TOOK NATEX YEAR AGO—HAD GOOD HEALTH EVER SINCE

Was Only Medicine This Highly Respected German Resident Ever Took That Brought Permanent Lasting Relief.

It is no mere accident that Natex so often brings relief to ailing people who have tried so many other medicines without being benefitted. This new prescription brings results because it is the best herbal medicine ever compounded, for the relief of stomach, liver, kidney, and bowel complaints, containing three times the amount of herbs found in ordinary tonics. Every day the Natex Specialist at Jaxol's Cut Rate Store hears from local people who have taken Natex with excellent results.

"It has been about a year since Natex ended my suffering and not one of my former ailments has returned," declared Mrs. Mary Deemer, 1312 S. Meadow St. "Out of all the different medicines I used, Natex was the only one that really gave relief.

"I used to suffer so badly with my stomach I lost all desire for my meals. Everything I ate seemed to disagree with me and caused so much gas that I was short of breath. I'd hardly be up from the table but what I'd suffer with indigestion and then for hours I'd feel miserable and depressed. I also suffered a lot with headaches and dizzy spells. I was so nervous I couldn't sleep, and dull pains in my back added to my misery.

"After taking so many other medicines without being helped, you can imagine how happy and surprised I felt when I discovered that Natex was doing me a lot of good. Natex seemed to go right to the root of my trouble, helped my appetite and put an end to the indigestion, gas and shortness of breath. Natex also ended the headaches and dizzy spells, quieted my nerves, improved my sleep and banished the pains I suffered in my back. As I mentioned before, all this happened about a year ago but I'm still enjoying perfect health."

Natex is being sold and recommended by all leading druggists everywhere and the Natex Specialist is at JAXOL'S CUT RATE STORE, 631 HAMILTON ST., daily explaining the merits of this new triple-strength prescription perfected by a college professor from nature's roots and herbs. See him today. Learn how Natex can also help you.

FIGURE 2.2

*Local lady took Natex year ago—had good health ever since. (*Source: Allentown Morning Call, *Allentown, Pa., May 27, 1935, p. 7.)*

tioners and educators. Even those who hold graduate degrees in the human services may be taken in by the seductive manner of a speaker's presentation. To test whether professionals could see through the fallacy of manner, Naftulin, Ware, and Donnelly (1973) hired an actor who "looked distinguished and sounded authoritative," and gave him the bogus title, "Dr. Myron L. Fox" (p. 631). The actor was given an impressive list of fictitious credentials and was coached to give a completely meaningless presentation, "Mathematical Game Theory as Applied to Physician Education." Those who cooked up the hoax coached Dr. Fox with a script that contained "excessive use of double-talk [ambiguous and deceptive talk], neologisms [new meanings for established words], non sequiturs [arguments in which the conclusion does not follow the premise] and contradictory statements" (p. 631). The distinguished-looking Dr. Fox was coached to intersperse humor and meaningless references to unrelated topics into his nonsense speech.

The fraudulent presentation was given before three audiences. The first audience of 11 psychiatrists, psychologists, and social work educators rated the nonsense presentation favorably on all 11 items on a rating form. Their comments included: "excellent presentation, enjoyed listening, has warm manner, good flow, seems enthusiastic" (Naftulin et al., p. 632). The second group of 11 psychiatrists, psychologists, and psychiatric social workers viewed a videotape of the nonsense presentation. Again, favorable responses far outweighed unfavorable ones. A

"I WOULDN'T BE WITHOUT NEW KONJOLA"

"Konjola Put Me Back on the Job, and I Feel Like a Different Person," Says Grateful Man.

The Konjola files contain a countless number of instances where this new medicine restored health so that the sufferer was able to go back to work after being forced to remain idle owing to illness.

The following happy experience with Konjola was recently related to the Konjola Man, by Mr. A. R. Sheckler, of Geneva, Pa., near Meadville. Mr. Sheckler said to the Konjola Man:

"Konjola put me back on the job and I feel like a different person. I had been troubled some time from neuritis, and stomach and kidney disorders. I suffered from neuritis as only one who

has had or still has this dread affliction can imagine. My kidneys caused their share of suffering and my stomach caused all the distress that usually accompanies an ailment of that kind. I had tried everything that I heard of in my vain search for relief, and my case was given up as hopeless.

"And then I heard of Konjola. I decided that I really owed it to myself to try this new medicine, and finally did. I shall never regret that decision, for this new medicine turned out to be just what I needed. By the time I had finished the third bottle, I felt immeasureably relieved. My neuritis eased up and has practically disappeared. My stomach and kidneys have been corrected, and never cause me the slightest trouble. I feel like a new man, and am back on the job working hard and feeling fine. I owe all this new health to Konjola, and am glad to recommend it to all who suffer as I did."

FIGURE 2.3
"I wouldn't be without new Konjola." (Source: The Tribune-Republican, *Meadville, Pa., August 20, 1929, p. 3.*)

third group of 33 educators and administrators was similarly taken in by Dr. Fox's captivating manner.

The perpetrators of the hoax concluded that, in spite of the educational sophistication of the members of the three audiences, Dr. Fox's style and wit fooled them into believing they had learned something substantive. Not a single member of the three audiences of professionals saw through the hoax!

Nor is the "Dr. Fox" effect unique to this group; it has been replicated repeatedly on other groups (Meier & Feldhausen, 1979; Ware & Williams, 1975; Williams & Ware, 1976).

Those who know how to use manner well can use it unscrupulously. Weinbach (1988), with tongue in cheek, gave advice to social work faculty members who wanted to sell their students particular ideas and to pump up their student evaluations. Weinbach advised that those who want to harness the fallacy of manner should, "consider wearing jeans and Reeboks, bring in a Big Mac to class. . . . drive a beat up Volkswagen, but be sure to admit that its [sic] a holdover from your poor student days" (p. 31).

This is not to say that instructors and practitioners who seek to describe their methods vividly should refrain from trying to hold their audience's attention. The **fallacy of manner** occurs when: (a) a speaker claims that something is true of clients or asserts that a particular method is effective; (b) the speaker uses very persuasive interpersonal skills (e.g., building up the audience's self-esteem, using anecdotes, engaging the audience in inane discussions, sometimes holding hands or hugging members of the audience, using frequent hand gestures and moving about the room, and listening with rapt attention to comments from the audience no matter how poorly reasoned the ideas may be); and (c) the speaker

FIGURE 2.4
Deaths, Deemer. (Source: Allentown Morning Call, Allentown, Pa., May 27, 1935, p. 7.)

Deaths

DEEMER—In this city, May 25, Mary A., widow of William Deemer, aged 49 years, 25 days.

Relatives, friends and members of the Citizens Welfare league, Division 4 are respectfully invited, without further notice, to attend the funeral services at the Derr funeral home, 46 East Susquehanna street Tuesday at 2 p.m., daylight saving time. Interment in Springfield cemetery. Viewing at the funeral home Tuesday from 7 to 9 p.m.

---

never addresses how effective a method may be, and/or presents *no* empirical evidence of the method's effectiveness.

Assuming Soft-Hearted Therefore Soft-Headed

The soft-hearted-therefore-soft-headed fallacy is a special case of "either-or" reasoning. The **either-or fallacy,** sometimes called the false dilemma, is committed when you do not consider all available alternatives and then accept only one (Seech, 1987, p. 106). For example, voters might be divided into either Democrats or Republicans—ignoring Independents, Socialists, and other less common political groups.

Those taken in by the **soft-hearted-therefore-soft-headed fallacy** assume that social workers are either sensitive, intuitive, and warm-hearted, or scientific, rational, and analytical. For example, Saleeby (1979) concluded that the increasingly scientific orientation to social work practice will lead to experimental controls that will spell the "dehumanization" of practice (p. 282). Haley (1980), a noted and skillful family therapist, argued that a therapist must be personally involved in the therapeutic process, whereas the scientist must be distanced and objective. Because of these two contrasting roles, Haley observed, "Today, it seems more apparent that the research stance and the posture of the therapist are the opposite of each other" (p. 17). Bierter (1977) warned against "the dangers of allowing social work to be invaded by science" (p. 789). He claimed that those who reason scientifically about their work with clients will necessarily lose empathy and closeness with clients. Bierter (1977) lamented:

> The "client" as a person is lost in the [scientific] process, and life itself vanishes from this artificially created situation. The "client" feels that violence is being done to him and experiences the role of object which is forced upon him as a denial of practical help and a withdrawal of love. (p. 192)

Figure 2.5 illustrates that there are alternatives to the soft-hearted-therefore-soft-headed fallacy. Ideally, social work practitioners can be both soft-hearted and hard-headed, that is, a Type I. A soft-hearted-hard-headed practitioner would be deeply concerned about child abuse, and would be concerned enough about abused children to apply hard-headed and analytical methods of science to best determine how reabuse can be prevented.

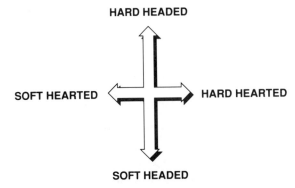

Type I
Soft Hearted / Hard Headed
(Ideal)

Concerned about effects of methods, persists when asking questions, asks specific questions, devises tests to measure effectiveness, bases conclusions on facts properly evaluated, tries to answer questions objectively, identifies key elements in arguments before reacting to them, not easily led in sheeplike fashion, believes in tests to verify ideas.

Type II
Hard Hearted / Hard Headed

HARD HEADED

Able to reflect feeling of others accurately, a good listener, more comfortable dealing with people than with things, senses when others need help, concerned about social injustice, resolves to help others, likely to put concerns of others ahead of own, finds others come to talk about problems.

SOFT HEARTED   **HARD HEARTED**

Uses the pronoun *I* excessively, more comfortable dealing with things than with people, believes that those in trouble must get themselves out, puts own concerns ahead of others, unconcerned about social justice, jumps in to tell of own problems when others talk of their problems, lacks empathy.

SOFT HEADED

Type III
Soft Hearted / Soft Headed
(Dangerous Combination)

Rarely questions effects of methods, easily discouraged or distracted when approaching a problem, gullible and swayed by emotional appeals, asks vague questions, thinks "one opinion is as good as another," reacts to arguments without identifying elements in the arguments, jumps to conclusions, follows the crowd, believes in magic.

Type IV
Hard Hearted / Soft Headed

FIGURE 2.5
Four practitioner types.

On the other hand, the Type III practitioner (soft-hearted and soft-headed) may be a deadly combination. Such a practitioner might establish a rapport with clients and gain their trust, but unknowingly apply ineffective or harmful methods. Type II (hard-hearted and hard-headed) and Type IV (hard-hearted and soft-headed) practitioners are less likely to gain the trust or cooperation of clients and may be avoided by them. Thus, these two types are less likely to do damage.

Without doubt, those who reflect feelings accurately, listen well, and convey empathy, warmth, and genuineness are exercising vital skills in the helping process. According to Hill (1982), although interpersonal skill is vital in the helping process, it alone is not enough to get results. Hill stated, "The summary of this research [regarding the helping process] indicates the importance of the therapeutic relationship is very necessary but not sufficient for client change" (p. 8). The other major component in the helping process is determining which method is effective and how to implement the method competently.

Further Reading About Practitioners' Fallacies

Literature on practitioners' fallacies is hard to find. Miller and Bogal (1977) have written about the fallacies of insufficient statistics (i.e., citing isolated, unrepresentative cases), not drawing a distinction between an argument's truth (i.e., are the basic premises correct?) and validity (i.e., does the conclusion follow logically from the premises?), and ignorance of hypothesis testing (i.e., how to test a hypothesis). Their article may have been the first about practitioners' fallacies written specifically for social workers. *The Biomedical Bestiary* (Michael, Boyce, & Wilcox, 1984) is a captivating menagerie of practitioners' fallacies in medicine, complete with "beastly" pictures. Paul Meehl's (1973) "Why I Do Not Attend Case Conferences" is a biting criticism of faulty reasoning by clinical psychologists. (Many of Meehl's fallacies, including all evidence is equally good, reward everything—gold and garbage alike, and the Barnum effect, will be explained in later chapters. We have already introduced one of Meehl's fallacies—identifying the soft-hearted with the soft-headed.) Discussions of "clinical reasoning" are relevant to social work but often are written in language that is too abstract to make the discussion of practical value (Arkas, 1981; Coggan, MacDonald, Camacho, Carline & Taylor, 1985; Nisbett & Ross, 1980; Susser, 1977; Tversky & Kahneman, 1974).

AVOIDING QUACK REASONING

Those who try to avoid practitioners' fallacies will want to be especially aware of quack reasoning. A quack is, "One who, with little or no foundation, pretends to have skill or knowledge in a particular field" (*Webster's New Universal Unabridged Dictionary,* 1983, p. 1471). Typically, we think of quacks in medicine, but there are quacks in every discipline, who claim to have knowledge without good reason. It is important for social work practitioners to be able to recognize features of quack reasoning. Here are earmarks of **quack reasoning:**

1. Promises quick, dramatic, miraculous cures (Herbert, 1983)
2. Speaks imprecisely and vaguely to describe the client's problem and intended outcome (Herbert, 1983)
3. Employs anecdotes and testimonials to support claims (Herbert, 1983)
4. Is bound to particular dogma, theory, or beliefs, and does not incorporate new ideas or methods based on their evidence (McCain & Segal, 1988, pp. 33–34)
5. Cries "foul" when asked to subject ideas to a test (Jarvis, 1987, p. 54)
6. Does not base methods on rationale or theory consistent with natural laws as we now understand them (*Alternative Therapy,* 1986, p. 62)
7. Joins cults that follow the techniques of a charismatic individual in which members consider themselves to be among the faithful (*Alternative Therapy,* 1986, p. 65)
8. Claims that their methods have effects "such that they cannot be tested by normal approved methods of clinical trial" (*Alternative Therapy,* 1986, p. 71)

9. Adopts a grab-bag approach to evidence by mixing bona fide versus bogus evidence in the same bag, just so the evidence supports some favored conclusion (Radner & Radner, 1982, pp. 54–55)

SUMMARY

This chapter presented definitions and illustrations of nine practitioners' fallacies that are often encountered in reasoning about social work practice:

- appealing to experience
- attacking the person rather than the person's argument
- appealing to authority
- accepting uncritical documentation
- appealing to popularity or numbers
- appealing to tradition or newness
- accepting testimonials
- acquiescing to the manner of a person presenting an idea
- assuming that practitioners who are soft-hearted must also be soft-headed

Social workers who are wary of such fallacies in their own reasoning, and in the reasoning of others, will most likely be able to help clients more effectively. The trick is being able to sniff out the fallacies. Hunting for fallacies is like trying to spot animals and birds in a dense forest; the underbrush of emotion, busy schedules, routine, and group pressure can obscure the view. Errors in reasoning frequently go unnoticed in discussions with agency colleagues, case conferences, and formal presentations at large workshops and conferences. So, just as those who want to observe creatures in the forest must train their eye, practitioners must practice detecting fallacies that can affect their practice. The following exercise will help.

FALLACY-SPOTTING EXERCISE

Instructions

The following describes events and statements made at a hypothetical workshop. This fictitious workshop, although concerning family therapy, might just as well be about methods for treating child abusers, motivating welfare recipients, counseling depressed individuals, training sex therapists, or other such field. All nine practitioners' fallacies are hidden somewhere in the dialogue. As you come to a parenthetical number in the dialogue, write the name of the fallacy that best applies on a separate piece of paper. You will probably get more out of the exercise if you name the fallacy and describe how it works, then check your answers against the key in the back of the book.

Background

You and your colleagues at the Springfield County Human Service Department have had a lucky break. Funds are available from your agency's professional education program allowing you to attend a workshop conducted by a national expert in conjoint family therapy, Dr. C. Michael Wiley. On the day of the conference, you arrive an hour early to register, collect your conference handouts, and get a good seat in the auditorium with your friends.

You are at the registration desk and you have just written a check to pay for your registration. The size of your check has made you feel fortunate indeed that the agency will reimburse you for the cost of the conference. As you lean over the registration table to fill out your name tag, you overhear two strangers discussing the conference.

FIRST STRANGER: You're going to love Dr. Wiley! *He has got to be one of the most effective conjoint family therapists who ever lived.* I could listen to that man for weeks and never get bored.

SECOND STRANGER: Oh? What's so special about him?

FIRST STRANGER: Dr. Wiley is so charismatic and persuasive that his enthusiasm spills over into the whole audience. You'll see! I get so excited when I hear him. I like the sound of his voice—and the way he treats the audience. He takes the microphone right down into the crowd to talk things out with them. If this conference is at all like the last one, Dr. Wiley will give us a demonstration of family sculpture. By the time he's done with that, he will have had 30 or 40 people from the audience directly involved—each one playing the role of a different family member. He kids each participant and has a little talk with them to discuss their role in the family sculpture. [*#1 Hint: What does the first stranger conclude about Dr. Wiley's effectiveness? What is the dominant form of argument used to support this reasoning?*]

SECOND STRANGER: Dr. Wiley certainly sounds dynamic. It is nice to know you think he is such an effective family therapist. What else do you think of Dr. Wiley's methods?

FIRST STRANGER: Well, just look around you. All these people can't be wrong. (You glance up from the table and notice how the crowd is thickening.) I have heard that Dr. Wiley's workshop in Michigan had so many applicants that they were forced to move it at the last minute to the largest auditorium in the city, and still the auditorium was packed. They had to bus people from the old meeting site to the larger auditorium rather than disappoint people. Nobody can put together a book of readings about conjoint family therapy without at least one chapter written by Dr. Wiley. Isn't this great! [*#2 Again, the second stranger has asked about Dr. Wiley's methods, and the first stranger has provided a fallacious argument.*]

Your registration complete, you look up and recognize two of your favorite co-workers. You exchange cheerful greetings and hustle into the auditorium to seats close to the podium. After about 30 minutes of good-natured humor and enjoyable discussion with your colleagues, the program begins with the introduction of Dr. Wiley.

(The master of ceremonies and Dr. Wiley go to the podium together. The audience stills in anticipation.)

MASTER OF CEREMONIES: For me, the high point of my professional lifetime is introducing to you Dr. C. Michael Wiley. No one is better qualified to speak to you about the effectiveness of conjoint family therapy than is Dr. Wiley. Dr. Wiley has been conducting family therapy for 40 years. In those 40 years he has worked intensively with approximately 5,000 families. No one is more experienced in conjoint family therapy than is Dr. Wiley. His past experience attests to the effectiveness of his methods. [*#3 What is the fallacy here?*] Furthermore, Dr. Wiley's educational achievements are monumental. Dr. Wiley has a total of 10 honorary doctoral degrees from American and European universities. He has served for five years as the family therapist in residence at the Vienna Family Therapy Institute. He has published 50 articles on family therapy methods. His educational achievements and administrative posts further attest to the effectiveness of his methods. [*#4 What is the fallacy here?*] Dr. Wiley has been, at one and the same time, a champion of tried-and-true methods and methods that are at the forefront of the conjoint family movement. Unquestionably, Dr. Wiley was the first to develop traditional conjoint family therapy methods based on his understanding of family systems and the need to discard traditional notions that therapists should focus on an identified client. More recently, Dr. Wiley has helped to develop strategic-behavior and solution-focused methods for working with families. Dr. Wiley's claims to effectiveness rest firmly on his experience with both time-honored methods and revolutionary new developments in the field. [*#5 What is the fallacy here?*]

DR. WILEY: Thank you very much for the generous introduction, Mr. Holcomb. I am honored by your kind words. I thought that the best way

to begin our program today would be to bring in members of families I have helped to discuss their experiences in family therapy. So today I have with me the Jones family: Mrs. Eleanor Jones, Mr. Robert Jones, and their two adolescent children, Jeff and Elaine. Perhaps Mrs. Jones would be willing to describe her early thoughts about family therapy and how the process has affected her.

MRS. JONES: (obviously a little nervous, but conveying an air of sincerity) I was a little reluctant at first to even consider speaking to you about how we participated in family therapy, but we are all so grateful to Dr. Wiley that we really thought we must tell our story. If you had seen our family two years ago you would have thought we were all candidates for the loony bin. My husband drank; I had insomnia and anorexia and was down to 90 pounds; Jeff fought with his peers and literally left his mark on them—he was compelled to bite other children—and Elaine would not accept our supervision. She was uncontrollable. We all went to Dr. Wiley at the suggestion of a school counselor and the social worker who had seen Elaine during one of her running-away periods. It has been a long hard road, but with Dr. Wiley's help, little by little, we began to see how our problems were interrelated.

(Mrs. Jones speaks for about 15 minutes, answers questions from the audience, and concludes:)

MRS. JONES: I was astounded by the effectiveness of Dr. Wiley's methods. I highly recommend him to you. [*#6 What is the fallacy here?*]

(The workshop continues as Dr. Wiley demonstrates the use of family sculpture and shows videotapes of himself working with families. After several hours of interaction with the audience, Dr. Wiley begins to conclude his presentation.)

DR. WILEY: As I see it, you're either a warm, caring, genuine, empathic person *or* you're a cold, insensitive, analytical, methodical scientist. You can't be both. There are those who say that as family therapists, we should adopt a critical attitude and should conduct scientific investigations to measure the effectiveness of our methods. I say to you, who needs such investigations? You who have worked with families: Do you need some measure to tell you what you already know? Of course not! You know when you are reaching a family and when you are not. And assume you were to try to measure effectiveness of family therapy. How would you do it? It would be like trying to hold a sunbeam in your hand. It would be like trying to measure the beauty of the sunset. Just as such things cannot be measured, so too effects of family therapy are too elusive, too subtle to be measured. [*#7 What is the fallacy here?*]

(A member of the audience raises her hand; Dr. Wiley beckons to her, and she goes to the center of the audience to stand next to him. She seems a little uncomfortable.)

UNCOMFORTABLE
QUESTIONER: Dr. Wiley, I sense that your methods may be effective. I very much enjoyed being here in the audience today, but I still wonder if I should adopt your methods. What evidence do you have, other than your experience, which is admittedly very extensive, and testimonials by many whom you have helped, to show that your methods are generally effective?

(Dr. Wiley stiffens, his knuckles paling as he grips the back of a chair in front of him.)

DR. WILEY: Always there are the doubting Thomases to question me. This gets very tiresome after awhile. [*#8 What is the fallacy here?*] Simply that others have written articles to support my methods should be enough to convince you. [*#9 What is the fallacy here?*]

REFERENCES

Alternative Therapy. (1986). British Medical Association, London: Chameleon.

Anderson, S. C., & Grant, J. F. (1984). Pregnant women and alcohol: Implications for social work. *Social Casework, 65,* 3–10.

Arkas, H. R. (1981). Impediments to accurate clinical judgment and possible ways to minimize their impact. *Journal of Consulting and Clinical Psychology, 49*(3), 323–330.

Bierter, W. (1977). The dangers of allowing social work to be invaded by science. *International Social Service Journal, 29*(4), 789–794.

Black, M. (1952). *Critical thinking.* Englewood Cliffs, NJ: Prentice-Hall.

Blenkner, M., Bloom, M., & Nielsen, M. (1971). A research and demonstration project of protective services. *Social Casework, 52*(8), 483–499.

Chase, S. (1956). *Guides to straight thinking.* New York: Harper & Row.

Coggan, P. G., MacDonald, S. C., Camacho, Z., Carline, J., & Taylor, T. (1985). An analysis of the magnitude of clinical-reasoning deficiencies in one class. *Journal of Medical Education, 60*(4), 293–301.

Coles, C. D., Smith, I. E., & Falek, A. (1987). Prenatal alcohol exposure and infant behavior: Immediate effects and implications for later development. *Advances in Alcohol and Substance Abuse, 6*(4), 87–104.

Cramp, A. J. (1921). *Nostrums and quackery.* Chicago: American Medical Association.

Cramp, A. J., & Simmons, G. H. (1936). *Nostrums and quackery and pseudo-medicine* (Vol. 3). Chicago: American Medical Association.

Crumb, F. W. (1973). Boos and bouquets for Fischer [Letter to the editor]. *Social Work, 18*(2), 124, 126.

Deaths, Deemer. (1935, May 27). *Morning Call,* p. 7.

Eau Claire Stop Smoking Center. (1981). At last a guaranteed way to stop smoking for good without withdrawals or gaining weight (pp. 1–5). (Available from 1119 Regis Court, Eau Claire, WI)

Evans, B. (1958). *The natural history of nonsense.* New York: Vintage.

Fearnside, W. W., & Holther, W. B. (1959). *Fallacy.* Englewood Cliffs, NJ: Prentice-Hall.

Fischer, J. (1973). Is casework effective?: A review. *Social Work, 18*(1), 5–20.

Foley, J. P. (1940a). The baboon boy of South Africa. *American Journal of Psychology, 53*(1), 128–133.

Foley, J. P. (1940b). The "baboon boy" of South Africa. *Science, 91*(2360), 291–292.

Foxx, R. M., & Azrin, N. H. (1973). The elimination of autistic self-stimulating behavior by overcorrection. *Journal of Applied Behavior Analysis, 6*(1), 1–14.

Funt, I. G. (1962). The application of casework principles in family life education. *Social Casework, 43,* 130–137.

Gula, R. J. (1979). *Nonsense: How to overcome it.* New York: Stein & Day.

Haley, J. (1980). *Leaving home.* New York: McGraw-Hill.

Harnadek, A. (1976). *Critical thinking: Book 1.* Pacific Grove, CA: Midwest Publications.

Herbert, V. (1983). Special report on quackery: Nine ways to spot a quack! *Health, 15*(10), 39–41.

Hill, C. E. (1982). Counseling process research: Philosophical and methodological dilemmas. *Counseling Psychologist, 10*(4), 7–19.

Iber, F. L. (1980). Fetal alcohol syndrome. *Nutrition Today, 15*(5), 4–9.

I wouldn't be without new Konjola. (1929, August). *Tribune Republican,* p. 3.

Jarvis, W. (1987). Chiropractic: A skeptical view. *The Skeptical Inquirer, 12*(1), 47–55.

Jones, K. L., Smith, D. W., Ulleland, C. N., & Streissguth, A. P. (1973). Pattern of malformation in offspring of chronic alcoholic mothers. *Lancet, 1,* 1267–1271.

Jurjevich, R. M. (1978). Emotionality and irrationality in psychotherapeutic fads. *Psychotherapy: Theory, Research and Practice, 15*(2), 168–179.

Local lady took Natex year ago—had good health ever since. (1935, May 27). *Morning Call,* p. 7.

McCain, G., & Segal, E. M. (1988). *The game of science.* Pacific Grove, CA: Brooks/Cole.

Meehl, P. E. (1973). Why I do not attend case conferences. *Psychodiagnosis: Selected papers* (pp. 225–323). Minneapolis: University of Minnesota Press.

Meier, R. S., & Feldhusen, J. F. (1979). Another look at Dr. Fox: Effect of stated purpose evaluation, lecture expressiveness, and density of lecture content on student ratings. *Journal of Educational Psychology, 71,* 339–345.

Michael, M., Boyce, W. T., & Wilcox, A. J. (1984). *Biomedical bestiary: An epidemiologic guide to flaws and fallacies in the medical literature.* Boston: Little, Brown.

Miller, J. (1988). AIDS heresy. *Discover, 9*(6), 63–68.

Miller, S. I., & Bogal, R. B. (1977). Logic as a tool for clinical training in social work. *Psychiatric Quarterly, 49*(1), 18–28.

Moore, B., & Parker, R. (1986). *Critical thinking: Evaluating claims and arguments in everyday life.* Palo Alto, CA: Mayfield.

Mykel, S. J. (1981). Fads and fallacies in psychoanalysis. *Issues in Ego Psychology, 4*(2), 33–37.

Naftulin, D. H., Ware, J. E., & Donnelly, F. A. (1973). The Doctor Fox lecture: A paradigm of educational seduction. *Journal of Medical Education, 48,* 630–635.

National Institute on Alcohol Abuse and Alcoholism. (1978). *Alcohol and Health,* Third Special Report to the Congress. Washington DC: U.S. Department of Health, Education and Welfare.

Nisbett, R., & Ross, L. (1980). *Human inferences: Strategies and shortcomings in social judgment.* Englewood Cliffs, NJ: Prentice-Hall.

Radner, D., & Radner, M. (1982). *Science and unreason.* Belmont, CA: Wadsworth.

Rosal, V. (1978). The nurse's role in the management of Parkinson's disease. *The Journal of Nursing Care, 11*(2), 10, 12, 30.

Saleeby, D. (1979). The tension between research and practice: Assumptions of the experimental paradigm. *Clinical Social Work Journal, 7*(4), 267–284.

Seech, Z. (1987). *Logic in everyday life.* Belmont, CA: Wadsworth.

Starr, P. (1973). Boos and bouquets for Fischer [Letter to the editor]. *Social Work, 18*(2), 124.

Susser, M. (1977). Judgment and causal inferences: Criteria in epidemiologic studies. *Journal of Epidemiology, 105*(1), 1–15.

Tversky, A., & Kahneman, D. (1974). Judgment under uncertainty: Heuristics and biases. *Science, 185,* 1124–1131.

Ware, J. E., & Williams, R. G. (1975). The Dr. Fox effect: A study of lecture expressiveness and ratings of instruction. *Journal of Medical Education, 50*(2), 149–156.

Warner, R. H., & Rosett, H. L. (1975). The effects of drinking on offspring. *Journal of Studies on Alcohol, 36,* 1395–1420.

Webster's New Universal Unabridged Dictionary (2nd ed.). (1983). New York: Simon & Schuster.

Weinbach, R. W. (1988). Manipulations of student evaluations: No laughing matter. *Journal of Social Work Education, 24*(1), 27–34.

Williams, R. G., & Ware, J. E. (1976). Validity of student ratings of instruction under different incentive conditions: A further study of the Dr. Fox effect. *Journal of Educational Psychology, 68*(1), 48–56.

Zingg, R. M. (1940). More about the "baboon boy" of South Africa. *American Journal of Psychology, 53*(3), 455–462.

Zingg, R. M. (1941). India's wolf-children. *Scientific American, 164*(3), 135–137.

3

Applying Scientific Reasoning to Social Work

For our purposes, reasoning well means applying basic principles of scientific thinking to common problems in social work. Being able to improve this reasoning is the subject of this chapter, which begins with a general definition of science, then describes 10 features of scientific thinking about social work. The remainder of the chapter is an exercise intended to help the reader apply scientific reasoning to case material.

THE SCIENTIFIC METHOD

Jacob Bronowski (1978), well known to television viewers for his nationally televised series, *Ascent of Man,* masterfully interpreted the meaning of science for the masses. Bronowski has stated that scientific thinking is to cultural history what crawling out of the ocean onto land was to mankind's evolutionary history— science is *that* basic to survival and advancement as a species. However, a universally accepted definition of the **scientific method** is as elusive as the abominable snowman (Caws, 1965).

Still, there are features common to all definitions of scientific method. Generally, the scientist begins an investigation motivated by a feeling of concern and wonder. Carl Sagan (1987) thinks this feeling—the wide-eyed wonder that children experience when they first begin to explore the world—is a principal force that propels scientific investigation. The scientist's wonder is then formulated more specifically into particular questions: How can we get electrons to move a shorter distance to increase the speed of a computer? Which of these endangered plants in the tropical rain forest will have medicinal effects? What factors determine whether children will adapt well to placement in a given type of foster home? What group counseling method will affect self-esteem among victims of incest most positively?

The imagination then conjures up explanations for the phenomenon, and each explanation is tested mentally for a fit against what is known about reality. Next, the imagination, based on personal experience, reading, discussion with others, and sometimes simply wild speculation, isolates a few of the most plausible explanations. Generally, such plausible explanations are then conceptualized by the scientist as hypotheses—specific statements formulated so clearly that they can be submitted to a test. Formulating hypotheses, and knowing how to test them, is the interface between imagination and the scientific method.

In social work this interface often concerns hypotheses about practice. The hypothesis that follows was formulated by a student social worker who wished to determine whether a certain program for anger-management training was successful in reducing a client's level of anger in a single case study:

> If Sarah participates in anger management training at the Centre for Psychological Services, baseline from April 1 to April 19, treatment from April 20 to May 11, and a second baseline from May 12 to May 21, Sarah's level of anger (as measured by the Navacco Anger Scale, 1975), will be at a significantly ($p < .05$) lower average level during her second baseline than during her first baseline. (Piehl, 1989)

Often such clearly formulated questions yield negative results, so the scientist tries again. Nobel laureate Sir Peter Medawar (1979) said of this trial-and-error process: "The day-to-day business of science consists not in hunting for facts but in testing hypotheses—that is, ascertaining if they or their implications are statements about real life" (p. 84). If the hypothesis does not reflect reality, the scientist rethinks the hypothesis and begins the investigation again. Thus, the scientific method is an active process; *science is a verb, not a noun.* Science is a self-correcting, systematic, deliberate procedure for determining what is true.

WHY SCIENTIFIC REASONING FOR SOCIAL WORKERS?

Accountability—A Professional's Tool

Accountability implies that the social worker is responsible to clients and funding agencies to achieve stated goals (Newman & Turem, 1974). For example, if social workers initiate a sex education program for adolescents in a local school system, students should then score higher on a test of their knowledge related to objectives of the program. Determining how to define a program's intended outcome, keeping records of that program's implementation and measuring the program's success rate are an essential part of accountability (Eldrige, 1984). Such definitions, records, and measures are also essential elements in scientific reasoning.

Evaluation Research

Initially, the evidence regarding evaluation research was grim. Fischer's (1973) review of 11 studies evaluating social casework's effectiveness as it was practiced from the 1950s and 1960s revealed, "that lack of effectiveness seems to be the rule" (p. 5). A few years later, Fischer's 1976 book, *The Effectiveness of Social Casework,* raised concerns about possible iatrogenic effects of social work: "It seems not only that professional casework, on the whole, is not helpful, but that often, clients are actually harmed by casework services" (p. 106).

More recent reviews report more optimistic conclusions about social work's effectiveness. According to Reid and Hanrahan (1982), more recent studies described more clearly defined interventions, interventions serving a wider range of client types, group methods that are more frequently applied than before, and intervention goals that are more limited although more specific. Reid and Hanrahan claimed that the majority of such studies done between 1973 and 1981 reported positive effects. Although Fischer (1983) argued that Reid and Hanrahan's review did not show unequivocally that social work is effective—because studies were too weak to be conclusive—more recent reviews have supported Reid and Hanrahan's conclusions. Rubin's (1985) review of studies done between July 1978 and June 1983 iterated grounds for optimism about social work's effectiveness, but Rubin was discouraged that only 12 studies met methodological criteria for inclusion in the review. His conclusions showed: (a) highly structured forms of practice (e.g., social-skills training for mentally retarded adults or stress-management training for women on public assistance) are effectively directed toward outcome goals; (b) individual differences among clients should be taken into account when matching clients with their interventions; and (c) positive outcomes are generally found for problem-solving and task-centered methods (Rubin, 1985, p. 494). Still more recent literature reviews (Videka-Sherman, 1988) have sought to determine which approaches are most effective with particular client groups against indices of treatment effect size (we will define effect size in Chapter 9). Videka-Sherman's review concluded that mental health clients benefit most when: (a) intervention is time-limited (scheduled to stop after a particular interval); (b) interventions have been specifically defined; (c) clients get homework tasks; and (d) therapists give clients advice.

Implementing CSWE Policy

The Council on Social Work Education mandates in its *Handbook of Accreditation Standards and Procedures* (1988) that, "Every part of the professional foundation curriculum should [because science produces useful knowledge] therefore help to bring students to an understanding and appreciation of the necessity of a scientific, analytic approach to knowledge building and practice" (p. 127). However, how best to implement these new standards to increase understanding and appreciation of the scientific method has not yet been determined. Although there are many approaches to teaching how to integrate research into social work practice (Barth, 1981; Beckerman, 1978; Bloom & Fischer, 1982; Epstein, 1981; Fortune, 1982; Rabin, 1985; Tripodi & Epstein, 1979), a review of the professional literature about practice education uncovered no studies examining the relative effectiveness of different approaches to teaching science to social workers (Sowers-Hoag & Thyer, 1985).

Although the Council mandated teaching a scientific approach, making scientific thinking "useful" to social work students and practitioners is another matter. A survey of undergraduate and postgraduate social work students showed perceived usefulness of social work research (which was low to begin with) varied little from lower to higher educational levels (Rosenblatt & Kirk, 1981). Another study, using Rosenblatt and Kirk's questionnaire, found that social work practitioners view research as being even less important and useful than do social work students (Rosen & Mutschler, 1982).

Of course, topics in research courses that will make greater practical sense to social work students and practitioners may be selected. Some typical content areas from a survey of baccalaureate social work research curricula are: problem formulation, variable relationships, hypothesis development, theory development, sampling techniques, experimental design, field research methods, document analysis, coding and data reduction, ethical standards, and evaluation research (Bogal & Singer, 1981, p. 47). While these are all excellent topics for a research course, their relevance to practice may not be clearly apparent. In an effort to make research more "useful" to social workers, some additional topics have been added to this text including: motivating students by showing how good intentions are not sufficient to help clients; identifying characteristics of the scientific approach for social workers; and helping students learn to spot practitioners' fallacies, generate questions about a method's effectiveness based on prevalent theory and practical experience, and pose such questions specifically enough to determine what works; defining goals with clients clearly enough to judge whether such goals have been achieved; systematically weighing study credibility and treatment effect size; using online computer procedures to locate quality evidence about particular problems in practice; and assessing client risk.

CHARACTERISTICS OF A SCIENTIFIC SOCIAL WORKER

Reasoning scientifically requires that the tenets of good thinking that apply across all disciplines are followed. For example, political scientists conducting a survey of voter preferences and medical researchers seeking the causes of a particular kind of tumor both try not to let their biases and preconceived notions influence them as they gather and analyze their data. Although social work is no exception to this rule, as with other disciplines, the particular subject matter demands that scientific principles be interpreted as they relate to particular problems within that discipline. The following attributes of a scientific approach to social work, while not all-inclusive, do reflect what social workers can actually do if they follow the guidelines in the research literature (Arkava & Lane, 1983; Atheron & Klemmack, 1982; Grinnell, 1985; Monette, Sullivan, & DeJong, 1990; Weinbach & Grinnell, 1987).

1. Asks: "Does the Method Work?"

Paul De Kruif (1926) studied great researchers, those whose ideas still profoundly shape our lives. He concluded that great researchers are not necessarily geniuses, but they all have one distinguishing feature in common—honesty! They all dared to ask embarrassing questions. Indeed, questioning basic assumptions is the first step in science (Bronowski, 1978, pp. 32–33).

Being skeptical about social work practice does not imply debunking every detail. It means questioning the big conclusions that concern the welfare of clients: Should adoption records be opened or closed to foster a good adjustment for children? Is conjoint family therapy more effective than individual family therapy? Both questions—adoptions (Curtis, 1986) and conjoint family therapy (Wells & Gianetti, 1986)—are still far from settled. Skepticism also means tackling the littler—individual—questions, for example: Concerning Brian, a developmentally disabled adolescent boy in an institution, are his self-feeding skills improving measurably?

Sometimes it takes gumption to ask whether methods used are effective. Imagine, for example, that you work at Rest Haven, a home for aged individuals who require skilled nursing care. Your supervisor has learned about validation therapy as a method for helping confused residents to reorient themselves. Your supervisor has attended Naomi Feil's Validation Training Institute and has obtained the nursing home administrator's support to institute a new validation therapy program at Rest Haven. Under such circumstances, would you dare to ask whether validation therapy is effective? How strongly would you press for good evidence before joining the movement to use validation therapy over reality orientation?

2. Tries To Be Objective

Objectivity is essential in the search for truth. This means looking for evidence that opposes one's own position as well as evidence that supports it. Objectivity implies avoiding total commitment to a single theoretical or technical model, being open to research evidence from other disciplines, and trying to weigh strengths and weaknesses of evidence fairly. Such commitment to seeking the truth is essential to the spirit and purpose of scientific investigation. Without a commitment to objectivity, as best it may be obtained, research methods would be an empty exercise.

Formulating impressions of clients based on their behavior, rather than on some preconceived notion or prejudice, indicates the practitioner's commitment to objectivity. In one study (Johnson, Kurtz, Tomlinson, & Howe, 1986) investigators asked diagnosticians to rate five videotaped interviews that used identical scripts, but different interviewees: an attractive young white woman, a middle-aged professional white man, a middle-aged white housewife, an attractive young black woman, and an elderly white man. The diagnosticians rated the young attractive white woman as being not only the most attractive, but also the most reliable source of information. Coincidence? Probably not. Preconceived notions about a client's personality (Arkes, 1981), social class (Franklin, 1986), and prior impressions of the client (Nisbett & Ross, 1980) can affect a practitioner's judgment.

Generally, objectivity is possible when one sets up a test to measure some outcome independent of the observers' thoughts and desires regarding the outcome. For example, observers might be asked to evaluate effectiveness of a delinquency-prevention program. If such observers can agree on how to measure delinquency and on what features constitute effectiveness in the program, then they are in a better position to evaluate the program's effectiveness against some outcome measure, for example, court records of convictions for new delinquent acts.

Some argue that objectivity is impossible in the social sciences and that simply by choosing some question for evaluation, a "valuation," or value judgment, has been made—thus rendering objectivity impossible. That is, by selecting one question instead of another values have interfered with the scientific process. A counterargument to this "valuation" argument is that while it is true that values have led to selecting one question over another—social workers make important value choices all the time—it does not follow that once the question has been selected based on some value position, that the scientist must abandon sound scientific methods while trying to answer the question. Another argument against objectivity is made by those who tell horror stories about a few scientists who have fabricated their data; such fabrication is said to prove that scientists cannot be objective. There are many such philosophical arguments against objectivity, but generally, on closer examination, they only illustrate the difficulty—not the impossibility—of being objective (Gibbs, 1983).

3. Distinguishes Between Questions of Fact and Questions of Value

Problems arise when questions of value are confused with questions of fact. A **question of value** is a state of uncertainty that cannot be answered by a procedure of verification (experimentation), but rests on an underlying belief, assumption, or feeling based on conscience. Questions of value are usually posed with the word "should" somewhere: Should adopted children adjust well socially? Should adopted children know who their biological parents are?

On the other hand, a **question of fact** can be resolved by setting up a test, a procedure for verification such that independent observers could agree if a given condition is met. A social worker wondering if adopted children should be informed of the names of their biological parents before such children reach age 18 might ask the following testable, verifiable, question of fact: Among the children placed for adoption in Kenwood County during the past 10 years, will scores on an index of social adjustment be higher for children who knew the name of their biological parent at the time of their adoption compared to those who did not?

Questions posed by social scientists always begin with some valuation (Myrdal, 1969), but problems arise when questions of value are confused with questions of fact. For example, a social worker who is deeply concerned about the welfare of adopted children may read an impassioned article about an adopted child who searched for years to contact his or her biological parents and the child's tearful reunion with them. In concluding the article, the writer might argue: "If you are sensitive at all, you will support legislation that supports open adoption records." This leap from sympathy felt toward one individual to a legislative change that may affect thousands ignores relevant questions of fact regarding whether self-esteem, interpersonal adjustment, and competency will be affected by open versus closed records. The confusion in the question is due to an "appeal to pity" (Gula, 1979, p. 26), which occurs when a speaker presents a pitiful and heartrending situation and then immediately calls for action as though a related question of fact had been settled.

4. States Problem and Goals in Measurable Terms

"Occasionally one hears that programs of social work produce outcomes so subtle they cannot be measured but that somehow without them [social worker programs] society would be worse off. When the outcome is not measurable, social workers are probably engaging in self-delusion" (Newman & Turem, 1974, p. 16). Newman and Turem were explaining why social workers need to become experts in measurement to determine whether they are actually achieving the noble goals that they set out to achieve with their clients. If, for example, social workers can measure "codependency," "self-esteem," and "marital adjustment," it becomes possible to establish whether any improvement has taken place in these areas. Measurement is essential to avoiding crippling vagueness. Such vagueness arises when, rather than referring to specific behaviors of clients, nebulous adjectives such as "somewhat improved," "better," or "severe," are used to describe clients' behaviors (Cutler, 1979, pp. 31–32). Vagueness also occurs when descriptions of clients are given in such general terms that the description may apply to any number of clients (Kadushin, 1963).

5. Uses Caution When Inferring What Caused Improvement

Miller and Bogal (1977) warned that social workers need to be cautious when inferring that their methods cause improvement. Experienced social workers may recognize this kind of causal reasoning:

- Mr. Heath's symptoms of depression became so debilitating that his wife finally convinced him to go to the Carson County Guidance Clinic for counseling. The social worker there met with him weekly for 4 months using a technique that she called "cognitive behavior therapy." At the end of the fourth month, Mr. Heath had none of the symptoms that had led to his referral. Apparently, cognitive behavior therapy was an effective method with Mr. Heath.

Simply because Mr. Heath's improvement followed cognitive behavior therapy does not prove that the therapy caused his improvement. Other intervening factors may have been the real cause: Mr. Heath may have a biochemical problem that corrected itself or was corrected by medication; or he might have changed jobs, inherited money, or resolved a conflict with his wife. Such factors may be the real cause of his improvement.

It is only through the systematic application of experimental design that causal inferences can be made with confidence. Successively more and more complex experimental designs allow us to be more and more sure of just what is actually causing the improvement.

6. Is Cautious When Making Generalizations

Deciding what is generally true about a given individual and what is generally true about groups of clients requires rigorous scientific thinking. Regarding an individual, a social worker watching a child throw a tantrum during a particularly stressful moment might conclude the child is often difficult. Regarding generalizations about whole classes of clients, social workers helping battered women in a refuge home for abused women might begin to see all men as being abusive.

Social workers who reason scientifically will recognize that criteria need to be set for making observations and representative samples of client behaviors need to be taken before generalizations can be made with confidence. Principles for sampling group and individual behavior, constructing clear questions, and collecting and analyzing survey data can be powerful tools for making better generalizations.

7. Asks Specific Questions

Vague questions yield vague answers, while specific questions help social workers and clients to focus their efforts.

Here is an example of a vague question (Arnold, 1988, p. 1):

- What effect has the constant sexual abuse and incest prevention via the media and school programming had in the reporting of fraudulent instances of the above?

Here is a related—but more specific—question (Arnold, 1988, p. 2):

- Will 300 Chippewa Falls elementary school students in grades kindergarten through six who are randomly assigned on May 2 to attend a Spiderman Program [Spiderman presents a program showing students the difference between appropriate and inappropriate touch] perform statistically significantly higher on a "Good Touch/Bad Touch" posttest on May 2 than those randomly assigned to the control group who did not attend the Spiderman Program?

Regardless of the complexity of an experimental design implied, questions posed by social workers can be made clearer against specific criteria. (Chapter 6 will describe how to clarify unspecific questions.)

8. Recognizes Golden Evidence

The eclectic approach to practice teaches that social workers should choose methods that are best supported by "golden" or empirical evidence (i.e., random assignment to treatment groups, attempts to control sources of error, and clear definition of outcome, Fischer, 1978). But how shall such evidence be weighed objectively?

One of the most pervasive and perplexing problems confronting eclectic practitioners is the way studies vary in quality and seem to contradict each other. (The Quality of Study Rating Form in Chapter 9 is designed to help practitioners to weigh study quality and treatment effect size.)

9. Knows How to Look for Golden Evidence

Valuable evidence must be found quickly and efficiently by practitioners who need it to guide their decisions. Library skills are essential to this search. Effective searching may involve old manual methods, but searching data bases electronically can uncover the same quality of evidence in less time (Gibbs & Johnson, 1983). Social workers need to know how to search for pertinent evidence manually and by using new computerized data bases including *Social Work Abstracts*.

10. Is Aware of Probability in Decision Making

Another difficult and ever-present problem in social work practice is uncertainty about a decision. All decisions reflect, at least implicitly, how probabilities have been weighed. For example, an intake worker in a psychiatric facility cannot admit all who are at risk; thus, the worker must assess the probability that individuals will harm themselves or others if they are not admitted. Protective service workers must weigh the chances that those who are referred to the agency will reabuse a child. Implicit in the primary counselor's intake interview with an alcoholic is likely to be weighing the probability of whether a client will improve more in in-patient or in out-patient treatment. Although such questions are incredibly complex, the scientific approach implies trying to identify such probabilities as explicitly as possible.

SUMMARY

This chapter began by underscoring the importance of applying the scientific method to social work practice and proceeded to identify 10 earmarks of a scientific social worker. The scientific social worker:

1. Asks: "Does the method work?"
2. Tries to be objective
3. Distinguishes between questions of fact and of value
4. States problem and goals in measurable terms
5. Uses caution when inferring what caused improvement
6. Is cautious when making generalizations
7. Asks specific questions
8. Recognizes golden evidence
9. Knows how to look for golden evidence
10. Is aware of probability in decision making

The Professional Thinking Form (PTF), presented below, is intended to be used both as an exercise to help social workers learn to identify errors that violate scientific reasoning about practice and as a research instrument to measure the ability to apply predominant principles of research methods to social work practice.

The PTF's first 11 items review concepts covered thus far in the text; the remaining 12 items provide a preview of forthcoming material.

THE PROFESSIONAL THINKING FORM

Purpose

How can social workers learn to apply principles of scientific reasoning to social work practice? How can scientific reasoning be made more useful to social workers? One possible answer concerns how common fallacies in reasoning also violate principles of research methods; for example, "hasty generalization," which occurs when an observer takes a look at a few cases and quickly generalizes to all cases (Moore & Parker, 1986, p. 247), violates the corresponding research principle that samples should be drawn representatively from a population (Kerlinger, 1986). Thus, students learning to spot fallacies in reasoning about social work practice may also be learning the essence of basic research methods.

The Professional Thinking Form (PTF) should be an effective way to help you to apply scientific reasoning to practice situations. It was designed as a review of knowledge of practitioners' fallacies that have already been explained

in this text (items 1–11) and as a preview of those to be explained in future chapters. Each of the 23 items on the PTF is intended to contain only one practitioner's fallacy, although there may be elements of other fallacies mixed in with each item. Try to identify the predominant fallacy in each item. Each item is based on a real situation, but names, dates, and locations have been changed.

You may best learn how to identify each fallacy by testing yourself as you go along: Read the instructions, label and describe each item's fallacy as best you can on a separate sheet of paper, and then consult Appendix C, the answer key. If you need help with any of the first 11 items, review key points of Chapter 2 and the first part of this chapter; items 12–23 are a preview—do the best you can. Have fun, but remember too that reasoning skills tested in the PTF concern the most vital decision making of all—that which can greatly affect other human lives.

PTF EXERCISES

The following items concern issues in practice. They test your ability to think analytically and critically about real issues that you may encounter in practice.

Please react to each item from the standpoint of scientific thinking. If any item is objectionable from this standpoint, specify what is wrong with it. If you are satisfied with the item as it stands, then mark it "OK." If you cannot make up your mind on one, then mark it with a question mark (?). Leave none blank.

The following two instructions apply only to use of the form in research:

- Do not put your name on this paper. Your responses will not be used to grade you nor to reflect negatively or positively on you in any way.

- Please be brief, and when you have finished, turn your paper over and leave it that way. You will be allowed a total of 40 minutes to complete the form.

Please react to the following statements:

1. Did you attend the workshop on Strategic Family Therapy? Marian Steinberg is such an excellent speaker, and her presentation was so convincing! She treated everyone in the audience like colleagues. She got us all involved in family sculpture, and she is such a warm person. I must use her methods!

2. Have you heard of the newest counseling method, "neurolinguistic programming"? It has just been developed as a counseling technique. You ought to keep up with the times and try the new method.

3. I know that group treatment for sexually abused girls is effective. I read an article in the February 1977 issue of *Social Casework* by Gagliano that says it is.

4. Bill has been a worker at the Dulaney Halfway House for 10 years. Bill presented evidence to the county board that the rate of residents' aggressive behavior went up recently. His evidence contradicts a report of a self-study that was sent to the Dulaney Board of Directors. Other workers think Bill sub-

mitted the report because he is angry about his salary, and they consider him untrustworthy because he was once convicted of assault. They don't believe him because of his anger and past behavior.

5. I know Ms. Sanchez has just completed a 2-year study with random assignment, control groups, and a 6-month follow-up to study the effects of our treatment for alcoholics here at Hepworth Treatment Center, but my experience indicates otherwise. My experience here as a counselor has shown me that Ms. Sanchez's results are wrong.

6. This is a conversation overheard at the Terceira Staff Luncheon among Bayberry County Guidance Clinic workers attending: "You mean you don't use 'provocative therapy'? I thought everyone 'in the know' used it by now. Provocative therapy is widely implemented at this facility. Most of the staff is trained in its use. We have all experienced great results with it."

7. Dr. Trevor H. Nohland has degrees from Harvard, MIT, and Stanford. He has held the prestigious Helms Chair of Human Studies for 10 years. He has been director of three university psychiatry departments and has served as a consultant to the U.S. Department of Health, Education, and Welfare. His stature attests to the truth of ideas in his book on neurolinguistic programming.

8. At a conference a professional leans over to you and says in a confidential whisper, "I don't understand how you would accept an opinion from Ms. Hughes. Just look at her. Her hair is unkempt and her slip is showing. How can we accept an idea from someone who looks like a fugitive from an insane asylum?"

9. Recently a director of an evaluation research consulting firm was overheard saying, "We conduct a lot of studies for agencies to determine how effective their treatment programs are. We never take a consultant job to do an evaluation unless we are sure that we can produce positive results."

10. Here is a statement made by an agency supervisor to a colleague: "Michelle is one of the most difficult workers to deal with. I asked her to decide between supporting ei-

ther nutritional or health programs to meet the needs of the elderly here in Dane County. She responded that she needed some time to get evidence to study the matter. She said that there may be other alternatives. As I see it, there are only two ways to go on this issue."

11. At a professional conference Dr. McDonald asked a family that had participated in "strategic family therapy" to tell the audience how the method worked for them. The husband said to the audience, "Frankly, I didn't think we had a prayer of saving our marriage. When my wife and I made our first appointment with Dr. McDonald I thought we would go through the motions of participating in counseling, and we would get a divorce. But, as Dr. McDonald requested, my wife and I brought our son David, 13, and our daughter Emily, 11, with us to counseling. All of us have been surprised, to say the least, by Dr. McDonald's approach. Instead of engaging in a lot of deep, dark discussions, we do exercises as a family. Last time we were requested to go on a treasure hunt with me as a leader for the hunt. Dr. McDonald's exercises have been fun to do as a family. These exercises teach us about our own family system. The methods have been extremely effective, and I highly recommend them to you."

Note: The remaining items are a preview of the rest of the text. Both the preceding and following items have been included in one place to keep the PTF intact as an instrument so that it can be used in its entirety as a measurement tool in evaluation studies.

12. Shortly after the City Area Planners announced their intent to build a vocational training facility, they were deluged with phone calls and letters from angry citizens protesting the plan. Planners were surprised that the whole community opposed the plan so strongly.

13. Most likely the client's suicide was due to depression.

14. Mr. Aimes has stated that he is able to use "cognitive behavior therapy" with great effectiveness. He illustrated how effective this method can be with the case of Mr. Roberts.

Mr. Aimes said, "Mr. Roberts could no longer go to work. Instead of working, Mr. Roberts 'called in sick' and remained home with his fears. His condition became so incapacitating that even at home he locked all the doors of the house, barricaded himself in the bathroom, and remained there for many hours. He worried that his daughter would be victimized by crime in a distant city, and worried that his savings would be lost. Mr. Roberts was finally brought by ambulance to Mercy Hospital where I began cognitive behavior therapy with him immediately. Within 6 short weeks, Mr. Roberts was well enough to go home. Cognitive behavior therapy is generally an effective method for treating acute anxiety if it is used promptly by a competent clinician."

15. You overhear the following question asked by an interviewer: "Will you be able to drive yourself to the hospital weekly and eat without dentures until January 1?"

16. The interviewer goes on to ask a female victim of domestic abuse the following question: "You don't really want to stay in a home with a violent wife-beater, do you?"

17. "Conjoint family therapy" is the most effective form of intervention for family problems.

18. One way of describing the clinician's perception of "progress" in clients who are working toward their independence from their families is that progress is the gradual increase in the clients' progress toward independence from their families.

19. The effectiveness of our program in family therapy is well documented. Before families enter treatment, we have them fill out a Family Adjustment Rating Scale (FARS). The scale has a Cronbach's alpha reliability of .98 and is validly associated with indices of sexual adjustment and marital communication. After treatment, we have family members fill out the FARS again. Statistically significant improvement in FARS scores show that our program is effective.

20. A social worker remarks to a client: "It is extremely difficult to work with people who have adolescent adjustment reactions. The problem is that adolescents have not had suf-ficient experience to reality test. This is why therapists who work with adolescents tend to use existential and reality-oriented approaches with them."

21. Don Jaszewski, a social worker at Parkview Elementary School, administered the Rosenberg Self-Concept Scale to all 100 students in the school's fifth and sixth grades. For the 5 students who scored lowest on the test, Don designed a special program to raise their self-esteem. All 5 participated in a weekly rap session, read materials designed to foster self-acceptance and self-assurance, and saw Don individually at frequent intervals during the academic year. When Don readministered the Rosenberg Self-Concept Scale at the end of his program, he was pleased to note his program participants' statistically significant improvement over their pretreatment scores. In fact, Don noted that 3 of the 5 students in his program scored almost average at posttreatment. Based on this evidence, Don urged the school administration to offer his program in the future.

22. With help from a noted researcher, the Cree County Social Service Department has developed a Screening Test (ST) for families to identify potential child abusers. Experience with the ST in the Cree County School District has shown that, among confirmed abusers who took the test, the result was positive (indicating abuse) for 95% of couples who did abuse their child within the prior year. Also, among nonabusers the test results were negative (indicating no abuse) for 95%. Cree County records also show that abuse occurs in 3 of 100 families in the Cree County School District. The ST has just been administered anew to all families in the Cree County School District. If the Donohue family's ST has been randomly selected, and their test is positive (indicating likely abuse), the chance, on a scale of 0% to 100%, is 95% that the child in the Donohue family has been abused. If you disagree with this statement, explain why and what you estimate the probability to be.

23. Mr. Rasmussen, director of Regional Alcoholic Rehabilitation Clinic (RARC), is proud of his treatment facility's success rate. RARC

draws clients who are generally leading citizens in the area and whose insurance companies are willing to pay premium prices for RARC treatment for their clients. Mr. Rasmussen points out proudly that 75% of those who complete RARC's treatment, according to a valid and reliable survey done by an unbiased consulting group, abstain completely from alcohol during the 6 months following treatment. In contrast, the consulting firm reports that alcoholics who complete treatment at a local halfway house for unemployed men have a 30% abstinence rate during the same 6 months. Mr. Rasmussen says: "The difference between 70% and 30% cannot be ignored. It is obvious that RARC's multidisciplinary team and intensive case-by-case treatment are producing better results than those at the halfway house."

REFERENCES

Allen, R. W., & Greene, L. (1975). *Propaganda game*. New Haven, CT: Autotelic Instructional Materials.

Arkava, M. I., & Lane, T. A. (1983). *Beginning social work research*. Newton, MA: Allyn & Bacon.

Arkes, H. R. (1981). Impediments to accurate clinical judgment and possible ways to minimize their impact. *Journal of Consulting and Clinical Psychology, 49*(3), 323–330.

Arnold, P. (1988). *Child sexual abuse prevention: The effectiveness of the Spiderman Program in the concept of good and bad touch*. Unpublished manuscript, University of Wisconsin-Eau Claire, Eau Claire, WI.

Atherton, C. R., & Klemmack, D. L. (1982). *Research methods in social work*. Lexington, MA: D. C. Heath.

Barth, R. P. (1981). Education for practice-research: Toward a reorientation. *Journal of Education for Social Work, 17*(2) 19–25.

Beckerman, A. (1978). Differentiating between social research and social work research: Implications for teaching. *Journal of Education for Social Work, 11*(2), 9–15.

Belson, W. A. (1981). *The design and understanding of survey questions*. Aldershot, Hants, England: Gower.

Bloom, M., & Fischer, J. (1982). *Evaluating practice: Guidelines for the accountable professional*. Englewood Cliffs, NJ: Prentice-Hall.

Bogal, R. B., & Singer, M. J. (1981). Research coursework in the baccalaureate social work curriculum: A study. *Journal of Education for Social Work, 17*(2), 45–50.

Bronowski, J. (1978). *Magic, science, and civilization*. New York: Columbia University Press.

Cannell, C. F., Lawson, S. A., & Hausser, D. L. (1975). *A technique for evaluating interviewer performance*. Ann Arbor, MI: University of Michigan, Survey Research Center of the Institute for Social Research.

Caws, P. (1965). *The philosophy of science*. Princeton, NJ: Van Nostrand.

Cook, T. D., & Campbell, D. T. (1979). *Quasi-experimentation: Design & analysis issues for field settings*. Boston: Houghton Mifflin.

Council on Social Work Education. (1988, March). *Handbook of accreditation standards and procedures*. Washington, DC: Council on Social Work Education.

Cunningham, F. (1973). *Objectivity in social science*. Toronto: University of Toronto Press.

Curtis, P. (1986). The dialectics of open versus closed adoption on infants. *Child Welfare, 65*(5), 437–445.

Cutler, P. (1979). *Problem solving in clinical medicine*. Baltimore: Williams & Wilkins.

De Kruif, P. (1926). *The sweeping wind*. New York: Harcourt, Brace, & World.

Eddy, D. M. (1982). Probabilistic reasoning in clinical medicine: Problems and opportunities. In D. Kahneman, P. Slovic, & A. Tversky (Eds.), *Judgment under uncertainty: Heuristics and biases* (pp. 249–267). Cambridge: Cambridge University Press.

Eldrige, W. D. (1984). Coping with accountability and evaluation: Some guidelines for supervisors of direct service staff. *Administration in Mental Health, 11*(3), 195–204.

Epstein, L. (1981). Teaching research-based practice: Rationale and method. *Journal of Education for Social Work, 17*(2), 51–55.

Evans, B. (1958). *The natural history of nonsense.* New York: Vintage.

Fearnside, W. W., & Holther, W. B. (1959). *Fallacy: The counterfeit of argument.* Englewood Cliffs, NJ: Prentice-Hall.

Fischer, J. (1973). Is casework effective? A review. *Social Work, 18,* 5–20.

Fischer, J. (1976). *The effectiveness of social casework.* Springfield, IL: Charles C Thomas.

Fischer, J. (1978). *Effective casework practice: An eclectic approach.* New York: McGraw-Hill.

Fischer, J. (1983). Evaluation of social work effectiveness: Is positive evidence always good evidence? *Social Work, 28,* 74–77.

Fortune, A. E. (1982). Teaching students to integrate research concepts and field performance standards. *Journal of Education for Social Work, 18*(1), 5–13.

Franklin, D. L. (1986). Does client social class affect clinical judgment? *Social Casework, 67,* 424–432.

Gibbs, L. E. (1983). Evaluation research: Scientist or advocate? *Journal of Social Service Research, 7*(1), 81–92.

Gibbs, L. E. (1985). Teaching critical thinking at the university level: A review of some empirical evidence. *Informal Logic, 7*(2&3), 137–149.

Gibbs, L. E., & Johnson, D. J. (1983). Computer assisted clinical decision-making. *Journal of Social Service Research, 6*(3/4), 119–132.

Gibbs, L. E., & Werner, J. S. (1988). *Integrating research into practice: Measuring ability to detect common clinicians' fallacies.* Unpublished manuscript, University of Wisconsin-Eau Claire, Eau Claire, WI.

Goiver, T. (1985). *A practical study of argument.* Belmont, CA: Wadsworth.

Grinnell, R. M. (1985). *Social work research and evaluation* (2nd ed.). Itasca, IL: F. E. Peacock.

Gula, R. J. (1979). *Nonsense: How to overcome it.* New York: Stein & Day.

Hammill, R., Wilson, T. D., & Nisbett, R. E. (1980). Insensitivity to sample bias: Generalizing from atypical cases. *Journal of Personality and Social Psychology, 39*(4), 578–589.

Johnson, R. H., & Blair, J. A. (1983). *Logical self defense* (2nd ed.). Toronto: McGraw-Hill.

Johnson, S. M., Kurtz, M. E., Tomlinson, T., & Howe, K. R. (1986). Students' stereotypes of patients as barriers to clinical decision-making. *Journal of Medical Education, 61*(9), 727–735.

Kadushin, A. (1963). Diagnosis and evaluation for (almost) all occasions. *Social Work, 8*(1), 12–19.

Kerlinger, F. N. (1986). *Foundations of behavioral research* (3rd ed.). New York: Holt, Rinehart and Winston.

Kirk, S. A. (1985). *Kirk-Rosenblatt research inventory (unpublished test).* School of Social Welfare, University of New York-Albany, Albany, NY.

Logan, C. H. (1976). Do sociologists teach students to think more critically? *Teaching Sociology, 4*(1), 29–48.

Mayer, V. J., & Richmond, J. M. (1982). An overview of assessment instruments in science. *Science Education, 66*(1), 49–66.

Medawar, P. B. (1979). *Advice to a young scientist.* New York: Harper & Row.

Meehl, P. E. (1973). *Psychodiagnosis: Selected papers.* Minneapolis: University of Minnesota Press.

Michael, M., Boyce, W. T., & Wilcox, A. J. (1984). *Biomedical bestiary: An epidemiologic guide to flaws and fallacies in the medical literature.* Boston: Little, Brown.

Miller, S. I., & Bogal, R. B. (1977). Logic as a tool for clinical training in social work. *Psychiatric Quarterly, 49*(1), 18–28.

Monette, D. R., Sullivan, T. J., & Dejong, C. R. (1990). *Applied social research* (2nd ed.). Ft. Worth: Holt, Rinehart, & Winston.

Moore, B. N., & Parker, R. (1986). *Critical thinking: Evaluating claims and arguments in everyday life.* Palo Alto, CA: Mayfield.

Myrdal, G. (1969). *Objectivity in social research.* New York: Random House.

Newman, E., & Turem, J. (1974). The crisis of accountability. *Social Work, 61*(19), 5–16.

Nisbett, R., & Ross, L. (1980). *Human inference: Strategies and shortcomings in social judgment.* Englewood Cliffs, NJ: Prentice-Hall.

Novacco, R. (1975). *Anger control.* Lexington, MA: Heath.

Peil, S. (1989). *Is anger management training successful in reducing the level of anger in a single-case study?* Unpublished manuscript, Social Work Department, University of Wisconsin-Eau Claire, Eau Claire, WI.

Rabin, C. (1985). Matching the research seminar to meet practice needs: A method for integrating research and practice. *Journal of Social Work Education, 21*(1), 5–12.

Reid, W. J., & Hanrahan, P. (1982). Recent evaluations of social work: Grounds for optimism. *Social Work, 27*, 328–340.

Rosen, A., & Mutschler, E. (1982). Social work students and practitioners' orientation to research. *Journal of Education for Social Work, 18*(3), 62–68.

Rosenberg, M. (1965). *Society and the adolescent self image.* Princeton, NJ: Princeton University Press.

Rosenblatt, A., & Kirk, S. (1981). A cumulative effect of research courses on knowledge and attitudes of social work students. *Journal of Education for Social Work, 17*(3), 26–34.

Rubin, A. (1985). Practice effectiveness: More grounds for optimism. *Social Work, 30*(6), 469–476.

Ruggerio, V. R. (1984). *The art of thinking: A guide to critical and creative thought.* New York: Harper & Row.

Sagan, C. (1987). The burden of skepticism. *The Skeptical Inquirer, 12*(1), 38–74.

Schuerman, J. R. (1983). *Research and evaluation in the human services.* New York: Free Press.

Smith, R. L. (1969). *At your own risk: The case against chiropractic.* New York: Pocket Books.

Sowers-Hoag, K., & Thyer, B. A. (1985). Teaching social work practice: A review and analysis of empirical research. *Journal of Social Work Education, 21*(3), 5–15.

Stein, L. I., & Test, M. A. (1980). Alternative to mental hospital treatment. *Archives of General Psychiatry, 37*, 392–412.

Stewart, C. J., & Cash, W. B. (1982). *Interviewing: Principles and practice.* Dubuque: Wm. C. Brown.

Tripodi, T., & Epstein, I. (1979). Incorporating knowledge of research methodology into practice. *Journal of Social Service Research, 2*(1), 65–78.

Videka-Sherman, L. (1988). Meta-analysis of research on social work practice in mental health. *Social Work, 33*(4), 325–338.

Weddle, P. (1978). *Argument: A guide to critical thinking.* New York: McGraw-Hill.

Weinbach, R. W., & Grinnell, R. M. (1987). *Statistics for social workers.* New York: Longman.

Wells, R. A., & Giannetti, V. J. (1986). Individual marital therapy: A critical reappraisal. *Family Process, 25*(1), 43–51.

4

Does a Method Cause Change?

Although they may not always be aware of it, social workers make numerous causal inferences in their everyday reasoning about clients. Clarifying how social workers make causal inferences and clearly defining the many causes other than intervention that can explain client change are the two major objectives of this chapter.

To illustrate how causal inferences are made informally in social work practice, we will describe Tilla Engen, an aged nursing home resident, and relate how the staff there made inferences that validation therapy has caused a sudden improvement in her previously confused thinking and irrational behavior.

Ms. Engen, and the staff members who help her, are fictitious, but their arguments that validation therapy helps Tilla Engen are those commonly heard in the halls and conference rooms of human service agencies across the country. Such arguments are based on "**cues-to-causality**" (Einhorn & Hogarth, 1986, p. 6), rough rules of thumb, generally implied rather than stated, that practitioners use to judge whether a method is causing a client's change.

Although helpful, cues-to-causality are not powerful enough on which to stake a life. Such cues-to-causality fail to rule out many alternate causes that may be the real cause of a client's change. Alternate causes that may be confounded with effects of intervention methods must be ruled out, to the greatest extent possible, to make a strong inference that intervention is effective.

INFERRING CAUSE IN SOCIAL WORK

Implicit in social work practice are questions about how best to help clients. Questions about helping include:

- Do depressed persons in support groups fare better than those in antidepressant drug treatments?

- How can I best help Mr. Venziano?

- Am I having an effect on Ms. Abram's behavior?

- Which of these methods—reality orientation, reminiscence groups, or validation therapy—is most effective with disoriented aged persons?

- Will young people take better precautions against AIDS if they are exposed to peer counseling or to an informational program conducted by their teachers?

Such questions imply causal reasoning. Statements about what most helps clients also reflect causal reasoning. For example, Gagliano (1987), a dedicated child welfare worker, stated: "In our experience, group counseling is the most effective method of therapy for sexually abused adolescents" (p. 102). Gagliano's statement implies that group counseling causes change somehow.

CAUSAL INFERENCE IN SOCIAL WORK PRACTICE

A causal inference is a statement that an event (cause) is responsible for producing a change in something else (the effect), for example the pinprick causes a twinge of pain. All of the questions about helping implied a causal inference, that is, event X (the method) caused event Y (outcome). Indeed, all questions regarding effects of applied methods imply a causal inference. For example, Will children whose parents attend parent effectiveness training (cause) perform more helpful tasks in the home (effect)? Or, Will families who attend strategic family therapy (cause) be able to fix the problem that led to their referral (effect), for example a child's bed-wetting.

Typical phrases—such as X is effective; X is linked to Y; X produced Y; X was responsible for Y; X led to Y; X was the factor behind Y; X created Y; X affected Y; X influenced Y; and Y was the result of X—can trigger quick recognition of causal reasoning. Whenever such phrases appear in social work literature, in discussions with professional colleagues, and in case conferences, mark the argument for analysis. Surely causal reasoning is embedded in the argument somewhere.

A Case Example

Background

Imagine that a few months ago you began employment as a social worker at Fairview Nursing Home, a 200-bed hospital-like facility, which sits in a grove of trees on the outskirts of a mid-sized town. At first, you were overwhelmed by the job's numerous procedural details and other responsibilities, including keeping institutional records, informing family members about the client's welfare, admitting residents, and learning to recognize the many faces and names, along with establishing yourself as a member of an interdisciplinary team. Having never worked in a nursing-home setting before, the institution's sights and sounds had a powerful effect on you. The endearing faces, and sometimes sad, resigned expressions of your first clients left vivid impressions. You recall well the first words of encouragement from your supervisor, and you remember the smell of antiseptics and illness on the nursing care ward.

Tilla Engen, one of the first clients assigned to you at Fairview, was discussed at your first interdisciplinary staff meeting. Weekly meetings are facilitated by your supervisor and include social workers, nurses, physical therapists, occupational therapists (or activity directors), and dieticians. One topic of discussion during this particular meeting was Tilla Engen's deteriorating condition.

Ms. Engen, an 81-year-old woman, ill with arthritis and stomach ulcers, had been admitted to Fairview 3 months earlier directly from a local hospital. The hospital social worker and Ms. Engen's daughter initiated the admission, because they judged that frail health had made it impossible for Ms. Engen to care for herself adequately alone in her little apartment. At the time of her admission, Ms. Engen had seemed slightly disoriented as to where she was, but in a few days she seemed to adjust well to her new surroundings and roommate. Then, about $2\frac{1}{2}$ months after her admission, an aide reported that Ms. Engen, who had been friendly to him and called him by name before, appeared not to recognize him. A nurse also noted that Ms. Engen, who used to enjoy the nurse's good-natured kidding, no longer even acknowledged her remarks. Then, during the past week, Ms. Engen sat alone by her window sometimes murmuring, "I hope Harold [her deceased husband] comes soon." When reminded that her husband is deceased, Ms. Engen would disagree or seem confused. Other recent entries on the patient's chart indicated that she was increasingly disoriented about time, place, and person. Concerned about these observations, the interdisciplinary team members agreed to work together on the problem and recommended that someone from the social work department work intensively with her for awhile to see what might be done to halt or at least diminish her sudden deterioration.

After the staff meeting, your supervisor listened sympathetically to your doubts about what to do and then suggested that you read some materials on validation therapy that might suggest an approach. You took the materials but did not get around to reading them before you made your first visit to see Ms. Engen the next day.

When you entered the client's room, you noticed first that her clothes and personal belongings were strewn about the room in disarray. Ms. Engen sat with her back to you by the window, the warm sunlight highlighting her gray hair. She did not acknowledge you as you called her name, nor did she turn to face you when you pulled a chair over and sat next to her. In response to your question about how she was feeling, she replied, "I know Harold will be here any time to get me." In response to your statement, "I'm sorry, Ms. Engen, you're here in Fairview Nursing Home. Don't you remember? Your daughter brought you here about 3 months ago; your husband is deceased; I'm your social worker," she simply repeated her statement more vehemently. She appeared sad, illogical, and disoriented as to time and location; though she knew who she was.

Some Evidence of Validation Therapy's Effectiveness

Ms. Engen's condition moved you to action. You read Babins's (1988) overview of validation therapy and Feil's (1981) original description of the method. The therapy's originator, Naomi Feil (1981) wrote that validation therapy is most effective for the disoriented elderly, "who are over age 80, have led happy productive lives, and typically denied [their feelings related to any] severe crisis during their lives and now show deterioration in their senses and their ability to remember recent facts" (p. 2). Such persons, according to Feil, are unlike those with Alzheimer's disease; Alzheimer's victims do not deliberately choose to disassociate themselves from reality to escape the painful present.

The validation therapist, unlike a reality orientation therapist, does not try to force an orientation to the present but reflects the client's feelings as portrayed even in disoriented thoughts. The validation therapist encourages the client to express feelings that may have been buried for a lifetime. The worker is "always ready to validate the person where they are, at the moment" (Feil, 1981, p. 41). Steps in the therapy involve taking a history, listening carefully, and with a gentle voice and prolonged eye contact to show interest, reflecting with words that acknowledge and legitimize whatever feelings are expressed, however disoriented the client's thinking (Feil, 1981, pp. 42–44).

Weak evidence supports validation's effectiveness. Babins (1988) used validation therapy to help five individuals and compared their functioning against that of an undisclosed number of persons in a comparison group. The five exposed to validation therapy participated biweekly, for 11 weeks, in validation groups. Both groups were rated by the therapist on an index of social behavior. According to Babins's ratings, participants in validation therapy had better social behavior at the end of the 11 weeks.

You read further that Peoples (1982) randomly assigned 29 residents of a nursing home (average age 87.7 years) to validation therapy ($N = 10$), reality orientation ($N = 8$), or a control group ($N = 11$). All three groups were pretested and posttested on three measures. According to Peoples, who conducted the measurements, the residents' only statistically significant improvement was indicated by higher scores on the Behavior Assessment Tool for the validation therapy group (pp. iii–iv). Although the study was well done and well conceptualized, you wonder about the possibility that bias may have entered into the experiment when Peoples rated the effects of her own validation therapy group compared to performance in the other groups.

You have also run across evidence that reminiscence groups may help the demented elderly, and you are encouraged because procedures in reminiscence groups resemble those in validation groups. Goldwasser, Auerbach, and Harkins (1987), together with their associates at Virginia Commonwealth University, randomly assigned 10 demented elderly subjects to each of three groups: a reminiscence group, a social support group, and a nontreated control group. Follow-up on the Mini-Mental State Exam, Beck Depression Inventory, and Katz Index of Activities of Daily Living show that those in the reminiscence group improved statistically significantly on the Beck over a 6-week period. There were no statistically significant differences in any other comparisons. As you read further, you noted also that a group for the demented elderly conducted by Cetingok and Hirayama (1983) did not produce successful results. All in all, given this evidence, it looked as though validation therapy was worth a try to help Tilla Engen.

Using Validation Therapy to Help a Client

During your first two validation sessions Ms. Engen spoke of her husband, their life together on a small midwestern farm, and their daughters to whom she referred as though they were still in grade school. During your third meeting, however, she reached out to you with a thin hand, placed it gently in yours, and asked, "What are we having for lunch today?" After that exhilarating breakthrough, other staff members began to notice changes in her behavior and thinking. The next day, the nurse reported that Ms. Engen, who had ceased making specific complaints about her physical discomfort, suddenly asked for still more medication, above that recently prescribed to ease the pain of her arthritis. The nurse saw the physician, and she changed the medication. Ms. Engen's daughter, who had not been visiting regularly, began to visit a couple of times a week.

Evaluating Arguments: Cues-to-Causality

Your client's progress became the principal subject of discussion at the next staff meeting. Everyone congratulated you, and they argued excitedly in various ways that your use of validation therapy had reversed Tilla Engen's deteriorating thinking and behavior. Here are some of their arguments:

Argument 1: Causal Chain Strength

YOUR SUPERVISOR: Excellent work! I'm so happy with your success in helping Tilla Engen. She does not have Alzheimer's Disease. She's an ideal candidate for validation therapy. This method really makes sense for her. She was merely tuning out her unpleasant surroundings and perhaps was dealing with unresolved conflicts. She is typical of aged residents who decide to disassociate themselves from reality to avoid the painful present. Your listening to her feelings without censuring her delusions has brought her back. Good job!

Argument 2: Contiguity

HEAD NURSE: At first when you said you would try to spend 20 minutes each day with Tilla Engen using validation therapy, I didn't think you'd be able to do it. As it worked out, I saw changes in her alertness *immediately* when you began validation therapy.

Argument 3: Temporal Order

WARD AIDE: Hmmmm. I didn't notice changes immediately. I observed the changes in her behavior a while *after* she began validation therapy. It was about 2 weeks after therapy began that I noticed Tilla Engen walking in the halls, which she hadn't done for several weeks. I was astounded when she looked me right in the eye and said, "Hello, Bill!" It was then that I knew something had been accomplished.

Argument 4: Covariation

PHYSICAL THERAPIST: Three times each week I work with Ms. Engen to improve her range of motion. I noticed that the longer you used validation therapy with her the more she seemed to be oriented to time and place. Recently, my impressions are that she's thinking as clear as a bell. She might be ready for a community options placement if we could find a suitable one.

Argument 5: Ruling Out Alternate Explanations

ACTIVITY DIRECTOR: I'm sure that the validation therapy was a big factor in Tilla Engen's improvement, but I wonder what effects her daughter's deciding to visit more frequently may have had. Also I noted in the chart that she has a history of depression. Maybe she was a little depressed for awhile as she adjusted to living here.

NUTRITIONIST: Yes, and have you also considered what effect the changes in medication may have had? Perhaps she's having less pain associated with her arthritis and stomach ulcers. Also, have her blood sugar levels been checked lately?

Arguments like these have begun to fascinate those who study how clinicians make their decisions (Abraham, 1986; Kleinmuntz, 1984). Einhorn and Hogarth (1986) are particularly interested in how causal inferences are made. A strength of Einhorn and Hogarth's work is how they have clarified cues-to-causality. Cues-to-causality, or just "cues," when present, increase the ability to infer a causal relationship between events. Einhorn and Hogarth list several such cues, including: causal chain strength, contiguity, temporal order, covariation, and ruling out alternative explanations—all illustrated in the staff meeting scenario. The presence of such cues can support an inference about probable cause, but cues do not establish cause without doubt (Einhorn & Hogarth, 1986, p. 13).

Discussion of Arguments

Argument 1, **causal chain strength**, refers to the reasonableness of the expected linkage between cause and effect (Einhorn & Hogarth, 1986, p. 12). In social work, the credibility of a theory that explains how a method is likely to effect change implies causal chain strength. A good theory should establish a direct link between elements in the intervention method and expected outcome and be supported by corroborating evidence.

It is much easier to generate a theory than to evaluate one. Is it reasonable to assume that aged nursing home residents who appear disoriented are choosing to be disassociated from reality? Are there other situations in which people in unpleasant surroundings have appeared disoriented in regard to time, place, and/or person? The only documented evidence on this subject appears to be that provided by Peoples (1982) and Babins (1988) regarding effectiveness of a therapy based on this theory. Other helpful evidence might be obtained by conducting a survey of aged persons to determine if those who have a higher level of unresolved conflicts become disassociated from reality at a higher rate than those with fewer unresolved conflicts.

Argument 2 applies the test of **contiguity** to infer cause. Contiguity means that X, the suspected cause, occurs together in time and space with Y, the suspected effect (Einhorn & Hogarth, 1986, p. 10). In social work practice, this implies that the practitioner has sufficient resources and power to bring together the client and the method intended to help the client. The causal inference is then made when an immediate change in the client's behavior appears contiguously with intervention.

In Argument 2, the head nurse did not think that the social worker would be able to meet with the client each day to implement the necessary validation therapy. In other words, the nurse did not think that the social worker would be able to bring the client and the therapy together in time and space in a way that would effect change. As it turned out, the nurse noted an immediate change, thus inferring that the change was caused by the therapy. The head nurse's judgment was based on contiguity.

There are two principal weaknesses with contiguity as a cue-to-causality in this context. First, there may be many alternate events that could have occurred simultaneously with the beginning of validation therapy. Such events might include a family member's increased interest resulting in frequent visits to see her, or changes in medication. Another problem with contiguity is that effects of intervention may not be detectable immediately, that is, contiguously with the inception of intervention. Such delayed effects of treatment are one problem in interpreting the treatment's effect size (Videka-Sherman, 1986, p. 22).

It is possible that the delay between human immunodeficiency virus—HIV—infection and the appearance of symptoms, on the average about 5 years (Redfield & Burke, 1988; Shilts, 1988, p. 460), may be a major factor in the tragic spread of AIDS. People may be relying too heavily on contiguity as a causal cue. Because they do not see immediate consequences experienced by those who do not take precautions against infection, they may not understand risks of infection.

Argument 3 applies the test of **temporal order** to infer cause: If event X (cause) precedes Y (effect) in time, then X has caused Y (Einhorn & Hogarth, 1986, p. 9). Bill, the ward aide who noted that validation therapy was followed 3 weeks later by Tilla Engen's eye contact and friendly greeting, assumed that validation therapy had caused the improved outlook.

Unfortunately, temporal order is a necessary but not sufficient condition to infer cause. If a method is to cause a given effect, it is essential that the method precede the change in the client's behavior; however, it is not enough in itself to cause a change in the client's behavior.

Assuming that temporal order proves cause is such a common error in reasoning that it has its own name: *post hoc ergo propter hoc*—after it, therefore because of it (Chaffee, 1988, p. 438; Gula, 1979, p. 115). Quacks capitalize on this classic fallacy to bamboozle clients into believing that they are being helped. The following lament by an honest physician describes this process: "If a person (a) feels poorly or is sick, (b) receives treatment to make him better, and (c) gets better, then no power of reasoning known to medical science can convince him that it may not have been the treatment that restored his health" (Medawar, 1967, pp. 14–15).

Causes other than intervention may have led to the client's improvement. Any of a collection of such alternate causes, broadly called "spontaneous recovery," occurs when clients improve on their own, without any intervention at all. Such improvement is thought to arise because of internal healing brought on by a client's inner resources and natural resiliency. Spontaneous recovery may account for change erroneously attributed to participation in intervention. Spontaneous recovery rates can be high. For example, based on a summary of 34 studies of patients in psychotherapy, the median spontaneous recovery rate was 43% with a range between 18% and 66% (Bergin & Lambert, 1978). Another review of studies of those treated for various forms of neurosis placed the spontaneous recovery rate at about two thirds over a 2-year period (Rachman & Wilson, 1980). Such rates must be interpreted with caution. Subotnic (1972) indicated that such rates may be due to the ways clients select themselves in and out of treatment.

Spontaneous recovery may follow a deceptive cyclical pattern. Figure 4.1 illustrates how cyclical remission for a client's recurrent problem may contribute to the illusion that clients have been helped. If treatment efforts begin during an acute phase of a client's cyclical problem (A in Figure 4.1), and improvement occurs naturally after the treatment begins (B in Figure 4.1), the improvement may be due to normal fluctuations in the problem rather than to the client's participation in treatment.

Argument 4, **covariation,** is commonly observed in two ways. First, we may observe instances where when X is present Y is also present, or when X is absent Y is also absent. Covariation may also be observed when an increase in the value of X corresponds to an increase in the value of Y, or when we may observe a strongly inverse relationship. Such covariation may be used to imply a causal relationship between X and Y (Einhorn & Hogarth, 1986). For example, the physical therapist observed that the more Tilla Engen received validation therapy the more her thinking improved. The physical therapist may have inferred that such covariation proved the effectiveness of validation therapy.

Clients who participate more intensely in intervention may improve most. Thus, we might, when observing such covariation, assume that more intensive involvement in intervention causes higher levels of success. For example, one might argue the following: Among elderly alcoholics who attended all group counseling meetings, or missed just one meeting, 90% were sober at the 6-month posttreatment follow-up; among those who attended less than half of the meet-

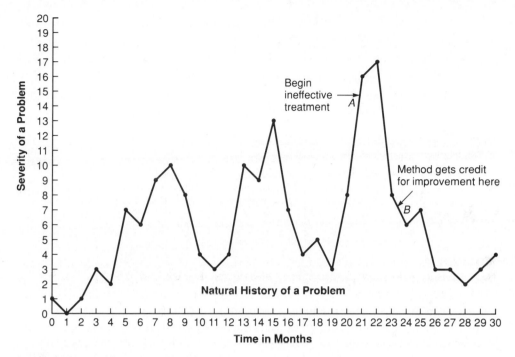

FIGURE 4.1
How a cyclical problem can foster the illusion that the client has been helped.

ings, only 30% were sober at the same 6-month follow-up. Therefore those who really got involved in treatment received the greatest benefits of treatment.

Such arguments ignore the "grand confounder" (Michael, Boyce, & Wilcox, 1984, p. 15). **Confounders** occur when what looks on the surface like a causal relationship between intervention and outcome is really a function of a totally unconsidered cause. Tilla Engen's improvement as she participated in more sessions of validation therapy may have been caused by changes in her medication, her daughter's more frequent visits, spontaneous changes in her health, or other unknown causes. The alcoholic clients who participated most intensely in treatment may have improved most—not because of the treatment, but because they were most motivated to change. Intensely involved clients may naturally function at a higher level than do less motivated clients.

Judging association can be tricky. To use association fairly to infer cause, we need to keep in mind: those who participate in the intervention who improve (successes), those who participate in intervention who do not improve (failures), those who do not participate in intervention and improve (spontaneous recovery), and those who do not participate in intervention and do not improve (untreated and unimproved). For those who find it helpful to visualize relationships, these four conditions appear as the four cells A–D in Figure 4.2.

Social psychologists who study human inference have made a fascinating discovery (Schustack & Sternberg, 1981)—generally, those who observe associ-

Client Outcome

	Improved	Not Improved

Client Participated in Treatment

Yes

Cell A
Successes
N = 75

Cell B
Failures
N = 25

$$\text{Proportion Successful} = \frac{A}{A + B} \times 100$$

No

Cell C
Spontaneous Recovery
N = 40

Cell D
Untreated, Unimproved
N = 60

$$\text{Proportion in Spontaneous Recovery} = \frac{C}{C + D} \times 100$$

FIGURE 4.2
Four elements involved in an association between treatment and outcome.

ations to infer cause rely far more frequently on confirming occurrences of the hypothesized cause and outcome (i.e., persons who fall in cell A of Figure 4.2), than they do on disconfirming cases (i.e., persons who fall into cells B and C of Figure 4.2). This principle, when extrapolated to social work practice, implies that we may judge effects of methods most by remembering successful cases. For example, those on the interdisciplinary team at Fairview may judge effects of validation therapy based on their positive experience with Tilla Engen, who fits into cell A of Figure 4.2.

A fair assessment of covariants implies that the team should also take a critical, analytical look at the possibly unpleasant information in the other three cells. Doing so is difficult because people tend to give weight to information provided in the cells in descending A, B, C, D order (Schustack & Sternberg, 1981, p. 111). A fair assessment would also take into account cases in which: (a) residents received validation therapy but did not improve, (b) residents did not receive validation therapy but improved nevertheless, and (c) the method was not used and the resident did not improve. (The two simple proportions in Figure 4.2 would help to make such comparisons.)

It would be ideal if we could just compute the proportion of successes [e.g., (75/100) × 100 = 75%] and the proportion in spontaneous recovery [e.g., (40/100) × 100 = 40%] and then compute the difference (75% − 40% = 35%) to conclude that the effect of the method was a 35% improvement. Unfortunately, it is not that simple. There are alternate causes to be considered.

Argument 5 concerns **considering alternate or confounding causes.** When viewing an apparent causal relationship between intervention and outcome, alternate causes are events other than the real cause that may be associated with intervention. Recall this reasoning in remarks made by the activity director and the nutritionist (p. 66) regarding alternate causes of Tilla Engen's improvement.

An argument that ignores alternate causes might be: If validation therapy helps Tilla Engen, then her confusion will lessen. Tilla Engen's confusion lessened. Therefore, validation lessened the confusion. This argument, although it may sound logical at first, is an example of a fallacy called "affirming the consequent" (Moore & Parker, 1986, pp. 208–209). It is true that if validation helps Ms. Engen, her confusion will lessen; but other factors may have lessened her confusion as well. These alternate effects must be ruled out somehow to make a sound causal inference.

Comments Regarding Cues-to-Causality

Although social work practitioners seldom label cues-to-causality, an analysis of causal reasoning in social work agencies will probably reveal their common use. Unfortunately, although the more cues present the more firmly a causal inference can be made, reasoning in social work practice typically does not represent the rigorous thinking needed to rule out confounding or alternate causes. Confounding causes may be the real source of change in many cases. We have no way of knowing unless we identify such confounders, and then try deliberately to rule them out. As the first step in that direction, the rest of this chapter defines confounding causes, or alternate explanations of client change; Chapter 5 will outline how successively more-complex experimental designs can be used as powerful tools to rule out alternate causes systematically.

CONFOUNDING CAUSES

Importance of Alternate Confounding Causes

Again, alternate causes—or confounders—are any events, other than the social worker's method, or methods used by other professionals, that are the real causes of a client's changed attitude or behavior. The term confounding cause is sometimes used because confounders occur concurrently with the social worker's intervention efforts, and they produce their own effects or intermingle their effects with that of the treatment. Confounding causes that involve how the method is applied, the client, any nontreated control or comparison group, the social worker, how outcome is measured, or the setting can weaken confidence that an intervention method is effective.

The cause-effect, or fishbone, diagram (Figure 4.3) presents a few of the most common confounding causes. Although such diagrams were developed initially to help experts define the cause of problems in production (Ishikawa, 1982), the fishbone can present a quick conceptualization of confounding causes in social work practice. Each major source of confounding causes appears as a major branch on the fishbone, for example, II. The Client. Each individual confounding cause is a smaller branch, for example IIA. The Client—Placebo Effect. The method's effect, or Client Outcome, is given at the far right. In Tilla Engen's case, the outcome is orientation to time, place, and person. (This outcome will be defined much more specifically as the dependent variable in a sample experiment in Chapter 5.)

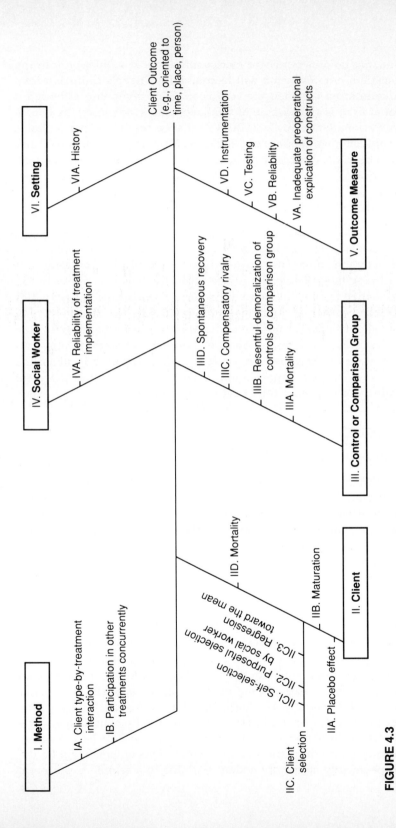

FIGURE 4.3
Fishbone diagram showing alternate causes of client change.

Only a portion of confounders mentioned in the literature, those most pertinent to social work, can be depicted in the fishbone diagram. Campbell and Stanley (1963) developed one list of confounders—"factors jeopardizing internal validity of experiments" (p. 5)—that can affect experiments. Cook and Campbell (1979) called their list "factors affecting validity and invalidity" (p. 37). More recently, Mark (1986) suggested that since so many authors have developed such lists of confounding causes that we should just speak of factors affecting "certainty of [causal] inferences in experiments" (p. 52). The fact remains that many of the confounding causes in Figure 4.3 were listed initially as possible threats to "internal validity," that is, enemies to sound causal inference in human service experiments (Cook & Campbell, 1979, p. 38).

Definitions of Confounding Causes

Although the citations in the following list give credit to the authors who originally defined confounding or alternate causes, definitions may have to be modified slightly to describe how they apply to social work.

I. *The Method*

A. Client Type-By-Treatment Interaction.   A method may be most effective with particular types of clients; it may be harmful to others. For example, Feil (1981, p. 2) claims validation therapy helps the disoriented elderly (age 80 or more); but it may not help those with Alzheimer's disease (Feil, 1981, p. 8). Such interactive effects may be confounders, which make it difficult to detect a treatment effect in which such clients are mixed in treatment. (More will be said about how to sort out interactions in the discussion of decision trees in Chapter 10.)

B. Participation in Other Treatments Concurrently.   Clients may get additional help elsewhere. Such concurrent participation in other facets of the helping process may be called **contamination.** In Tilla Engen's case, regular physical therapy and reduced pain or a change in medication may have accounted, either entirely or in part, for her improvement.

II. *The Client*

A. Placebo Effect.   The term *placebo effect* has been used variously and imprecisely (Berg, 1983; Senger, 1987). For our purposes, **placebo effect** means a change in a client's condition that is caused, not by the specific action or procedure engaged in by the client, but merely by the client's expectation that something good will happen. Placebo effects can be negative if clients have negative expectations (Lesse, 1964). The client's expectation may be encouraged by the professional's sympathetic ear, a warm presence, and reassurance that something is being done to help. Effects of such procedures have been demonstrated in medicine (Brody, 1980, p. 8) and psychiatry, where changes induced by psychotherapy may not be significantly greater than those induced by placebo (Prioleau, Murdock, & Brody, 1983, p. 283).

A related phenomenon, the Hawthorne effect, was the subject of a review by Adair (1984). Adair stated that, although variously defined in basic psychology

textbooks, the general consensus has been that the Hawthorne effect refers to changes that participating as a subject in a study has on subject behavior (p. 335). Adair's review of research on the Hawthorne effect indicates that it is not just the participation that affects behavior, but more importantly the subject's definition of the meaning and purpose of the experiment (p. 341). Adair's review has implications for therapeutics: If people expect to improve they may—sometimes solely because of those expectations.

Where applied to validation therapy, to infer that validation caused Tilla Engen to change, it would be necessary to show that someone who just listened to her and offered friendship would not have induced the same change in Ms. Engen's condition. In other words, the method should have some specific effect beyond those attributable to expectations generated by the interpersonal relationship between client and social worker.

B. Maturation. **Maturation** refers to "processes within the respondents operating as a function of the passage of time" (Campbell & Stanley, 1963, p. 5). In Tilla Engen's case, she may have become less physically ill, or her depressed mood might have improved with the passage of time. Such internal processes may be the real cause of her changed orientation to time, place, and person.

C. Client Selection—1. Self-Selection.   Individuals being studied may differ in important ways from the larger population that they are assumed to represent, or from a second group of people with whom they are supposedly comparable. The reason often lies in the way individuals become study subjects (Michael, Boyce, & Wilcox, 1984, p. 31).

For example, assume an evaluator asks residents of Fairview Nursing Home to volunteer for a validation therapy group. All those who volunteer are assigned to the treatment or validation group. An equal number of nonvolunteers are chosen from the home and are assigned to a nontreated comparison group. Later, after the treatment group is finished, the group leader finds that those in the self-selected validation group were much less disoriented than were the persons in the comparison group. The leader concludes that validation therapy is effective. This is not necessarily so. Think of all the ways that the volunteers may be different from nonvolunteers and how that can affect performance. Volunteers are likely to have been more motivated, more oriented to their surroundings in the first place, in better health, and so on, than were the nonvolunteers.

C. Client Selection—2. Purposeful Selection by Social Worker.   Here, instead of volunteers selecting themselves for intervention, the social worker handpicks those who receive intervention and those to be assigned to a comparison group. For example, if younger residents were chosen by a social worker for inclusion in a validation group, later differences in functioning across those treated and not treated might be due to these age differences; younger residents may very likely function at a higher level. The social worker's selection bias need not be consciously applied nor intentional.

C. Client Selection—3. Regression Toward the Mean.   Selecting subjects for intervention based on their extremely high or low scores, administering treatment, and posttesting on the same measure will likely yield misleading scores at posttest (Campbell & Stanley, 1963, p. 5; Michael et al., 1984, pp. 75–81). When subjects are selected for intervention because of their extremely high or low scores, a regression effect can cause a problem during comparison of their pretest and posttest scores. Groups of clients who initially fell into very high or very low groups at pretest (before treatment), will most likely move toward, or regress toward, the mean at posttest (after treatment). Regression occurs because scores of clients who were initially at the highest or lowest ends of a distribution of scores tend to have an unusual component of error in their scores. At posttest these individuals are not likely to have such an unusual component of error in their scores again. For example, if on the first day of the month we computed a confusion score for each of 100 aged residents' functioning that day, selected the 10 highest and lowest functioning individuals, and gave the same measure on the last day of the month, both the 10 highest (fewest wrong) and the 10 lowest (most wrong) scorers on pretest would likely regress toward the mean on posttest, as shown in Figure 4.4.

D. Mortality.   **Mortality** refers to "differential loss of respondents from comparison groups" (Campbell & Stanley, 1963, p. 5). Assume an evaluation is being

FIGURE 4.4
How the regression effect can make the lows score higher and the highs score lower on posttest.

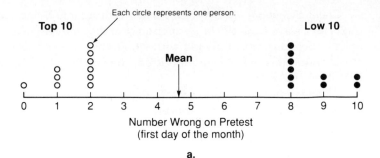

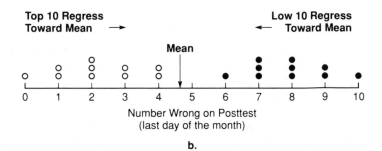

done to compare effects of validation therapy on groups of clients such as Tilla Engen, compared against a nontreated group of similar-aged clients in a comparison group. If a higher proportion of clients from either group dies, or becomes unavailable, such differential loss could obscure causal inferences about effects of the therapy. This is because those subjects lost may have been the ones less or more likely to improve after intervention.

III. The Control or Comparison Group

A. Mortality (See IID)

B. Resentful Demoralization of Controls or Comparison Group.
Nontreated respondents may perceive that they are getting less-desirable care and may become demoralized (Cook & Campbell, 1979, p. 55). Subjects confined to nontreated control or comparison groups may feel denied or punished and may deteriorate on that account. This effect can account for an experiment's results even when subjects have been randomly assigned to treatment or to control groups.

Demoralization might occur if a group of aged residents were selected to participate in a validation group, but other residents were not. Nonparticipants might deteriorate because they thought they were hopeless cases or because they believed themselves to be less competent or less worthy.

C. Compensatory Rivalry.
Instead of becoming demoralized, participants in a study may feel a sense of rivalry with those in a treatment group (Cook & Campbell, 1979, p. 55). Nonparticipants might become motivated to prove that they were wrongfully omitted from the group or they may want to prove that they did not need treatment. Such an effect can be a threat to experiments even when

subjects have been randomly assigned to treatment and to a nontreated control group.

D. Spontaneous Recovery. This refers to improvement in the client's condition due to internal resources (as defined earlier in this chapter). Spontaneous recovery may be thought of as a special case of maturation among nontreated subjects.

IV. The Social Worker

A. Reliability of Treatment Implementation. There are many factors that can affect how the social worker implements an intervention (Cook & Campbell, 1979, p. 43; Cronbach, 1982, pp. 262–266). A beginner who conducts validation therapy may apply that method reasonably well but may still be just learning. A more experienced worker might apply the method differently and possibly more effectively. Other sources of variation in how intervention is administered include the social worker's level of interpersonal skill, rapport with a particular client or group of clients, and how well the social worker motivates clients to participate regularly in intervention.

V. The Outcome Measure

A. Inadequate Preoperational Explication of Constructs. When applied to social work, this term (Cook & Campbell, 1979, p. 64) implies that it is impossible to determine a causal relationship between a client's intervention and outcome if both intervention and outcome are not defined clearly in valid and measurable terms. How could we know if the former causes the latter if we do not know what the terms mean? (To illustrate this principle, Chapter 5 will include a measure to define level of orientation more clearly using a Short Portable Mental Status Questionnaire [Pfeiffer, 1975], which would have been helpful in Tilla Engen's case.) Defining validation therapy, the independent variable, is more difficult.

B. Reliability. Reliability concerns consistency in measurement. Such consistency is vital to determining a causal relationship. If so much variation occurs in measurement that it obscures a subject's real performance, it becomes impossible to establish a causal relationship between intervention and such an unreliably determined outcome.

C. Testing. "The effects of taking a test upon the scores of a second test" may be a factor in judging causal relationships (Campbell & Stanley, 1963, p. 5). Here the testing procedure itself causes a change in the client's behavior. For example, if Ms. Engen were questioned each day about her orientation to time, place, and person, her being repeatedly tested might help her to rehearse her answers and therefore score higher on later tests simply because she recalls items on the previous test and remembers the answers, rather than because of her exposure to validation therapy.

D. Instrumentation. "Changes in the calibration of the measuring instrument or changes in the observers or scorers used may produce changes in the obtained measurements" (Campbell & Stanley, 1963, p. 5). If the social worker who daily measures Tilla Engen's degree of disorientation decides to take a vacation, another staff member, who takes over measurement responsibilities, might apply the measurement or score the results differently. Thus, changes in scores obtained by the new grader might be caused by changes in measurement procedures, rather than by the effects of validation therapy.

VI. *The Setting*

A. *History.* "The specific events occurring between the first and second measurement in addition to the experimental variable may account for changes in client behavior" (Campbell & Stanley, 1963, p. 5). Regarding evaluation of validation therapy, changes in the nursing home environment other than participation in validation therapy might have led to changes among the residents. For example, the administration might have decided to relocate residents from one floor to another. Such stressful relocation might profoundly affect the level of orientation among residents relocated. Thus, if a group of participants in a validation therapy group were pretested and posttested over the interval of relocation, lower scores at posttest might reflect the negative effects of resident relocation.

CONCLUSIONS REGARDING CONFOUNDING CAUSE

The sheer number of confounding causes listed in the previous section, among them any *one* that might account for a client's changed attitudes or behavior, underscores the complexities in drawing a causal inference about effects of our methods. Even more disconcerting is the fact that the list is incomplete. Mark (1986), who summarized several lists of confounding causes that had been compiled by prominent researchers, reminds us that such lists are not exhaustive. Each particular evaluation of an intervention must take into account confounding causes that may be specific to a particular evaluation, at a particular time, with particular clients, involving a particular method (p. 59).

Applying cues-to-causality, as we have seen, is not an effective countermeasure to confounding causes. Although cues are used informally in social work practice, and are somewhat helpful for judging a method's effects, they are not applied systematically enough in practice to rule out confounders. We need better guides for causal reasoning.

SUMMARY

Intended to clarify ways in which informal causal reasoning is applied in everyday social work practice, this chapter provided an illustration of various causal inferences, which are also known as cues-to-causality, through the case of Tilla Engen, an aged nursing home resident who has recently begun to display confused thinking and irrational behavior. Tilla Engen's social worker has decided to implement validation therapy. A case conference is featured, in which the various professionals responsible for Ms. Engen's care discuss the factors that may have contributed to the client's subsequent improvement, including the possibility of the positive effect of validation therapy.

Cues-to-causality covered in the chapter include:

1. Causal chain strength: Does a given theory make a plausible link between cause and effect?

2. Contiguity: Do the suspected cause and effect occur together in space and time?
3. Temporal order: Does the suspected cause precede the effect in time?
4. Covariation: Does the suspected cause appear when the suspected effect appears? Does the suspected cause *not* appear when the suspected effect does not appear? Is there an increase in the suspected cause that corresponds with an increase in the effect? Is there a *decrease* in the suspected cause that corresponds with the decrease in the suspected effect?

5. Ruling out alternate explanations: Are there other likely causes that may explain an apparent cause-effect relationship?

Also included in this chapter is a fishbone diagram, which depicts the various confounding causes that concern the method, the client, the control or comparison group, the social worker, the outcome measure, and the setting.

This discussion of cues-to-causality shows their fallibility as guides to practice with clients and underscores the importance of experimental designs that incorporate these cues systematically and logically into their structure.

EXERCISES REGARDING CUES-TO-CAUSALITY

Using cues-to-causality does not necessarily involve fallacious reasoning. Cues are often all that is available in practice to judge a method's effectiveness. If one recognizes that cues are merely fallible indicators of a method's effectiveness, no fallacious reasoning has occurred. Fallacious use occurs only when it is assumed without question, based on a cue-to-causality, that a method is effective.

Following are four hypothetical statements regarding practice effectiveness. These statements each exemplify one fallacy. Label the four fallacious statements, and describe why each of these four statements is fallacious.

1. There is no doubt in my mind that our survivor group for battered women works. I saw *immediately* an improvement in members' self-esteem during our very first meeting.
2. I am sure that noncompliance among outpatients with bipolar affective disorders decreases due to our program. Before participating in our program, fewer took their

lithium as prescribed by their doctor; *after* participating in the social work department's program for noncompliant outpatients a greater proportion took their lithium as prescribed.
3. Triniteam works—90% of juveniles who participated in all of our Project Aware meetings were nondelinquent 6 months after the group ended. Only 10% of those who attended less than half the Project Aware meetings were nondelinquent 6 months after the group ended.
4. I know reality orientation (RO) works. It just *makes sense* that it should. Reality orientation involves reminding the disoriented elderly in many ways who they are, where they are, what time it is, and what is expected of them. For example, our nursing home has an RO Board on each wing of every floor. The board gives the location, date, next meal to be served, and any prominent news of personal interest to the residents. Our activities constantly remind residents of such things.

EXERCISES REGARDING CONFOUNDERS

The fishbone diagram (Figure 4.3) lists possible alternate causes for client change. Review the definition for each confounder, then read the following hypothetical case material. Name the possible confounders (they are numbered as in Figure 4.3) as they appear in the case material, and describe why each confounder might explain the group's improvement.

Case Material

Adolescent suicide is the fourth leading cause of death for those under age 15 (U.S. Bureau of the Census, 1989, p. 79). Recognizing the gravity of this threat to the lives of our young people, we at the Eastern Crisis Center have developed a multiple method approach to prevent suicide among adolescents at risk. *We think our approach is one of the most effective treatments devised to help the suicidal adolescent.*

5. Typically, we accept as clients adolescents whose families are from higher socioeconomic backgrounds since we are a private agency supported by client fees that are paid directly to us or by the client's insurance plan (IIC2).
6. Generally, adolescents we see come to us voluntarily (IIC1), although sometimes reluctantly, at the insistence of concerned parents, school counselors, social workers, or other professionals. Although there is considerable variation among them, the profile of our typical adolescent clients includes: history of emotional distance and physical abuse by parents or other caregivers, low cohesiveness and angry judgmental communication patterns in the family, low perception of self-worth, chemical dependency, and academic failure and truancy that is often accompanied by high expectations.
7. Initially, during the crisis period, we work closely with a psychiatrist who often prescribes antidepressant medication and inpatient services, if warranted. The psychiatrist also may continue to see clients as outpatients. We advise that professionals consult closely with the psychiatrist and that cases be managed conservatively to avoid litigation in the event of a suicide. Once the crisis has subsided, we begin highly successful (IB) individual treatment.
8. As a general rule, among those clients who stay with the treatment regimen throughout its entire course (about 70%), all suicide ideation and suicidal behavior has been eliminated by the end of treatment (IID).

REFERENCES

Abraham, I. L. (1986). Diagnostic discrepancy and clinical inference: A social-cognitive analysis. *Genetic, Social and General Psychology Monographs, 112*(1), 41–102.

Adair, J. G. (1984). The Hawthorne effect: A reconsideration of the methodological artifact. *Journal of Applied Psychology, 69*(2), 334–345.

Babins, L. (1988). Conceptual analysis of validation therapy. *International Journal of Aging and Human Development, 26*(3), 161–168.

Berg, A. O. (1983). The placebo effect reconsidered. *The Journal of Family Practice, 17*(4), 647–650.

Bergin, A. E., & Lambert, M. J. (1978). The evaluation of therapeutic outcomes. In S. L. Garfield & A. E. Bergin (Eds.), *Handbook of psychotherapy and behavior change: An empirical analysis* (2nd ed., pp. 139–189). New York: Wiley.

Brody, H. (1980). *Placebos and the philosophy of medicine.* Chicago: The University of Chicago Press.

Campbell, D. T., & Stanley, J. C. (1963). *Experimental and quasi-experimental designs for research.* Chicago: Rand McNally.

Cetingok, M., & Hirayama, H. (1983). Evaluating the effects of group work with the elderly: An experiment using a single-subject design. *Small Group Behavior, 14*(3), 327–335.

Chaffee, J. (1988). *Thinking critically.* Boston: Houghton Mifflin.

Cook, T. D., & Campbell, D. T. (1979). *Quasi-experimentation: Design and analysis issues for field settings.* Boston: Houghton Mifflin.

Cronbach, L. J. (1982). *Designing evaluations of educational and social programs.* San Francisco: Jossey-Bass.

Einhorn, H. J., & Hogarth, R. M. (1986). Judging probable cause. *Psychological Bulletin, 99*(1), 3–19.

Feil, N. (1981). *Validation/fantasy therapy.* Cleveland, OH: Edward Feil Productions.

Gagliano, C. K. (1987). Group treatment for sexually abused girls. *Social Casework, 68*(2), 102–108.

Goldwasser, A. N., Auerbach, S. M., & Harkins, S. W. (1987). Cognitive, affective and behavioral effects of reminiscence group therapy on demented elderly. *International Journal of Aging and Human Development, 25*(3), 209–222.

Gula, R. J. (1979). *Nonsense: How to overcome it.* New York: Stein and Day.

Ishikawa, K. (1982). *Guide to quality control* (2nd rev. English ed.). Tokyo: Asian Productivity Organization.

Kleinmuntz, B. (1984). The scientific study of clinical judgment in psychology and medicine. *Clinical Psychology Review, 4*(2), 111–126.

Lesse, S. (1964). Placebo reactions and spontaneous rhythms. *American Journal of Psychotherapy, 18*(1), 99–115.

Mark, M. M. (1986). Validity typologies and the logic and practice of quasi-experimentation. In W. M. K. Trochim (Ed.), *Advances in quasi-experimental design and analysis* (pp. 47–66). San Francisco: Jossey-Bass.

Medawar, P. B. (1967). *The art of the soluble.* London: Methuen.

Michael, M., Boyce, W. T., & Wilcox, A. J. (1984). *Biomedical bestiary: An epidemiologic guide to flaws and fallacies in the medical literature.* Boston: Little, Brown.

Moore, B. N., & Parker, R. (1986). *Critical thinking: Evaluating claims and arguments in everyday life.* Palo Alto, CA: Mayfield.

Peoples, M. (1982). *Validation therapy versus reality orientation therapy as treatment for disoriented institutionalized elderly.* Unpublished master's thesis, College of Nursing, Akron, OH.

Pfeiffer, E. (1975). A Short Portable Mental Status Questionnaire for the assessment of organic brain deficit in elderly patients. *American Geriatrics Society, 23*(10), 433–441.

Prioleau, L., Murdock, M., & Brody, N. (1983). An analysis of psychotherapy versus placebo studies. *The Behavioral and Brain Sciences, 6,* 275–310.

Rachman, S. J., & Wilson, G. T. (1980). *The effects of psychological therapy* (3rd ed.). Oxford: Pergamon.

Redfield, R. R., & Burke, D. S. (1988). HIV infection: The clinical picture. *Scientific American, 259*(4), 90–99.

Schustack, M. W., & Sternberg, R. J. (1981). Evaluation of evidence in causal inference. *Journal of Experimental Psychology: General, 110*(1), 101–120.

Senger, H. L. (1987). The "placebo" effect of psychotherapy: A moose in the rabbit stew. *American Journal of Psychotherapy, 41*(1), 68–81.

Shilts, R. (1988). *And the band played on: Politics, people and the AIDS epidemic.* New York: Penguin.

Subotnik, L. (1972). Spontaneous remission: Fact or artifact. *Psychological Bulletin, 77*(1), 32–48.

U.S. Bureau of the Census (1989). *Statistical abstracts of the United States* (109th ed., p. 109). Washington, DC: U.S. Government Printing Office.

Videka-Sherman, L. (1986). Alternative approaches to aggregating the results of single-subject studies. *Social Work Research & Abstracts, 22*(1), 22–23.

5

Experimenting to Judge a Method's Effect

THE NEED TO KNOW THE LOGIC OF EXPERIMENTAL DESIGN

Confounding causes can be disconcerting to those who want to help others, but there are ways to deal with them. Practitioners who can recognize confounders have taken a giant step forward; those who know about confounding causes can keep a watchful eye out for them. Vigilant practitioners may be less likely to practice social work in a blissful ignorance that permits ineffective, and possibly harmful, methods. Also, knowing about confounders can move a practitioner to action. Stronger causal inferences can be drawn by practitioners who know how to apply the basic logic of a few experimental designs.

Absolutely essential to experimentation, regardless of the discipline and the level of the experiment's sophistication, is a spirit of inquiry that demands proof for any assertion. The scientist believes that important assertions must be submitted to a test and that "propositions that are not testable are worthless—you have to be able to check assertions out" (Sagan, 1987, p. 11). When it comes to determining what really helps clients, the adage rings true for practitioners: "In God we trust. All others must use data" (Walton, 1986, p. 96).

The practitioners' informal use of cues-to-causality shares common principles with the logic of experiments: Practitioners who utilize causal cues apply *imprecisely* the same principles that experimenters apply *more precisely* to the logic of their experiments. Cues-to-causality relate to principles of experiment design in many ways. For example a practitioner determines a client's addiction to heroin and, after referring the client to methadone treatment, later checks the client's arm for needle marks to see if the client's addiction may have been reduced by the referral (temporal order). The scientist-practitioner, also aware of temporal order's importance, administers a pretest of addictive behavior before treatment and administers the same measure again after treatment to make a comparison. A school social worker, wondering how effective a school's pregnancy-prevention program has been, reviews a list of girls who became pregnant that semester and notices names of those who regularly attended the school's prevention program (covariation). The scientist-practitioner, also aware of the importance of covariation, uses inferential statistics to compare the proportion pregnant who participated against those who are pregnant and did not participate in the school's pregnancy-prevention program. A nursing home administrator wonders if an aged resident became less disoriented because of: participating in validation therapy, a change in medication, adjusting to living in a nursing home, fluctuation in her recurrent history of depression, or some other reason (ruling out spurious factors). More systematically, the scientist-practitioner may try to control for effects of confounders in an experiment by randomly assigning subjects to validation therapy or to some other intervention. The scientist-practitioner may also use a nontreated control or comparison group.

Although logic in experiments has roots deep in commonsense reasoning, experiments are more credible than common sense. Causal inferences derived through experimentation are more trustworthy because experiments can incorporate many conditions for inferring cause simultaneously. Experiments also are more systematic in their measures and procedures, thus ruling out common sources of bias in inferences about practice. Successively more complex experimental designs can help to rule out more and more confounding causes.

DEFINITIONS OF RELATED TERMS AND SYMBOLS

Before discussing the hierarchy of a few experimental designs as applied to evaluating effects of validation therapy, let us define terms relevant to experimental design using an experiment in mental health.

An **experiment** is a systematic procedure intended to answer a specific question. This question is formulated into a testable hypothesis. Experimentation involves manipulating and objectively observing independent and dependent variables, recording results, and making logical inferences based on what is observed. Scientists generally conduct experiments to better understand and control the events they study.

In social work, experiments generally address a most pressing and practical question: Which method works? For the purposes of our mental health example, such a question might be: Is a particular community treatment program for the mentally ill effective?

Before going on to the mental health study that we will use to illustrate key terms and symbols of experimental design, special note should be taken of three concepts: random selection, simple random assignment, and block random assignment.

The first concept, **random selection,** helps to insure the ability to generalize the results of an experiment to some population, the second, **simple random assignment,** helps to insure the ability to draw a causal inference about the

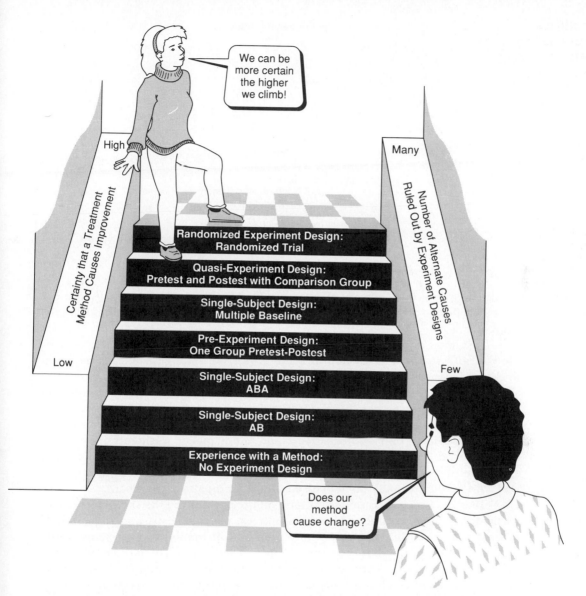

treatment's effects; and, the third, **block random assignment,** helps to insure that one can draw a sound causal inference about the effects of an intervention while keeping the number of subjects in treatment and control groups balanced. More will be said about these topics later in this chapter.

Experimental Design: An Application of Key Terms and Concepts

M.A. Test and L.I. Stein, concerned about the fate of mentally ill persons who developed a "revolving door syndrome," designed an experiment to evaluate a Training in Community Living Program for chronically mentally ill patients. Such patients regularly entered and reentered wards at the local Mendota Mental

FIGURE 5.1

Symbols used to diagram the Test and Stein study.

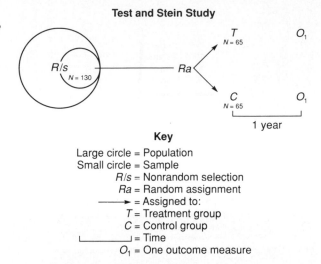

Test and Stein Study

Key

Large circle = Population
Small circle = Sample
R/s = Nonrandom selection
Ra = Random assignment
———➤ = Assigned to:
T = Treatment group
C = Control group
⌊_____⌋ = Time
O_1 = One outcome measure

Health Institute in Madison, Wisconsin (Test & Stein, 1977, p. 8). Figure 5.1 shows the design of their experiment; the following discussion further defines each symbol.

Test and Stein's 130 chronically mentally ill subjects were selected, or sampled (small circle), for study nonrandomly (*R/s*) from among chronically mentally ill clients being treated at the Mendota Mental Health Institute; that is, particular subjects were selected from the larger pool of Madison's chronically mentally ill clients in such a way that those selected did *not* each have an equal chance of being chosen from among the larger group, or population (marked by a larger circle). To select their subjects, Test and Stein picked residents from Dane County, aged 18 to 62, who did not have a diagnosis of severe organic brain syndrome or alcoholism, who were referred to Mendota Mental Health Institute, and who would normally have been admitted for inpatient treatment.

Test and Stein's community treatment program pitted the skills of a team of dedicated professional social workers, nurses, psychologists, and psychiatrists against problems that the chronically mentally ill tended to experience while trying to live independently in the Madison area. The team exerted an all-out effort to help clients to remain in the community by coordinating their efforts closely with local community agencies, coming to the aid of clients at any time (day or night) in cases of emergency, teaching clients social skills in group settings such as sheltered workshops, monitoring medications, and deciding how best to enlist the support of the client's family or friends.

To evaluate the program's effects, Test and Stein's 130 subjects were assigned (→) to either a 65-member (*N* = 65) treatment, or experimental, group, *T*, whose subjects received the community treatment, or to a 65-member control group, *C*, whose subjects did not receive special treatment (although they received the usual services available). Subjects were assigned to treatment and control groups randomly (*Ra*).

Table 5.1 is an example of how simple random assignment is used to assign subjects to treatment or control groups. Follow these steps:

1. Number 130 blank spaces. Spaces are allotted (column 1) for every subject, to be filled in with clients' names as subjects are admitted to the experiment.

2. Locate in a statistics text, or generate by computer, a column of random one-digit numbers. All digits in column 2 in Table 5.1 had an equal chance of occurring at each position. They were generated using a MINITAB computer program (Ryan, Joiner, & Ryan, 1976).

3. As clients become available for treatment, assign each one to the control group if their random number is odd. Assign clients to the community treatment program if their number is even (column 3). It is best that someone completely disinterested in the results of the study completes this assignment and keeps client records.

Note that proportions in treatment and control groups are often uneven in simple random assignment (column 4).

If Test and Stein had followed simple randomization, their random number tables might have assigned uneven numbers of subjects—this is unlikely for such a large experiment—to the treatment and control groups by the time 130 subjects were assigned. Uneven assignment is much more likely in smaller experiments (Lachin, 1988). Tables define the probability of lopsided proportions in experiments by numbers of subjects in the experiment (Lachin, 1988, p. 315). Important dissimilarities between treatment and control groups can occur with random as-

TABLE 5.1

Example of Simple Random Assignment to Treatment or Control Groups

Subjects	Random Digit	Assigned to Treatment or Control	Proportion in Treatment Group
1. _____	4	T	100%
2. _____	5	C	50%
3. _____	0	T	66%
4. _____	6	T	75%
5. _____	3	C	60%
6. _____	8	T	67%
7. _____	6	T	71%
8. _____	5	C	63%
9. _____	5	C	56%
10. _____	0	T	60%
11. _____	5	C	56%
12. _____	1	C	50%
13. _____	1	C	46%
14. _____	8	T	50%
15. _____	8	T	53%
⋮			
⋮			
130. _____	5	C	50%

signment, although, like disproportion, dissimilarities are less common in larger experiments.

The following block randomization procedure (Zelen, 1974), provides steps for balancing proportions of subjects to avoid disproportionate groups while still assigning subjects randomly (see Table 5.2):

1. Number 130 blank spaces. A space is allocated (column 1) for every subject, to be filled in with client's names as subjects are admitted to the experiment.

2. Determine how often you would like to be sure that treated and nontreated groups are equal in size. For the Test and Stein example that contains 130 subjects, we will balance the proportions as every 4th subject is added to the experiment. This means on the 4th, 8th, 12th, 16th, and so on, up to the 128th subject, there will be equal proportions in the treatment and control groups (column 4).

3. Determine how many possible patterns there are for arranging two treatment and two control subjects. See the bottom of Table 5.2 for the six possible arrangements, numbered from 1 through 6.

4. Following a column of randomly generated numbers that range from 1 to 6 (column 2), select possible arrangements listing these arrangements in sequence until the required number of subjects has been assigned (column 3).

Simple random assignment and block randomization insure, as much as possible given the chance occurrence of dissimilarities, that treatment, *T,* and nontreated control, *C,* subjects will be similar to each other prior to treatment, therefore posttreatment differences will most likely be due to the intended intervention, rather than to some initial dissimilarity (Meinert, 1986, pp. 67–68). Random assignment is a very important feature of experimental design. Designs that incorporate random assignment, as we will see in the section on levels of experimental design, enable one to rule out many confounding causes.

In every experiment there is a suspected, or hypothesized, causal relationship between an independent variable and a dependent variable. The term **variable** refers to events to which we can assign numerical values. In social work, the **independent variable** is generally our method. In Test and Stein's study, the independent variable is the chronically mentally ill subject's participation in the community treatment program, or the control's nonparticipation. The treatment method (suspected causal event X) can be manipulated by the social worker; thus, the independent variable is sometimes called the **manipulated variable.** In social work, the **dependent variable** is generally the outcome of our intervention. This event, Y, is the intended result of our efforts; thus, the dependent variable is sometimes called the **responding variable.** In the Test and Stein study, one dependent variable, or outcome of the experiment (O_1), was the client's readmission/nonreadmission to a mental hospital during the year after being assigned to the treatment or control group. Test and Stein (1977) found that only 12 of the 65 treatment participants were hospitalized during the first year; 58 of the 65 control group members were hospitalized during that same 12 months (p. 15).

Not all experiments follow the classic experimental design used by Test and Stein, but their experiment helped us to define symbols that we can use to de-

TABLE 5.2

Example of Block Random Assignment to Treatment or Control Groups

Subjects	Randomly Selected Block	Assigned to Treatment or Control	Proportion in Treatment Group
1. _____	2	C	00%
2. _____		C	00%
3. _____		T	25%
4. _____		T	50%*
5. _____	1	T	60%
6. _____		T	67%
7. _____		C	57%
8. _____		C	50%*
9. _____	5	T	56%
10. _____		C	50%
11. _____		C	45%
12. _____		T	50%*
13. _____	6	C	46%
14. _____		T	50%
15. _____		T	53%
16. _____		C	50%[a]
:			
:			
128. _____		T	50%*

All Possible Arrangements of Four Subjects That Have Two Treatment and Two Control Subjects Each

		Arrangements			
1	2	3	4	5	6
T	C	T	C	T	C
T	C	C	T	C	T
C	T	T	C	C	T
C	T	C	T	T	C

*Treatment and control groups equal.

scribe other designs to follow. Test and Stein's experiment was a good one for us to start with because, although they did not use random selection, they followed the principles of randomized trial, one of the strongest designs.

SINGLE-SUBJECT DESIGNS

Why Single-Subject Designs?

The image of a practitioner who applies research to practice—a person who is empathic and caring but also hard-headed—seems to be coming into focus as the ideal in the minds of those who influence social work practice. Practitioners who embrace the new role, variously termed "scientist-practitioner" (Barlow, Hayes, & Nelson, 1984, pp. 3–37), "accountable professional" (Bloom & Fischer, 1982, p. ix–xi), or "practitioner-researcher" (Howe, 1974, p. 18), should be able to integrate single-subject experiments into practice to evaluate their effects. Those conducting single-subject experiments may be able to develop entirely new practice models by synthesizing, with the help of their colleagues, evidence from many single-subject experiments (Blythe & Briar, 1985; Corcoran, 1985).

Advocates of the movement claim that single-subject experiments, especially those that apply less rigorous designs, are more likely to be implemented in human service agencies than multiple-subject experiments (Barth, 1981). Another advantage of single-subject designs is their usefulness for evaluating intervention with a particular individual. Because single-subject designs can evaluate a particular method's effect on a particular individual, some argue that such designs enable a practitioner to answer specific questions about subject-by-treatment interactions better than designs that involve groups of subjects who are lumped together in treatment or experimental groups (Hersen, 1982, p. 169). There are also several practical advantages of single-subject designs. Whereas multiple-subject designs can require years and hundreds of thousands of dollars to finish, single-subject designs can be completed in weeks or months. And, because single-subject designs require so few resources relative to group designs, the practitioner is more likely to have the means to apply them, thus reducing the researcher/practitioner gap (McReynolds & Thompson, 1986, p. 197). Furthermore, the way a practitioner and a client collaborate on a single-subject evaluation can focus the efforts of both on a specific objective, thus increasing the chances that their objective will be achieved.

Single-subject designs have structured evaluation of a wide variety of problems, including: a grade-school child's noncompliance with parental discipline (Szykula & Morris, 1986), a low level of exercise among mental patients (Thyer, Irvine & Santa, 1984), children's infrequent use of automobile seat belts (Sowers-Hoag, Thyer, & Bailey, 1987), and problems with independent living among residents of a halfway house (Stocks, Thyer, & Kearsley, 1987).

Principal Features

Single-subject designs can be referred to using a variety of terms, such as $N = 1$, single-case, intrasubject-replication, and single-system designs. The term **single-system design** refers to the idea that subjects of the experiment might be a single family, group, or organization that is being evaluated to test the effects of some intervention (Nuehring & Pascone, 1986, p. 361), however, typically, the subject is an individual.

Generally, in single-subject designs, causal inferences are based on subjects serving as their own controls. To draw the causal inference, the frequency of the subject's behavior is plotted over days, weeks, or months, both during nontreatment (baseline) and treatment periods. Various designs involve comparing the frequency of baseline behavior against the frequency of behaviors during treatment periods to see if patterns during treatment periods are different from those during the nontreated baseline periods. Causal inferences are generally based on changes in patterns of behaviors. In contrast, multiple subject or group designs, for example the Test and Stein (1977) study, base causal inferences on a comparison across treatment and control groups.

Perhaps the best way to define single-subject designs and to illustrate how they apply to practice is by example. A fictitious case involving Dr. Samuel Bradley will demonstrate how a simple design might be used to evaluate effects of validation therapy. The example will show how single-subject designs are superior to the type of causal reasoning that occurred in the case conference regarding Tilla Engen in Chapter 4. As you read the example, keep in mind that there is a wide range in the degree of rigor in single-subject designs, and thus a wide range in the strength of causal inferences that can be drawn from these designs (Barth, 1981; Gambrill & Barth, 1980).

Five Steps in Single-Subject Evaluations: Application of AB and ABA Designs

The student social worker who used validation therapy to help Tilla Engen might have wondered whether Tilla's sudden reorientation to her surroundings resulted from the effects of that particular method or from some confounding cause. We will assume that the student social worker, encouraged by Ms. Engen's progress, has decided to implement a single-subject experiment to evaluate validation's effect with another client, Samuel Bradley. We further assume that the social worker has become familiar with informative sources on how to apply single-subject designs to social work practice (Bloom & Fischer, 1982; Jayaratne & Levy, 1979) and that the student social worker has chosen Dr. Bradley for the single-subject evaluation.

Dr. Samuel Bradley is an 82-year-old man who has been physically and intellectually active throughout his life. Raised in the South, he migrated to a Northern city when he was 30 years old. This resourceful and intelligent man worked days on a construction crew and studied at night until he finished his undergraduate degree at age 35, and then earned a medical degree and practiced until age 70. He and his wife raised three children.

After the death of his wife, Dr. Bradley remained in solitary retirement until he was admitted at age 80 to Fairview Nursing Home. Records at Fairview show that Dr. Bradley has had a long history of high blood pressure and has now been diagnosed as having arteriosclerosis. He had a mild stroke a year ago, which resulted in impaired speech, although he can still make himself understood. However, like Ms. Engen, Dr. Bradley has become increasingly disoriented during the past few weeks.

To implement an AB single-subject design in order to evaluate validation therapy in this case, we take a five-step approach.

Step 1: Select a Behavior That Needs Change
Bloom and Fischer (1982) suggest "prioritizing problems" as a first step (p. 59). Ideally, prioritization should be done collaboratively with the client, because cli-

ents who are personally involved with the treatment tend to progress better (Coulton, 1985), but assume that Dr. Bradley is not rational enough to help with prioritizing. Consequently, an inventory of Dr. Bradley's problems has been made by the student social worker and by members of the interdisciplinary team. The client's problem should be observable, countable, clearly stated, verifiable by an observer, and targeted as something to be increased or decreased in frequency (Bloom & Fischer, 1982, pp. 60–62). The team's members have decided that his major problem is disorientation, as evidenced by many of the same behaviors that Ms. Engen exhibited.

Step 2: Select or Develop a Repeatable Measure

According to Feil (1981), the expected benefits of validation therapy are that the client should "return to present reality" and that one should observe that the client's "speech improves" (p. 9). Feil, who devised validation therapy, feels that a person participating in validation therapy should become less disoriented, therefore, a measure to evaluate an aged person's level of orientation should be appropriate to evaluate the therapy's effects.

The student social worker, trying to measure effects of treatment, might choose Pfeiffer's (1975) Short Portable Mental Status Questionnaire (SPMSQ) to measure Dr. Bradley's level of disorientation daily. The SPMSQ (see Figure 5.2) can usually be administered easily in less than 5 minutes (Pfeiffer, 1975), and its reliability and validity have been evaluated with satisfactory results (Nelson, Fogel, & Faust, 1986). The test consists of 10 questions about the subject's degree of orientation to time, place, person; recall of past events; and ability to do simple calculations. Dr. Bradley's total score would be the number of errors on the SPMSQ, ranging from 0 (no errors) to 10 (all items incorrect).

Step 3: Select a Treatment Method

Ideally, methods that hold the most promise based on empirical investigations should be selected. (The section on cues-to-causality in Chapter 4 contains a review of a few studies regarding effects of validation therapy and similar methods [Babins, 1988; Goldwasser, Auerbach, & Harkins, 1987; Peoples, 1982] as well as a description of validation therapy [Feil, 1981]). Such nonspecificity is common for descriptions of treatments that have been developed by nonbehaviorists (Nelsen, 1981). Social work practice requires that treatments be defined in behaviorally specific terms because treatment definition is vital to evaluating intervention programs (Yeaton & Sechrest, 1981).

Step 4: Select a Single-Subject Design and Implement It

The student social worker who evaluated validation therapy's effect on Dr. Bradley's disorientation could choose from among a hierarchy of less to more rigorous single-subject experimental designs (Barth, 1981, p. 22; Mahoney, 1978, p. 666; Paul, 1967, p. 115). Entire volumes describing such designs are available (Kazdin, 1982). More complex designs are appealing because they allow stronger causal inferences; however, the final choice of design must be determined by what is ethical and feasible.

The weakest, but perhaps the most common, single-subject design is AB. Bloom and Fischer (1982) point out that there is no "design for all seasons," but

Instructions: Ask questions 1–10 in this list and record all answers. Ask question 4A only if patient does not have a telephone. Record total number of errors based on ten questions.

_____   1. What is the date today?

_____   2. What day of the week is it?

_____   3. What is the name of this place?

_____   4. What is your telephone number?

_____   4A. What is your street address? (Ask only if patient does not have a telephone.)

_____   5. How old are you?

_____   6. When were you born?

_____   7. Who is the President of the U.S. now?

_____   8. Who was President just before him?

_____   9. What was your mother's maiden name?

_____   10. Subtract 3 from 20 and keep subtracting 3 from each new number, all the way down.

_____   Total Number of Errors

INSTRUCTIONS FOR COMPLETION OF
THE SHORT PORTABLE MENTAL STATUS QUESTIONNAIRE (SPMSQ)

Ask the subject questions 1 through 10 in this list and record all answers. All responses to be scored correct must be given by subject without reference to calendar, newspaper, birth certificate, or other aid to memory.

Question 1 is to be scored correctly only when the exact month, exact date, and the exact year are given correctly.

Question 2 is self-explanatory.

Question 3 should be scored correctly if any correct description of the location is given. "My home," correct name of the town or city of residence, or the name of hospital or institution if subject is institutionalized, are all acceptable.

Question 4 should be scored correctly when the correct telephone number can be verified, or when the subject can repeat the same number at another point in the questioning.

Question 5 is scored correct when stated age corresponds to date of birth.

Question 6 is to be scored correctly only when the month, exact date, and year are all given.

Question 7 requires only the last name of the President.

Question 8 requires only the last name of the previous President.

Question 9 does not need to be verified. It is scored correct if a female first name plus a last name other than subject's last name is given.

Question 10 requires that the entire series must be performed correctly in order to be scored as correct. Any error in the series or unwillingness to attempt the series is scored as incorrect.

FIGURE 5.2

Short Portable Mental Status Questionnaire (SPMSQ) (Source: Reprinted with permission from the American Geriatrics Society, "A Short Portable Mental Status Questionnaire for the Assessment of Organic Brain Deficit in Elderly Patients," by Eric Pfeiffer, M.D., JOURNAL OF THE AMERICAN GERIATRICS SOCIETY, Vol. 23, No. 10, pp. 440–441, 1975.)

AB's simplicity makes it their choice for an "all-purpose design" (p. 385). Figure 5.3 diagrams a hypothetical AB experiment to evaluate Dr. Bradley's level of disorientation before and during validation. Prior to his treatment, the first phase or baseline, A, was a week-long, no-treatment period that served as a benchmark for measuring changes in his level of orientation. Gambrill and Barth (1980) claim that keeping such a baseline is so essential to responsible practice that failure to do so is a threat to good service. Ideally, during the baseline phase, Dr. Bradley's disorientation should have remained relatively constant so that, by contrast, a pattern of change would be evident during the treatment phase, B. Treatment— the intervention phase—began immediately after the week-long baseline period.

Step 5: Interpret the Results

There are two ways to judge whether validation therapy changed Dr. Bradley's level of disorientation. Most likely, the student social worker would utilize the graphic approach by drawing a line that connects the observation points in the baseline phase and another line connecting the observation points during the treatment phase; then, the slope and level of the baseline and treatment phases

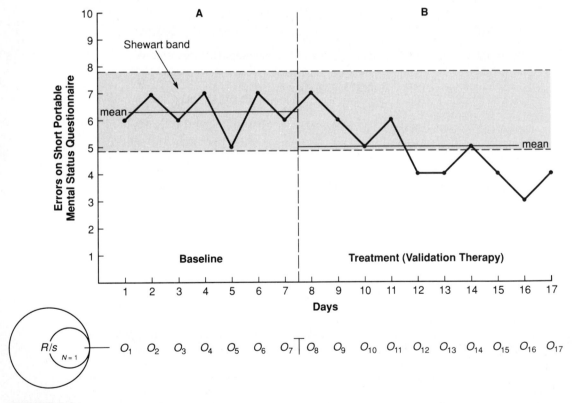

FIGURE 5.3
Dr. Bradley's level of orientation before and during validation therapy (higher scores mean less disorientation).

could be compared graphically. If, as in Figure 5.3, the slope of points is downward after treatment began (lower scores indicate that Dr. Bradley had answered fewer questions incorrectly on SPMSQ), and the mean of the points were at a lower level during the treatment phase, the student might judge that the method caused Dr. Bradley to improve. Also, the student social worker might judge that before validation therapy, Dr. Bradley's mean level of intellectual impairment was within the "severe intellectual impairment" range according to Pfeiffer's (1975, p. 441) criteria. During treatment, Dr. Bradley's mean level had changed to the "moderate intellectual impairment" range. Such a difference might have practical significance because the later score puts Dr. Bradley within the range of intellectual impairment for residents who are allowed moderate freedom within Fairview.

Unfortunately, interpretations of graphs can yield inconsistent results. Experts often disagree about whether particular patterns of graphed behaviors indicate change. For example, Ottenbacher (1986) asked 46 occupational therapists to view five hypothetical AB graphs of single-subject behaviors and to judge whether a clinically significant change had occurred across baseline and treatment phases. Ottenbacher (1986) reported considerable disagreement about how to interpret the five graphs; two of the five showed agreement that was close to a level expected by chance alone (p. 467). Finding the same kind of disagreement among 11 judges, Jones, Weinrott, and Vaught (1978) questioned the worth of visual comparisons and urged that visual comparisons be supplemented by statistical procedures for comparing baseline and treatment phases (p. 282).

Simple statistical procedures can provide more consistent and reliable judgments about whether Dr. Bradley's behavior has changed. Statistical procedures are useful because they reduce uncertainty about whether behavior has actually changed by providing a definite rule for inferring change. There is a wide variety of such statistical procedures for use with both simpler (Gingerich, 1983) and more complex single-subject designs (Kazdin, 1979). The Shewart Chart is one example of a simple statistical procedure that can illustrate the judgment process in Dr. Bradley's case.

The Shewart Chart is an industrial quality-control procedure that can be adapted to clinical use (Gottman & Leiblum, 1974). According to Gingerich (1983, p. 709), to construct a Shewart Chart from baseline data (see Figure 5.3), one should (a) plot the baseline observations, (b) compute the mean of the baseline observations (in Dr. Bradley's case, the mean is 6.3), (c) compute the standard deviation of the baseline observations (.7 in Figure 5.3), (d) draw two horizontal dotted lines (these Shewart bands lie 2 standard deviations above [+ 1.4] and below [− 1.4] the baseline mean), and (e) plot the treatment observations. If two consecutive treatment observations fall outside a Shewart band, a significant change has occurred (as on days 12 and 13 of Dr. Bradley's performance). Because Dr. Bradley's SPMSQ falls outside the band on these occasions, the test indicates he has changed according to the Shewart Chart test. Gingerich (1983) cautions that the Shewart Chart assumes that baseline observations are distributed normally, that each observation is independent of the others, and that the length of the treatment phase should equal the length of the baseline.

Strengths and Weaknesses of AB Design

Although the AB design just described is the weakest single-subject design, AB has strengths that case studies (e.g., Tilla Engen's case study in Chapter 4) lack. If implemented correctly, AB designs rule out one troublesome confounding cause: inadequate preoperational explication of constructs. If Dr. Bradley's treatment and outcome were not defined specifically, how would it be possible to determine if there were a causal relationship between treatment and outcome? Conversely, if AB is done appropriately, those applying it will define treatment and outcome operationally in measurable terms. Such clear definition is essential to establishing a causal relationship between treatment and outcome—validation therapy is not clearly defined in the literature. Another major advantage of AB design over case study is that AB can rule out iatrogenic effects of treatment; that is, if clients improve during treatment on a given measure, they cannot very well be harmed relative to that criterion. Ruling out iatrogenic effects may not sound like much of an accomplishment, but harmful effects of social casework have been well documented (Fischer, 1976, pp. 98–109).

On the weaknesses side, it is impossible, using this particular design, to isolate effects of validation therapy from effects of other events in Dr. Bradley's life that could have caused his improvement. Many alternate or confounding causes can discredit validation therapy as the reason for Dr. Bradley's improvement. In addition to history, maturation, testing, instrumentation, and statistical regression as confounders for AB designs (Kazdin, 1982, p. 92), others, including purposeful selection by the social worker, may be responsible for Dr. Bradley's reduced disorientation. Although not intending to bias the study, the social worker might have selected Dr. Bradley for study because he had a better chance of changing than did other residents at Fairview. Also, reliability of treatment implementation might be a confounder here. If treatment was administered by the student social worker either in an inexpert way, or in an unusually enthusiastic way, for example, the experiment might not have been a true test of the method's effects. Additionally, Dr. Bradley might have changed just because he perceived someone's kind efforts to help him and he learned to expect change for himself (placebo effect). Dr. Bradley may also have changed because he was particularly suited to benefit from validation therapy (client type-by-treatment interaction).

Additional Single-Subject Designs

Withdrawal designs—so called because they involve withdrawing treatment to test its effects (Hersen, 1982, p. 180)—are simply alternate phases of baseline and treatment designated ABA (baseline-treatment-baseline) or ABAB. Such designs can be visualized easily as extensions of the design in Figure 5.3. In Dr. Bradley's case, an ABA design would involve simply applying the same procedure as in the AB design already described and then withdrawing treatment to see if his disorientation returned during a second baseline. Withdrawal designs, by alternating treatment and baseline phases, can support stronger causal inferences (McReynolds & Thompson, 1986, pp. 198–199). Here the causal argument is analogous to what happens when a child learns to twist a water faucet: Turning the effect on and off repeatedly demonstrates a causal relationship.

Does the thought of withdrawing Dr. Bradley's treatment to see if he again becomes disoriented sound unethical? That it may be unethical to withdraw apparently successful treatment to test its effects is a common and serious objection to withdrawal designs in social work practice (Arkava & Lane, 1983, p. 133; Bloom & Fischer, 1982, p. 310). Another is the potential irreversibility of certain changes. Perhaps, once Dr. Bradley becomes familiar with SPMSQ, he will remember the proper answers, then his behavior would not return to initial baseline levels during a withdrawal phase.

Irreversible treatment effects and ethical concerns about withdrawal are problems avoided in **multiple baseline across subjects designs.** A social worker using this type of design selects several clients who have the same kind of problem; for example, a social worker at Fairview Nursing Home might select three residents who were moderately disoriented. Then, simultaneously, the social worker begins a baseline on all three clients by recording daily SPMSQ scores. After a week of baseline collection, the first client would begin receiving validation therapy, but the other two would remain on baseline. The next week, while the first client continues with validation, the second would begin validation, and so on until all three receive validation therapy. The three clients would get the same treatment from the same worker, but clients would begin treatment at staggered intervals, as diagramed in Figure 5.4. The multiple baseline across subjects design is essentially several AB designs begun at the same moment with baselines of differing length.

Multiple baseline designs, because they do not require withdrawing treatment, are probably the least obtrusive (Thomas, 1978, p. 29) and most appropriate single-subject designs in social work practice (Arkava & Lane, 1983, p. 139). In addition to multiple baselines across subjects, multiple baseline designs may also be applied across several behaviors for the same client or across settings (Barlow & Hersen, 1984, chap. 7).

Unfortunately, multiple baseline designs present some problems. Sometimes one or more baselines are not stable. Without stable baselines, it is difficult to determine change. In such cases, Bloom and Fischer (1982) suggest that workers wait until baselines stabilize and then base causal inferences on these stable baselines (p. 336). Another problem may be that because of the need to solve multiple problems, the social worker must begin two or more interventions simultaneously. Bloom and Fischer (1982) recommend doing what is necessary to help the client, but they caution that if the client does change during multiple treatments, it may not be clear whether the change is due to one treatment or the other, or to the combination (p. 337).

Drawing Causal Inferences

Withdrawal and multiple baseline designs rule out history, maturation, and inadequate preoperational explication of constructs as confounding causes, but do not deal effectively with other confounders including:

- **testing**—procedures for measuring outcome—that can have reactive effects on client behavior (Mizes, Hill, Boone, & Lohr, 1983)

- **self-selection** and **purposeful selection** by the social worker—selecting clients who would have a good prognosis no matter what the treatment
- **instrumentation**—a lack of consistency in measurement when social workers become less objective (Thomas, 1978, p. 27)
- **client type-by-treatment interaction**—concerns which clients benefit most by particular interventions (these effects can be investigated by more sophisticated single-subject designs, Barlow & Hersen, 1984, p. 193)
- the **placebo effect.**

Still, single-subject designs are a great advance over unstructured case observations. In addition to their ability to rule out iatrogenic effects and certain confounding causes, single-subject designs help practitioners and their clients direct their energies toward specific goals.

NONRANDOM GROUP DESIGNS

Preexperimental Design: One-Group Pretest-Posttest

Strong single-subject designs tell more about effects of a method than weak multiple-subject or group designs (experiments that involve five or more subjects concurrently) can. First, let us examine a weak but extremely common group design called preexperimental design; that is, one-group pretest-posttest (Cook & Campbell, 1979). This design is depicted in Panel a in Figure 5.5. To conduct such a study at Fairview, the social worker there might locate 10 disoriented residents, pretest them on the SPMSQ a week before validation therapy, expose them to validation therapy group for 2 months, and posttest them all on the SPMSQ a week after the group terminates. A validation group might include reminiscing, talking about feelings for lost loved ones, listening to music from bygone eras, and dancing (Feil, 1981).

Although a one-group pretest-posttest design uses multiple subjects, it supports weaker causal inferences than ABA or multiple baseline across subjects can. All of the confounding causes listed in Figure 4.2 roam around unharnessed in this simple group design, except those confounders pertaining to control groups. Even history and maturation, confounders ruled out in more complex single-subject designs, are a problem in this particular group design. For example, regarding maturation, a pretest to posttest decline over a 10-week period among validation therapy group members might reflect normal deterioration in residents so old, especially since one of Feil's (1981) criteria for validation therapy is that residents should be aged 80 or older (p. 2). Regarding history, residents' participation in a validation group might have been adversely affected by an outbreak of food poisoning at Fairview that stressed and weakened the health of Fairview's residents. Such a traumatic event might have caused a decline from pretest to posttest. The one-group pretest-posttest design has been called "preexperimental" because of just such weaknesses (Campbell & Stanley, 1963, p. 6).

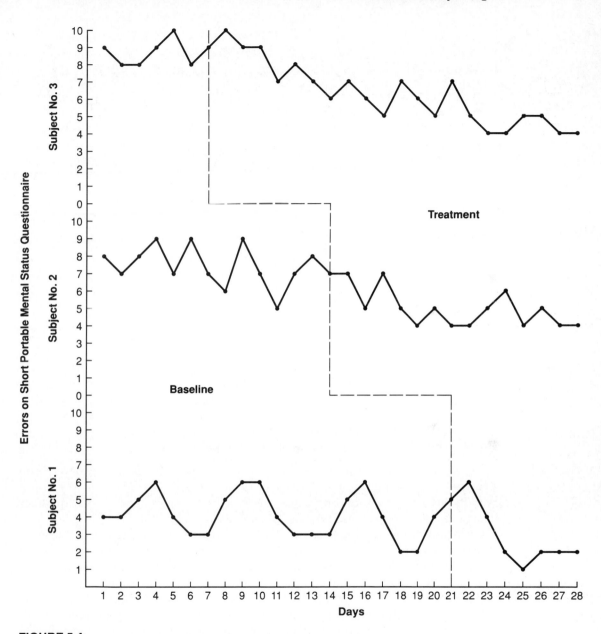

FIGURE 5.4
Multiple baseline across three subjects receiving validation therapy.

On the positive side, this design helps rule out iatrogenic effects by documenting measurable improvement. Also, larger numbers of subjects in this design mean a method's effects can be generalized more accurately than in single-subject designs.

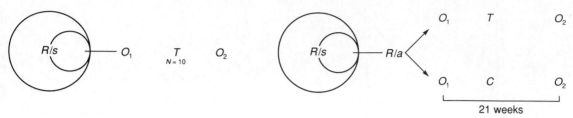

Pre-Experiment Design: Pretest-Posttest
(Cook & Campbell, 1979, p. 99)

a.

Quasi-Experiment Design: Untreated Control Group
(Cook & Campbell, 1979, p. 103)

b.

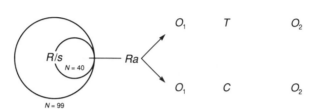

Experiment Group-Control Group: Randomized Subjects
(Kerlinger, 1986, p. 306)

c.

FIGURE 5.5
Three common group designs.

Quasi-Experimental Design:
Pretest-Posttest with a Comparison Group

This quasi-experimental design (Panel b, Figure 5.5) uses a **comparison group**—subjects nonrandomly assigned to participate in the nontreated group—to rule out some confounding causes. Nonrandom assignment is what qualifies designs as quasi-experimental (Campbell & Stanley, 1963, p. 2).

To implement a pretest-posttest with a comparison group design at Fairview, an evaluator might talk to staff members and residents to select, and then pretest using the SPMSQ, residents who are most willing and likely to benefit from a validation group. A similar comparison group of residents would be pretested simultaneously with the SPMSQ. Then, a week after pretesting, those selected for the validation group would begin their 2 months of group participation. Later, possibly 3 months after the group ends, comparison and treatment subjects would again simultaneously answer the SPMSQ.

A pretest-posttest with a comparison group design negates some confounding causes, but leaves others intact to besmirch causal inference based on the design. Because treatment and comparison groups both experience the same interval between pretest and posttest, and they may be tested with identical procedures (in this case the SPMSQ), the confounders history, maturation, instrumentation, and testing should not be a problem. The design's major weakness is that possible initial dissimilarities between treatment and comparison groups might account for later differences at posttest. For example, the social worker who chose residents of Fairview for the validation group might have chosen those most likely to improve between pretest and posttest. The social worker might have unintentionally chosen group members who were younger, in better health, or more alert. This initial dissimilarity, though not evident in a comparison across pretest scores, could be the result of any of the following confounders: self-selection, purposeful selection by the social worker, placebo effect, client type-by-treatment interaction, and possibly, for those less-disoriented subjects who might realize that they are in a nontreated comparison group, resentful demoralization of respondents receiving less desirable treatments.

RANDOMIZED EXPERIMENTAL DESIGN: RANDOMIZED TRIAL

Absolutely impregnable experiment designs cannot be designed and conducted. Confounders challenge *every* experiment, no matter how dedicated the experimenters or how compliant the subjects. Still, if a strong evaluation of validation therapy could be devised to test effects of validation as a method, how might one proceed?

Panel c in Figure 5.5 outlines a stronger evaluation of validation therapy. This more powerful design might include random selection of eligible subjects from Fairview, random assignment of these subjects to treatment and control groups, and posttesting control and treatment subjects after treatment is completed. Because subjects are randomly assigned to treatment and control groups, assuring as much as possible that these groups are initially similar, posttest differences are likely due to the effects of the treatment alone. Still, although this design addresses most of the confounders in Figure 4.3, placebo effect, resentful demoralization of controls or comparison group, and compensatory rivalry may still interfere with causal inferences based on randomized trials in which subjects know that they are participating in treatment or control groups. In general though, the randomized experiment design is the type of study that gives us the greatest certainty that our methods cause change.

Features of a Randomized Design

A randomized design to test effects of validation therapy versus no treatment would have 10 important features:

1. *Specific Inclusion and Exclusion Criteria*
Individuals might be included in the experiment if they meet these eligibility criteria: (a) they are healthy enough to participate in validation groups, that is, can walk or be wheeled into a meeting room; (b) they score from 2 through 8 on SPMSQ, that is, they experience some disorientation but not so severely that their behavior would be disruptive in the group; and (c) they say they would be willing to participate in the group. By specifying such criteria, the evaluator helps potential consumers of the research to determine whether their particular clients are similar enough that results from the study might apply to their clients.

TABLE 5.3
Example of random selection for inclusion in an experiment

List of All 99 Subjects	First Random Numbers to Appear in a Table of Random Numbers
1. _____	53
2. _____	62
3. _____	90
4. _____	10
5. _____ [a]	32
6. _____	54
7. _____	42
8. _____ [a]	73
9. _____ [a]	21
10. _____ [a]	9
11. _____	63
12. _____	98
13. _____	87
14. _____	5
15. _____	75
16. _____	76
17. _____	26
18. _____	8
19. _____	59
20. _____	49
↓	⋮
99. _____	N

[a]Numbers among first 20 randomly selected among first 20 random numbers.

2. Random Selection from the Population (Rs)

Assume that we would like to generalize the study's results to the population at Fairview who meet the criteria. To select a manageable number of subjects, perhaps 40, in such a way that results of the experiment could be generalized to the larger group of 99, one would:

- Determine, through discussions with staff members at the nursing home, which residents are sufficiently mobile to attend validation groups. Then administer SPMSQ to these mobile individuals to determine which meet SPMSQ criteria. Assume that there are 99 (see Table 5.3, column 1).

- Randomly select individuals to be included in the study, in this example, 40. To select these 40, begin at any two-digit column on a random numbers table and read down that column selecting for study those individuals whose numbers appear. Contact these subjects sequentially until 40 willing subjects are found (see Table 5.3, column 2).

- Be sure to keep a record of those who did and did not meet each inclusion-exclusion criterion and the number who where contacted who refused to participate. An honest reporting of the study's findings should clarify exactly how subjects were selected for study and who was excluded for what reasons.

3. Include Enough Subjects to Accomplish the Study's Purpose
Many trials fail to find statistical significance for meaningful outcome differences across treatment and control groups because too few subjects were included in the study (Freiman, Chalmers, Smith, & Kuebler, 1978). Procedures are available for determining how many subjects to include in an experiment (Kraemer & Thiemann, 1987).

4. Clearly Describe the Treatment Method
Those who administer validation therapy in group treatment should describe it so specifically that others could apply the method uniformly according to the same procedures used in the trial.

5. Select Valid Outcome Measures
All subjects should be pretested using a measure sensitive to the program's purpose. In the case of validation therapy, the outcome measure is the Short Portable Mental Status Questionnaire (Pfeiffer, 1975).

6. Make Sure Those Conducting Measurements
Are Disinterested and Are Masked if Possible
Those who administer outcome measures should have no vested interest in the study's outcome. Those employed at an organization other than Fairview, who have no chance to lose or gain from the study's outcome, should measure outcome. Those measuring outcome should also be masked as to which subjects were in the control and experimental groups so that such knowledge cannot bias the way they administer the measures.

7. Train Evaluators to Administer Outcome Measures Reliably
Those who administer outcome measures should be trained to follow identical procedures with all clients in order to minimize variation in measurement due to error. (Reliability, meaning consistency in measurement, will be discussed in Chapter 7.)

8. Randomly Assign Subjects to Treatment and Control Groups
Procedures for randomly assigning subjects to treatment or control groups have been shown in Tables 5.1 and 5.2. Those assigning subjects randomly to validation therapy or to a control group should not see the numbers before the assignment is made, and they should not be in a position to alter the random assignment procedure. To assure this, seal sequentially numbered envelopes—each containing the randomly determined word "treatment" or "control"—and keep them secure. Make sure that subjects are assigned as they are referred for treatment according to the group assignment given in the envelopes.

9. Try to Mask Experimental and Control Subjects
If controls and experimentals—those receiving validation therapy and those not receiving validation therapy—become aware of their membership in such groups and the expectations that group membership implies, this awareness can affect

the experiment's result. That is, resentful demoralization of controls and compensatory rivalry and placebo effect can be confounded with the treatment's effect. To counter these confounders, it may be advisable to give controls an enjoyable recreational experience or some other activity that makes them feel special but does not have therapeutic value. Technically, when subjects do not know if they are in a treatment or control group, they are **blinded**. The process by which they are blinded is called **masking**.

10. Have the Analysis Done by a Disinterested, "Blind," Person

Bias may enter into an experiment during the analysis phase. If the person doing the analysis doesn't know who is an experimental or control subject, bias is less likely to occur. Those who do the analysis without knowing whether the data are from treatment or control subjects are said to be **blinded**. If efforts to mask subjects and those who administer the experiment are successful, then the experiment is said to be **double blind.**

LEVEL OF GENERALIZATION

If validation therapy causes clients at Fairview to change, will it have the same effect on disoriented clients at another nursing home? Or conversely, if the method has been effective elsewhere, will validation therapy be effective at Fairview? Such information is vital to practitioners who want to select methods for their own clients. Such generalization is the last issue to be discussed in this chapter.

Experiments are said to be **externally valid** if their causal findings generalize across places, times, and clients (Campbell & Stanley, 1963, p. 5). Since Campbell and Stanley first coined this term, and defined several threats to external validity, so many lists of threats to external validity have been developed that a more generally applicable term might be an experiment's **level of generalization** (Mark, 1986, p. 52).

Ideally, validation therapy's level of generalization would be greatest if subjects in the experiment were drawn representatively from some population of clients. **Random selection** means that each individual has an equal and independent chance of being selected for study from the population. For example, if all 400 disoriented nursing-home residents in Monroe County were listed, their names numbered, and 50 subjects for the experiment were randomly selected from the list, then effects determined in the experiment would be most representative of the method's effects in Monroe County. However, it is difficult to select subjects randomly for study. In the Monroe County example, it would take a coordinated effort to measure all 400 residents at the four different nursing homes in the county. Then the 50 residents randomly selected for study would need to be transported to some central location to participate in validation groups or some nontherapeutic activity group. The stress of moving and disrupting residents might interfere with the results of the experiment. It might even endanger the health of some. The cost might still be high if 50 single-subject experiments were conducted by a single therapist, who would have to shuttle between the four nursing homes.

Given that random selection is difficult, how can results of studies be generalized? There is no simple answer. The following problems menace a study's level of generalization. Intervention as intended and described may not actually be what happens (Cronbach, 1982, p. 93). Subjects in one agency, perhaps because they are highly motivated or competent in a particular way, may be particularly likely to benefit from a particular method—interaction of selection and treatment (Cook & Campbell, 1979, p. 73)—and similarly, subjects in a certain type of agency, with its unique configuration of programs and personnel, may also benefit most from a particular method—interaction of setting and treatment (Cook & Campbell, 1979, p. 74).

Practitioners who wonder if their own clients would experience treatment effects as reported in a study elsewhere have two tools. One is replication. Group designs provide a form of replication for a method's effects if the general trend for many subjects in a group experiment is toward statistically significant improvement. Group studies replicated at different agencies and times provide still more convincing evidence in favor of a study's level of generalization. Unreplicated single-subject studies constitute very weak evidence. However, multiple single-subject studies administered by different practitioners in different settings, at different times, with different client types may, if analyzed collectively for interactions, tell us more about a particular method's effects with particular client types than group designs can (Barlow & Hersen, 1984, p. 56).

The practitioner's other ally for making generalizations is a systematic look at similarities and differences across subjects and settings. Such comparisons should include client assessment criteria, client demographic characteristics, and a description of the level of expertise of practitioners who applied the method elsewhere. The greater the similarity, the greater the likelihood that a method found effective elsewhere will be effective in one's own setting.

SUMMARY

This chapter has outlined some key features of experimental design so that practitioners can learn to reason about the causal inferences that they make every day. (For a more complete description of how to conduct various experimental designs consult texts that deal exclusively with single-subject designs [Barlow & Hersen, 1984; Bloom & Fischer, 1982; Drew & Hardman, 1985; Kazdin, 1982] and multiple-subject designs [Box, Hunter, & Hunter, 1978; Cook & Campbell, 1979; Das & Giri, 1986; Petersen, 1985].) The causal inference hierarchy showing levels of designs, given in Figure 5.1, although helpful as a guide, is only an approximation. Single-subject designs and group designs each have their own strengths and should be used to augment each other (Shine, 1975). Single-subject designs may be more appropriate to assess measures, to explore treatments, and to evaluate interventions with particular types of clients; group designs, unless they are designed specifically to test for interactions, may be more appropriate to determine how generally effective a method may be. By illustrating some of the complexities involved in drawing a causal inference in social work practice, this chapter will encourage practitioners to be cautious when drawing causal inferences. It is also hoped that practitioners who are aware of the problems caused by confounders may turn to experimentation to draw their causal inferences.

EXERCISES

1. If you have access to clients, select a client you intend to help and plan a single-subject study to evaluate the client's progress.

2. Plan a group study to evaluate effects of a method. What are the strengths and weaknesses of the design that you chose to guide your evaluation?

REFERENCES

Arkava, M. L., & Lane, T. A. (1983). *Beginning social work research.* Newton, MA: Allyn & Bacon.

Babins, L. (1988). Conceptual analysis of validation therapy. *International Journal of Aging and Human Development, 26*(3), 161–168.

Barlow, D. H., Hayes, S. C., & Nelson, R. O. (1984). *The scientist practitioner: Research and accountability in clinical and educational settings.* New York: Pergamon.

Barth, R. P. (1981). Education for practice-research: Toward a reorientation. *Journal of Education for Social Work, 17*(2), 19–25.

Bloom, M., & Fischer, J. (1982). *Evaluating practice: Guidelines for the accountable professional.* Englewood Cliffs, NJ: Prentice-Hall.

Blythe, B. J., & Briar, S. (1985). Developing empirically based models of practice. *Social Work, 30*(6), 483–488.

Box, G. E. P., Hunter, W. G., & Hunter, J. S. (1978). *Statistics for experimenters,* New York: John Wiley.

Campbell, D. T., & Stanley, J. C. (1963). *Experimental and quasi-experimental designs for research.* Chicago: Rand McNally.

Cook, T. D., & Campbell, D. T. (1979). *Quasi-experimentation: Design & analysis issues for field settings.* Boston: Houghton Mifflin.

Corcoran, K. J. (1985). Aggregating the idiographic data of single-subject research. *Social Work Research & Abstracts, 21*(2), 9–12.

Coulton, C. J. (1985). Research and practice: An ongoing relationship. *Health and Social Work, 10*(4), 282–291.

Cronbach, L. J. (1982). *Designing evaluations of educational and social programs.* San Francisco: Jossey-Bass.

Das, M. N., & Giri, N. C. (1986) *Design and analysis of experiments* (2nd ed.). New York: John Wiley.

Drew, C. J., & Hardman, M. L. (1985). *Designing and conducting behavioral research.* New York: Pergamon.

Feil, N. (1981). *Validation/fantasy therapy.* Cleveland: Edward Feil Productions.

Fischer, J. (1976). *The effectiveness of social casework.* Springfield, IL: Charles C Thomas.

Freiman, J. A., Chalmers, T. C, Smith, H., & Kuebler, R. R. (1978). The importance of beta, the Type II Error and sample size in the design and interpretation of the randomized control trial. *New England Journal of Medicine, 299*(13), 690–694.

Gambrill, E. D., & Barth, R. P. (1980). Single-case study designs revisited. *Social Work Research & Abstracts, 16*(3), 15–20.

Gingerich, W. J. (1983). Significance testing in single-case research. In A. Rosenblatt & D. Waldfogel (Eds.), *Handbook of clinical social work.* San Francisco: Jossey-Bass.

Goldwasser, A. N., Auerbach, S. M., & Harkins, S. W. (1987). Cognitive, affective and behavioral effects of reminiscence group therapy on demented elderly. *International Journal of Aging and Human Development, 25*(3), 209–222.

Gottman, J. M., & Leiblum, S. R. (1974). *How to do psychotherapy and how to evaluate it: A manual for beginners.* New York: Holt, Rinehart and Winston.

Hersen, M. (1982). Single-case experimental designs. In A. S. Bellack, M. Hersen, & A. E. Kazdin (Eds.), *International handbook of behavior modification and therapy.* New York: Plenum.

Howe, M. W. (1974). Casework self-evaluation: A single-subject approach. *Journal of Social Service Research, 48*(1), 1–50.

Jayaratne, S., & Levy, R. L. (1979). *Empirical clinical practice.* New York: Columbia University Press.

Jones, R. R., Weinrott, M. R., & Vaught, R. S. (1978). Effects of serial dependency on the agreement between visual and statistical inference. *Journal of Applied Behavior Analysis, 11*(2), 277–283.

Kazdin, A. E. (1979). Data evaluation for intra-subject-replication research. *Journal of social service research, 3*(4), 79–97.

Kazdin, A. E. (1982). *Single-case research designs.* New York: Oxford University Press.

Kerlinger, F. N. (1986). *Foundations of behavioral research* (3rd ed.). New York: Holt, Rinehart & Winston.

Kraemer, H. C., & Thiemann, S. (1987). *How many subjects?* Newbury Park, CA: Sage.

Lachin, J. M. (1988). Properties of simple randomization in clinical trials. *Controlled Clinical Trials, 9*(4), 312–326.

Mahoney, M. J. (1978). Experimental methods and outcome evaluation. *Journal of Consulting and Clinical Psychology, 48*(4), 660–672.

Mark, M. M. (1986). Validity typologies and the logic and practice of quasi-experimentation. In W. M. K. Trochim (Ed.), *Advances in quasi-experimental design and analysis* (pp. 47–66). San Francisco: Jossey-Bass.

McReynolds, L. V., & Thompson, C. K. (1986). Flexibility of single-subject experimental designs. Part I: Review of the basics of single-subject designs. *Journal of Speech and Hearing Disorders, 51*(3), 194–203.

Meinert, C. L. (1986) *Clinical trials.* New York: Oxford University Press.

Mizes, J. S., Hill, G. P., Boone, S. E., & Lohr, J. M. (1983). Reactivity of measurement: A single-subject investigation of effects of participant observers. *Psychological Reports, 53*(2), 663–668.

Nelsen, J. C. (1981). Issues in single-subject research for non-behaviorists. *Social Work Research & Abstracts, 17,* 31–37.

Nelson, A., Fogel, B. S., & Faust, D. (1986). Bedside cognitive screening instruments: A critical assessment. *The Journal of Nervous and Mental Disease, 174*(2), 73–83.

Nuehring, E. M., & Pascone, A. B. (1986). Single-subject evaluation: A tool for quality assurance. *Social Work, 31*(5), 359–365.

Ottenbacher, K. J. (1986). Reliability and accuracy of visually analyzing graphed data from single-subject designs. *American Journal of Occupational Therapy, 40*(7), 464–469.

Paul, G. L. (1967). Strategy of outcome research in psychotherapy. *Journal of Consulting Psychology, 31*(2), 109–118.

Peoples, M. M. (1982). *Validation therapy versus reality orientation as treatment for the institutionalized disoriented elderly.* Unpublished master's thesis, University of Akron, OH.

Peterson, R. G. (1985). *Design and analysis of experiments.* New York: Marcel Dekker.

Pfeiffer, E. (1975). A Short Portable Mental Status Questionnaire for the assessment of organic brain deficit in elderly patients. *American Geriatrics Society, 23*(10), 433–441.

Ryan, T. A., Joiner, B. L., & Ryan, B. F. (1976). *MINITAB: Student handbook.* North Scituate, MA: Duxbury.

Sagan, C. (1987, February 1). The fine art of baloney detection. *Parade Magazine,* p. 11.

Shine, L. C. (1975). Five research steps designed to integrate the single-subject and multi-subject approaches to experimental research. *Canadian Psychological Review, 16*(3), 179–184.

Sowers-Hoag, K. M., Thyer, B. A., & Bailey, J. S. (1987). Promoting automobile safety belt use by young children. *Journal of Applied Behavior Analysis, 20*(2), 133–138.

Stocks, J. T., Thyer, B. A., & Kearsley, M. (1987). Using a token economy in a community-based residential program for disabled adults: An empirical evaluation leads to program modification. *Behavioral Residential Treatment, 1*(3), 174–185.

Szykula, S. A., & Morris, S. B. (1986). Strategic therapy with children: Single-subject case study demonstrations. *Psychotherapy, 23*(1), 174–180.

Test, M. A., & Stein, L. I. (1977). A community approach to the chronically disabled patient. *Social Policy, 8*(1), 8–16.

Thomas, E. J. (1978). Research and service in single-case experimentation: Conflicts and choices. *Social Work Research & Abstracts, 14*(4), 20–31.

Thyer, B. A., Irvine, S., & Santa, C. A. (1984). Contingency management of exercise by chronic schizophrenics. *Perceptual and Motor Skills, 58*(2), 419–425.

Walton, M. (1986). *The Deming management method.* New York: Dodd, Mead.

Yeaton, W. H., & Sechrest, L. (1981). Critical dimensions in the choice and maintenance of successful treatments: Strength, integrity, and effectiveness. *Journal of Consulting and Clinical Psychology, 49,* 156–167.

Zelen, M. (1974). The randomization and stratification of patients to clinical trials. *Journal of Chronic Diseases, 27,* 365–375.

6

How to Ask a Specific Question About a Method's Effectiveness

WHY ASK SPECIFIC QUESTIONS?

Learning to pose relevant, clear, and answerable questions may help bridge what many perceive to be a gap between scientific reasoning and social work practice (Bierter, 1977; Heineman, 1981; Saleebey, 1979). This chapter may be particularly important if, as some believe (Bushnell & O'Brien, 1977, pp. 178–179), a major reason for the gap between research and practice can be traced to researchers not posing questions of importance to practitioners.

Because social work practitioners use methods that can affect the survival and well-being of a wide variety of clients, the questions they pose are far from trivial. Clients face a multitude of perplexing and resistant problems; therefore practitioners' questions can be as challenging as they are complex.

To provide examples of practice-related questions, during each year of a 6-year period, social workers in western Wisconsin have responded to various versions of a Researchable Question Form (see Exercises section). The form, created for use in a Methods of Social Work Research course, asks practitioners to pose questions about the effects of their methods.

Dozens of different topics were mentioned in the 207 questions submitted by practitioners during the 6-year period. Among them were questions on the effect of:

- a family treatment weekend on participants in a chemical dependency program
- an AIDS information program on condom use by undergraduates
- a time-saving procedure on a social service department's productivity

- an educational program on antagonistic relationships between geriatric and mentally ill residents of an institution
- a Child and Family Services Parent Aid Program on the recidivism of child abuse among families served by the program
- a Community Options Program on rehospitalization rate for the mentally ill
- Spiderman's Good Touch-Bad Touch Education Program on children's knowledge of appropriate touching behavior
- regular contact with their biological parents on the adjustment of adopted children compared with adjustment of those who do not have such contact
- adult day care on the well-being of aged persons
- an Immediate Care Unit versus a regular unit in an institution for emotionally disturbed adolescents
- a daily "assurance call" on a client's frequency of calls to a social service agency
- a widow's support group on stress levels
- an employee assistance program on employee absenteeism
- electroconvulsive shock therapy when administered before or after psychotropic drugs
- brief versus longer treatment for chemically dependent clients
- a public utility company's Early Identification Program for those needing health and social services
- group counseling for chemically dependent clients in mixed-sex or homogeneous-sex groups
- high versus low parent involvement on performance of students in Head Start Programs
- family-based services or traditional out-of-home placement on children's psychosocial adjustment
- an eating disorders (bulimia and anorexia) counseling program at a local hospital

Given the vital nature of such topics, social workers who know how to formulate incisive questions have a better chance of obtaining well-founded answers. The alternative is allowing someone else to ask—and subsequently answer—the question. Because others may have posed their question unspecifically and without a systematic procedure for answering it, simply accepting their answer can put clients at risk.

OVERVIEW

This chapter outlines, as precisely as possible, how to formulate specific answerable questions about topics such as those just presented. The chapter's first section discusses how to sharpen question clarity. To demonstrate ways to pose questions clearly, 12 criteria for a specific, answerable question are defined and applied to questions actually asked by practitioners.

Because this text is intended to sharpen reasoning about effective practice, questions posed here only concern evaluation of a method. Evaluative questions name or imply an independent variable (method) and a dependent variable (intended outcome). In asking evaluative questions, investigators seek to establish a causal link between the two by manipulating the independent variable according to the logic of a particular experimental design (one reason why the chapter on experimental design was presented *before* this chapter on how to pose a question). Evaluative studies are distinct from descriptive studies that seek to "discover facts or describe reality" (Monette, Sullivan, & DeJong, 1986, p. 5), as would a survey.

Example Questions

Following are several example questions that we will use in our discussion. The first three imply a single-subject design:

- Will weekly home visits reduce an elderly person's many calls each day to the Grace Lutheran Foundation (Evavold, 1986)?

- Does play therapy as a method of treatment for a sex abuse victim under age 12 increase the victim's feelings of self-control (Bredesen, 1988)?

- Will using behavior modification result in a decrease in the number of self-injurious behaviors exhibited every day by a profoundly retarded male resident of an institution (Howe, 1988a)?

Here is a question posed by a social worker regarding effects of a sexual-abuse victims' group:

- We are conducting two kinds of groups right now: counseling for female sexual abuse victims and an Informal Disposition Group. We are offering both groups on a time-limited basis and it would be helpful to know their effectiveness. I am especially interested in what effects the sexual abuse group is producing. Also, I'm interested in the client perceived value of the Informal Disposition Group (Roth, 1986).

Here is a question posed by a physician regarding effects of an AIDS information program for undergraduate students (Kark, 1988):

- Will the AIDS information program result in the increased usage of condoms among University of Wisconsin—Eau Claire (UW—EC) students?

This question was posed by a school counselor (Paloski, 1988):

- It appears that most students who are referred to the School-Age Parents Program have at least some knowledge about the various forms of birth control and access to it but are, nevertheless, pregnant. Other issues such as codependency in the family, addictive relationships, sexual abuse, the student's assumptions that life options are limited, and our society's perpetuation of promiscuous sexual behavior frequently appear to enter into the picture of teenage pregnancy in this country.

All students are required to take a ninth-grade health class that presents in-formation regarding birth control. However, not all of the other abovementioned issues are dealt with as possible causes of teenage pregnancy and presented to all students.

Both Memorial and North high schools have drop-out prevention programs that maintain students as a control group during their sophomore and junior years. It would be useful to determine if additional information regarding these other possible causes of teenage pregnancy presented over a 2-year period to one control group would affect the pregnancy rate as compared to the other group to which no additional information and activities were presented.

TWO COMMON PROBLEMS IN QUESTIONS POSED BY PRACTITIONERS

Although the example questions concern important issues and were posed by competent, dedicated, and highly respected professionals, none were formulated specifically enough to elicit specific answers. Practitioners need to sharpen their questions to make them answerable. To make questions more specific, it is necessary to state who will receive the special treatment, how effects of the treatment are to be measured, over what interval the outcome is to be measured, and how features of experimental design will be used to structure the implied test.

To illustrate the need for greater specificity, let us examine the example questions. How would increased condom use be measured in order to judge effects of the AIDS-prevention program? Would the judgment be inferred by increased condom sales? Might more accurate estimates be obtained by confidential questionnaires or by structured interviews? As for the question regarding self-abusive behavior by a resident of an institution, would a single-subject evaluation involve an AB design or perhaps an ABA withdrawal design? Regarding the teenage pregnancy-prevention program, what specific components would the program contain?

In addition to question clarity, factors that can affect study feasibility need to be examined. Feasibility factors can determine whether steps implied to be examined. Feasibility factors can determine whether steps implied in the question can be accomplished. For example, ethical concerns may preclude random assignment to treatment groups, costs of a study may be too high for an agency to bear, necessary cooperation may not develop among agency personnel, or too few subjects may be available to submit the program to a fair test.

To illustrate potential problems with feasibility, think of whether a local board of education might accept randomly assigning some—but not all—students to a special teenage pregnancy-prevention program. Might some controls hear about the special program and want to be included? Regarding the self-abusive, developmentally disabled resident of an institution, would staff members have the time to monitor the resident's behavior frequently enough to determine whether it was changing? For the moment, consider only the problem of question specificity—there will be more on feasibility later in this chapter.

THE ROLE OF AN UNDERLYING THEORY
IN QUESTION CONSTRUCTION

A **theory** is a set of interrelated propositions or statements that seek to explain clearly defined events (Nagel, 1961, pp. 90–97). For example, corrections theoreticians Sutherland and Cressey (1974) sought to explain delinquency as being caused by "differential association" with delinquent peers (pp. 75–91). Differential association theory includes these propositions:

> Criminal behavior is learned. . . . The principal part of the learning of criminal behavior occurs within intimate personal groups. . . . The specific direction of motives and drives is learned from definitions of the legal codes as favorable or unfavorable. . . . A person becomes delinquent because of an excess of definitions favorable to violation of the law. (Sutherland & Cressey, 1974, pp. 75–76)

Theory has implications for practice when it is used to justify trying a particular intervention. Practitioners in corrections who subscribe to differential association theory might reason that if delinquent behavior is learned through association with peers, then nondelinquent behavior can be learned in peer group counseling if nondelinquent definitions are substituted for delinquent ones.

Whether a theory is explicitly stated or not, any intervention is based on some underlying theoretical proposition. Ellis and Harper (1975) included these theoretical propositions underlying cognitive behavior therapy in their work: (a) people who have problems with dysfunctional behavior may have such problems because they think inaccurate and self-defeating thoughts about themselves; (b) typical dysfunctional thoughts are that situations are terrible and that one cannot stand the terrible situation; (c) a way to help people to overcome dysfunctional behavior is to teach them to substitute more positive, constructive cognitions for their negative, counterproductive ones. Consequently, various procedures have been developed by cognitive behavior therapists to help people change their self-defeating cognitions (Kazdin, 1984, pp. 211–225; Lewinsohn & Hoberman, 1982, pp. 420–421).

When formulating a research question, it helps to consider the reasons or propositions that underlie the intervention. Even if the reasoning is not as explicit as just outlined, theories that are clearly stated and well-supported by empirical evidence are more likely to generate effective intervention.

CRITERIA FOR MAKING QUESTIONS MORE SPECIFIC

Regardless of the investigator's theoretical orientation, proposed study design, and resources to conduct a study, explicit criteria can help to formulate a specific and answerable question. The criteria given in Figure 6.1 are essential to a clearly formulated question about a method's effect. These criteria may be applied to single-subject and group designs and may be "rubber-stamped" onto student papers right next to their questions in order to rate their answerability.

There are 12 criteria on the stamp; each criterion is worth 2 points for a total of 24 possible points. Each criterion earns 2 points if the part of the question

____	1. Is a Question of Fact	____	7. "When" of Treatment Is Stated
____	2. "Who" Is Selected	____	8. "When" of Outcome Is Specified
____	3. Method Is Stated		
____	4. Study Design Is Evident	____	9. Is Single-Barreled
____	5. Dependent Variable Is Identified	____	10. Is Simple and Direct
		____	11. Demonstrates Feasibility
____	6. "Where" of Evaluation Is Cited	____	12. Specifies Conditions Needed to Answer Question

FIGURE 6.1
Criteria for question answerability: Clarity-of-Question Stamp.

concerning that criterion meets the condition stated, 1 point if it can be made clear only by interpreting from other parts of the question or from discussion accompanying the question, and no points if the question does not meet the criterion.

Criterion 1: Is a Question of Fact

Chapter 3 drew a distinction between a question of fact and a question of value. Questions of value concern what outcomes *should* be obtained (e.g., better nutrition for children) and the acceptability of risks to obtain those outcomes. In contrast, questions of fact concern which methods are most likely to produce particular outcomes. To guide the search for effective methods, a question of fact must specify how a particular test is to be run to answer the question in a particular context. Questions of fact are stated in an if/then format: If certain conditions are met in a test, then will there be a particular outcome? The following example is a question of fact concerning whether Brian will decrease the frequency with which he bashes his head against tables, walls, and other objects, or hits objects, or hits his head with his hand. The related question of value, obviously answered in the affirmative, is: Should Brian's self-abusive behavior be stopped? The example question (Howe, 1988b) is posed so specifically that it may be submitted to a test:

- Will Brian, a resident of Northern Center for the Developmentally Disabled, have a statistically significantly ($p < .05$) lower rate of self-injurious behavior during the Positive Practice Treatment Program, from November 1 to December 1, than during his baseline, from October 1 to October 31?

This question receives 2 points for being a question of fact. It meets Criterion 1 because it implies that if a particular set of conditions is met, the answer will be found. The question does not ask a value question; it is not posed with the word *should* implied in the question, nor is *should* used specifically in the question. The question is posed in a way that does not imply that the answer is a forgone conclusion, as would a question that asks if the reduction in self-abusive behavior during the treatment phase will be from 1% to 19% or greater than 20%. A question posed with such alternatives assumes that outcome could only involve some degree of improvement; however, Brian might deteriorate during treatment.

Criterion 2: "Who" Is Selected

In a single-subject study, "who" would be the client. If the client's identity needs to be protected, a pseudonym or number could be used to designate the particular client.

In a group study, the "who" would be the diagnostic label or general inclusion/exclusion criteria that describe a whole group of clients participating in the study, for example, "alcoholics in treatment." Assign a question 2 points if a name or diagnostic label is used to describe who, generally, is participating in the study.

Here is a question about Deborah:

- If Deborah's nightmares are counted daily during a baseline from January 1 through 15, and are also counted during the period of her play therapy at the Family Support Center from January 16 through January 31, will the frequency of her nightmares be significantly lower ($p < .05$) during the treatment phase?

Elaboration that might accompany the question, as in an "impressions" section of a case record, would give more detailed information to describe Deborah's history as a victim of sexual abuse and other dynamics thought to be related to her nightmares. Literature might be cited indicating how play therapy might be effective in her case (Federation, 1986; Mitchum, 1987). Elaboration in a group study, perhaps a study to evaluate effects of a program for alcoholics, might include criteria—the Substance Abuse Modified Diagnostic Interview Schedule (SAMDIS)—for assessing if clients are alcoholics (Hoffmann & Harrison, 1984). A distribution of subject scores on SAMDIS would further define the "who" in such a group experiment.

Criterion 3: Method Is Stated

Criterion 3 is met—give 2 points—if the investigator merely names the method to be used, for example: Victim's Support Group, Social Skills Training Group versus Alternate Training Group, and Family Incest Team Treatment. In the example question (Meiske, 1988), the method is designated by the title "Medication Counseling":

- Among the first 50 noncompliant patients admitted to Sacred Heart Hospital's Psychiatric Unit beginning November 1, will the 25 randomly assigned to Medication Counseling in the Social Services Department receive significantly higher scores ($p < .05$) on the Behavioral Scale of Medication Compliance 3 months after the date of their discharge than will 25 randomly assigned to a control group?

Although a question would meet Criterion 3 if it named the treatment, defining treatment much more specifically would be essential in any discussion section of a proposed study. Licht's (1979) exemplary Staff-Resident Interaction Chronograph might provide a model for treatment definition. Licht has developed a procedure for rating five resident behaviors and 21 kinds of staff reactions to those behaviors to describe treatment for the mentally ill and mentally retarded in institutions. Although his procedure takes 6–8 weeks to learn, during $4\frac{1}{2}$ years of experience with it, users have achieved high, long-run interrater reliabilities ($r = .99$).

Other factors that might be specified about the treatment include: the time clients spend participating, manuals and videotape materials describing specifically methods used, costs, special equipment, special training necessary to administer the treatment, and levels of experience of those administering treatment. Morris and Fitz-Gibbon (1978) have written an entire volume about how to describe treatment program implementation.

Criterion 4: Study Design Is Evident

Any question about a method's effects implies an experimental design that structures the question, whether that design is a single-subject or group design. To meet Criterion 4, a question should list essential features of a single-subject or group design implicit in the question. In a single subject ABA design, for example, the question might concern performance differences between the first and second baseline periods, or a difference between baseline and treatment for an AB design.

Similarly, key features of group designs need specification, including whether subjects have been randomly or nonrandomly assigned to treatment groups, control groups, or comparison groups and whether measures will be administered as pretests, posttests, or both. Recall from Chapter 5 that random selection and random assignment refer to different procedures. Random selection refers to how subjects are chosen from among a population of potential subjects for inclusion in the experiment. (This concerns generalizability of the experiment's results to others.) Random assignment refers to a procedure for assigning subjects to alternate treatment groups or to control groups. (This concerns causal inference.) The following example question (Kresbach, 1988) illustrates how essential features of a randomized trial's design can be incorporated into a question:

- If approximately 60 volunteer freshman girls from South Junior High School are randomly assigned to a Self-Awareness Class (to run from September 5 to June 3) or to a control group, will experimentals have a lower proportion pregnant ($p < .10$) during the period June 3 to June 2 the following year than will controls?

This question clearly states that volunteers will be randomly assigned to treatment or control groups and that there will be a comparison made at a particular time after the program ends. From the question's wording, it would be possible to diagram key features of this pregnancy-prevention study.

Assign a question 2 points for specifying enough features to diagram its study design; 1 point for one feature omitted (e.g., random assignment); and no points for two or more features omitted.

Criterion 5: Dependent Variable Is Identified

In the previous question, the dependent variable, or intended outcome, is the proportion pregnant. Drawing a circle around this dependent variable helps to clarify an expected causal relationship between the independent variable (method) and the dependent variable (intended outcome). Give 2 points for circling the dependent variable.

Criterion 6: "Where" of Evaluation Is Cited

The "where" of an evaluation refers to the location at which the evaluation is to take place. To meet Criterion 6 and receive 2 points, the name of the facility where treatment takes place is sufficient. In the discussion section of a proposal, greater specificity might include: the address of the facility, department name, name of persons responsible for administering the treatment and the study, and features of the facility that make it suitable as a place to administer the treatment. The following sample question (Schwamb, 1986) lists the Eau Claire County Department of Human Services as the location:

- Will approximately 10 sexually abused adolescents, who participate in a Sex Abuse Victims' Group from March 25 to July 1 at the Department of Human Services have a higher mean score ($p < .10$) on an Index of Self-Esteem (Hudson, 1982) administered on July 1 than they did on March 18?

Criterion 7: "When" of Treatment Is Stated

The "when" refers to the exact times that treatment begins and ends. In the previous question, those dates are March 25 to July 1. In a single-subject experiment, the time would be the period between the beginning of repeated measures during a treatment phase and the end of that treatment phase. Assign 2 points for specifying both beginning and ending time, 1 point for specifying just one or the other, and no points for neither.

Specifying time in treatment clarifies for others how much effort went into treatment and aids in estimating the potential costs for implementing the method elsewhere. A more detailed discussion accompanying this question might include the number of meetings attended and the length of time spent at each of the meetings.

Criterion 8: "When" of Outcome Is Specified

Specifying the interval for measuring outcome fulfills Criterion 8. In a single-subject question, the beginning and ending of the baseline and treatment periods can specify the when of the outcome. In a group study, the time of the outcome would refer to the date of any pretests and/or posttests. In the following sample question (Suske, 1985), the when of the outcome is the interval from March 1 to September 30 for both treatment and control groups:

- If residents of the Dunn County Health Care Center are randomly assigned to a delayed treatment control group or to participate in a Reality Orientation

(RO) Group from March 1 through August 31, will RO Group members have higher mean change scores ($p < .05$) on the Kahn-Goldfarb Mental Status Questionnaire (Kahn, Goldfarb, Pollack, & Peck, 1960) from March 1 to September 30 than will controls measured over the same interval?

Assign 2 points for specifying both times for measuring outcome in a pretest-posttest design or the one time in a posttest-only design. In a single-subject study, assign 2 points for specifying clearly all baseline and treatment periods. Assign 1 point if just one time is omitted, no points if two or more times are omitted.

Criterion 9: Is Single-Barreled

Multiple-barreled questions list more than one outcome in the same question. For example, in the sample question that cited the Kahn-Goldfarb Mental Status Questionnaire, including the Mini-Mental State Examination as an outcome also (Folstein, Folstein, & McHugh, 1975) would have made the question double-barreled. Any multiheaded question gets 0 points on Criterion 9.

Multiple-barreled questions are impossible to interpret. What if the scores improve on one outcome measure but decline on another? How then would the question be answered? True, most studies pose several questions, but making each question explicit simplifies analysis, helps investigators avoid the "fishing expedition" approach to research, and teaches skills of question formulation that can be applied to each individual question of a multiple question study.

Criterion 10: Is Simple and Direct

Scientific writing implies a simple and direct approach. Such writing pares away all unnecessary words, avoids vague and ambiguous words and phrases, and states the essentials. The following question (Bender, 1988) needs to be shortened:

- Of 44 patients admitted to Luther Hospital Mental Health Unit between June 1 and January 31 with a diagnosis of severe depression (major depressive disorder, bipolar depression, schizoaffective depression, and depressive neurosis), will 22 patients randomly assigned to electroconvulsive shock therapy (ECT) experience a longer time period between successful treatment and recurrence of severe depressive symptoms (relapse), measured at 3-, 6-, 9-, and 12-month intervals following completion of inpatient treatment than will 22 patients randomly assigned to antidepressant drug therapy treatment measured at identical posttreatment intervals?

The question is longer than necessary. It uses almost 90 words; the revision below, fewer than 60. The original question is also four-barreled, because the comparison across treatment groups could be made at any one of four points in time. A more concise version reads:

- If approximately 44 severely depressed patients admitted to Luther Hospital's Mental Health Unit between June 1 and January 31 are randomly assigned to receive electroconvulsive shock therapy (ECT) or antidepressives as a first treatment, will the average number of days to relapse during the 12 months immediately postadmission (for those discharged) be significantly lower ($p < .05$) in the ECT first treatment group?

Any question that cannot be rewritten and reduced by more than five words without sacrificing its meaning receives 2 points on Criterion 10. A question gets 1 point if it can be reduced by 6–10 words, again, without sacrificing meaning, and 0 points if it can be reduced by 11 or more words.

Criterion 11: Demonstrates Feasibility

Many factors that are difficult to anticipate and rate enter into a study's feasibility. Major ethical problems could stop a study dead in its tracks or make the study's results uninterpretable. Assign a question 2 points for feasibility if no major problems are anticipated, 1 point if one major problem seems evident, and 0 if two or more problems are evident. What makes a problem "major" enough to threaten the study's feasibility is purely a matter of interpretation, but the following section suggests some possibilities.

Feasibility: Ethical Problems Regarding Treatment of Subjects

Although posed clearly enough for testing, questions can still be unanswerable for ethical reasons, or at least they *should* be unanswerable. For example, just after World War II, the world found out how horribly those doing experiments could violate ethical principles. During World War II, a German physician by the name of Rascher conducted experiments on human subjects at Dachau Concentration Camp. Following is a question that, while meeting Criteria 1–10, totally violates the rules of ethical experimentation. Dr. Rascher's heinous experiment was described in evidence presented before the International Military Tribunal (1947, p. 545) in Nuremberg, Germany, at the Nazi War Crimes Trial:

- If healthy residents of Dachau Concentration Camp, dressed in complete flying suits, are nonrandomly assigned on August 15, 1942 to immersion in water (3°C) until their internal body temperature reaches 28°C, will more survive immediate efforts to revive them if the back of their head and neck were allowed out of the water compared with those not so allowed?

This grisly question is presented here to make the point very strongly that methodologically sound questions—questions that clearly pose a question of fact—must still be examined for their underlying value implications. The Nazis who conducted such experiments were missing something—a conscience. Further documentation proves that Dr. Rascher was not just an isolated case of unethical behavior during the Nazi era (Lifton, 1986).

Rules for Protecting Human Subjects.   Since the Nuremberg Trials, human experimentation has undergone an evolution. The trend has been toward systematic assessment of both the methodological and ethical appropriateness of research before it is conducted. Initially, the Nuremberg Code, resulting from the events described at the trials, established 10 guidelines for human experimentation. Principal facets of the Code include voluntary and informed consent of subjects, assessment of risks to subjects, minimizing risks to subjects, and freedom of subjects to withdraw from experiments at any time (Katz, 1972, pp. 305–306).

In the United States during the 1960s, several incidents called attention to questionable practices regarding human subjects. These questionable actions included: leaving black male victims of syphilis in a longitudinal experiment untreated even after penicillin was discovered (Jones, 1981); giving subjects injections of live cancer cells without their knowledge (Beecher, 1966); and leading participants in a psychological experiment to believe that they were administering an intense harmful shock to others (Milgram, 1963).

Such publicized events led to a series of Congressional Hearings, culminating in the establishment of the National Research Act (Public Act 93-348), signed into law in July 1974. At the same time, the National Commission for the Protection of Human Subjects of Biomedical and Behavioral Research was established. In 1978, this Commission issued the Belmont Report, which further clarified moral principles involved in research by promoting the following ideals: respect for persons (assuring right of subjects to make their own choices and the need to protect those who are not able to make their own choices), beneficence (doing no harm and maximizing possible benefits), and justice—certain groups (e.g., welfare recipients) should not bear a disproportionate weight of risks in experiments, and all should share equally in the benefits of the research (National Institute of Health and the Food and Drug Administration, 1987; Office of the Federal Register, 1979, pp. 23193–23194).

Currently, *Code of Federal Regulations 45 CFR 46* (Office of the Federal Register, 1987), although applying only to federally supported research, outlines principles with widest jurisdiction for protecting human subjects in the United States. The Code mandates that there be Institutional Review Boards (committees of at least five male and five female members including representatives of a variety of professions and one nonscientist) to review proposed research with an eye toward protecting the rights of human subjects. Principles from the Code include the following guidelines for evaluating the ethical feasibility of research:

1. *Minimal Risk.* There is some discomfort and uncertainty for subjects in all experiments, so every effort should be made to minimize necessary risks. Sound research design assures that subjects will not participate in weak and uninterpretable research. Investigators can minimize risks by discussing potential problems with colleagues and members of review boards. Conducting pilot studies with a few carefully monitored subjects can help avert greater problems in a later, full-scale study.

2. *Reasonable Risk to Subjects.* Determining whether risks to subjects are reasonable implies conducting preliminary estimates of costs and potential benefits to subjects. It is hoped that, in the long run, the knowledge gained will outweigh the risks taken. Experiments that provide useful information that can improve human life should be done; experiments that can only produce trivial knowledge should not. Former U.S. Senator William Proxmire's Golden Fleece Awards paid mock tribute on an annual basis to this second type of experiment.

3. *Equitable Selection of Subjects.* Populations that are particularly vulnerable—children, the mentally ill, prisoners, the mentally retarded, the elderly—should be afforded special protection. The investigator needs to make it clear who is chosen to be a subject and why. Definite steps should be taken to protect especially vulnerable subjects from disproportionate risks in experiments. The underlying principle is that all strata of society should share the risks as well as the benefits of research.

4. *Privacy and Confidentiality.* Information about subjects should be protected so that it can never be used in a way that would embarrass or hurt them. Generally, identifying subjects by number only should begin as early as possible in a study. The key to a subject numbering system should be kept locked in a place separate from subject files and both should be kept in a secure location.

5. *Informed Consent.* Subjects should fully understand the risks that participating in the study holds for them along with any potential benefits. To ensure that subjects fully understand the conditions of their participation and the potential risks, the investigator should be sensitive to educational levels, language differences, and cultural background when discussing the possibility of participation. Usually consent is obtained by having a subject sign a form that outlines such risks and benefits. Proper procedure always assures subjects that their participation is voluntary and may be withdrawn at any time. (A sample consent form is presented in Appendix A.)

6. *Data Monitoring.* The data should be monitored continuously so that the experiment can be stopped early on if results begin to show clearly that controls are suffering because of their "nonparticipation" or that experimentals are experiencing iatrogenic effects. Estimation procedures are available for stopping trials when the data indicate positive or negative effects before the trial's planned termination (DeMets & Halperin, 1982; Hilsenbeck, 1988; Meinert & Tonasica, 1986).

All of these points are included in federal documents (Office of the Federal Register, 1987, pp. 137–138). Again, such principles are intended to protect human subjects in experiments that are vital to the well-being of all in our society. Federal agencies are one source of guidelines; many professions also have their own.

The Code of Ethics of the National Association of Social Workers contains many of the same principles as those in the *Code of Federal Regulations.* The NASW Code's five principles concerning research read:

> Scholarship and Research—The social worker engaged in study and research should be guided by the conventions of scholarly inquiry.
>
> 1. The social worker engaged in research should consider carefully its possible consequences.
> 2. The social worker engaged in research should ascertain that the consent of participants in the research is voluntary and informed, without any implied deprivation or penalty for refusal to participate, and with due respect for participants' privacy and dignity.
> 3. The social worker engaged in research should protect participants from unwarranted physical or mental discomfort, distress, harm, danger, or deprivation.
> 4. The social worker who engages in the evaluation of services should discuss individuals only for professional purposes and only with persons directly and professionally concerned with clients.
> 5. Information obtained about participants in research should be treated as confidential. (National Association of Social Workers, 1980, p. 4)

Ethical Feasibility of a Study: An Example from Adoptions

Complexity often arises when applying ethical principles to a proposed study. Here is a specific, testable question (Hale, 1988), posed by a social worker about adoptions, that raises ethical issues:

- Among adolescents served by the Department of Community Services who are randomly assigned, from January 1 to December 31, to a group that will have contact with their birth parent or to a group that will not, will those not having contact have higher mean Coopersmith Self-Esteem Inventory scores ($p < .05$) on June 30 of the following year?

The social worker who posed this question was concerned about a perplexing problem in contemporary adoptions: Are children of closed adoptions better adjusted than children of open adoptions? The terms "open" and "closed" are variously defined by different child-care experts, but generally, **open adoption** refers to an agreement that adoptive parents and the child's biological parents will share their identities and will work out some kind of agreement as to how to relate to each other during the child's upbringing (Sorich & Siebert, 1982, p. 213). **Closed adoption** means contacts between the biological parents and the adoptive family, including the adopted child, are severed completely (Pannor & Baran, 1984, p. 246; Sorich & Siebert, 1982, p. 213). A related question, but one not considered here, is what effect opening adoption records once the child reaches age 18 may have (Flynn, 1979).

Because the question of open versus closed adoption concerns a vital area the question appears to meet the first criterion of the NASW Code presented earlier and that part of *Federal Regulations* requiring that experiments provide useful knowledge that can improve human life. Furthermore, experimenting to find an answer seems warranted because adoption experts are at opposite poles on the question. According to Pannor and Baran (1984), "All adoptions, including the placement of newborn infants, should now be open, in the best interests of the child, birth parents, and adoptive parents" (p. 246). On the opposite pole are Kraft, Palombo, Mitchell, Woods, and Schmidt (1985) who state: "Contact between birth parents and adoptive parents, either directly or indirectly through the agency staff, may interfere [with bonding between adopting parents and child] in a most subtle and most serious way" (p. 81).

Which viewpoint is correct? The welfare of children requires an answer. Unfortunately, there is not much to go on in the way of research evidence. Some speak in favor of open adoptions, basing their position on their own case-by-case experience (Blotcky, Looney, & Grace, 1982; Sorich & Siebert, 1982), but others take the opposite position, basing their position on their own impressions and on relevant child-development theory (Kraft et al., 1985). No studies that investigate the question directly are available (Kraft et al., 1985, p. 71; Triseliotis, 1985, p. 21). Obviously, a well-conceived and well-conducted study would help to settle this vital question.

Even though the question is vital to the welfare of children, it may still be unanswerable because, as the question is posed, the answer may violate the rights of human subjects. The principle of harm in the NASW Code and the section on risks in *Federal Regulations* should be considered. Would it be ethical to prohibit adolescents, on a random basis, to contact their biological parents and other birth relatives with whom they have bonded? In addition to the pain of such a severance, might there be harmful effects on the adolescent's development? If adolescents are informed, according to principles of informed consent, that they have the right to refuse to participate and can withdraw their consent at any time, would adolescents give their consent? Such questions might make the study involving adolescents as posed unanswerable for ethical reasons. A more practical and ethically defensible experiment might involve infants who are adopted.

Feasibility: Design Practicality
Superficially, arguments against experimentation in human service agencies may focus on resources to conduct a study, but the real obstacle may be the staff's

deeper disbelief in experimentation. Following are common arguments against experimentation and counterarguments favoring experimentation in single-subject and group experiments. Study feasibility may depend on how such arguments are clarified, honestly discussed, and resolved within the agency. Perhaps these arguments and counterarguments will forearm those who want to evaluate effects of agency procedures.

Arguments Against and For Single-Subject Designs
Argument 1

AGAINST: I simply don't have the time to conduct single-subject designs with each of my 70 clients.

FOR: Perhaps a few representative types of clients, or those whose problems are most critical, could be chosen for single-subject evaluation. Integration of single-subject designs is not an either-or situation. Try it with a few.

Argument 2

AGAINST: Effects of my methods are too subtle to measure.

FOR: If effects are too subtle to measure, then effects may not be substantial enough nor worth the effort and resources that you and the client are expending.

Argument 3

AGAINST: This whole idea of using science to help clients leaves me cold. I can't maintain a meaningful, empathic relationship with clients and try to measure their progress.

FOR: This is the soft-hearted therefore soft-headed fallacy. Practitioners need to be both soft-hearted and hard-headed to get results.

Argument 4

AGAINST: I can't tell clients that I am going to set goals for them and measure their progress toward those goals. I have no power to tell them what to do.

FOR: This is a "straw man" argument (Moore & Parker, 1986, p. 109), which misrepresents appropriate procedures for a single-subject study and then attacks that misrepresentation. Ideally, clients should act as partners in single-subject experiments by collaborating on goal setting.

Just as there are arguments against using single-subject designs to evaluate treatment programs, there are arguments against using group designs. Following are arguments against random assignment in group designs and corresponding counterarguments. There are other arguments against group designs, but generally the most common bone of contention in group designs is random assignment.

Arguments Against and For Random Assignment in Group Designs
Argument 1

AGAINST: We admit that we may not know if our method is effective because we lack empirical evidence about its effects; however, randomly assigning subjects to treatment or control groups would deny treatment that our experience has shown us to be effective. We simply cannot put clients at risk by denying them a particular treatment.

FOR: Admittedly there are risks to clients in any experiment, but isn't it more ethical, when studies are not available, to put a small number of clients at risk under controlled conditions, than to use untested methods on a wide scale? (Remember the fallacy of experience described in Chapter 1? Failure to recognize the fallacy of experience can be costly.)

Argument 2

AGAINST: Random assignment is too disruptive to our work with clients. It takes too much time, it would inconvenience staff, and it would cost us money.

FOR: Random assignment helps to rule out confounding causes more effectively than does any other procedure, so random assignment should be used wherever practically and ethically possible in group experiments. Weak studies allow only weak causal inferences.

Argument 3

AGAINST: Random assignment to a nontreated control group is out of the question unless clients choose to be in a nontreated group. It would be unethical to deny treatment to some. Our job is helping, not turning people away from treatment.

FOR: If a control group is impossible, subjects might be randomly assigned to two or more alternate treatments that are believed to be effective, thus avoiding ethical problems that arise when subjects are denied treatment. In situations where limited resources require that treatment must be delayed for some, those in a delayed treatment group can serve as controls while the experimentals are receiving treatment. Randomly assigning clients to a delayed treatment group may be the most equitable way to assign clients, because all will have an equal chance of being assigned to one.

Argument 4

AGAINST: We can't simply tell clients that they will be randomly assigned to one of two treatments. This would shake client confidence in our services by implying that we don't know which is more effective.

FOR: Absolutely! We can't simply tell clients that they will be randomly assigned to one of two treatments; they must be informed about the conditions of an experiment before consenting to participate in a randomized trial. However, in situations in which equally competent, experienced, and ethical professionals in two camps believe their method is effective, why not tell clients that current knowledge indicates both methods are believed to be effective, and we want to determine if one is more effective than the other?

Feasibility: Time to Do the Study

Unless the evaluator is very experienced, evaluations tend to take more time than anticipated. Following are a few aspects that commonly take more time than allotted:

1. Time to locate and copy previous studies that may help to plan the present evaluation

2. Time to start up treatment because details of treatment and forms for collecting data need to be worked out

3. Evaluation of a proposal for its ethical implications by nine different human-subjects committees and gaining permission to see client records (The consent form in Appendix A has been approved by nine human-subjects committees.)

4. Demands on clients' time—including traveling, participating in treatment, keeping records, and responding to follow-up

5. Demands on staff time—including attending meetings, keeping records, administering treatment, answering questions about the evaluation, and traveling to the treatment site

6. Length of treatment necessary

7. Time to devise an outcome measure, especially if a literature search fails to locate a good outcome measure

8. Time to pretest and modify outcome measures

9. Time to locate respondents at follow-up

10. Analyzing and writing up results—especially if records are not impeccable

Feasibility: Costs of Materials and Services

Clear assessment of study feasibility implies anticipating major costs. Here is a list of items whose costs are commonly underestimated:

1. Copyrighted measures, for example a study to evaluate effects of a parent training program for abusive parents might use the Adult-Adolescent Parenting Inventory at a cost of $43.50 for 40 tests and a Test Handbook (Family Development Associates, undated)

2. Transporting clients

3. Special consultants who are essential to making the method work

4. Materials essential to the treatment

5. Telephone charges for regularly following individuals

6. Clerical help to type reports and measures and implement quality control to check coding of responses

7. Copying measurement tools, coding sheets, and reports

8. Rental charges for special equipment including films and videotapes

9. Room rental

10. Stamps and mailing supplies

11. Computer time, software for analyzing data

12. Statistical consultants and other experts

Criterion 12: Specifies Conditions Needed to Answer Question

This 12th and final condition helps show the relationship between a researchable question and a hypothesis. Following is a researchable question (MacLeod, 1988) regarding the effects of two group approaches to helping abused women:

> If 30 women who have been victims of domestic violence are assigned randomly to a Structured Group or to a Support Group at Bolton Refuge House from November 1 to March 15, will those in the Structured Group experience greater average positive change scores ($p < .01$) on the Coopersmith Self-Esteem Inventory from November 1 to March 15 than *will* those in the Support Group over the same interval?

This question, because it has been stated specifically enough, can be changed to a researchable hypothesis by altering it slightly. Just move the word "will" to transform the question into a testable statement (MacLeod, 1988), or hypothesis:

- If 30 women who have been victims of domestic violence are assigned randomly to a Structured Group or to a Support Group at Bolton Refuge House from November 1 to March 15, those in the Structured Group *will* experience greater average positive change scores ($p < .05$) on the Coopersmith Self-Esteem Inventory from November 1 to March 15 than those in the Support Group over the same interval.

The research question is now posed in testable form because it: (a) meets criteria 1–11, (b) has been transformed into a hypothesis, (c) the hypothesis states exactly what comparison is to be made, that is, that mean change scores will be compared across the two treatment groups, and (d) the p level for this comparison will be made at the .05 level. Assign 2 points for meeting criterion 12 if the question meets all of these criteria; score it 0 if it does not meet all of them. Incidentally, to compute mean change scores for each group subtract the pretest score from the posttest score for all individuals in the group and compute the mean for these score changes.

SUMMARY

Questions posed by social work practitioners about effects of their methods are often too vague to answer. Such vagueness has serious implications for practice, because specific answers about effects of methods cannot come from vaguely posed questions. Therefore, as a vital first step toward effective practice, we must learn to pose specific questions about our methods' effects.

As an aid to those formulating researchable questions, this chapter reduced the art of question formulation to 12 specific principles that can be applied to single-subject and group experiments. These principles are intended to be used as a guide. They should also be specific enough to be used to identify and rate problems in question wording. Although studies typically ask multiple questions, it is hoped that these 12 criteria will help pose each one more specifically. To review, the 12 criteria for posing a researchable question are:

1. Is a question of fact
2. "Who" is selected
3. Method is stated
4. Study design is evident
5. Dependent variable is identified
6. "Where" of evaluation is cited
7. "When" of treatment is stated
8. "When" of outcome is specified
9. Is single-barreled
10. Is simple and direct
11. Demonstrates feasibility
12. Specifies conditions needed to answer question

EXERCISES

Here are two questions—actually posed by practitioners—that need clarification. The first requires a group design; the second a single-subject design. Please pose one clear question according to the information that follows the practitioner's question. Information necessary to posing the questions accompanies each question, following the outline in Figure 6.1.

Posing the question may be much easier if you first diagram the study according to the symbols in Figure 5.1 and Figure 5.3 from the information given following each practitioner's question and then pose your researchable question.

1. Practitioner's Question 1: "Will the AIDS Information Program result in the increased usage of condoms among University of Wisconsin-Eau Claire students?" This question (Kark, 1988) was posed by a concerned physician whose practice includes UW-EC students. Here is additional information to help you to clarify your researchable question:
   a. Is a Question of Fact: The physician assumes that his question regarding AIDS among students is important; he values their survival. Thus, the physician has decided a question of value. The physician's question of fact concerns how effective a prevention program may be.
   b. "Who" Is Selected: Entering UW—EC students will participate as subjects in the experiment.
   c. Method Is Stated: Two treatment groups and one control group are to be assigned. The first treatment is a 2-hour AIDS information program. The second is a 2-hour informational program plus a brief talk and question/answer session conducted by an AIDS victim who is the same age as the students. Controls will receive no treatment.
   d. Study Design Is Evident: Subjects will be randomly assigned to the two treatment groups and to one control group, but no information is available on how many students can participate from among the entering freshman class. Resources would determine the number who could participate.
   e. Dependent Variable Is Identified: The dependent variable is self-reported condom use. Use will be determined by how students answer *one* specially constructed

question that will be inserted into a questionnaire about AIDS knowledge (Goodwin & Roscoe, 1988). Here is that question: "During the past 6 months . . . , if I had sexual intercourse, my partner and I used a condom on every occasion: _____yes, _____ no, _____did not have intercourse" (Shipley, 1989, pp. 2–3).

f. "Where" of Evaluation Is Cited: The educational program is to be conducted at UW—EC.

g. "When" of Treatment Is Stated: The two hypothetical programs will be conducted for 2 hours on September 25.

h. "When" of Outcome Is Specified: The outcome will be measured on or about March 25 of the following year.

i. Is Single-Barreled: Additional questions in this study might concern differences in knowledge of AIDS across the two treatment groups, each treatment group compared with the control, proportion using condoms across treatment groups, and each treatment group's use of condoms compared with the control group. Another question is whether the proportion of condom use reported in *both* treatment groups is higher than the proportion of condom use among controls. That is, if condom use is greater in one treatment group over controls, but not greater in both treatment groups over controls, the answer to the question is still negative. This is an unusual way to pose a question, but sometimes an unusual approach is best. For our purposes here, only one question—with a single outcome—should be posed.

j. Is Simple and Direct: The question should include all of the key points listed here and be as clear and brief as possible.

k. Demonstrates Feasibility: As this book is being written, the feasibility of answering the question is just being investigated. Resources are limited, and use of a control group may be challenged on ethical grounds.

l. Specifies Conditions Needed to Answer Question: The question will be considered to have been answered affirmatively if a higher proportion ($p < .05$) of students uses

condoms in both of the treatment groups, compared with those in the control group. As stated earlier, the question can be posed for different comparisons, possibly for proportion of condom use among those in the information-only group compared with that of controls.

At this point, please stop and pose your version of the researchable question according to the information given. Then check the answer key in Appendix C.

2. Practitioner's Question 2: "How effective is behavior modification in getting students back 'on-task'?" Although posed in a way that implies that a group study might be used, the question (Teske, 1989) was actually answered with a single-subject design. Here is information relevant to this question:

a. Is a Question of Fact: Andy is a learning-disabled student at a local high school. The social work student, involved in other aspects of Andy's program at the school, has decided, in collaboration with Andy's teacher, that another problem with his school performance is that Andy just sits in his seat and never remains engaged for very long on on-task behaviors—studying, reading, doing homework. The question of value is whether Andy should spend more of his time on-task. The question of fact concerns whether he does stay on-task according to the following criteria.

b. "Who" Is Selected: Andy.

c. Method Is Stated: The treatment method for increasing Andy's on-task behavior is a program for rewarding such behavior.

d. Study Design Is Evident: The proposed study is an ABAB design.

e. Dependent Variable Is Identified: The dependent variable is Andy's on-task behavior, as measured on a Teacher Observation Code Sheet. This Code Sheet is based on other instruments (Hodge, 1985; Zigmond, Kerr, & Schaeffer, 1988).

f. "Where" of Evaluation Is Cited: North High School in Eau Claire, Wisconsin.

g. "When" of Treatment Is Stated: The first treatment period is from April 17 through

April 30; the second is from May 1 through May 16.

h. "When" of Outcome Is Specified: Outcome will be observed at 7-minute intervals by his teacher during randomly chosen time periods during each class day during the first baseline period (April 1 through April 16) and the second treatment period (May 1 through May 16).

i. Is Single-Barreled: This question concerns only a comparison between the first baseline and the second treatment period of an ABAB design. Other comparisons could include first baseline against second baseline, or first treatment against second treatment.

j. Is Simple and Direct: State the question in as few words as possible but still include all elements of the question.

k. Demonstrates Feasibility: This study was actually accomplished.

l. Specifies Condition Needed to Answer Question: This question implies a visual inspection of plotted behavior to draw an inference about whether Andy's behavior changed.

At this point, please stop and pose your version of the researchable question according to the information given. Then consult the answer key (Appendix C).

Using the Researchable Question Form

The researchable question can forge a bond between a Research Methods class and the reality of client care, current practice methods, and concerns about practice effectiveness. Typically, although vital to what actually goes on in practice, practitioners' questions are not sufficiently precise to make them answerable without clarification.

To pose an answerable question from a researchable question use the following form:

- Contact a social work practitioner who works with clients and uses methods that interest you

- Assure the practitioner that you are planning how you would conduct an evaluation study

- Ask the practitioner to pose a researchable question about the effectiveness of some method that he or she is using (e.g., alternate methods for terminating counseling, grief group, modeling socially appropriate behaviors, problem solving)

- Review the criteria for question answerability on the Clarity of a Question Stamp

- With the criteria on the Clarity of a Question Stamp as an outline for your discussion, contact the practitioner again to provide information you will need to pose your specific question

- Using your notes of this information, pose your question

- Revise your question repeatedly as your literature review and further discussions with the practitioner sharpen your understanding.

Researchable Question Form (To Be Filled Out by Field Instructor)

Name of Agency: _____
Name of person who could clarify the "Researchable Question": _____
Address of agency: _____
Agency phone number: _____
Type of client served by agency: _____
_____

Number of clients served per month by agency:
_____

What important question concerns you about your agency's effectiveness? You may wonder which of two new approaches to treating residents who have Alzheimer's disease has the longer period of self-sufficiency for your residents. You may wonder if preschool children who are exposed to sex education films falsely report sexual abuse more frequently than do children who are not exposed to such material. Such questions concerning effectiveness are very important and generate interest for students in our Research Methods course.

Please use the space below and the back of this page to state your question as clearly as possible. Please define key words in your question.

_____   _____
_____   _____
_____   _____
_____   _____
                           _____
                           _____

REFERENCES

Beecher, H. K. (1966). Ethics and clinical research. *New England Journal of Medicine, 274*(24), 1354–1360.

Bender, P. (1988). *Depression in remission: ECT versus psychotropic drugs.* Unpublished manuscript.

Bierter, W. (1977). The dangers of allowing social work to be invaded by science. *International Social Science Journal, 29*(4), 789–794.

Blotcky, M. J., Looney, J. G., & Grace, K. (1982). Treatment of the adopted adolescent: Involvement of the biologic mother. *Journal of the American Academy of Child Psychiatry, 21*(3), 281–285.

Bredesen, T. (1988). *Researchable question.* Family Support Center, Chippewa Falls, WI.

Bushnell, J. L., & O'Brien, M. St. L. (1977). Strategies and tactics for increasing research production and utilization in social work education. In A. Rubin & A. Rosenblatt (Eds.), *Sourcebook in research utilization.* New York: Council on Social Work Education.

DeMets, D. L., & Halperin, M. (1982). Early stopping in the two-sample problem for bounded random variables. *Controlled Clinical Trials, 3*(1), 1–11.

Ellis, A., & Harper, R. A. (1975). *A new guide to rational living.* Englewood Cliffs, NJ: Prentice-Hall.

Elmer, L. A. (1989). *A single-subject evaluation of a child's on task behavior.* Unpublished manuscript, University of Wisconsin-Eau Claire, Social Work Department, Eau Claire.

Evavold, S. (1986). *The effectiveness of home visits in treating the depressed elderly.* Unpublished manuscript, University of Wisconsin-Eau Claire, Social Work Department, Eau Claire.

Family Development Associates. (Undated). (Available from Family Development Associates, P.O. Box 94365, Schaumburg, IL 60194)

Federation, S. (1986). Sexual abuse: Treatment modalities for the younger child. *Journal of Psychosocial Nursing, 24*(7), 21–24.

Flynn, L. (1979). A parent's perspective. *Public Welfare, 37,* 28–33.

Folstein, M. F., Folstein, S. E., & McHugh, P. R. (1975). Mini-mental state: A practical method for grading the cognitive state of patients for the clinician. *Journal of Psychiatric Research, 12,* 189–198.

Goodwin, M., & Roscoe, B. (1988). AIDS: Students' knowledge and attitudes at a midwestern university. *Journal of American College Health, 36*(4), 214–222.

Hale, J. (1988). *Open adoption: Does it really benefit the child?* Unpublished manuscript, University of Wisconsin—Eau Claire, Social Work Department, Eau Claire.

Heineman, M. B. (1981). The obsolete scientific imperative in social work research. *Social Service Review, 55*(3), 371–397.

Hilsenbeck, S. G. (1988) Early termination of a phase II clinical trial. *Controlled Clinical Trials, 9*(3), 177–188.

Hodge, R. D. (1985). The validity of direct observation measures of pupil classroom behavior. *Review of Educational Research, 55*(4), 469–483.

Hoffmann, N. G., & Harrison, P. A. (1984). Substance Abuse Modified Diagnostic Interview Schedule. *Psychological Documents* #14-10.

Howe, S. (1988a). *Researchable question.* Northern Center for the Developmentally Disabled, Chippewa Falls, WI.

Howe, S. (1988b). *Reinforcement and over correction: Will they extinguish self-injurious behavior in a single case?* Unpublished manuscript, University of Wisconsin—Eau Claire, Social Work Department, Eau Claire.

Hudson, W. W. (1982). *The Clinical Measurement Package: A field manual.* Homewood, IL: The Dorsey Press.

International Military Tribunal. (1947). *Trial of the major war criminals before the International Military Tribunal: Vol. 25* (Documents and other material and evidence, No. 001-PS to 400PS). Nuremberg, Germany: International Military Tribunal.

Jones, J. H. (1981). *Bad blood.* New York: The Free Press.

Kahn, R. L., Goldfarb, A. I., Pollack, M., & Peck, A. (1960). Brief objective measures for the determination of mental status in the aged. *American Journal of Psychiatry, 117,* 326–328.

Kark, R. (1988). *Researchable question.* University of Wisconsin—Eau Claire Health Services, Eau Claire.

Katz, Jay (1972). *Experimentation with human beings.* New York: Russell Sage Foundation.

Kazdin, A. E. (1984). *Behavior modification in applied settings* (3rd ed.). Homewood, IL: Dorsey.

Kraft, A. D., Palombo, J., Mitchell, D. L., Woods, P. K., & Schmidt, A. W. (1985). Some theoretical considerations on confidential adoptions, Part II: The adoptive parent. *Child and Adolescent Social Work, 2,* 69–81.

Krebsbach, J. (1988). *Using sexual awareness in the school setting to reduce pregnancy rates.* Unpublished manuscript, University of Wisconsin—Eau Claire, Social Work Department, Eau Claire.

Lewinsohn, P. M., & Hoberman, H. M. (1982). Depression. In A. S. Bellack, M. Hersen, & A. E. Kazdin (Eds.), *International handbook of behavior modification and therapy.* New York: Plenum.

Licht, M. H. (1979). The Staff-Resident Interaction Chronograph: Observational assessment of staff performance. *Journal of Behavioral Assessment, 1*(3), 185–197.

Lifton, R. J. (1986). *The Nazi doctors.* New York: Basic Books.

MacLeod, R. (1988). *An evaluation of structured group therapy for women of domestic abuse.* Unpublished manuscript, University of Wisconsin—Eau Claire, Social Work Department, Eau Claire.

Meinert, C. L., & Tonasica, S. (1986). *Clinical trials: Design, conduct, and analysis.* New York: Oxford University Press.

Meiske, C. (1988). *An evaluation of social workers' effect on medication compliance among hospital patients.* Unpublished manuscript, University of Wisconsin—Eau Claire, Social Work Department, Eau Claire.

Milgram, S. (1963). Behavioral study of obedience. *Journal of Abnormal and Social Psychology, 67*(4), 371–378.

Mitchum, N. T. (1987). Developmental play therapy: A treatment approach for child victims of sexual molestation. *Journal of Counseling and Development, 65*(6), 320–321.

Monette, S. R., Sullivan, T. J., & DeJong, C. R. (1986). *Applied social research.* New York: Holt, Rinehart and Winston.

Moore, B. N., & Parker, R. (1986). *Critical thinking: Evaluating claims and arguments in everyday life.* Palo Alto, CA: Mayfield.

Morris, L. L., & Fitz-Gibbon, C. T. (1978). *How to measure program implementation.* Beverly Hills, CA: Sage.

Nagel, E. (1961). *The structure of science.* New York: Harcourt, Brace & World.

National Association of Social Workers. (1980). *Code of ethics of the National Association of Social Workers.* Silver Spring, MD: NASW.

National Institutes of Health and the Food and Drug Administration. (1987). *The Belmont Report: Basic ethical principles and their application.* (Cassette Recording). Bethesda, MD: Office for Protection from Research Risks, National Institutes of Health.

Office of the Federal Register, National Archives and Records Service, General Services Administration (April 18, 1979). *Federal Register.* Part 4, 44(76). Washington, DC: U.S. Government Printing Office.

Office of the Federal Register, National Archives and Research Services, General Services Administration (1987). *Code of Federal Regulations. 45 CFR 46* (Public Welfare), pp. 131–150. Washington, DC: U.S. Government Printing Office.

Paloski, L. (1988). *Researchable question.* School Age Parents Program, Memorial High School, Eau Claire, WI.

Pannor, R., & Baran, A. (1984). Open adoption as standard practice. *Child Welfare, 63*(3), 245–250.

Roth, F. (1986). Researchable question. Eau Claire Department of Human Services, Eau Claire, WI.

Saleebey, D. (1979). The tension between research and practice: Assumptions of the experimental paradigm. *Clinical Social Work Journal, 7*(4), 267–284.

Schwamb, J. F. (1986). *Final proposal: Group therapy for sexually abused victims.* Unpublished manuscript, University of Wisconsin—Eau Claire, Social Work Department, Eau Claire.

Shipley, L. K. (1989). *An assessment of AIDS education and condom use among college students.* Unpublished manuscript, University of Wisconsin—Eau Claire, Social Work Department, Eau Claire.

Sorich, C. J., & Siebert, R. (1982). Toward humanizing adoption. *Child Welfare, 61*(4), 207–216.

Suske, L. (1985). *An evaluation of effectiveness of the Reality Orientation Group held at the Dunn County Health Care Center.* Unpublished manuscript, University of Wisconsin-Eau Claire.

Sutherland, E. H., & Cressey, D. R. (1974). *Criminology* (9th ed.). Philadelphia: J. B. Lippincott.

Teske, E. (1989). *Researchable question.* Learning Disabilities Program, North High School, Eau Claire, WI.

Triseliotis, J. (1985). Adoption with contact. *Adoption and Fostering, 9*(4), 19–24.

Zigmond, N., Keer, M. M., & Schaeffer, A. (1988). Behavior patterns of learning disabled and non-learning disabled adolescents in high school academic classes. *RASE, 9*(2), 6–11.

7

Principles of Measurement

OVERVIEW

Recall that each question posed in Chapter 6 contained a clearly identifiable dependent variable. Such dependent variables included, for example, the number of incidents of a developmentally disabled client's self-injurious behavior, the number of nightmares experienced by a victim of abuse, and the score on a behavioral scale of medication compliance. Measuring the dependent variable in a research question entails formulating a clear concept to describe one particular client outcome, devising ways to observe events (thoughts, feelings, or behaviors) that indicate that outcome, and assigning numbers to indicators to quantify whether the client or clients have indeed changed. *Measurement* is a way to assign numbers to objects or events according to certain specified rules (Kerlinger, 1986, p. 392).

Measuring client change in single-subject and group experiments is the primary concern of this chapter, though principles of measurement apply to client assessment too. This chapter addresses how to define and evaluate the criteria by which we can know if we are helping our clients.

The chapter begins by illustrating why measurement is especially vital to social work practice—it helps practitioners avoid bias and vagueness in the ways they perceive clients and clarifies client assessment and outcome. The chapter then outlines some suggestions for locating measures and concludes by demonstrating how to judge the quality of a measure.

WHY SOCIAL WORK PRACTITIONERS NEED MEASUREMENT

Measurement Helps Us Avoid Bias

Without measurement to serve as a guide, the practitioner's mind may construct an inaccurate picture of the client. This **observation bias**—a tendency to act toward a client or group of clients in a way that is consistently based, not on the client's behavior, but rather on the worker's inaccurate perceptions of the client—can be especially harmful if it forms the basis for decisions about the client.

Observation bias has been traced to superficial aspects of the client's personal appearance, information provided about the client prior to an interview, and the practitioner's tendency to jump to premature conclusions or to convey an expectation to the client about what the client *should* say during an interview. The following features of the client's physical appearance and mannerisms have been empirically demonstrated as sources of observation bias in evaluations by human service workers: status as a young white woman (Kurtz, Johnson, & Rice, 1989), race (Cousins, Fischer, Glisson, & Kameoka, 1986), personal attractiveness (Johnson, Kurtz, Tomlinson & Howe, 1986; Nordholm, 1980), and verbal expressiveness (Cousins et al. 1986). Bias has also been traced to information provided to interviewers beforehand, including being told that the person to be interviewed had "severe emotional problems" (Harvey, Yarkin, Lightner, & Town, 1980, p. 563; Yarkin, Town & Harvey, 1981, p. 295), that the interviewee was "extroverted" or "introverted" (Fong & Markus, 1982; Snyder & White, 1981), that the person to be observed was unusual (Langer & Imber, 1980), or that the client came from a middle or lower social class (Franklin, 1986). Professionals may be vulnerable to bias because they tend to formulate hypotheses about clients before all the relevant data are in (Voytovich, Rippey, & Suffredini, 1985), and/or because they may be influenced by stereotypes about clients (Nurcomb & Fitzhenry-Coor, 1982). Clients may unknowingly feed the bias by sensing what the interviewer expects and answering questions in a way that supports such preconceptions (Snyder & Swann, 1978).

Because measurement seeks to objectify client assessment and outcome, it can go a long way toward overcoming the sources of bias. Measures foster fair treatment based on the client's real needs and performance, rather than on some stereotype or superficial characteristic.

Measurement Helps Us Avoid Vagueness

Have you ever wandered about in dense fog? Shapes are obscured or vague. Sometimes objects are not what they first appear to be. In fog, the mind can play tricks by filling in details of objects that are only half-perceived. Much is only half-seen, and much goes by totally undetected. Without measurement as a guide, social workers can be in a verbal fog. Worse than being in a real fog, social workers in a verbal fog are unaware that they are not communicating and have the illusion of having communicated.

Unfortunately their communication may be too vague to be effective. Such **vagueness**—having unspecific multiple meanings or different meanings to different practitioners—can be traced to several sources, including inexact quantifying adjectives, universally applicable terms, jargon, and tautology.

Four Sources of Vagueness

Inexact quantifying adjectives—imprecise terms used to relate how frequent, how often, or how severe a client problem or behavior may be—convey multiple meanings to those who hear them. Inexact quantifying adjectives often appear in statements about clients:

1. The client *often* missed appointments with his probation officer.

2. The couple *frequently* argued about their sexual relationship.

3. According to Margaret, she has had *frequent* emotional outbursts since the fire, and as a result, her children have become frightened and hide from her. Her husband has also missed a *considerable amount* of work because Margaret is afraid to be home alone (Scott, 1988, p. 1).

4. The child *not uncommonly* remained at home.

Table 7.1, containing the same adjectives as those used by Cutler (1979, p. 31) in a similar experiment, was constructed by asking 18 social work students to rate—on a scale from 0% (certain not to happen), to 50% (as likely as not to happen), to 100% (certain to happen)—20 quantifying adjectives according to what percentage of the time the adjective implied.

The data in table 7.1 show why quantifying adjectives add to the fog of imprecision in reasoning about practice. The last two columns on the right, giving

TABLE 7.1

Variable meanings for quantifying adjectives as rated by social workers (N = 18)

Quantifying Adjective	Mean Percent of Occurrence Implied	Standard Deviation (%)	Range (%)
1. Never	.3	1	0–5
2. Always	93.1	24	0–100
3. Rarely	8.5	5	1–25
4. Uncommonly	14.4	10	5–40
5. Frequently	73.3	18	20–98
6. Usually	78.9	14	49–99
7. In most cases	81.8	12	51–98
8. Probably	68.5	12	50–90
9. Commonly	75.3	11	50–95
10. Most likely	79.0	10	51–95
11. Possibly	51.3	13	25–85
12. Certainly	91.7	8	75–100
13. Suggestive of	45.5	17	5–75
14. Unequivocal	76.2	37	10–100
15. Many	73.4	15	25–90
16. Some	47.0	19	12–85
17. Few	18.3	10	5–40
18. Not uncommonly	63.1	25	7–97
19. Not infrequently	66.6	22	0–99
20. Not unusually	59.3	28	0–99

Note: These data are from social work students in field work, but the list of adjectives was developed by Cutler (1979, p. 32).

the standard deviation and range of values for each adjective, show the range of meanings implied by each adjective. If such a wide range in meaning exists, quantifying adjectives can only foster confusion. To avoid imprecision caused by inexact quantifying adjectives, refer to counts of specific behaviors whenever possible, or report scores on client assessment and outcome measures.

Social workers may unknowingly use **universally applicable terms** to describe clients and the effects of interventions in terms that are so vague as to be absolutely meaningless, even though they may think their assessments are perfectly clear. Clients, too, may fail to detect vague assessments of their problem; they may even consider universally applicable statements to be penetratingly perceptive. For example, the statement "At times you have a little difficulty relating to persons of the opposite sex" applies to almost everyone at some time. Astrologers and fortune-tellers play on people's gullibility by using such vague, generally true statements that could apply to most people.

To test whether a universally applicable client assessment that would be acceptable to professional social workers could be written, Alfred Kadushin (1963) cooked up this assessment:

> [The client] is reacting to a difficult life situation. . . . A considerable amount of emotional energy is being absorbed by internal conflicts so that limited energy is available to deal constructively with environmental difficulties. . . . The client is basically insecure, having experienced some rejection by parents and peers. (p. 17)

This statement contains **Aunt Fanny Talk,** so called because it is so vague that an astute reaction to it would be: "so does my Aunt Fanny" (Kadushin, 1963, p. 12). Kadushin divided 60 graduate school social workers, who were supervising master's level social work students in their field placements, into three groups and asked the members of each group to read a long and detailed case description. One group read about a boy of 5 with ulcerative colitis, the second group read about a girl of 15 who felt painfully self-conscious around peers, and the third group read about a woman in her late 30s whose husband was dying of cancer. After the social workers had read the assigned case descriptions, Kadushin asked all 60 to rate the client assessment on a scale from 1 (definitely inadequate) to 7 (definitely superior) according to how well the assessment portrayed the client in the case description they had read. Kadushin did not tell the social workers that he had given the *identical assessment statement* to all the social workers, regardless of which case they'd read.

Kadushin found that no matter which case the social workers had read, they all rated the assessment as being above average. None of the 60 social workers objected to the assessment statement's vagueness.

In another study, psychology students could not detect pure Aunt Fanny Talk when given a universally applicable assessment about themselves. On the contrary, the psychology students, who were not aware that every student in the class had received the same assessment to interpret their personality test's results, thought the bogus assessment did an excellent job of capturing their unique personality profile (Forer, 1949):

> You have a tendency to be critical of yourself. . . . while you have some personality weaknesses, you are generally able to compensate for them. . . . disciplined and self controlled outside, you tend to be worrisome and insecure inside. . . . at times you have serious doubts as to whether you have made the right decision or done the right thing. . . . (p. 120)

Forer reported that when the students found out how they had been tricked they took it with good humor.

A third source of vagueness occurs when a professional uses terms—**professional jargon**—that the client cannot readily understand. For example, a chemical-dependency counselor may use the word *codependence* to describe any destructively submissive way to relate to another person (Brown, 1988). If the word *codependence* is used without defining clearly how it applies to the client, the client cannot be expected to understand. Jargon is counterproductive because clients may feel alienated when they hear professionals use it (Alexander & Tompkins-McGill, 1987) and because it interferes with clear communication between worker and client (Bloom, 1980; Hardman, 1977). Following is an example of jargon used in an explanation of a therapy group's purpose:

> The purpose of this group is to facilitate better communications within families re-
> garding . . . expectations-role definitions, to enhance coping mechanisms in areas of
> both emotional stress and reality pressures. (Bloom, 1980, p. 336)

Professional jargon may sometimes convey a clear meaning among professionals; however, even professionals may not always have a clear understanding
of their own terms. A Systematic Buzz Phrase Projector ("New Peak for Newspeak," 1968) generates meaningless jargon. The Systematic Buzz Phrase Projector presented in Table 7.2 was constructed from terms used by social workers. Note
that many phrases, though randomly generated, actually seem to make sense.

A fourth source of vagueness, **tautology,** introduces imprecision into communication by including the term to be defined in its own definition. For example,
a practitioner might say that a client's assertiveness is improved. Then to define
assertiveness, the practitioner might explain that assertiveness means that the
client acts more assertively, without describing specifically what the client does
that shows greater assertiveness compared with previous behavior. To avoid tautology, reference should be made to specific assertive behaviors on an assertion
inventory, such as the client's self-rated discomfort in various situations, for example, asking for a raise, admitting ignorance in some area, initiating a conversation with a stranger, accepting a date (Gambrill & Richey, 1987, pp. 90–91).

Vague terms are counterproductive for social workers and for the clients
they serve. Vague assessment terms (e.g., not uncommonly depressed, acceptable
foster home, high risk for reabuse, borderline personality) may cause social workers to misdirect their efforts in the helping process. Vague outcome terms (e.g.,
overall higher self-esteem, better interpersonal skill, less depressed) can obscure
effects of interventions and may even lead to continued use of ineffective
methods.

Levels of Definition

A major step toward overcoming vagueness in social work practice is understanding the differences between: (a) an undefined term (highest and least specific level

TABLE 7.2

Buzz-Phrase Projector for social workers (A surefire way to produce meaningless jargon)

1. Functional	1. Role	1. Pattern
2. Integrated	2. Family	2. Status
3. Compatible	3. Community	3. Relationship
4. Responsive	4. Group	4. Expectation
5. Dysfunctional	5. Individual	5. Definition
6. Satisfactory	6. Transition	6. Coping Mechanism
7. Supportive	7. Treatment	7. Purpose
8. Structured	8. Milieu	8. Contingency

Directions. Randomly select any three numbers that range from 1 through 8, for example
5, 8, and 1. Select the corresponding words from each column and there you have it—social
work jargon.

Note: The original format for the Systematic Buzz Phrase Projector came from "New peak for
newspeak," May 6, 1968, *Newsweek,* p. 104. The jargon is from social work.

of abstraction), (b) a term that has been defined conceptually (intermediate level), and (c) a term that has been defined operationally (lowest and most specific level of abstraction). Recognizing level of abstraction is one of the great contributions of the science of semantics (Condon, 1985, p. 48). If practitioners are aware of when they are using terms at these three levels of abstraction, much can be done to overcome vagueness. Level of abstraction increases as we move further away from directly observing the object of study, through descriptions, to the highest level of abstraction, in which words stand for whole classes of events.

The four examples of vagueness discussed (inexact quantifying adjectives, universally applicable terms, professional jargon, and tautology) all concern the highest level of abstraction: **undefined terms**—single words or short phrases used without further explanation. To demonstrate vagueness of undefined terms, ask a group of social workers to write definitions of *child abuse* and read their varied definitions aloud while tallying the different criteria listed, or read Hakeem's (1985) account of the variety of meanings for *psychopath* and related terms.

Any term that is defined exclusively with other words is known as a concept or construct. Typically, a **conceptual definition** will consist of descriptive terms and examples but does not state in step-by-step fashion the operations or procedures necessary to measure a variable. For example, here is a conceptual definition of the term *depression:*

> a morbid state characterized by mood alterations, such as sadness and loneliness; by low self-esteem associated with self-reproach; by psychomotor retardation [slow thinking and slow moving] and at times agitation; by withdrawal from interpersonal contact and at times a desire to die; and by such vegetative symptoms as insomnia and anorexia. (Freedman, Kaplan, & Sadock, 1976, p. 1294)

Typically, a conceptual definition lists distinguishing characteristics. For example, Chapman's (1967, p. 33) definition of depression lists "pessimism" and feelings that one is "inadequate, incapable, worthless and defeated" and has "profound feelings of guilt over . . . minor failings and small misdeeds."

Conceptual definitions can help clarify the meaning of a concept such as depression, especially when the definition includes examples. The following quote (Chapman, 1967, p. 33) shows how depressed persons can have feelings of inadequacy: "I recall a depressed patient who felt that she was mentally retarded with an I.Q. of 60, despite the fact that she held a doctor's degree from a leading university and had done outstanding professional work in her field."

A concept (for example, depression) can be greatly clarified through a process called **operational definition.** The process begins with a conceptual definition, such as that given for depression. Next, indicators—specific, observable events (e.g., complaints about guilt feelings) that show the presence of the concept—are selected. An operational definition then describes the specific steps, procedures, or rules that are followed to measure indicators of a variable. An operational definition may be thought of as a manual for measuring a concept. Technically, once a concept becomes defined by operation, it becomes a variable.

The process for developing an operational definition of depression was followed by Zung (1965), who developed the Self-Rating Depression Scale (SDS)

TABLE 7.3

The Zung Self-Rating Depression Scale (SDS)

Items	A A Little of the Time	B Some of the Time	C Good Part of the Time	D Most of the Time	Item Weights*			
					A	B	C	D
1. I feel down-hearted and blue					1	2	3	4
2. Morning is when I feel the best					4	3	2	1
3. I have crying spells or feel like crying					1	2	3	4
4. I have trouble sleeping at night					1	2	3	4
5. I eat as much as I used to					4	3	2	1
6. I still enjoy sex					4	3	2	1
7. I notice that I am losing weight					1	2	3	4
8. I have trouble with constipation					1	2	3	4
9. My heart beats faster than usual					1	2	3	4
10. I get tired for no reason					1	2	3	4
11. My mind is as clear as it used to be					4	3	2	1
12. I find it easy to do the things I used to					4	3	2	1
13. I am restless and can't keep still					1	2	3	4

that appears in Table 7.3. The SDS was selected as a sample operational measure for this chapter because it is brief, clear, concerns an important problem, and can be used both in assessment and as an outcome measure.

To develop the SDS, Zung analyzed the major features of three conceptual definitions of depression. Based on that analysis, Zung isolated 20 features of depression that appeared in all three definitions, for example, crying spells, thoughts of suicide, and disturbed sleep patterns. Zung next developed the 20-item SDS, each item serving as an indicator of the variable, depression. Note that the steps in the instructions, the steps followed by respondents who rate themselves on each item as they feel currently, and the scoring instructions collectively, constitute an operational definition for level of depression. Scores below 50, 50–59, 60–69, and 70 or over designate, respectively, no psychopathology, minimal to mild, moderate to marked, and severe depression.

TABLE 7.3

continued

Items	A A Little of the Time	B Some of the Time	C Good Part of the Time	D Most of the Time	Item Weights*			
					A	B	C	D
14. I feel hopeful about the future					4	3	2	1
15. I am more irritable than usual					1	2	3	4
16. I find it easy to make decisions					4	3	2	1
17. I feel that I am useful and needed					4	3	2	1
18. My life is pretty full					4	3	2	1
19. I feel that others would be better off if I were dead					1	2	3	4
20. I still enjoy the things I used to do					4	3	2	1

*Item weights should not appear on actual measure.

Instructions for Administration: Tell the client,"I am going to ask you to answer a series of 20 questions according to how you feel right now. Please answer each question according to the one response that best applies to you, "A Little of the Time, Some of the Time, Good part of the Time, Most of the Time." (Then read each question and record the client's answer. If the client asks you to clarify the question; reread the question and ask that the client answer it according to the item's meaning on how they interpret it.

Instruction for Scoring: Sum the weights for the client's response to all 20 items. Compute the subjects score by dividing the subjects score by 80 and multiplying by 100 to get a percent. For example, for a score of 56, this would be the score (56/80) 100 = 70%. An explanation of how to interpret this score goes beyond space available here, but generally, the higher the value the more depressed the client.

Operational Definition's Superior Clarity: A Demonstration

Does the use of operational definition to determine a client's problem foster greater consensus among observers than conceptual definition? Following is a research question concerning an experiment that has been conducted repeatedly in research methods classes to compare the clarity of operational against conceptual definitions:

- If Methods of Social Work Research students in Lab. A01 of the Spring class at UW—EC are asked to view a videotaped client interview, will students rating the client report lower variation on the Self-Rating Depression Scale (Zung, 1965) than they will on any of the following three conceptual definitions of depression: Definition 1 (Freedman et al., 1976, p. 1294), Definition 2 (Chapman, 1967, p. 33), and Definition 3 (American Psychiatric Association, 1987, pp. 222–223)?

To conduct the experiment, students were asked to construct a list of the features of depression that are listed in each of the three conceptual definitions. (The Diagnostic and Statistical Manual of Mental Disorders—DSM-III-R—presents guidelines for classifying mental disorders. The DSM-III-R definition for depression has features of a weak operational definition, so let us classify it with the other two conceptual definitions.) Then students viewed a videotaped interview of a student who role played a moderately depressed person. The role player was instructed to display several symptoms of depression that appear in the definitions given. The role player also answered all 20 questions on the SDS. Then the students in the lab were asked to compute the proportion of symptoms of depression that appeared in each conceptual definition and in the SDS.

The distribution of proportions in Figure 7.1 shows the dispersion of eight students' scores for the three conceptual definitions and for the SDS. Scores on the SDS (the operational definition) show the lowest variation among the student ratings. Lower variation for the operational definition implies clearer understanding of how to rate a particular subject's level of depression. This experiment has been replicated five times; each time the operational definition has resulted in the least confusion as demonstrated by less dispersion.

LOCATING A USEFUL MEASURE

Whole volumes just begin to do justice to the topics of how to locate or develop a measure for use in practice. See Table 7.4 for a list of sources of published measures that can be used by social workers.

LEVELS OF MEASUREMENT

All measures do not lend themselves to the same statistical manipulations and uses. In a sense, there is a hierarchy of measures. Understanding the four levels of measurement can help us classify measures for better understanding.

Nominal measures consist of unordered, named categories. Nominal categories have no numerical meaning; categories cannot be ordered or added. If numbers are used to designate classes, they only designate class membership; they do not represent a hierarchy of classes. Recidivism/no recidivism, suicide/no suicide, abused/not abused, reabused/not reabused, dead/alive, and improved/not improved are examples of nominal classes. The classification of clients into alcohol dependence/no alcohol dependence in Figure 7.2 (page 153), according to criteria listed in DSM-III-R (American Psychiatric Association, 1987), is one example of a nominal measure.

Nominal measures are not always two-categoried. For example, one classification of alcoholics divides alcoholics into four types (Gibbs & Hollister, 1989). All nominal measures should classify individuals into categories that are mutually exclusive (all individuals fall into one and only one category) and comprehensive or exhaustive (all individuals have a place in the classification and no individuals are not classifiable).

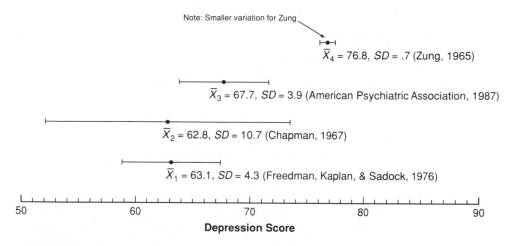

FIGURE 7.1
Variation among four definitions of depression.

Ordinal measures consist of categories that can be ranked or ordered on some characteristic or property. Ordinal numbers indicate rank and nothing more. Nothing is said about the size of the interval between the ordered categories. Ordinal measures usually contain from 3 to 10 categories. One form of an ordinal measure is the classification of persons who meet DSM-III-R criteria for depression into "mild," "moderate," or "severe, without psychotic features" categories (American Psychiatric Association, 1987, p. 223).

Another example of an ordinal scale might be a risk of reabuse scale that classifies abused children into "low risk," "intermediate risk," and "high risk" categories (Palmer, undated, pp. 16, 17, 33, 38). Such scales are ordinal because risk falls into a rough hierarchy, but the relative size of the risk in each category may vary substantially.

Interval measures possess the characteristics of nominal and ordinal scales, including the ranking of classes, but numerically equal distances divide units in the scale being measured. Interval measures may be added and subtracted. For example, the 20 items of the Zung Self-Rating Depression Scale (see Table 7.3) may be added to yield a total score.

Ratio measures possess the characteristics of the previous three measures—nominal, ordinal, and interval—and are also based on absolute zero, which has an empirical meaning. Individuals who have a score of zero have the complete absence of some quality. Ratio measures may be multiplied and divided; for example, a ratio scale might be dollars repaid by delinquents who are making restitution for property they have vandalized. A bar graph indicating amount of restitution paid could have a meaningful zero at "no restitution repaid"; if the delinquents repaid $400, they would have repaid exactly twice the amount repaid when they were at the $200 mark.

TABLE 7.4

Sources containing useful measures for practice

Cautela, J. R. (1977). *Behavior analysis forms for clinical intervention.* Champaign, IL: Research Press.	The 36 assessment forms included in this volume were developed by Cautela and his collaborators for use in a behaviorally oriented practice with adults. The forms primarily concern behavioral assessment.
Cautela, J. R., Cautela, J., and Esonis, S. (1983). *Forms for behavior analysis with children.* Champaign, IL: Research Press.	The 44 forms included in this volume were developed for use in a behaviorally oriented practice with adults. The forms concern problem assessment, reinforcer surveys, and outcome ratings.
Corcoran, K., & Fischer, J. (1987). *Measures for clinical practice.* New York: The Free Press.	The 128 measures in this volume are classified into instruments concerning adults, children, couples, and families. The measures were selected because they are short, easy to score and administer, and are useful as assessment and outcome measures for a range of common client problems. In addition to sections on basic principles of measurement, types of measurement tools, advantages and disadvantages of rapid assessment tools, and sources of such measures, the authors construct a useful introduction to each measure that includes the source of each measure, norms for interpreting scores, scoring instructions, reliablity, and validity for each measure.
Perloff, E. (undated). *Health Instrument File [online database].* 354 Victoria Bldg., University of Pittsburgh, Pittsburgh, PA 15261.	The Health Instrument File is an online database that contains about 2,000 measures that are useful to social workers, psychologists, nurses, and persons working in public health. The instruments include questionnaires, observation checklists, and interview forms. Files are available only online using procedures such as those outlined in Chapter 9.
Hudson, W. (1982). *The clinical measurment package.* Homewood, IL: The Dorsey Press.	This manual includes nine scales that measure depression, self-esteem, marital discord, sexual discord, parent-child relationships as seen by the parent, the child's perception of his or her relation to the mother, the child's perception of his or her relation to the father, intrafamilial stress, and peer relationships. This manual includes instructions for administering and scoring the scales plus reliability and validity data.
Mash, E. J., & Terdal, L. G. (Eds.). (1988). *Behavorial assessment of childhood disorders* (2nd ed.). New York: Guilford.	Mash and Terdal and their coauthors have compiled descriptions and actual text of measures that cover a wide range of childhood disorders. The measures in most cases can be used both for assessment and outcome monitoring. Literature regarding nonincluded measures and the quality of measures included is impressively compiled.
Lettieri, D. J., Nelson, J. E., & Sayers, M. A. (1985). *NIAAA treatment handbook series 2: Alcoholism treament assessment research instrument.* (DHHS Publication No. ADM 85–1380). Washington, DC: U.S. Government Printing Office.	The 45 instruments in this volume pertain to all aspects of alcoholism treatment including assessment and follow-up. Accompanying each instrument is a description of the instrument, information on its availability, and relevant published literature regarding the instrument's applications and evaluation.
Robinson, J. P., & Shaver, P. R. (1973). *Measures of social psychological attitudes.* Ann Arbor, MI: Survey Research Center, Institute for Social Research.	The 127 attitude measures included in this volume concern 10 areas of concern including the self, other people, values, and so on. Discussion accompanying each scale concerns the variable being measured, a description of the measure, and an evaluation of the scale in whatever contexts it has been used.

COMMON FEATURES OF GOOD MEASURES: CRITERIA FOR SELECTING OR DEVELOPING MEASURES

Remembering the criteria for good measurement can help in developing or locating a good measure. The rest of this chapter defines and illustrates criteria for judging the quality of measures. There are several factors to consider when judging **utility**—how practical the measure may be for achieving one's purpose—including the measure's cost, ease of scoring, length, ease of interpretation, sensitivity to intended change in the client's behavior, and time required to administer.

Another important criterion for judging a measure's quality is **nonreactivity,** meaning that the measure's score is not altered by multiple administrations. Recall Chapter 5's illustration of how the Short Portable Mental Status Questionnaire (SPMSQ) was administered repeatedly to Dr. Bradley, a resident of a nursing home. SPMSQ's items included questions regarding who the president is, who the previous president was, and the client's date of birth. Reactivity in measurement would occur if Dr. Bradley's score improved not because of an underlying change in his level of orientation to time, place, and person, but simply because he recalled answers to repeatedly asked questions. Reactivity may be a problem for repeated measures on multiple question tests such as the Self-Rating Depression Scale.

Directness, another criterion of a good measure, refers to how the client's score reflects observations of the variable being measured. Plotting observations of an alcohol-dependent client's daily alcohol consumption is a more direct measure than scores on a questionnaire such as the Short Michigan Alcoholism Screening Test would be (Pokorny, Miller, & Kaplan, 1972).

RELIABILITY

A **reliable measure** will yield consistent results each time it is administered. Ideally, scores on reliable measures fluctuate only because of variation in the phenomenon being measured—not because of error in measurement.

In general, reliability is important for practice research for four principal reasons. First, if client change can be measured consistently, we can be more certain that changes reflected in a measured outcome are due to the intervention's effect, rather than an error in the way outcome is being measured. For example, if members of an eating disorders support group are weighed consistently each week (on the same scale, at the same time of day, according to the same procedures, with shoes and coats always removed and results recorded legibly and immediately), changes in weight will be more likely due to the support group's effect than if group members are weighed in hit-or-miss fashion. Inconsistency in judging outcome appears to be a significant problem among social workers. Proctor and Rosen (1983) found that social workers asked to read a case summary listed inconsistently what they thought were the principal problems and desired outcomes as described in a case summary.

Second, a reliable outcome measure can help to focus the efforts of social worker and client, because both will have greater confidence that their effort is causing change if the client's behavior is measured consistently.

Third, reliable assessment is essential to judging client type-by-treatment interaction. For example, if an experiment evaluates whether alcoholics with high social stability will improve more in outpatient treatment than in inpatient treatment, a reliable way to categorize alcoholics into high/low social stability groups is essential before studying the hypothesized interaction. Unreliable assessment could mask such interaction.

Finally, because tests of statistical significance can serve as one criterion for judging a method's effectiveness, and statistical significance reflects measurement variation and sample size, more reliable outcome measures can reduce the number of subjects required in an evaluation study (Fleiss, 1986, pp. 1–8).

Sources of Error in Measurement

The following formula illustrates an important fact about measurement (Kerlinger, 1986, p. 407). The client's total score, X_t, is equal to the client's true score, X_∞, plus or minus an error component, X_e

$$X_t = X_\infty \pm X_e$$

Here the infinity symbol, ∞, signifies a theoretically true score that one would obtain if measurement conditions were perfect. Theoretically, the true score lies at the mean of an infinite number of independent administrations of the measure. The formula shows that any measure will be affected by an error component.

Random error and systematic error are the two sources of the error term in the formula above. **Random error** is chance error that sometimes contributes to overestimating, and sometimes underestimating, the client's true score. The effect of random error is analogous to static in a television picture. The greater the error, the more obscure the true picture becomes until, in extreme cases, the picture of the client's true behavior is lost entirely. As an example of random error, a coder who knows nothing of the study might encounter an ambiguous answer on an alcohol-use questionnaire and interpret the respondent's mark incorrectly, or a respondent may not hear the interviewer's question clearly, or the researcher may hit a wrong key while entering a client's data at a computer terminal.

Random errors tend to cancel each other out in the long run. For this reason, they are not usually as serious as systematic errors, but they can obscure a method's effect. To help rule out random error: make sure that the respondent understands questions and instructions, use measures with higher proven reliability, and use good quality control procedures that include proper training of those who will administer and score measures. (Later sections on reliability coefficients and types of reliability will clarify how to judge a measure's ability to overcome random error.)

Systematic error—variation in measurement that tends to favor one conclusion over another—is always a serious problem because it causes an underestimation or overestimation of the phenomenon being measured. In addition to causing problems with reliability, error that tends in one direction or another can profoundly affect the validity of a measure (more on this topic later). Those who use measures in practice should make every effort to avoid introducing systematic errors into the measurement process.

The subject (client) is one potential source of systematic error. Subjects who report observations of their own behavior in single-subject studies or group studies may want to please their social worker enough that they will report events inaccurately. The subject may also, in response to real or imagined pressure from the social worker, give inaccurate answers to questions on outcome measures. Recall the tragic case of Mary Deemer, in Chapter 2, whose testimonial appeared on the same page as her obituary.

Practitioners who follow principles of good measurement to evaluate client outcome are basing their inferences on much firmer ground than if they rely on **testimonials**—statements given by recipients of treatment to prove that a treatment works. The client's own stated experience serves as the evidence to prove the method's effectiveness, not some deliberate, systematic measure of client performance. Measurement far surpasses testimonial as credible evidence because: (a) a testimonial appeals to emotions so strongly as to block analytical inquiry about the method's effectiveness; (b) the client's testimonial evidence may reflect not clearly defined and measurable change, but the client's perceptions of real or imagined pressure to report positive change; and (c) clients may be chosen to give testimonials because they can be counted on to provide glowing reports about the treatment's effectiveness.

The **evaluator** is another potential source of bias. To avoid systematic bias: (a) select someone who does not have anything to gain or lose by the study's outcome to measure outcome; (b) train those who measure outcome carefully and continue to monitor their reliability, because reliability can decline if it is not continuously monitored (Romanczyk, Kent, Diament, & O'Leary, 1973); and (c) consider using computerized assessment and outcome evaluations that have been found to be at least as consistent as those administered by interviewers (Griest, Klein, Erdman, & Jefferson, 1983).

Scientist-practitioners who knowingly introduce systematic error are responsible for *intentional bias* or cheating. Intentional bias is less difficult to detect than one might expect. A recent case of cheating in an evaluation study involved Dr. Stephen Breuning, who faked data to support his hypothesis that violent mentally retarded clients' IQs miraculously doubled when their neuroleptic medications were withdrawn (Roman, 1988, p. 52). Dr. Breuning's lie has resulted in his public censure (Safer, 1988) and his indictment on criminal charges ("Researcher Indicted on Criminal Charges," 1988). Those in universities may be pressured into such actions by the need to publish their work to get tenure or a promotion (Angell & Relman, 1988). Another pressure to cheat may come from peers and administrators who want proof that interventions are working.

Environmental factors are a third source of systematic error in measurement. Such factors leading to underestimating a client's true ability include, for example, distractions in the measurement situation (e.g., noise, cold temperature in the room where the measurement is taking place), and illegible test items due to faint print or the client's needing glasses.

Coefficients of Reliability

Reliability is typically quantified according to some coefficient that reflects the degree of consistency in measurement. Various coefficients are most appropriate to nominal, ordinal, interval, or ratio measures. Typically, a reliability coefficient ranges between -1 and $+1$. If there is no consistency at all (a degree of consistency that one would expect by chance) the coefficient would be zero or close to it. A positive coefficient, shown by a value above zero, indicates that an increase in scores on one variable is associated with an increase in scores on another variable, or that raters agree on how to classify clients. A negative coefficient indicates consistent disagreement. The magnitude of the association, whether positive or negative, is reflected in the size of the coefficient. That is, a coefficient of .80 is better than one of .70. As a very rough rule of thumb, reliability coefficients are sufficiently large if they reach or exceed .70. Higher coefficients might be called for if profoundly life-affecting decisions, for example, child abuse assessment, are to be based on the measure.

Five Types of Reliability

Judging **test-retest reliability**—a measure's degree of consistency over time— is a simple procedure: Administer the measure once to a group of clients, wait a short time, readminister the measure to the same clients, and then compute a coefficient of reliability. Procedures for both administrations of the test should be as identical as possible (e.g., same time of day, same explanation for observing behaviors); and no events should have taken place in the lives of clients between test and retest that might greatly affect their score on retest. One trick in evaluating test-retest reliability is judging how long the test-retest interval should be: Too long an interval and life events will become confounded with test results, too short an interval and those measured will recall previous answers. Reliability coefficients tend to be larger for short intervals and smaller for longer intervals. Test-retest reliability can also be affected by the respondent's sensitization to the content of the measure in a way that affects later performance. Test-retest reliability may not be feasible in a human service agency because of the time and inconvenience of arranging two appointments to evaluate a measure.

(Test-retest reliability is occasionally confused with pretest-posttest differences in an experiment. Pretest refers to measurement before an intervention begins; posttest, the measurement after an intervention is completed. Pretest-to-posttest differences are intended to measure effect of treatment, not consistency of measures.)

As an example of how test-retest reliability relates to a research question, here is a question (Farrell, 1989) regarding the relative effectiveness of two alternate approaches to helping members of groups for child abusers:

- Among approximately 20 child abusers referred to child and family services, who are randomly assigned to a support group with parent nurturing training or to support groups with no parent nurturing training, from April 3 to July 17, will those in the support plus nurturing training group have statistically significant ($p < .10$) higher mean General Positive Child Care Scale scores than will those in the exclusively support group on October 17?

Before describing how test-retest reliability would be evaluated for the measure listed in this question let us look at the General Positive Child Care Scale (GPCCS). The 15-item GPCCS is a subscale of the 99-item Childhood Level of Living Scale (CLL) (Polansky, Chalmers, Buttenwieser, & Williams, 1978, pp. 443–444). The 99 items of CLL were developed for professional child-care workers to summarize the quality of a child's living environment on five dimensions: General Positive Child Care, State of Repair of House, Negligence, Quality of Household Maintenance, and Quality of Health Care and Grooming. The 15-item General Positive Child Care Scale (GPCCS) was chosen as the study's outcome measure because its items reflect nurturing, which is what this training program is trying to improve. GPCCS items include: "Mother sometimes leaves child to insufficiently older sibling. . . . Child receives at least 9 hours of sleep most nights. . . . Mother enforces rules about going into the street" (pp. 443–444). Child care workers rate GPCCS items as yes or no for all 15 items. Answers indicating positive parenting get 1 point each for a total of 15 possible points.

To evaluate the GPCC Scale's test-retest reliability, let us assume that Child and Family Services workers collected data from 15 families who were similar to, but not among, those who would be participating in treatment. Then, 2 months later, the same workers went back to the same homes and readministered the GPCCS. Table 7.5 gives hypothetical data for such a test-retest and a very satisfactory Pearson r (.93). This value is close to 1, a perfect positive correlation.

The following tests of reliability require only a single administration. **Split-half** reliability involves administering a measure on one occasion, dividing the items or behaviors on the measure into two halves according to odd-even item

TABLE 7.5
Hypothetical test-retest data for General Positive Child Care Scale

Family Number	Test	Retest
1	4	5
2	10	9
3	11	11
4	12	10
5	14	12
6	8	6
7	7	7
8	10	11
9	6	8
10	0	1
11	7	7
12	5	3
13	9	10
14	4	3
15	9	9

Note: Pearson r = .93.

number or by random division, computing a total score for each half for each subject, listing two columns that consist of total scores on each half for each individual, and finally, computing a correlation between the two columns. To test **parallel forms** reliability, develop two separate measures that quantify the same variable: administer one form, then the other immediately after, and compute the correlation between the two. **Internal consistency** reliability tests the assumption that all items in a particular scale measure the same dimension. Special reliability coefficients that quantify the amount of shared variance among the measure's items are used as coefficients of internal consistency (e.g., Cronbach's alpha or Kuder-Richardson formula 20).

The extent of consistency among two or more raters who independently measure the same event is commonly called **interrater reliability.** Here the concern is with extent of consistency among raters of equal status, not with how well a measure agrees with a more credible gold standard. Tinsley and Weiss (1975, p. 359) draw a fine distinction between interrater agreement (extent to which different raters make exactly the same judgment about a rated subject, or derive exactly the same score for rated subjects) and interrater reliability (extent to which scores given by one judge are associated with scores given by another). Tinsley and Weiss's distinction may help to clarify that the following discussion concerns nominal agreement of judgments across raters, where the index of agreement is whether raters make exactly the same judgment to classify a client.

Nominal interrater agreement is by far the most important form of reliability for social workers because social workers typically make go/no go, act/do not act decisions. For example, a worker's assessment of a foster home must classify the home as either suitable or unsuitable for children. The social worker cannot report that a foster home is half suitable, because the worker must decide either to place or not to place a child in that home. Similarly, protective service workers determine whether children are at high risk or low risk for being reabused. Those at high risk receive aggressive and prompt attention. The same kind of act/do not act thinking is often implied in judgments about client outcome. For example, a single-subject evaluation of a client's performance might include a daily judgment about whether the client does or does not consume any alcohol. At the first sign of alcohol consumption, prompt corrective action might be taken. Because the realities of social work practice so often demand either/or decisions, knowing how to rate interrater agreement for nominal categories is essential.

An Example of Nominal Interrater Agreement

The Diagnostic and Statistical Manual of Mental Disorders (DSM-III-R) (American Psychiatric Association, 1987) presents guidelines for classifying mental health clients by disorder. One of those disorders, alcohol dependence, may be used to illustrate how to assess interrater agreement. DSM-III-R lists nine symptoms of alcohol dependence, any three of which will be sufficient to classify a client as being alcohol dependent (pp. 167–168). The nine symptoms include loss of control (person drinks more over longer period than intended); interference with work, school, or home responsibilities (intoxicated during these responsibilities); and tolerance (need for more alcohol to get the same desired effect). DSM-

III-R's nine criteria, and other criteria for other forms of chemical dependency and abuse, have been condensed into a Substance Use Disorder Diagnostic Schedule (SUDDS) interview guide and scoring manual (Harrison & Hoffmann, 1985).

Figure 7.2's hypothetical data summarize the extent of agreement between two chemical-dependency assessment workers. To conduct a test of interrater agreement, Worker 1 might classify subjects in the morning according to the client's answers on SUDDS into Alcohol Dependence or No Alcohol Dependence

FIGURE 7.2
Hypothetical interrater agreement on DSM-III-R criteria for alcohol dependence.

		Worker 2: Alcohol Dependence	Worker 2: No Alcohol Dependence	Row Totals (across)
Worker 1	Alcohol Dependence	50 Expected Frequency = 37.8 Cell n_{11}	4 Cell n_{12}	54 $n_{1\cdot}$
Worker 1	No Alcohol Dependence	6 Cell n_{21}	20 Expected Frequency = 7.8 Cell n_{22}	26 $n_{2\cdot}$
	Column Totals (down)	56 $n_{\cdot 1}$	24 $n_{\cdot 2}$	$n = 80$

f_o = Frequency of observed agreement
= Total for cells having the same row and column numbers
= 50 + 20
= 70

P_o = Proportion of observed agreement
= f_o/n
= 70/80
= .88

f_e = Frequency of expected agreement
= $\sum_{i=1}^{T} n_{i\cdot} n_{\cdot i}/n$
= multiply the Row 1 total by the Column 1 total and divide by n; multiply the Row 2 total by the Column 2 total and divide by n; sum these values
= $[(54 \times 56)/80) + (26 \times 24)/80]$
= 37.8 + 7.8
= 45.6

P_e = f_e/n
= 45.6/80
= .57

$$K = \text{kappa} = \frac{P_o - P_e}{1 - P_e} = \frac{.88 - .57}{1 - .57} = .72$$

categories; then Worker 2 would do the same in the afternoon. High agreement across Workers 1 and 2 would reflect whether independent raters know what they are doing when they assess a client.

Proportion of agreement is a common but unsophisticated way to judge nominal interrater agreement. Notice in Figure 7.2 that Cells A and C in the upper left and lower right, respectively, indicate cases of agreement, that is, instances in which Worker 1 judges a client to be Alcohol Dependent and Worker 2 judges a client to be Alcohol Dependent (Cell A), or an identical classification for clients who are Not Alcohol Dependent (Cell C). Proportion of observed agreement, P_o, is equal to the frequency of observed agreement, f_o, divided by the total number of subjects, n; so P_o in this case is .88 or 88%.

Proportion of agreement is a poor indicator of interrater reliability because P_o is profoundly affected by the proportion of clients who have the problem (prevalence rate or base rate) among persons being rated. It stands to reason that if the raters are using an instrument to pick out which clients are alcohol dependent among a group where 50% are alcohol dependent, greater agreement would be expected purely by chance than where the prevalence rate is only 5%.

Reliability in single-subject studies is often quantified in terms of percent of agreement between two raters who observe the same client behavior (Hartmann, 1977). To compute percent of agreement between raters, note item by item the number of instances in which two raters agree with each other by recording the same behavior. Note also the total number of ratings. Divide the number of instances of agreement by the total number of behaviors rated and multiply by 100. This will be the percent of agreement.

Cohen's (1960) **kappa coefficient of agreement** is a more conservative coefficient of nominal interrater agreement than percent. Kappa compensates for chance agreement. Kappa has extremely wide acceptance. Cohen's article on kappa has been cited more than 810 times since the article was published (Institute for Scientific Information, 1986, p. 18). To compute kappa, first compute the frequency of expected agreement, f_e, according to the formula in Figure 7.2, compute the proportion of expected agreement, P_e, and then compute kappa according to the formula at the bottom of Figure 7.2.

Note that the effect of expected agreement, P_e, is a component of the kappa formula. Compensation for expected agreement accounts for why kappa (.72) is lower than proportion of agreement (.88) in the Figure 7.2 example. Finding that kappa is lower is consistent with comparisons elsewhere between kappa and percent of agreement among raters (Hartmann, 1977).

Kappa is a true reflection of interrater agreement only when raters work independently, when clients do not affect each others' classification, and when clients to be classified all have a place in the classification but only one place. Like other coefficients, kappa ranges from -1 through 0 (chance agreement) to $+1$ (perfect agreement), except that kappa may reach an upper limit below $+1$ in instances where the rate of the problem to be classified is below about 5% (Spitznagel & Helzer, 1985, p. 726). Kappa can be computed for 3×3 and larger nominal classifications and for more than one rater (Soeken & Prescott, 1986). Significance tests are also available (Chan, 1987; Hubert, 1977). Because coefficients of nominal agreement that may be less affected by base rate are available, some advocate that alternative coefficients be used instead of kappa (Spitznagel & Helzer, 1985), but others discredit this argument strongly enough (Shrout, Spitzer, & Fleiss, 1987) to indicate that kappa will probably remain the dominant standard for judging reliability of nominal agreement. Orme and Gillespie (1986) maintain that kappa has been unjustifiably ignored as an index of agreement in social work.

It should be noted that interval and ratio measures can be checked for interrater reliability too. The best coefficient for this purpose is generally the **intraclass correlation coefficient** (Berk, 1979). (This coefficient will not be described here because of social work's concern with nominal judgment in decision making.)

VALIDITY

A measure is considered **valid** if it measures accurately what we think it should be measuring. More narrowly, judging a measure's validity implies checking a measure against some other observation that serves as a criterion (Cronbach, 1971, p. 443). There is no single procedure for determining validity; that is, there are several commonly used ways to compare a measure against other measures or observations. Ideally, any measure should be subjected to several different tests of its validity.

The reader should note that there is some variation among texts regarding how different forms of validity are defined. For example, Monette, Sullivan, and DeJong (1986) do not draw a distinction between content validity and face validity, but Babbie (1989) does.

The following discussion of validity tries to be true to a central tendency among authors about the meaning of the following types of validity: face validity, two forms of criterion-related validity (predictive and concurrent validity), and construct validity. These three forms of validity are arranged in order of their increasing complexity and the demands they make on resources to evaluate them. Examples from social work illustrate each validity type.

Face validity refers to a commonsense judgment about whether the measure actually reflects what the measure is intended to measure. To judge face validity, one must first formulate the measure's purpose clearly. Then the content of the measure should be carefully examined to see if it suits this purpose. Face validity is the quickest and easiest form of validity to check, but it is also the least precise. Always keep in mind that clients and their social workers may be in substantial disagreement about what the nature and severity of the client's problem was initially and whether it has been alleviated (Mutschler & Rosen, 1980). In such instances, if measures were used, social worker and client would be disagreeing about the validity of the measure. Ideally, measures should reflect both the worker's and the client's selection of an outcome measure.

The following (Nett, 1988) is a researchable question concerning effectiveness of an eating disorder's treatment program and a discussion of the dependent variable's face validity:

- Will bulimics [sufferers of an eating disorder characterized by bingeing and purging] treated at Sacred Heart Hospital, who receive outpatient treatment from April 1 to October 31, have statistically significantly lower scores at 6-month posttest on the Body Dissatisfaction Subscale of the Eating Disorder Inventory than at pretest given when the bulimics began their outpatient treatment?

Because distorted body image—seeing oneself as too heavy even when one is below the norm—is a common problem for bulimics (Schlesier-Stropp, 1984), correcting distorted body image is a major goal of the eating disorders program. Helping bulimics, who are primarily young women, to correct their body image often relies on positive imaging during deep muscle relaxation, exploring the origins of body image in early sexual and other experiences, exploring similarities in mother-daughter body image, and so on.

Because changing body image was one objective of the eating disorders program at Sacred Heart, the student planning to evaluate the program's effects chose the nine-item Body Dissatisfaction Subscale of the Eating Disorder Inventory (EDI) as a dependent variable (Garner, Olmstead, & Polivy, 1983). Here are six of the scale's nine items: "I think my stomach is too big; I think my thighs are too large; I think that my stomach is just the right size; I feel satisfied with the shape of my body; I like the shape of my buttocks; I think my hips are too big (Garner & Olmstead, 1984, p. 22). To these items of the scale, respondents are asked to rate truthfully whether the items apply to themselves: always, usually, often, sometimes, rarely, or never (Garner & Olmstead, 1984).

Judgment about the scale's face validity rests on whether such items measure body image in a way that reflects the goal of the eating disorders treatment program. If questions about the shape of the body and size of hips and thighs are appropriate for the purpose of the measure, then the measure has face validity. Face validity requires only a judgment call without an empirical standard, but sometimes such judgment is all that busy practitioners have time for.

Incidentally, body weight might be another measure that has face validity, as determined by a systematic, carefully monitored, weigh-in procedure, the results of which could be compared to tables of weight norms. Body weight, measured according to operationally defined procedures, would be a less reactive form of measure.

Criterion-related validity concerns the extent of agreement between a measure and a criterion that serves as a more direct measure of the event, that is, does the measure agree with a "gold standard" of some kind? What a client actually does or will do provides such a standard. Predictive validity, one form of criterion-related validity, is so important for assessing clients and client outcome in social work practice that it is the major topic of Chapter 10 (which concerns risk assessment and decision making). A useful and clear distinction between two forms of criterion-related validity is based on the comparison of a measure's finding against the gold standard (Monette, Sullivan, & DeJong, 1986, p. 97).

According to Monette and colleagues, in predictive validity, results of a measure are compared with the client's later behavior to see if the instrument successfully predicted what the client would actually do. A suicide risk scale's ability to predict later survival or death provides a grim but vivid example of predictive validity (Pokorny, 1983). High predictive validity is also critical to instruments that are designed to sort children who are being placed for adoption into high and low risk categories (Barth, Berry, Yoshikami, Goodfield, & Carson, 1988). If such a risk-assessment instrument has predictive validity, those classified into the high-risk category should identify a high proportion whose adoption will later be disrupted. Intensive services might go to high risk placements. Obviously, predictive validity is essential to decision making.

Concurrent validity requires that the measure and the gold standard be compared at the same time or over a very short interval of time. As an example of concurrent validity, Pokorny et al. (1972, p. 344) administered a 10-item Brief Michigan Alcoholism Screening Test to 60 male veterans who had been diagnosed as alcoholics and who were being treated for alcoholism. Concurrently, they administered the Brief MAST to a second group of 62 randomly chosen male veterans who were in treatment but who had mixed psychiatric diagnoses that excluded alcoholism. The gold standard in this check of validity is membership in the group being treated for alcohol dependency, or membership in the group being treated for some problem other than alcohol dependency.

To classify subjects as having or not having a drinking problem according to the Brief MAST, respondents answered yes or no to 10 items that included (Pokorny et al., 1972, p. 343) the following: "Have you ever been arrested for drunk driving or driving after drinking ('yes' = 2 points)?" or "Have you ever gotten into trouble at work because of drinking ('yes' = 2 points)?" Alcoholic responses on Brief MAST are weighted, usually with 2 points, and these weights are added up to get a total score that can range from 0 (no alcohol problems) to 29. Those who exceed a 5-point cutoff score were classified as having an alcohol problem.

Figure 7.3, based on the data of Pokorny and others (1972, p. 344), demonstrates the extent of agreement between Brief MAST and criterion group membership. In 115 (94%) of the cases the Brief MAST classified subjects correctly (i.e., [60 + 55]/122). The Brief MAST identified only 7 false positives (persons classified by Brief MAST as having an alcohol problem when psychiatrists had not diagnosed an alcohol problem).

In addition to a credible expert's opinion as the standard, another measure may be used as a criterion. For example, those conducting support groups for female victims of domestic violence wanted to evaluate their program's effects on the self-esteem of group members (Hoffman, 1989). Low self-esteem is a common problem for such clients (Mitchell & Hodson, 1983), so Hoffman planned a study of the group's effect on its members' self-esteem. The Rosenberg Scale consists of 10 items, for example, "I feel that I have a number of good qualities" and "I take a positive attitude toward myself," to which the respondent is asked to rate extent of agreement or disagreement (p. 306). If the Rosenberg Self-Esteem Scale (1965, pp. 303–307) were to be used to evaluate the program, its concurrent validity might be computed by administering the Rosenberg Scale and the Hudson Index of Self-Esteem (1982, p. 9) concurrently to the same group of clients. The correlation between the scales would reflect either scale's concurrent validity.

FIGURE 7.3
Extent of agreement between Brief MAST and criterion group membership.

Brief MAST	Criterion Groups: Alcoholics in Alcoholism Treatment	Criterion Groups: Nonalcoholics in Psychiatric Treatment
Alcoholic	60	7
Nonalcoholic	0	55

n = 122

Now let us turn to the last form of validity. A **construct** is a concept that has been deliberately invented or adopted for a particular scientific purpose. Learning theory's constructs include behavior, positive reinforcer, and negative reinforcer. Such concepts are essential to theory because constructs, as defined by measures, designate the events that a theory tries to explain. Constructs, and measures that reflect them, are essential to understanding and testing a theory. If the theory-based measure performs as the theory predicts it should, the measure is said to have **construct validity.**

Nunnally (1967, p. 87) outlined a series of three steps to determine construct validity. Performing these steps usually extends beyond the methodological expertise and time available to practitioners, but practitioners can look for the three steps in discussions of construct validity.

Nunnally's first step involves specifying a construct as clearly as possible and determining which observations should be indicators of the construct. To illustrate how each step applies to a measure, let us apply them to how a measure was developed to assess which type of alcoholic should receive inpatient or outpatient treatment.

Theoreticians (Straus & Bacon, 1951) and persons who have done multivariate statistical studies (Morey & Blashfield, 1981) have speculated that social stability is a dimension related to improvement among those treated for alcoholism. Some point to evidence that alcoholics with higher social stability should benefit most from outpatient treatment; lower social stability alcoholics should benefit most in inpatient treatment. A review of 45 studies by Gibbs and Flanagan (1977, pp. 1130–1133) derived a list of indicators of social stability that includes: older at age of admission into treatment, few arrests, married or cohabiting, stable marriage, high-status occupation, steady work history, and higher level of education. Such indicators were chosen as the basis for the Social Stability Scale

Nunnally's (1967, p. 87) second step for establishing construct validity determines the extent to which indicators of the construct correlate with each other as a group or cluster of mutually correlated indicators. To accomplish this, Gibbs (1980): (a) developed a list of 50 characteristics of alcoholics that had been found statistically associated with treatment outcome for alcoholics (prognostic indicators); (b) hypothesized, according to social stability theory, which indicators should correlate or cluster together; (c) measured the 50 prognostic indicators among 121 alcoholics; (d) used multivariate statistical procedures to cluster correlated prognostic indicators; (e) compared the hypothesized social stability cluster with the cluster formed by the computer to see if they were the same—they were very similar—thus confirming a social stability dimension.

Nunnally's third step is determining whether the measure—in this case social stability—measures what it is supposed to. To check whether the Social Stability Scale acted as it should, raters were taught to classify alcoholics reliably according to high or low social stability. Then the scale was replicated among alcoholics in Duluth, Minnesota, treatment facilities to be sure that it was not a scale unique to where it was developed in southern Wisconsin. Higher social stability alcoholics were found to have higher, but not statistically significantly higher, sobriety rates among outpatients than among inpatients (Gibbs & Hollister, 1989).

CONTRASTS BETWEEN RELIABILITY AND VALIDITY

My grandfather used to tell a story that clearly demonstrates two features of the relationship between reliability and validity. Grandfather knew a fellow—an inventor of Imperial Gold Seal Wonder Soap—who could be counted on to tell a lie *every time* he came to the canning factory. The fellow might rattle off how many cords of wood he had split and piled at so much money per cord on various occasions and what the total was for various weeks. Grandfather got to checking the figures with a pencil and paper and, amazingly, the total earned for each week came out right every time. The fellow was consistent, but according to others who came to the canning factory, the fellow hadn't been in the woods when he said he was, or he hadn't split as much as he said he did, or he wasn't paid as much as he said he was. He was consistent, he was reliable—he lied every time! However, he wasn't truthful; what he said wasn't valid. The story illustrates, first, that reliability (consistency in measurement) is possible without validity and second, that the reverse is not true. Had the fellow been truthful (valid) he would also have had to be reliable (consistent) in his account. Thus, a second principle—that measures that are valid must also be reliable (consistent).

Relating these principles to social work practice, if child-service workers have kappas exceeding .90 on an instrument to predict adoption disruption, but the instrument does not predict for which placements the disruption will occur, then the instrument, although reliable, is useless because it is not also valid. On the other hand, if the instrument consistently predicts disruption it will also have to be reliable.

SUMMARY

This chapter began with a discussion of measurement's importance as a tool for avoiding the bias and vagueness in social work practice. Vagueness can be traced to imprecise quantifying adjectives, assessment and outcome statements that can be applied to anyone, jargon, and tautology. It was further demonstrated that an operational definition is superior to a conceptual definition for establishing a common understanding of what was meant by "level of depression" when applied to a single role played case.

Next, sources of measures were described that contain complete measurement instruments that are invaluable for social work practice. To judge the quality of such measures, one should evaluate a measure's utility, reactivity, directness, reliability, and validity. Interrater agreement is the most important form of reliability for social workers. The coefficient of such agreement is generally kappa. Ideally, different forms of validity should be checked, but the one that has the most practical significance for practitioners is criterion-related validity.

EXERCISES

Assume that your agency's training program teaches child-care workers to assess the suitability of prospective adoptive parents. Further assume that you and your co-workers are concerned that consistency of adoption workers' judgments should be higher than the average of 45% agreement reported in Brown and Breiland's simulation (1975, p. 294).

To test your workers' interrater agreement, you have conducted a study to compare your workers' decisions to accept or reject applicants. Following are data comparing the judgments of two adoption workers in your agency who have viewed 20 two-hour videotapes of adoption study interviews conducted at another agency to test how consistently your workers rated the suitability of the videotaped applicants: Worker 1 and Worker 2 agree on 40 cases that are acceptable to

both; Worker 1 and Worker 2 agree on 30 cases that are unacceptable; in 10 cases Worker 1 thinks the family is acceptable, but Worker 2 thinks the family is unacceptable; and in 15 cases Worker 1 thinks the family is unacceptable, but Worker 2 thinks they are acceptable.

1. What is the proportion of agreement for judgments by the two workers? (Draw a 2×2 table for Worker 1's judgments against Worker 2's judgments and fill in the values in all four cells based on the values given.)
2. What is the kappa for the level of interobserver agreement in this example?
3. Does this kappa exceed the conventional .70 level for a reliability coefficient?
4. Why would interrater agreement be especially vital for adoption workers?

REFERENCES

Alexander, R., & Tompkins-McGill, P. (1987). Notes to the experts from the parent of a handicapped child. *Social Work, 32*(4), 361–362.

American Psychiatric Association. (1987). *Diagnostic and Statistical Manual of Mental Disorders: DSM-III-R.* (3rd ed.). Washington, DC: American Psychiatric Association.

Angell, M., & Relman, A. S. (1988). Fraud in biomedical research: A time for congressional restraint. *The New England Journal of Medicine, 318,* 1462–1463.

Babbie, E. (1989). *The practice of social research.* Belmont, CA: Wadsworth.

Barth, R. P., Berry, M., Yoshikami, R., Goodfield, R. K., & Carson, M. L. (1988). Predicting adoption disruption. *Social Work, 33*(3), 227–233.

Berk, R. A. (1979). Generalizability of behavioral observations: A clarification of interobserver agreement and interobserver reliability. *American Journal of Mental Deficiency, 83*(5), 460–472.

Bloom, A. A. (1980). Social work and the English language. *Social Casework, 61*(6), 332–338.

Brown, S. (1988). Jargon: Confusing the issues. *Professional Counselor, 3*(3), 24.

Brown, E., & Brieland, D. (1975). Adoptive screening: New data, new dilemmas. *Social Work, 20*(4), 291–295.

Chan, T. S. C. (1987). A DBASE III program that performs significance testing for the Kappa coefficient. *Behavior Research Methods, Instruments, & Computers, 19*(1), 53–54.

Chapman, A. H. (1967). *Textbook of clinical psychiatry*. Philadelphia: Lippincott.

Cohen, J. (1960). A coefficient of agreement for nominal scales. *Educational and Psychological Measurement, 20*(1), 37–46.

Condon, J. C. (1985). *Semantics and communication*. (3rd ed.). New York: Macmillan.

Corcoran, K., & Fischer, J. (1987). *Measures for clinical practice*. New York: The Free Press.

Cousins, P. S., Fischer, J., Glisson, C., & Kameoka, V. (1986). The effects of physical attractiveness and verbal expressiveness on clinical judgments. *Journal of Social Service Research, 8*(4),59–74.

Cronbach, L. J. (1971). Test validation. In R. L. Thorndike (Ed.), *Educational measurement* (2nd ed., pp. 443–507). Washington, DC: American Council on Education.

Cutler, P. (1979). *Problem solving in clinical medicine*. Baltimore: Williams & Wilkins.

Farrell, T. (1989). *The effectiveness of a parent nurturing program implemented into the Parent Anonymous program*. Unpublished paper, University of Wisconsin—Eau Claire.

Fleiss, J. L. (1986). *The design and analysis of clinical experiments*. New York: Wiley.

Fong, G. T., & Markus, H. (1982). Self-schemas and judgments about others. *Social Cognition, 1*(3), 191–204.

Forer, B. R. (1949). The fallacy of personal validation: A classroom demonstration of gullibility. *Journal of Abnormal and Social Psychology, 44*(1), 118–123.

Franklin, D. L. (1986). Does client social class affect clinical judgment? *Social Casework, 67,* 424–432.

Freedman, A. M., Kaplan, H. I., & Sadock, B. J. (1976). *Modern synopsis of comprehensive textbook of psychiatry II* (2nd ed.). Baltimore: Williams & Wilkins.

Gambrill, E., & Richey, C. (1987). Assertion inventory. In K. Corcoran & J. Fischer (Eds.). *Measures for clinical practice* (pp. 88–91). New York: The Free Press.

Garner, D. M., & Olmstead, M. P. (1984). *The Eating Disorder Inventory Manual*. Odessa, FL: Psychological Assessment Resources.

Garner, D. M., Olmstead, M. P., Polivy, J. (1983). Development and validation of a multidimensional eating disorders inventory for anorexia nervosa and bulimia. *The International Journal of Eating Disorders, 2*(2), 15–30.

Gibbs, L. E. (1980). A classification of alcoholics relevant to type-specific treatment. *The International Journal of the Addictions, 15*(4), 461–488.

Gibbs, L., & Flanagan, J. (1977). Prognostic indicators of alcoholism treatment outcome. *The International Journal of the Addictions, 12*(8), 1097–1141.

Gibbs, L. E., & Hollister, C. D. (1989) *Matching alcoholics with treatment: Reliability, replication and validity of a treatment typology*. Unpublished manuscript.

Greist, J. H., Klein, M. H., Erdman, H. P., & Jefferson, J. W. (1983). Clinical computer applications in mental health. *Journal of Medical Systems, 7*(2), 175–185.

Hakeem, M. (1985). The assumption that crime is a product of individual characteristics: A prime example from psychiatry. In R. F. Meier (Ed.), *Theoretical methods in criminology*. Beverly Hills, CA: Sage.

Hardman, D. G. (1977). What really happened at Babel. *Social Work, 22*(4), 301–303.

Harrison, P. A., & Hoffmann, N. G. (1985). *Substance Use Disorder Diagnosis Schedule (SUDDS)*. St. Paul, MN: Ramsey Clinic, Department of Psychiatry.

Hartmann, D. P. (1977). Considerations in the choice of interobserver reliability estimates. *Journal of Applied Behavior Analysis, 10*(1), 103–116.

Harvey, J. H., Yarkin, K. L., Lightner, J. M., & Town, J. P. (1980). Unsolicited interpretation and recall of interpersonal events. *Journal of*

Personality and Social Psychology, 38(4), 551–568.

Hoffman, J. (1989). *Battered women and the role of support groups in improving self-esteem.* Unpublished manuscript, University of Wisconsin—Eau Claire.

Hubert, L. (1977). Kappa revisited. *Psychological Bulletin, 84*(2), 289–297.

Hudson, W. (1982). *The clinical measurement package.* Homewood, IL: Dorsey Press.

Institute for Scientific Information. (1986). This week's citation classic. *Current Contents (Social and Behavioral Sciences), 18*(3), 18.

Johnson, S. M., Kurtz, M. E., Tomlinson, T., & Howe, K. R. (1986). Students' stereotypes of patients as barriers to clinical decision-making. *Journal of Medical Education, 61*(9), 727–735.

Kadushin, A. (1963). Diagnosis and evaluation for (almost) all occasions. *Social Work, 8*(1), 12–19.

Kerlinger, F. N. (1986). *Foundations of behavioral research* (3rd ed.). New York: Holt, Rinehart and Winston.

Kurtz, M. E., Johnson, S. M., & Rice, S. (1989). Students' clinical assessments: Are they affected by stereotyping? *Journal of Social Work Education, 25*(1), 3–12.

Langer, E. J., & Imber, L. (1980). Role of mindlessness in the perception of deviance. *Journal of Personality and Social Psychology, 39*(3), 360–367.

Mitchell, R. E., & Hodson, C. A. (1983). Coping with domestic violence: Social support and psychological health among battered women. *American Journal of Community Psychology, 11*(6), 629–653.

Monette, D. R., Sullivan, T. J., & DeJong, C. R. (1986). *Applied social research.* New York: Holt, Rinehart and Winston.

Morey, L. C., & Blashfield, R. K. (1981). Empirical classifications of alcoholism. *Journal of Studies on Alcohol, 42*(11), 925–937.

Mutschler, E., & Rosen, A. (1980). Evaluation of treatment outcome by client and social worker. In *National Conference on Social Welfare, the Social Welfare Forum, 1979: Official proceedings, 106th annual forum.* New York: Columbia University Press.

Nett, C. (1988). *One effectiveness study of outpatient treatment of bulimics.* Unpublished manuscript, University of Wisconsin—Eau Claire.

New peak for newspeak. (1968, May 6). *Newsweek,* 104–104b.

Nordholm, D. L. A. (1980). Beautiful patients are good patients: Evidence for the physical attractiveness stereotype in first impressions of patients. *Social Science and Medicine, 14A,* 81–83.

Nunnally, J. C. (1967). *Psychometric theory.* New York: McGraw-Hill.

Nurcomb, B., & Fitzhenry-Coor, I. (1982). How do psychiatrists think? Clinical reasoning in the psychiatric interview: A research and education project. *Australian and New Zealand Journal of Psychiatry, 16*(1), 13–24.

Orme, J. G., & Gillespie, D. F. (1986). Reliability and bias in categorizing individual client problems. *Social Service Review, 60*(1), 161–174.

Palmer, M. (undated). *Risk assessment models: A comparative analysis, Working Paper 1.* University of Southern Maine: National Child Welfare Resource Center for Management and Administration.

Pokorny, A. D. (1983). Prediction of suicide in psychiatric patients. *Archives of General Psychiatry, 40,* 249–257.

Pokorny, A. D., Miller, B. A., & Kaplan, H. B. (1972). The Brief MAST: A shortened version of the Michigan Alcoholism Screening Test. *American Journal of Psychiatry, 129,* 342–345.

Polansky, N. A., Chalmers, M. A., Buttenwieser, E., & Williams, D. (1978). Assessing adequacy of child caring: An urban scale. *Child Welfare, 57,* 439–449.

Proctor, E. K., & Rosen, A. (1983). Problem formulation and its relation to treatment planning. *Social Work Research & Abstracts, 19,* 22–28.

Researcher indicted on criminal charges (1988). *Human Research Report, 3*(8), p. 3.

Roman, M. B. (1988, April). When good scientists turn bad. *Discover, 9*(4), 51–58.

Romanczyk, R. G., Kent, R. N., Diament, C., & O'Leary, K. D. (1973). *Measuring the reliability of observational data: A reactive process. Journal of Applied Behavior Analysis, 6*(1), 175–184.

Rosenberg, M. (1965). *Society and the adolescent self-image.* Princeton, NJ: Princeton University Press.

Safer, M. (1988, January 17). *The facts were fiction.* [Interview with Steven Breuning and Thomas Gualtieri]. *60 Minutes.* New York: CBS News.

Schlesier-Stropp, B. (1984). Bulimia: A review of the literature. *Psychological Bulletin, 95*(2), 247–257.

Scott, P. (1988). *Writing techniques: Interviewing and recording.* Unpublished manuscript, Department of Social Work, University of Wisconsin—Eau Claire.

Shrout, P. E., Spitzer, R. L., & Fleiss, J. L. (1987). Quantification of agreement in psychiatric diagnosis revisited. *Archives of General Psychiatry, 44,* 172–177.

Snyder, M., & Swann, W. B. (1978). Hypothesis-testing processes in social interaction. *Journal of Personality and Social Psychology, 36*(11), 1202–1212.

Snyder, M., & White, P. (1981). Testing hypotheses about other people: Strategies of verification and falsification. *Personality and Social Psychology Bulletin, 7*(1), 39–43.

Soeken, K. L., & Prescott, P. A. (1986). Issues in the use of Kappa to estimate reliability. *Medical Care, 24*(8), 733–741.

Spitznagel, E. L., & Helzer, J. E. (1985). A proposed solution to the base rate problem in the Kappa statistic. *Archives of General Psychiatry, 42,* 725–728.

Straus, R., & Bacon, S. D. (1951). Alcoholism and social stability: A study of occupational integration in 2023 male alcoholic patients. *Quarterly Journal of Studies on Alcohol, 12,* 231–260.

Tinsley, H. E. A., & Weiss, D. J. (1975). Interrater reliability and agreement of subject judgments. *Journal of Counseling Psychology, 22*(4), 358–376.

Voytovich, A. E., Rippey, R. M., & Suffredini, A. (1985). Premature conclusions in diagnostic reasoning. *Journal of Medical Education, 60*(4), 302–307.

Yarkin, K. L., Town, J. P., & Harvey, J. H. (1981). The role of cognitive sets in interpreting and remembering interpersonal events. In J. H. Harvey (Ed.), *Cognition, social behavior, and the environment* (pp. 289–308). Hilldales, NJ: Lawrence Erlbaum Associates.

Zung, W. W. K. (1965). A Self-Rating Depression Scale. *Archives of General Psychiatry, 12,* 63–70.

Using On-Line Computer Procedures to Locate Evaluation Studies

The purpose of this chapter is not to provide a comprehensive discussion of how to conduct a library search of any topic of interest to social workers: Engeldinger and Stuart's (1989) thorough review of texts in social work has identified research texts that do this well (Berger & Patchner, 1988; Grinnell, 1981; Monette, Sullivan, & DeJong, 1986). Nor is this chapter intended to be a general introduction to computers in human services. LaMendola (1987) has listed topics that might be in such an introduction. This chapter *does* demonstrate how busy practitioners can use on-line computer technology to locate appropriate and current evaluation studies quickly and efficiently.

Recent advances in computer technology and resourceful adaptations of that technology by librarians have provided quicker and more efficient access to appropriate studies than ever before possible. Until just recently, however, the necessary technology was inaccessible to all but a select few. Now practitioners and students who are willing to learn a few on-line procedures can access bibliographic **data bases** (files of references and citations compiled especially for rapid search by computer). Commonly, access is by a computer terminal that is connected by a **modem** (*mo*dulator-*dem*odulator unit that transforms digital electronic symbols into impulses transmittable by phone lines and back again) and a telephone line to a distant data base, hence the term **on-line** (open to communication with other computers).

THE NEED FOR INFORMATION TO GUIDE PRACTICE

As an example of a need for a search, a family therapist might want to read a review of research regarding effects of methods used to help divorcing couples.

The therapist might also want to evaluate family therapy's effects against a particular outcome measure, but the therapist might not have the time nor the expertise to develop such a measure. Using conventional library methods, searching these two topics could take hours or even days. A manual library search would involve going to a library, searching through relevant abstracts by hand, writing down promising references, going to the shelves to retrieve journal articles, copying the articles retrieved, and filling out interlibrary loan request cards for articles that are not in the collection.

A PROMISING SOLUTION: END USER
SEARCHING IN ON-LINE DATA BASES

In contrast to manual search methods, the family therapist might have had a microcomputer, a modem, and an account with a **data base vendor** (a company that maintains and sells access to data bases). The therapist could then have used the computer to dial a data base, interact with the data base according to established procedures to locate citations and abstracts, and save references on a disk to be printed later—all in just a few minutes. This process of doing one's own search without help from a librarian is called **end user** searching.

To illustrate how the family therapist might have fared by using end user search methods, let us perform the therapist's on-line search using our profession's data base, *Social Work Abstracts* produced by the National Association of Social Workers, Inc. The search located, in 3 minutes and 20 seconds, from an office terminal, a record for Sprenkle and Storm's (1983) article, "Divorce Therapy Outcome Research: A Substantive and Methodological Review." (See Table 8.1 for this article's citation.) Relevant to the family therapist's second request, the same search also located Snyder, Wills, and Keiser's (1981) article, "Empirical Validation of the Marital Satisfaction Inventory: An Actuarial Approach."

The Sprenkle and Storm **record** (a unit of information in a data base) reproduced in Table 8.1 contains much useful information. Each document has its own unique **accession number** (e.g., 11905) to identify it. The update code 853 indicates that the document was added to the data base during the third quarter of 1985. The next three **fields** (sections of the record that apply to the storage of a particular piece of information) designate the author's last name and initials (AU), the title of the article (TI), and the source (SO), indicating that the article appeared in the *Journal of Marital and Family Therapy,* volume 9, issue 3, pages 239 through 258, in the year 1983. The address (AD) of the primary author may be especially helpful to practitioners because it provides a way to contact an expert who may be able to give valuable suggestions about the study's implications for practice. The hardcopy (HC) citation is the issue of *Social Work Research & Abstracts* that contains this article. The **descriptor** (DE) is the term or terms that identify the principal content of the article. **Code descriptors** identify the principal content of the article. Descriptors for articles in the on-line data base *Social Work Abstracts* are listed in the *User's Guide to Social Work Abstracts* (Beebe & Payne, 1989). The **classification code** (CC) is a broad descriptor that classifies articles according to a list of general categories that appear in the *User's Guide*

TABLE 8.1

A typical record retrieved through the Social Work Abstracts Database.

```
AN  ACCESSION NUMBER: 11905. 853.
AU  AUTHOR/S: *Sprenkle-D-H. Storm-C-L.
TI  TITLE: Divorce therapy outcome research: a substantive and
       methodological review.
SO  SOURCE: Journal of Marital and Family Therapy, 9(3):
       239-58, 1983.
AD  ADDRESS: *Marriage and Family Therapy Program, Purdue
       Univ., West Lafayette, Ind.
HC  HARDCOPY: 21(1), 1985, No. 304.
DE  CODE DESCRIPTOR/S: Research: on outcome of divorce therapy
       Divorce-therapy: research on outcome of.
CC  CLASSIFICATION CODE: RESEARCH (CC4030).
PT  PUBLICATION TYPE: JOURNAL (J).
AB  ABSTRACT: A substantive and methodological review of
       twenty-two empirical studies related to divorce therapy
       provided strong evidence for the superiority of mediation
       to traditional adversary methods for custody and
       visitation disputes. Conciliation counseling appeared to
       increase the number of reconciliations in the short term.
       Other conclusions, however, must remain tentative.
       Although the methodologies of the studies reviewed were
       weak, there were wide variations in quality.
       Investigations of divorce mediation used the best designs
       and studies of separation techniques the worst. What
       social scientists and psychotherapists know and what they
       need to know about divorce therapy is addressed
       critically, and suggestions are made for future research
       and practice. (Journal abstract, edited. Curtis Janzen.)
```

Source: Social Work Abstracts, BRS Information Technologies and National Association of Social Workers, Inc.

to *Social Work Abstracts* (Beebe & Payne, 1989, pp. 14–15). **Publication type** (PT) denotes whether the record is a book (B), journal article (J), or dissertation (D). The **abstract** (AB) is a concise summary of the content of the source document.

EVIDENCE REGARDING RELATIVE MERITS OF MANUAL VERSUS ON-LINE SEARCHING

Table 8.2 sums up nine studies that compared on-line versus manual searching methods. The table's first column lists the study's author(s), the second lists the titles of articles making the comparison, and the third describes procedures used to make the comparison. The content of the second and third columns indicates that manual versus on-line searching has been compared in a variety of disciplines—pharmacy, biology, business, research methods, and general interest. None of the investigators assigned searchers randomly to manual or to on-line procedures; generally, the same individuals conducted both kinds of searches in a nonrandomly determined order. In three of the nine experiments, students were taught to do their own on-line and manual searches and their efficiency was evaluated.

TABLE 8.2

Relative merits of on-line versus manual search methods

Author(s)	Article Title	Procedures for Making Comparison	Principal Findings		
			Effectiveness	Time Needed	

Author(s)	Article Title	Procedures for Making Comparison	Effectiveness	Time Needed
Akaho, Bandai, & Fujii (1986)	Comparison of manual and online searches of *Chemical Abstracts*	The authors divided 134 pharmacy students into five groups; each group was assigned to search one topic using both manual and online methods. Students received 1 hour of instruction in doing manual searches and 1 hour of instruction in doing online searches.	When considering online charges and the hourly wage of a typical researcher, the manual search was more expensive. For a part-time worker, the manual search would be less expensive (p. 61). The average manual search got 74% as many appropriate articles as the online method.	Students spent 50–100 minutes less time on the online search.
Bayer & Schwerzel (1982)	A comparison of online and manual searching in selected areas of research	Instructors of a research methods course had students do manual searches on two topics; then, after the students learned to do their own online seraches, the students searched the two topics online.	Students increased the number of documents in the online search over the manual search ranging from 130% to 3,000%.	The manual searches averaged 5 hours per search; the online searches averaged less than ½ hour.
Bernstein (1988)	The retrieval of randomized clinical trials in liver diseases from the medical literature: Manual versus MEDLARS searches	Bernstein obtained results of another investigator's manual search (Poynard & Conn, 1985) about randomized trials to evaluate the treatment of liver disease. Then Bernstein did an online search of MEDLARS on the topic.	Bernstein's online search recalled 48.7% of the documents compared with 99.5% retrieved by Poynard's manual search (p. 25).	Poynard's manual search took 400 hours; the online search, though not reported, probably took less than ½ hour.
Hartley (1983)	A "laboratory" method for the comparison of retrieval effectiveness in manual and online searching	Hartley collected 10 typical request topics from library records and had 10 librarians (who were equally experienced with manual and online methods) do one manual and one online search among the 10 topics.	Online retrieval effectiveness was about equal.	No comparison made.

Reference	Title	Study	Findings	Cost comparison
Houghton, Smith & Webster (1983)	A comparison of *Excerpta Medica* and *Medline* for the provision of drug information to health care professionals—conclusions	The authors randomly selected from their files 14 manual searches that they had done for library patrons in *Index Medicus* and *Excerpta Medica*. Then they did online searches on each manual search topic.	In only one of the searches was a single source located manually that was not located online. "In every other online search the number of references retrieved was greater or equal to the number retrieved manually" (p.291).	For *Excerpta Medica*, the average manual search was 2½ hours per search. The corresponding online searches averaged 10 minutes, 48 seconds. For *Index Medicus*, the average manual search took 1 hour 12 minutes per search, but the corresponding online search took an average of 9 minutes in *Medline* (the online equivalent of *Index Medicus*).
Maciuszko (1987)	Hardcopy versus online searching: A study in retrieval effectiveness	Maciuszko had six students formulate 22 questions regarding issues in biology, business and general interest. Six librarians from six different libraries conducted 88 searches regarding the questions using manual and online methods.	Manual searches found a higher "recall" of documents, but online searches had greater "precision" (p. 308). "The most striking finding of the experiment was that neither mode of searching offered an overall noteworthy advantage over the other" (p. 309).	No comparison made.
Naber (1985)	Online versus manual literature retrieval: A test case shows interesting results in retrieval effectiveness and search strategy	Naber located an article by Boers & Ben-Asher that contained 105 articles regarding ways to collect rainwater. Naber then searched the same topic online.	The manual literature search [Boers & Ben-Asher's published article] produced 33.2% of the total number of relevant titles found. The online search found 86.7% (p. 24).	No comparison made.
Reese (1988)	Manual indexes versus computer-aided indexes: Comparing the *Readers' Guide to Periodical Literature* to *Info Trac II*	Seventeen students at an open admission junior college were given a topic to research manually in the *Readers' Guide* or using CD-ROM files or *Info Trac II*.	83% of the manual searches were successful; 63% of the *Info Trac II* searches were successful (p. 388).	No comparison made.
Rollins (1983)	Some economies of online searching: Experience of Houston Public Library	Staff at the Houston Public Library kept careful records, including online charges and staff time, of costs to do searches for library patrons.	Online searches average $15.75; manual searches average $22.50.	No comparison made.

Column 4 of Table 8.2 summarizes studies comparing the effectiveness of on-line and manual searches. Given their wide range of measures and conflicting findings, it is difficult to come to a clear conclusion; still, it appears that on-line methods save time but do not find substantially better evidence. This finding appears to agree with Hartley's (1983) review of six studies that compared the number and quality of references, but not time spent to locate them.

A study using social work fieldwork students found that on-line methods located the same quality of evidence in less time than manual methods. Gibbs and Johnson (1983) randomly assigned students in four social work fieldwork methods sections to on-line or manual search groups. Each student was asked to identify a client with whom they were working and to pose a question regarding the evaluation research that would be most appropriate to their work with that client. The instructor did a search of an on-line data base that contained evaluation studies and gave the search to the on-line group to get them started on their library searches. The manual search group got no help. Students in the on-line group spent a statistically significant smaller amount of time in the library, but there were no differences between the groups regarding number of references, reference appropriateness, or study quality.

AN EXPLANATION OF ON-LINE SEARCH PROCEDURES

Social Work Abstracts (SWAB) is the only data base in the *Directory of Online Databases* (1989) that is specifically listed under "Social Work." It is the primary data base for our profession's literature. The sample record that appears in Table 8.1 came from SWAB.

Although *Abstracts for Social Workers* began in 1965, SWAB's approximately 20,000 documents go back only to 1977. Approximately 500 records are added quarterly. Most (90%) of the documents loaded into the SWAB data base are published in 34 core professional social work journals. Abstractors select the rest from social work dissertations and approximately 200 additional journals. Documents are included in SWAB because they contain information, reviews, descriptions and evaluations of new or old techniques, new programs and theories, or new and special topics of interest to social workers (Beebe & Payne, 1989, p. 2).

SWAB contains a wide variety of documents regarding topics of interest to social workers, including: Fields of Service, Aging and the Aged, Alcoholism and Drug Addiction, Civil Rights, Crime and Delinquency, Economic Security, Employment, Family and Child Welfare, Health and Medical Care, Housing and Urban Development, Mental Health, Mental Retardation, Schools, Social Policy and Action, Service Methods, Practice Methods, and Administration (Beebe & Payne, 1989). Within each of these major topics there are many subtopics that concern important practice-related issues.

EQUIPMENT USED TO CONDUCT ON-LINE SEARCHES

Since September 1985, SWAB has been available on-line through BRS Information Technologies. To access the SWAB data base on-line, or any data base for

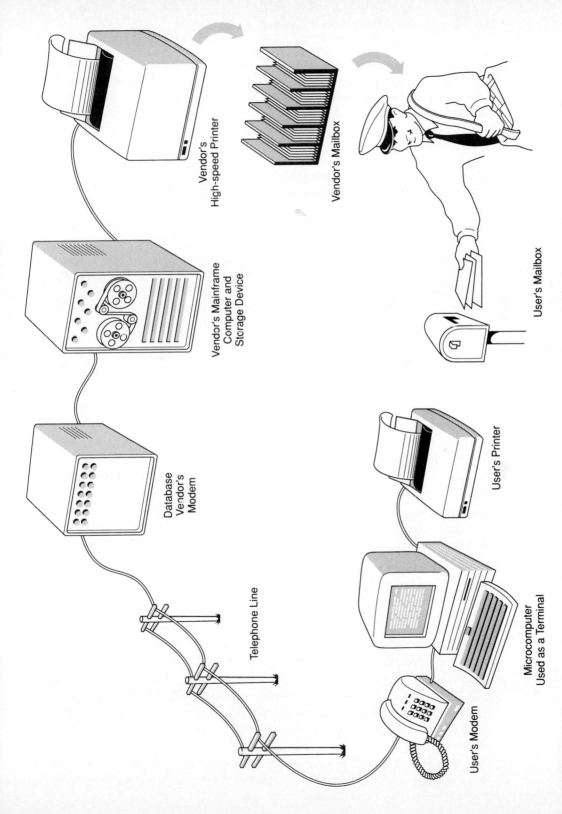

Vendor's
High-speed Printer

Vendor's Mailbox

User's Mailbox

Vendor's Mainframe
Computer and
Storage Device

Database
Vendor's
Modem

User's Printer

Telephone Line

Microcomputer
Used as a Terminal

User's Modem

FIGURE 8.1
Components of an on-line system.

that matter, the user sits at a terminal or a microcomputer that serves as a terminal to contact—over telephone lines—a data base that is kept in the memory of a distant computer. Access requires both hardware and software. Figure 8.1 outlines **hardware** (actual pieces of equipment in a computer system) that are required to access any data base. **Software** refers to the programs and/or instructions that implement the user's instructions. Essential hardware includes:

1. *Microcomputer Used As a Terminal.* Most small desktop computers can be adapted to serve as a terminal.

2. *User's Modem.* The modem allows the user to access and interact with a data base through a phone line. It converts electronic signals to auditory signals and then back again, thus allowing the computer to "converse" by telephone with a data base. An external modem, as shown in the lower left of Figure 8.1, is a small box about the size of a telephone's base. (An internal modem does the same job, via a "card" in the computer.) Modems are designed to operate at different communication speeds, or baud rates. A 1200 baud modem can transmit or receive about 120 **characters** (letters or numbers) per second; a 2400 baud modem can handle about 240 characters per second.

3. *Telephone Line.* The user connects with the data base by punching in a phone number using the computer keyboard, or by using a program that dials the number automatically. It is possible to connect with many distant data bases through a local Telenet or Tymnet number. Once connected, the user can interact with the data base through the computer's screen and keyboard by responding to the data base's prompts.

4. *Vendor.* The company or organization that sells the data base to users is known as the vendor. It may maintain for sale, at an hourly connect cost or per-document cost, many different data bases.

5. *Data Base Vendor's Modem.* On the other end of the phone line, the data base vendor's modem connects the user with the vendor's computer. This modem can handle many users almost simultaneously as they wait in a queue (line-up of users whose jobs await processing).

6. *Mainframe Computer.* The vendor's large, full-scale computer and its software interact with each user in the queue. The computer performs the search operations requested by the user and also retrieves records from memory and transmits these records to the user's screen. Users who store search results in their own computer's memory, or on a disk to be printed later, are said to be **downloading** the results of their search.

7. *Disk Storage.* The vendor maintains the data base on a large, quickly accessible memory device, a tape, hard disk, or CD ROM (a thin disk of metal foil sandwiched between two layers of transparent plastic which is read by a small laser beam which deciphers the patterns of small holes in the foil layer).

8. *User's Printer.* The user's printer can be used to print the user's commands as they were executed during the search and the search's retrieved records.

9. *Vendor's Printer*. Users can choose to download results of their search directly, or they can ask that the vendor's high speed printer print the search and mail it at some additional cost.

STEPS FOR CONDUCTING AN ON-LINE
SEARCH IN THE SWAB DATA BASE

The following steps outline the search process. The steps and basic logic described here can be applied to any search of a computerized bibliographic data base.

1. Write out your question as specifically as you can in **natural language** (everyday words you would use in conversation). Ideally, the question should be clearly stated and single-barreled, but it is not necessary to construct a question as specifically as the research questions were posed in Chapter 6. Here is an example of a question that has been posed in natural language: What is the most effective method for preventing the spread of AIDS among sexually active college students?

2. Construct a search table (see Table 8.3) to outline your question's key search concepts. Your question can provide the skeleton for your search. To construct your table, list horizontally, at the head of empty columns, each of the key concepts from your question. The first row of Table 8.3 contains four key words or phrases from the question above, including: "most effective method," "preventing," "AIDS," and "college students."

   Glance at any literature that you might have about the topic and discuss your question with knowledgeable colleagues to help you identify commonly used synonyms for your question's key words. Record these natural language synonyms in the second row of your table in the appropriate column.

   Then, if the data base has a **thesaurus** (a list of subject terms or phrases that indexers use to catalog each record in a data base), record the thesaurus's descriptors below the natural language words. (See the descriptors row of Table 8.3.) The descriptors in the example search came from the *User's Guide to Social Work Abstracts* (Beebe & Payne, 1989). *Descriptors,* as opposed to natural language, are the data base's controlled vocabulary that is standardized for the data base.

   In the fourth row, identify any root words that can be formed by **truncation** (cutting off or removing a portion of a word to reveal a root that is shared in common with other synonyms and/or descriptors). The $ is used for truncating words in BRS/After Dark. The root words *Universit$* and *College$* capture *university/universities* and *college/colleges*.

3. Combine search terms according to two basic principles of Boolean logic (basic principles of set theory). The row marked "Search Terms Chosen" at the very bottom of Table 8.3 contains the root terms and most promising descriptors for limiting the search. These terms should be the ones most likely to locate the highest proportion of appropriate documents. The next step is combining these likely terms to make the search specific. The OR command

TABLE 8.3
Search table for an example question

| | Search Terms | | | |
	First Concept	Second Concept	Third Concept	Fourth Concept
Word or Phrase from Your Question	Most effective method	Preventing	AIDS	College students
Natural Language Synonyms	Subjects assigned randomly Random assignment Control groups Control group Comparison group Comparison groups Experimental group Experimental groups Statistically significant Statistical significance Single-subject $N = 1$ Single case experimental design	Prevention Preventable Prevent	Acquired Immune Deficiency Syndrome	College students University students
Descriptors		Preventicare Prevention Preventive instruction Preventive services	Acquired Immune Deficiency Syndrome HIV Human T-Cell Lymphotropic virus HTLV-III	Universities University Colleges

TABLE 8.3
continued

	First Concept	Second Concept	Third Concept	Fourth Concept

Root Words	Random
	   Control group
	Experimental
	   group
	Comparison
	   group
	Statistical
	   significance
	Single-subject
	$N = 1$
	Single case
	   experimental
	   design
		Prevent	No truncation	University
				College

Search Terms Chosen	Random$
	Control group$
	Comparison
	   group$
	Experimental
	   group$
	Statistical$
	   significan$
			Acquired
			   Immune
			   Deficiency
			   Syndrome
			HIV
			Human T-cell
			Lymphotropic
			   virus
			HTLV-III
				Universit$
				College$

lumps documents together into one larger set of documents, which may or may not overlap with each other (see Figure 8.2). To combine all documents in each column together into one set, combine the terms vertically in each column with the *OR* command. For example, to combine several terms to identify studies, the user typed in the search command: *Random$ OR control group$ OR experimental group$ OR comparison group$ OR statistical$ significan$*. The resultant Set A of 1,013 documents (see Figure 8.2) contains these terms somewhere in the abstract, title, citation, or descriptor list.

There were 1,074 documents in Set B that contained the root word *prevent$* somewhere in the document. There were 97 documents in Set C where any descriptors for AIDS appeared anywhere in the document, and there were 2,466 documents in Set D that contained the search terms *universit$ OR college$*. Each of the four sets at the top of Figure 8.2 contains documents that can have as few as one of the search terms present or as many as all of the search terms present.

In contrast to the *OR* command that broadened the search, the *AND* command narrows the search and reduces the number of documents retrieved. It would be ideal to find documents concerning studies (Set A) about the prevention (Set B) of AIDS (Set C) among college students (Set D); however, Figure 8.2 shows

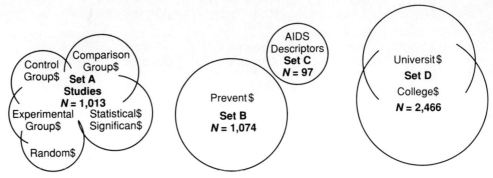

a. Sets Formed Using the OR Command

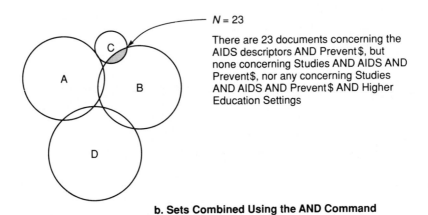

N = 23

There are 23 documents concerning the
AIDS descriptors AND Prevent$, but
none concerning Studies AND AIDS AND
Prevent$, nor any concerning Studies
AND AIDS AND Prevent$ AND Higher
Education Settings

b. Sets Combined Using the AND Command

FIGURE 8.2
The AND and OR commands for limiting a search.

no such intersection between Sets *A AND B AND C AND D*. Secondly, it would
be fortunate to find documents about studies that investigated ways to prevent
AIDS, but there are none in SWAB that concern Sets *A AND B AND C*. Finally,
there are 23 documents that concern preventing AIDS that are designated by the
intersect between Sets *B AND C*.

Although search fledglings will probably find the *AND* and *OR* commands
to be the most versatile and high powered, those with more experience may try
other commands in BRS, including the *SAME, WITH,* or *NOT*.

An example of the *SAME* command is: *HIV SAME PREVENT$*. Both the
AIDS descriptor, *HIV,* designating the Human Immunodeficiency Virus and *PRE-
VENT$* must appear together somewhere in the same paragraph or field of a
document.

An example of the *WITH* command is: *HIV WITH PREVENT$*. Both the
descriptor *PREVENT$* and the acronym *HIV* must appear in the same sentence
somewhere in the document.

An example of the *NOT* command is: *HIV NOT PREVENTION*. Only the acronym *HIV* must be present in the document somewhere. Any document that contains the descriptor *PREVENT$* will be eliminated from among those about *HIV*.

SOME HELPFUL HINTS FOR END USER SEARCHING

Wygant (1986, pp. 128–129) cautions that students who attempt end user searches must guard against the illusion that because the printer has spewed out a ream of perfect hard copy that the search was thorough. Only careful preparation can make searches thorough. Careful preparation involves selecting and combining search terms according to the steps listed.

Wygant referred to three other common errors in search logic. The *NOT* command is tricky. If documents are likely to include terms interchangeably, for example *UNIVERSIT$* and *COLLEGE$,* and the user uses the command *UNIVERSIT$ NOT COLLEGE$;* this use of the *NOT* command is likely to zap the many documents in which the two terms are used interchangeably. Wygant also describes problems with natural language when used as search terms. Many words in common use are imprecise. For example, it has already been pointed out that the term *AIDS* can designate both a verb and noun that mean something other than *Acquired Immune Deficiency Syndrome*. Beware also of multiple Boolean operators in a single sentence. For example, a searcher wanting information about abused children and abused aged persons might be tempted to combine the *AND* and the *OR* commands into one set of commands: *CHILDREN OR AGED AND ABUSE*. This will pull out anything about children plus abused elderly. It would be better to: search *ABUSE$ AND CHILDREN* (set A), search *ABUSE$ AND AGED* (set B), then search *A AND B*.

Not specifying the field to search widens the search; using commands that designate a particular field in a record narrows the search. For example, in SWAB, one can search the title of documents by specifying the term *TI* in the search (see Table 8.1). This will pull out only those documents that contain the search term in the title field of the record.

Training Students to Conduct End User Searches in the Social Work Abstracts Data Base

Appendix B was written to make end user searches easier for inexperienced users. It outlines, step-by-step, how to complete a search, but it is specific to IBM equipment, Kermit communication software, and the BRS-SWAB data base. However, Appendix B may serve as a guide for other end user on-line procedures.

Appendix B was used to train two student volunteers from each of three Methods of Social Work Research labs. These six students, none of whom had any experience with on-line searching, met for 2 hours one evening for training in how to locate evaluation studies.

A BRS-SWAB Search Conducted by Students

After 2 hours of training, the volunteers met to conduct additional searches for themselves and their classmates during special evening lab meetings. The search given in Table 8.4 was conducted by a team of two undergraduate social work students in the Social Work Abstracts (SWAB) data base available through BRS Information Technologies (1987). The students, both planning single-subject studies for their own class assignments, were trying to locate references concerning single-subject studies. The students were also trying to locate references for a classmate who had requested information about cognitive therapy for depressed elderly persons.

At the time the team conducted the search they had already done searches for 11 other classmates, so they had already refined their skills a bit. The search team's system involved a division of labor: One sat at the computer to execute commands; the other, watching on a large screen, read the steps aloud and checked them off as they were accomplished. The partial text of their search—most references were deleted to save space—appears in the left-hand column of Table 8.4. The right-hand column of Table 8.4 presents an explanation for commands and the search results.

The search took about 11 minutes, or about $5\frac{1}{2}$ minutes per search topic. This compares favorably with average search times for professional librarians of 7 minutes per search (Pujat & Schutzer, 1982, p. 23), and $17\frac{1}{2}$ minutes (Rollins, 1983, p. 16) and 12 minutes for nonlibrarians (Myers, 1986).

What End User Searching Has Taught Us

Experience with on-line SWAB searching has taught us some useful lessons. Here are the positive ones:

1. Student volunteers can, in approximately 2 hours, learn to conduct their own independent BRS-SWAB searches.

2. A rough poll of students from previous Methods of Social Work Research classes, compared with those who now have access to SWAB, indicates that SWAB students spend about one-third the time in the library locating 10 sources to plan an evaluation study.

3. Student volunteers located 10 references for most classmates at a cost of less than $2.50 per search.

4. A particular descriptor that may work well in many data bases to locate evaluation studies is designated by Set A in Figure 8.2.

5. One trick that Engeldinger and Stuart (1989) call "citation searching" was especially helpful. Students often find one or two articles that are specific to their topic. Often these articles contain an extensive bibliography that, in addition to being selectively compiled, also contains a concentration of useful references.

Experience with on-line searching for social work literature has not been all positive. Here are its disadvantages:

1. Phone lines sputter occasionally. This static generates literally any kind of character possible. Such characters can disconnect the line, cause the printer font to produce tiny letters, underline everything indiscriminately, or stop abruptly. You must use your word processing program to identify and kill strange characters that stop the printer. You can patiently reboot the system and start all over when disconnected. Phone line problems can be alleviated by: (a) moving the equipment to a new, more static-free phone line (having all the equipment on one cart helps); (b) disconnecting any phone line accessories, including telephone answering machines; and (c) switching to a lower baud setting on the modem.

2. Teaching students to use the system takes about 2 hours.

3. The older and more complex communication software is frustrating to learn. Newer software, including Smartcomm, Procomm, and Procomm Plus might be simpler.

4. Buying and installing a modem took time that could have been reduced by consulting an expert beforehand.

ON-LINE DATA BASES AVAILABLE IN
THE APPLIED SOCIAL SCIENCES

Large vendors sell access to collections of data bases. These vendors include: BRS Information Technologies' BRS/After Dark, DIALOG Information Retrieval Corporation's KNOWLEDGE INDEX, and BRS/Saunders Colleague. In 1989 there were 4,062 data bases available—there had been just 400 in 1979 (Directory of Online Databases, 1989, p. v). For a list of data bases and their descriptions, consult the *Directory of Online Databases* (1989).

SOME OBJECTIONS—AND RESPONSES—
TO ON-LINE TECHNOLOGY

People often fear computers. Experience frequently allays such fear. Those who investigated the correlates of resistance to new technology among librarians found that a lack of experience with computers was strongly associated with "computer anxiety" (Sievert, Albritton, Roper, & Clayton, 1988, p. 343). Among factors most associated with computer anxiety were: no previous computer courses, no hands-on experience, no computer available in one's present library position, and no experience with on-line catalogue searching (Sievert et al., 1988, p. 248). The message for social workers in all this: Try it.

On-line technology has not been explained in social work literature. Astonishingly, a recent on-line search showed that not a single article had appeared in *Social Work Research & Abstracts* with the term *online, on line,* or *on-line* anywhere in the citation, descriptor list, or abstract. Apparently, social work has not yet picked up on a major advance of our time.

Frequently, abstracts do not find their way into data bases until a year or two after publication. Thus, manual searches are more current than on-line

TABLE 8.4
Text of a social work abstract search through the BRS data base

Computer Screen Shows	Explanation
	Prior to conducting the search, the students connected the modem, identified themselves to BRS by typing in passwords, and prepared their disk drive to record the search so it could be printed later (see Appendix C for these steps).
| ```
              BRS/AFTER DARK
                 MAIN MENU
SERVICE                        NUMBER
Search Service                    1
BRS/After Dark Update (1/5/89)    11
How To Use BRS/After Dark         12
Customer Services                 13
ENTER SERVICE NUMBER OR H FOR HELP → 1
``` | The students selected the *Search Service* option from among options listed. |
| ```
 BRS/AFTER DARK SEARCH SERVICES LIBRARIES
LIBRARY NAME                    LABEL
Science and Medicine            SCME
Busines and Finance             BUSI
Reference                       REFE
Education                       EDUC
Social Science and Humanities   SOCS
Practice Databases              PRAC
ENTER LIBRARY OR DATABASE LABEL →  SWAB
``` | Instead of waiting for a long list of data bases to be printed, the students selected the one they wanted: SWAB. |
| ```
SWAB 1977-4TH QTR 1988
ENTER Y TO DISPLAY DATABASE DESCRIPTION
OR PRESS ENTER TO BEGIN SEARCHING →
ENTER SEARCH TERMS, COMMAND, OR H FOR
HELP
SEARCH 1 → SINGLE-SUBJECT
   ANSWER 1  13 DOCUMENTS FOUND
``` | Specifying the term, *SINGLE SUBJECT* will pull out of SWAB those references that have the term *single subject* anywhere in the document. There were 13 such documents. |
| ```
ENTER SEARCH TERMS, COMMAND, OR H FOR
HELP
SEARCH 2 → D
``` | The students enter *D* to print the documents selected. |
| `ENTER ANSWER NUMBER → 1` | The students ask only that documents from Search 1 be printed. |
| ```
ENTER TI (TITLE ONLY), S (SHORT FORMAT),
M (MEDIUM FORMAT), L (LONG FORMAT),
TD (TAILORED DISPLAY)→ L
``` | The students ask for a longer, more informative printout that includes each document's citation, descriptors, and an abstract. |
| ```
ENTER DOCUMENT NUMBERS → 1-13
*ANSWER 1 SWAB SCREEN 1 OF 27*
  1
AN ACCESSION NUMBER: 19131. 889.
AU AUTHOR/S: Cooper-M.
TI TITLE: Behavioral treatment of a
  client with an obsessive-compulsive
  disorder: a single subject design.
``` | All 13 Abstracts from *Answer* 1 are requested. <br><br> This first reference is a doctoral dissertation from New York University by M. Cooper. |

the authors in their local telephone directory. Such sleuthing is called moving up the "bibliographic chain" (Davis & Parker, 1979, p. 49).

Data bases for professional literature can present indexing problems that make accessing the information difficult. **Indexing** means classifying articles that are being added to a data base according to a list of descriptors in the data base's thesaurus. Indexing may not be reliable. Bernstein (1988, p. 28) found that sources located during a manual search but not by computer were most often missed by the computer because the indexer had misclassified the articles. The user's best solution to this problem may be to reduce the precision of a search. An example would be **search free text** (a mode of searching where all words in a record or citation may be used as retrieval search terms; Wood, Horak, & Snow, 1986, p. 278). Searching free text will locate more false positives, thus reducing search precision.

The user may locate on-line an ideal citation that is unavailable at the local library. In such cases, most libraries can obtain a copy through their interlibrary loan department. To get a copy, telephone the citation in to the local library, or fill out a request through the local library's interlibrary loan department.

FUTURE TRENDS IN END USER SEARCHING

Recent advances in information technology may eventually rank with the invention of the printing press in importance. In 1987, DIALOG, one of our nation's largest information data base vendors, made a commitment to offer on-line search training to students, from elementary and high school level through professional level (Kesselman, 1988, p. 64). Such end user searching may become particularly useful to social workers because DIALOG has begun offering a "One Search" option that permits searching a topic in as many as 20 different data bases simultaneously (Kesselman, 1988, p. 63). Thus, a social work practitioner might be able to search for information on "in-home care" in the SWAB and in *Medline* data bases simultaneously.

Early experience with end user searching has been primarily in the life and physical sciences. The Bio-Medical Library at the University of Minnesota-Minneapolis began teaching end user searching in regular for-credit classes in January of 1984 (Glasgow & Foreman, 1986). Experience with these classes has been positive. Administrators at the University of Maryland's Health Sciences Library have made their facilities available for end user access to BRS/After Dark to save library staff time and to make it more convenient for library patrons (Simon, 1986). Brooks (1982) taught biology students at Oregon State University to conduct their own on-line searches. According to Brooks, "The students are most enthusiastic about their ability to directly conduct a search whenever they wish, and they do not envision a time when they will not run their own searches" (p. 37).

In the early 1980s, the IRCS Medical Science group of journals went on-line to users with the full text of IRCS journals, not just citations and abstracts (Buckingham, Franklin, & Westwater, 1983; Collen, Flagle, & Deng, 1985).

On-line journals, if the format becomes widely available to users in the applied social sciences, may have a profound effect on human services practice. Full text searches would allow the user to identify a topic, immediately retrieve an article concerning it, use commands to locate the section most pertinent to a problem in the article, and print that section for later reference.

Books, too, are now available on-line. The author of one such book that is available *only* on-line predicts that **virtual libraries** (libraries available electronically) will become widespread (Wheeler, 1987). Wheeler's projection may not be as absurd as it sounds. The text of all 750,000 volumes of a medium-sized university library, minus their illustrations, can now fit on approximately 2,100 CD ROM disks—and these $4\frac{3}{4}'' \times \frac{1}{20}''$ disks could all fit into a 15" cube. Such technology may foster great opportunities for end user searching in social work.

SUMMARY

Recent advances in computer technology make it possible for practitioners to access current research to guide their practice quickly and conveniently. Practitioners can locate practice-relevant evaluation studies according to client type, intervention method, setting, features of study design, and outcome measures that would have taken prohibitively too much time to locate using manual search methods. Clearly, based on studies that compare manual search methods with on-line methods, the latter are much faster, although not necessarily able to find better evidence.

This chapter illustrated how, in a couple of hours, social work students can learn the rudiments of end user searching, described the format of information retrieved from *Social Work Abstracts,* and outlined strategies for planning a search.

On-line access to data bases may profoundly affect the way practitioners make decisions in their practice. Full text journals have already become available to health-care professionals, and only about 1% of these professionals reported that the search process was not "user-friendly" (Collen & Flagle, 1985, p. 2768). Electronic publication is no longer a distant vision, but an inevitability (Seiler, 1989, p. 66). Such changes, plus knowing that almost any computer can be modified for less than $300 to allow on-line searching, warrant teaching social work students to make use of on-line search technology in their own preservice training programs.

EXERCISE

This class project requires:

1. Hardware: a computer with a serial port, two disk drives, 1200 or 2400 baud modem, telephone line, *BRS/After Dark User's Manual* (BRS Information Technologies, 1987), and a *User's Guide to Social Work Abstracts* (Beebe & Payne, 1989).
2. Communications Software: for example, Smartcomm, Avatalk, Procomm.
3. A User's Account: a minimum of about $150 in a BRS/After Dark account.
4. A large display screen: an 8" × 10" CRT display will allow up to four students to view a search comfortably; 60 students can view a search projected onto a movie screen by an overhead projector through a liquid crystal display.

Procedures

Unless someone in the group is familiar with computer hardware, arrange for someone who knows the technology well to set up and test the equipment and test the phone line for interference. The instructor should become familiar enough with the search process to develop a short step-by-step

manual for logging onto the data base, saving a file, and logging off (see the sample manual in Appendix B). With this manual in hand, follow steps for planning and conducting a search as outlined in the previous section of this chapter marked: Steps for Conducting an On-line Search in the SWAB Data Base.

REFERENCES

Akaho, E., Bandai, A., & Fujii, M. (1986). Comparison of manual and online searches of *Chemical Abstracts. Journal of Chemical Information and Computer Sciences, 26*(2), 59–63.

Bayer, B., & Schwerzel, S. W. (1982). A comparison of online and manual searching in selected areas of research. In M. E. Williams & T. H. Hogan (Compilers), *National Online Meeting: Proceedings—1982* (pp. 23–27). Medford, NJ: Learned Information, Inc.

Beebe, L., & Payne, A. H. (1989). *User's guide to social work abstracts* (2nd ed.). Silver Spring, MD: National Association of Social Workers.

Berger, R. M., & Patchner, M. A. (1988). *Implementing the research plan: A guide for the helping process*. Newbury Park, CA: Sage.

Bernstein, F. (1988). The retrieval of randomized clinical trials in liver diseases from the medical literature: Manual versus MEDLARS searches. *Controlled Clinical Trials, 9*(1), 23–31.

Brooks, K. M. (1982). Non-mediated usage of online retrieval systems in an academic environment. In M. E. Williams & T. H. Hogan (Compilers), *National Online Meeting: Proceedings—1982* (pp. 35–39). Medford, NJ: Learned Information.

BRS Information Technologies. (1987). *After Dark user's manual*. Latham, NY: BRS Information Technologies.

Buckingham, M. C. S., Franklin, J., & Westwater, J. (1983, December 6–8). RCS on-line: Experiences with the first electronic biomedical journal. *7th International Online Information Meeting, London* (pp. 105–109). Oxford: Learned Information.

Collen, M. F., & Flagle, C. D. (1985). Full-text medical literature retrieval by computer. *Journal of the American Medical Association, 254*(19), 2768–2775.

Collen, M. F., & Flagle, Deng, C. D. (1985). Full text medical literature retrieval. *Journal of the American Medical Association, 254*, 2768–2774.

Davis, G. B., & Parker, C. A. (1979). *Writing the doctoral dissertation*. Woodbury, NY: Barrons Educational Series.

Directory of online databases (Vol. 10, No. 1). (1989). New York: Cuadrá/Elsevier.

Engeldinger, E. A., & Stuart, P. (1989, March 5). *The library in social work research: A review of research textbooks*. Paper presented at the 35th annual meeting of the Council on Social Work Education, Chicago, IL.

Gibbs, L. E., & Johnson, D. J. (1983). Computer assisted clinical decision making. *Journal of Social Service Research, 6*(3/4), 119–132.

Glasgow, V. L., & Foreman, G. (1986). U-Search: A program to teach end user searching at an academic health sciences library. In M. S. Wood, E. B. Horak, & B. Snow (Eds.), *End user searching in the health sciences* (pp. 137–147). New York: Haworth Press.

Grinnell, R. (Ed.) (1981). *Social work research and evaluation*. Itasca, IL: F. E. Peacock.

Hartley, D. (1983, December 6–8). A "laboratory" method for the comparison of retrieval effectiveness in manual and online searching. *7th International Online Information Meeting, London* (pp. 157–166). Oxford: Learned Information.

Houghton, B., Smith, J., & Webster, M. (1983, December 6–8). A comparison of *Excerpta Medica* and *Medline* for the provision of drug information to health care professionals—Conclusions. *7th International Online Information Meeting, London* (pp. 283–304). Oxford: Learned Information.

Kesselman, M. (1988). Online update. *Wilson Library Bulletin, 62*(8), 63–65.

LaMendola, W. (1987). Teaching information technology to social workers. *Journal of Teaching in Social Work, 1*(1), 53–69.

Maciuszko, K. L. (1987, May). Hardcopy versus online searching: A study in retrieval effectiveness. *National Online Meeting Proceedings—1987, New York,* (pp. 305–310). Medford, NJ: Learned Information.

Monette, D. R., Sullivan, T. J., & DeJong, C. R. (1986). *Applied social research.* New York: Holt, Rinehart and Winston.

Myers, F. J. (1986). Physician searching: A rural hospital experience. In M. S. Wood, E. B. Horak, & B. Snow (Eds.), *End user searching in the health sciences* (pp. 189–196). New York: Haworth Press.

Naber, G. (1985, February). Online versus manual literature retrieval: A test case shows interesting results in retrieval effectiveness and search strategy. *Database, 8*(1), 20–24.

Poynard, T., & Conn, H. O. (1985). The retrieval of randomized clinical trials in liver disease from the medical literature. A comparison of MEDLARS and manual methods. *Controlled Clinical Trials, 6,* 271–279.

Pujat, D., & Schutzer, C. (1982). Database searching in the hospital library. *Science and Technology Libraries, 3*(1), 19–28.

Rabin, C. (1981). The single-case design in family therapy research. *Family Process, 20*(3), 351–366.

Reese, C. (1988). Manual indexes versus computer-aided indexes: Comparing the *Readers' Guide to Periodical Literature* to *Info Trac II. Reference Quarterly, 27*(3), 384–389.

Rollins, G. (1983). Some economies of online searching: Experience at Houston Public Library. *Public Library Quarterly, 4*(2), 13–18.

Schorr, A. L. (1988). Other times, other strategies. *Social Work, 33*(3), 249–250.

Seiler, L. H. (1989). The future of the scholarly journal. *Academic Computing, 4*(1), 14–16, 66–69.

Sievert, M. E., Albritton, R. L., Roper, P., & Clayton, N. (1988). Investigating computer anxiety in an academic library. *Information Technology and Libraries, 1*(3), 243–252.

Simon, M. (1986). The BRS/AFTER DARK search service in a health sciences library. In M. S. Wood, E. B. Horak, & B. Snow (Eds.), *End user searching in the health sciences* (pp. 163–178). New York: Haworth.

Snyder, D. K., Wills, R. M., & Keiser, T. W. (1981). Empirical validation of the Marital Satisfaction Inventory: An actuarial approach. *Journal of Consulting and Clinical Psychology, 49*(2), 262–268.

Sprenkle, D. H., & Storm, C. L. (1983). Divorce therapy outcome research: A substantive and methodological review. *Journal of Marital and Family Therapy, 9*(3), 239–258.

Wheeler, H. (1987). *The virtual library: The electronic library developing within the traditional library.* [available electronically]. Los Angeles, CA: Doheny Documents.

Wood, M. S., Horak, E. B., & Snow, B. (Eds.). (1986). *End user searching in the health sciences.* New York: Haworth.

Wygant, A. C. (1986). Teaching end user searching in a health sciences center. In M. S. Wood, E. B. Horak, & B. Snow (Eds.), *End user searching in the health sciences* (pp. 127–135). New York: Haworth.

How to Evaluate Studies to Guide Practice Systematically

MOTIVATION AND OVERVIEW

The Filter Approach to Evaluating Evidence

Those who master on-line computer methods quickly encounter a new problem—how to make practical use of studies once they have been retrieved. Any on-line search will uncover both strong and weak studies, often with contradictory findings, that report various levels of effectiveness against different outcome measures. The problem is further complicated by the sheer number of methods from which to choose. Herink (1980) has described over 250 methods available to practitioners in the applied social sciences.

Two approaches for assimilating evaluation studies come to mind. Those who apply the first approach absorb information from many studies, become immersed in the content and hope that doing so will suggest some course of action. This **sponge approach** (Browne & Keeley, 1981, p. 2), assumes that concentration and memory will yield useful conclusions. But this approach has a serious disadvantage: It lacks a system for sifting through the studies to determine which contain the largest and most substantial grains of truth.

The **filter approach** (Browne & Keeley, 1981, p. 2) is the exact opposite of the sponge approach. Those who apply the filter approach have a set of criteria in mind while reading evidence and constantly apply those criteria while listening to or reading an argument. In a sense, the applied criteria serve as pores of a filter—allowing evidence of less substance to be discarded and leaving solid evidence behind.

Primitive practitioners looking for ways to use study results.

As a guide for making decisions about practice, the filter approach is so far superior to the sponge approach that failure to apply it constitutes another practitioners' fallacy, the **reward everything**—gold and garbage alike—**fallacy** (Meehl 1973, p. 228). Here it is at work in a group leader's thinking during a staff conference at a human services agency:

> Several family service workers are discussing how best to help the Cunninghams, a divorcing couple seen by several workers in the agency. The couple has tried unsuccessfully to resolve their differences, but in spite of the staff's competently and empathically given help, both Mr. and Mrs. Cunningham have decided that their incompatibility is too great to be resolved. Now they have begun to argue over how to determine the custody arrangements of their two children. The staff's leader, who will see the couple tomorrow, is asking staff members for advice on how to deal with the situation.

STAFF LEADER: What do you think I should tell the Cunninghams tomorrow?

FIRST STAFF MEMBER: I think we should urge them to try divorce mediation and I think we should make referrals to mediation more often. There seems to be some pretty convincing evidence that it works. (The staff member searches through some papers and retrieves some notes.) Although I haven't done a thorough re-

view, I ran across a pretty strong study last week that evaluated divorce mediation. In a 1982 Denver mediation study, Pearson and Thoennes randomly assigned about 300 couples to free divorce mediation services or to a control group and then followed the couples to see what happened. About 80% of the mediated couples reached an agreement before their divorce hearing, while only 50% of the nonmediated group reached an agreement. Of couples participating in mediation, 70% agreed to joint custody of their children, but only 15% of the controls did. Of course about 50% of the couples who were offered mediation declined—that may make these results difficult to interpret.

In a 1987 study, in which the rate of those declining to participate in mediation was much lower than in the Denver study, Emery and Wyer found that among couples randomly assigned to mediation or a control, those assigned to mediation had a 67% lower rate of cases proceeding to court. Mediation looks promising. Let's recommend that the Cunninghams try mediation.

STAFF LEADER: Good point! Maybe we should advise them to give mediation a try. Does anyone else have an opinion about this?

SECOND STAFF MEMBER: I would advise against mediation. I referred a family to the Tri-County Mediation Center 2 months ago, and they wound up in a bitter court dispute anyway. I think that once a couple has decided to divorce there is nothing anyone can do to help them to resolve their differences. They're past reasoning.

STAFF LEADER: Good point! Maybe we should let the Cunninghams head directly for family court. It's difficult to decide what to recommend.

In this example the group leader has given identical credence to both staff members' arguments: the one who cited empirical evidence and the one who described a personal experience with a single case. This is the reward everything fallacy—giving equal weight to weak and strong arguments indiscriminately.

The staff leader may have believed that all professionals on the staff have a right to their opinion and should be heard. That is certainly true, but it does not follow that because staff members have a right to an opinion, they necessarily have a well-informed opinion. Where client care is at stake, what benefits clients should dominate over other concerns.

Why Develop a Quality of Study Rating Form?

Practitioners can avoid the reward everything fallacy by having objective criteria for filtering evidence. Practitioners can use these criteria to filter evidence and choose practice methods that are supported by the strongest empirical evidence. This empirically based approach has been described as the "eclectic approach" to social work practice (Fischer, 1978, p. 67). Practitioners who find only weak evidence might humbly admit that they simply do not know with certainty what is most effective.

Because eclecticism relies heavily on a practitioner's ability to weigh evidence fairly, the question of whether studies can be evaluated objectively becomes paramount. Weighing studies' objectivity is difficult or impossible without the guidance of a rating procedure. Lord, Ross, and Lepper (1979) identified 24 undergraduate psychology students whose attitude was strongly in favor of capital punishment as a way to deter murder. The investigators also identified 24 students who were strongly against capital punishment. Lord and his colleagues asked these two groups of students to rate the results and procedures of two fictitious studies, "one seemingly confirming and one seemingly disconfirming their existing beliefs about the deterrent efficacy of the death penalty" (p. 2098). The results of their experiment are not encouraging: Students in both groups rated study quality higher if it supported their bias, even though the two studies used methodology of comparable quality. Furthermore, although they had been asked to read an equal number of studies that favored and refuted capital punishment—suggesting an equivocal answer to the question of the deterrent effects of capital punishment—the students did not become less certain about their own beliefs. On the contrary, they ended up feeling stronger about their original position than they had before they read the studies! Apparently, seeing the equivocal studies *intensified* their bias.

Even full-fledged professionals find it difficult to be objective when trying to filter important evidence. Mahoney (1977) randomly submitted five different versions of an article to 75 professionals who reviewed articles for a particular journal. The article's versions were identical except that each had a different discussion and conclusion section. A higher proportion of the reviewers accepted the version of the article that supported their own position. Mahoney concluded that the reviewers' judgment was biased.

Those who review articles for social work journals may also be unknowingly influenced by bias. Epstein (1989) found a not statistically significant but nonetheless positive association between a bogus article's positive findings and its rate of acceptance by 33 core social work journals. Among the 33 journals, 47.1% accepted or conditionally accepted the positive version—meaning that the social worker's intervention was successful; 25.0% accepted the negative version—a difference of 22.1% favoring the positive version (p. 16). Among less prestigious social work journals, acceptance was statistically significantly in favor of the positive version (p. 16). Epstein has been criticized by angry editors for not telling journal editors and reviewers about his experiment (Feinberg, 1988).

Given the need to weigh studies objectively so they can be used to guide decision making, it is essential to find a way to evaluate study quality against clearly defined criteria. This chapter shows how to apply the Quality of Study Rating Form (QSRF). The form, designed for busy practitioners, may be used as a template by which to measure a study's prominent features.

THE QUALITY OF STUDY RATING FORM (QSRF)

Purpose

The Quality of Study Rating Form is intended to: (a) provide a quick, systematic, and reliable guide for busy practitioners who need to synthesize evaluation research for its practice implications; (b) summarize a few prominent features of an evaluation study; (c) help those who have limited exposure to research methods to rate an index of study quality reliably; (d) help those who have a limited exposure to concepts of meta-analysis compute two simple indices of a treatment method's effect size; and (e) help practitioners compare and synthesize these indices to select a method.

Background

Practitioners who want to use evaluation studies to guide their practice soon find that evaluation studies concern widely different designs, outcome measures, client types, intervention methods being evaluated, and magnitudes of outcome differences. Such variability across many studies can overwhelm a rational interpretation, because it is difficult to compare study quality and levels of client improvement systematically.

The QSRF was designed to meet the need for a reliable, brief, and relatively simple way to rate evaluations of social service methods. Standards for study quality, already discussed in previous chapters of this text and elsewhere in the research literature (Atherton & Klemmack, 1982; Grinnell, 1988; Monette, Sullivan & DeJong, 1986), are the basis for most of the criteria of the QSRF.

The QSRF builds on, or parallels, the work of others who have been concerned about how to rate study quality (Davitz & Davitz, 1967; Katzer, Cook, & Crouch, 1978; Soeken, 1985). At least three forms for rating evaluation studies now exist. These forms are a major step in the right direction. Chalmers et al. (1981) have developed a form for rating a randomized trial in medical research, but the form's criteria do not apply specifically to social work research, and its reliability for independent raters has not been measured (T. C. Chalmers, personal communication, October 8, 1987). A second form, created by Glass, McGaw, and Smith (1981), includes criteria for rating studies of effects of psychotherapy but, like the Chalmers form, it was not developed to measure social work interventions and was not evaluated for its interrater reliability. Fischer (1981) has developed a form for rating exploratory, descriptive, and experimental studies in social work, but it asks the rater to classify each of 80 study criteria as low to high without providing clear criteria for such classification. Fischer's form also has not been tested for its interrater reliability (J. Fischer, personal communication, October 14, 1987).

In addition to being based on criteria for a strong evaluation study, the QSRF is based on elementary principles of meta-analysis. **Meta-analysis,** a term coined by Glass (1976), also sometimes referred to as "data synthesis" (Nurius, 1984; Tripodi, 1982), is the "statistical analysis of a large collection of analysis results from individual studies for the purpose of integrating the findings" (Glass, 1976, p. 3). Those who use meta-analysis regard data from entire studies—rather than from individual subjects—as the unit of analysis. Those conducting meta-analysis combine studies for their collective wisdom by computing an index of treatment effect size for each study. The index is then compared across studies to make judgments. The QSRF contains two indices of treatment effect size.

Description

The QSRF and its explanation for criteria (see Table 9.1) are designed to help users to compute reliably one index of study quality and two indices of treatment effect size. The QSRF includes: (a) a section for identifying client type, treatment method, source of the study following APA format (American Psychological Association, 1983), and one outcome measure used to compute treatment effect size; (b) 15 weighted criteria concerning study quality that are added to compute a Total Quality Points Index; and (c) two common indices of treatment effect size (ES1 and ES2). The explanation for criteria (given in next section of this chapter) that accompanies the form gives an item-by-item description of each numbered criterion on the QSRF. Ideally, forms should be compiled for particular methods, client types, and outcome measures to make comparisons across methods, client types, and type-by-method interactions. However, conventional meta-analysis is computed across intervention only. For studies in which there are multiple outcome measures and multiple comparisons, averages of ES1 and ES2 can be computed.

To compute Total Quality Points (item 16), rate the study according to criteria 1–15, record each item's weight in the space provided beneath the criterion, then add the weights for items 1–15 and write the sum in column 16. That is the Total Quality Points (TQP) value.

Although users may disagree with item weighting and may want to apply their own weights, the form is presently arranged to allow TQP to range from 0 to 100. The first 15 items are assigned all-or-nothing weights because intermediate weights would have complicated the explanation for criteria and might have reduced overall reliability.

Items 16 and 17 rate common indices of treatment effect size: The first, ES1, is based on means, and the second, ES2, on proportions. These two indices provide standard metrics for comparing effect size across treatments.

Now examine the QSRF (given in Table 9.1) carefully and read the explanation for criteria (see following section). The form reviews concepts explained in previous chapters. As you read the form and its explanation for criteria, think of how you would rate the items on a study. You will be asked to rate a study that appears immediately following the form.

TABLE 9.1
Quality of Study Rating Form

Client Type(s)

Treatment Method(s)

Outcome Measure to Compute ES1

Outcome Measure to Compute ES2

Source (APA Format)

Criteria for Rating Study

Clear Definition of Treatment					6. Subjects randomly assigned to treatment or control (20 pts)	7. Subjects randomly selected (4 pts)	8. Nontreated control group (4 pts)
1 Who (4 pts)	2 What (4 pts)	3 Where (4 pts)	4 When (4 pts)	5 Why (4 pts)			

Criteria for Rating Study (cont.)

9. Number of subjects in smallest treatment group exceeds 20 (4 pts)	10. Outcome measure has face validity (4 pts)	11. Treatment outcome measure was checked for reliability (5 pts)	12. Reliability measure has value greater than .70 or percent of rater agreement greater than 70% (5 pts)	13. Outcome of treatment was measured after treatment was completed (4 pts)	14. Test of statistical significance was made and $p < 0.5$ (20 pts)

Criteria for Rating Study (cont.)   Criteria for Rating Effect Size

15. Follow-up greater than 75% (10 pts)	16. Total quality points (TQP)	17. Effect Size (ES1) $$ES1 = \frac{\bar{x}_t - \bar{x}_c}{s_c} = \frac{\text{(mean of treatment)} - \text{(mean of alternate treatment or control)}}{\text{standard deviation of control or alternate treatment}}$$		18. Effect Size (ES2) $ES2 = P_t - P_c$ = (proportion improved in treatment) − (proportion improved in control group or alternate treatment)

Note: From "Quality of Study Rating Form: An Instrument for Synthesizing Evaluation Studies" by L. E. Gibbs, 1989, *Journal of Social Work Education, 25*(1), p. 67. Copyright 1989 by The Council on Social Work Education. Adapted by permission.

Explanation of Criteria

In the Client Type and Treatment Methods sections, state briefly and specifically what the key identifying features are for client type (e.g., adult victims of sex abuse). Also list the principal treatment method and outcome measure. Use one form for each treatment comparison.

   Give either zero points or the particular point value indicated if the study meets the criterion, as numbered and described below:

1. The author describes *who* is treated by stating the subjects' average age, standard deviation of age and sex or proportion of males and females, and diagnostic category, for example, child abusers, schizophrenics.

2. The authors tell *what* the treatment involves so specifically that you could apply the treatment with nothing more to go on than their description, or they refer you to a book, videotape, or article that describes the treatment method.

3. Authors state *where* the treatment occurred so specifically that you could contact people at that facility by phone or by letter.

4. Authors tell the *when* of the treatment by stating how long subjects participated in the treatment in days, weeks, or months or tell how many treatment sessions were attended by subjects.

5. Authors either discuss a specific theory that justifies *why* they used one or more treatment methods or they cite literature that supports the use of the treatment method.

6. The author states specifically that subjects were *randomly assigned* to treatment groups or refers to the assignment of subjects to treatment or control groups on the basis of a table of random numbers or other accepted randomization procedure (see Chapter 5). Randomization implies that each subject has an equal chance of being assigned to either a treatment or control group. If the author says subjects are randomly assigned but assigns subjects to treatments by assigning every other one or by allowing subjects to choose their treatment groups, subjects are *not* randomly assigned.

7. As discussed in Chapter 5, *selection* of subjects is different from random *assignment*. Random selection means subjects are taken from some potential pool of subjects for inclusion in the study by using a table of random numbers or other random procedures; for example, if subjects are chosen randomly from among all residents in a nursing home, the results of the study can be generalized more confidently to all residents of the nursing home.

8. Members of the *nontreated control group* do not receive a different kind of treatment; they receive *no* treatment. An example of a nontreated control group would be a group of subjects who are denied group counseling while others are given group counseling. Subjects in the nontreated control group might receive treatment at a later date, but do not receive treatment while experimental group subjects are receiving their treatment.

9. Those in the treatment group or groups are those who receive some kind of special care intended to help them. It is this treatment that is being evaluated by those doing the study. The results of the study will state how effective the treatment or treatment groups have been when compared with each other or with a nontreated control group. In order to meet this criterion, the *number of subjects in the largest treatment group must be at least 21*. Here, "number of subjects" means total number of individuals, not number of couples or number of groups.

10. *Face validity of an outcome measure* is present if the outcome measure used to determine the effectiveness of treatment makes sense to you. A good criterion for the sense of an outcome measure is whether the measure evaluates something that should logically be affected by the treatment. For example, drinking behavior has face validity as an outcome measure for treating alcoholism. An intelligence quotient may not have face validity as an indicator for alcoholism treatment effect.

11. Some criterion or criteria must be used to measure the effectiveness of a treatment. Examples of such outcome measures might include number of days spent in the community after release from treatment before readmission, score on a symptom rating scale, or number of days after release from treatment during which no alcohol was consumed. For this criterion, it is not enough to merely state that outcome was measured in some way, the author must cite a measurement procedure or describe how the outcome was measured and evaluate the measure's reliability. *Reliability*—the consistency of measurement—is frequently measured in an outcome evaluation study by comparing the findings of investigators who independently rate the performance of individuals in treatment or nontreated control groups. Another less frequently used way to measure reliability of outcome measures is to have the same individual rate the performance of subjects and then rerate performance. In single-subject studies, two raters may rate the subject's behavior independently for cross-rater comparison.

    The reliability criterion is satisfied only if the author of the study affirms that evaluations were made of the outcome measure's reliability or interrater agreement, and the *author lists a numerical value of some kind for this measure of reliability*. Where multiple outcome criteria were used, a reliability check of one or more outcome criteria satisfies number 11.

12. The *reliability coefficient discussed in number 11 is .70* or greater (70% or better).

13. *At least one outcome measure was obtained after treatment was completed.* After release from the hospital, after drug therapy was completed, after subjects quit attending inpatient group therapy—all are posttreatment measures. For example, if subjects were released from the mental hospital on November 10, and some measure of success was obtained on November 11, then the study meets criterion 9. Outcome measured both during treatment and after treatment ended is sufficient to meet this criterion.

14. *Tests of statistical significance* are generally referred to by phrases such as "differences between treatment groups were significant at the .05 level" or "results show statistical significance for outcome." Give credit for meeting this criterion *only* if author refers to a test of statistical significance by name (e.g., analysis of variance, chi square, *t* test) *and* gives a *p* value, for example *p* < .05, *and* the *p* value is equal to or smaller than .05.

15. The proportion of subjects *successfully followed-up* refers to the number contacted to measure outcome compared with the number who began the experiment. To compute this proportion followed-up for each group studied (i.e., treatment group, control group), determine the number of subjects who initially entered the experiment in the group and determine the number successfully followed-up. (If there is more than one follow-up period, use the longest one.) Then for each group, divide the number successfully followed-up by the number who began in each group and multiply each quotient by 100. For example, if 20 entered a treatment group, but 15 were followed-up in that group, the result would be: (15/20)100 = 75%. Compute the proportion followed-up for all groups involved in the experiment. If the *smallest* of these percentages equals or exceeds 75%, the study meets this criterion.

16. Total quality points (TQP) is simply the sum of the point values for criteria 1–15.

17. Effect size (ES1) is a number that summarizes the strength of effect of a given treatment. The index can be computed as follows:

$$ES1 = (\bar{x}_t - \bar{x}_c)/(S_c)$$

$$= \frac{\text{(mean of treatment)} - \text{(mean of control or alternate treatment group)}}{\text{standard deviation of control or alternate treatment}}$$

This formula is for computing ES1 when outcome means of treatment groups and control groups are given. To compute an effect size from information presented in an article, select two means to compare; for example, outcome might be a mean of a treatment group compared with a mean of a nontreated control group. Subtract the mean of the second group from the mean of the first group and divide this value by the standard deviation of the second group. (Standard deviations are indicated by various signs and symbols, including *s.d., S, s, SD,* or σ.) ES1 may be a negative or positive number. If the number is positive, the first group may have the greater treatment effect—this assumes that positive outcome on the outcome measure implies larger numbers on that measure. If the ES1 is negative when comparing a treatment group against a control group, the treatment may produce a harmful or iatrogenic effect. If the number is negative when comparing two alternate treatments, the first treatment is less effective than the second. The larger a positive ES1 value, the stronger the effect of treatment.

18. We can also compute ES2 for proportions or percentages, using the formula:

$$ES2 = P_t - P_c = \left(\frac{\text{number improved in treatment}}{\text{total number in treatment group}} \times 100 \right)$$
$$- \left(\frac{\text{number improved in alternate treatment or control}}{\text{total number in alternate treatment or control}} \times 100 \right)$$

Assume that we are comparing the proportion in a treatment group who are improved against the proportion in a control group who are improved. Let us say that 70% of those in the treatment group are improved and 50% of those in the control group are also improved for a particular outcome measure. ES2 then equals 70% minus 50%, or 20%. Thus, the proportion of improvement attributable to the treatment may be 20%. As a general rule, ES1 and ES2 can be interpreted with greater confidence in studies with a higher TQP. However, even in stronger studies, results may be affected by factors other than those listed in the QSRF.

USING QSRF TO RATE A STUDY

The study presented in Figure 9.1 is an evaluation of an abduction- and sex-abuse prevention program for kindergartners and first- and second-graders at an urban elementary school in Denver. (Only the segments of the evaluation pertaining directly to parts of the QSRF are included.) Each part of the article that is relevant to a particular section on the QSRF is numbered according to the appropriate section of the QSRF. A short explanation of why the study meets or does not meet the QSRF's criterion appears next to each number. A completed QSRF (Table 9.2) contains the rating on each criterion.

  The last three pages of the article have been omitted to save space. In the final pages of their article, Kraizer, Fryer, and Miller (1988) argue that their program teaches children how to avoid an abduction without making them fearful. They also include a reference list on the last page.

Steps for Making Comparisons across Several Studies

Practitioners may conduct their own reviews using the QSRF, or they may collaborate with others who know how to use the QSRF to make comparisons across methods. Below are steps to follow when using the QSRF to select an intervention method:

1. Locate as many sources—ideally they will be studies—as you can that investigate the effectiveness of a *particular method* with a *particular client type*.

2. Rate each study—raters can work independently to share results because rating can be done reliably—according to criteria on the QSRF.

3. Make a table of the five sources concerning each method that score highest on TQP (see the blank Table 9.3).

Programming for Preventing Sexual Abuse and Abduction: What Does It Mean When It Works?

SHERRYLL KERNS KRAIZER
GEORGE E. FRYER
MARILYN MILLER

This article is
from *Child Welfare*,
1988, *67*(1), 69-78.

*Many kinds of educational programs and other
approaches to teaching children about the dangers of
sexual abuse and abduction by strangers can have the
"side effect" of creating new anxieties in the children.
The program described in this article is effective without
introducing negative, anxiety-producing stories,
examples, and other warnings.*

As the missing children campaign gathered steam in the mid-'80s and messages about strangers surrounded children, sexual abuse and abduction prevention programs became widespread. It is now the prevailing opinion that the missing children statistics were substantially inflated, which has unfortunately diminished the enthusiasm for addressing this problem with children in classrooms [Spitzer 1986; Hartmark 1986; Griego and Kilzer 1985; Gelman

*Sherryll Kerns Kraizer, M.S., is Director, Health Education Systems and Coalition
for Children, Palisades, NY. George E. Fryer, Jr., M.A., M.S.W., is Senior Instructor,
Department of Pediatrics, University of Colorado School of Medicine, Denver, CO.
Marilyn Miller, M.A., is Associate Director, Health Education Systems and Coalition
for Children, St. Louis, MO.*

0009-4021/88/010069-10 $1.50 © Child Welfare League of America

Where—The article
locates the authors
well enough to
contact them.

Where—This
address appears
on the article's
last page.

*(Address requests for a reprint to Sherryll Kerns Kraizer, Director, Health Education
Systems, Inc., Box GG, Palisades, NY 10964.)*

FIGURE 9.1

An application of QSRF. (Source: Reprinted with permission from Child Welfare 67(1),
January/February, 1988, pp. 69–74.)

70   CHILD WELFARE / Volume LXVII, Number 1 / January–February 1988

et al. 1986; USA Today 1986]. What was created which has not been addressed, however, is a pervasive and insidious anxiety on the part of vast numbers of young children in this country, as reflected by a Roper survey [1986] that reported 76% of the children were "worried that they might be kidnapped." While it is known that the vast majority of abuse takes place at the hands of people known to the child, not strangers, this does not diminish the need to provide prevention training for children to prevent both the fear and the reality of abduction.

Ask any child what she thinks a stranger is. The most common answer for children of all ages in all parts of the country is some version of, "Strangers are people who kidnap you, poison you, cut off your head and you never see your mommy and daddy ever again." Many prevention programs have reinforced this mentality and fed into the existing fear children have that they might at any moment become a "milk-carton child." This has been justified in many circles with statements such as, "I'd rather have my children be afraid and safe."

More recently, consideration has been refocused on the whole child, and concern has been expressed that messages of this kind may be damaging to children, that children may be more afraid and anxious after prevention programs are presented than before, and that these programs may not be effective in teaching the desired prevention skills [Conte et al. 1985a, 1985b; Kraizer 1986; National Committee for the Prevention of Child Abuse 1986]. The National Committee for the Prevention of Child Abuse points to this as a key issue in their Guidelines for Child Sexual Abuse Prevention Programs. "Sexual abuse prevention is a topic that can look deceptively simple. Some program materials foster this misconception by ignoring negative side effects, by assuming that new concepts will result in new and effective behavior."

(5) *Why*—No theory or evidence are cited to support the method; only evidence is cited to show that other programs may be harmful.

This article reports on an evaluation of a primary prevention program that parts from traditional ways of talking about strangers with children [Kraizer 1981]. It introduces documentation that education of children geared to prevention of abduction and abuse by strangers can be effective without introducing negative, anxiety-producing stories, examples, or other warnings.

The evaluation measured the actual behavioral change attributable to a prevention program and assessed the relationship of those results to more proximate measures normally associated with evaluation of such programs [Fryer et al. 1987a]. These results are discussed here in the context of what has been learned that can inform existing and future prevention efforts in the area of stranger awareness in particular, and more generally in the related areas of prevention of sexual abuse and safety for children in self-care.

(1) *Who*—Clients are children who might be abducted, but nowhere does the article give the necessary sex and age data.

FIGURE 9.1
continued

The Program

The "Children Need To Know: Personal Safety Training Program," developed in 1981, is a scripted primary prevention program designed to be used in a group classroom setting [Kraizer 1981]. It teaches prevention of sexual abuse by people known to the child, safety for children in self-care, and prevention of abuse and abduction at the hands of strangers—the focus of this evaluation. It begins by allowing children to voice their misconceptions about strangers, followed by discussion about what the word really means, acknowledges the predominance of nice strangers in the world and sets parameters for when children should be concerned with following rules about strangers. The primary messages are:

> A stranger is anyone you don't know.
>
> Most people are strangers and most of them are nice.
>
> You can't tell by looking who is nice and who isn't.
>
> When you are with an adult who is taking care of you, that adult is principally responsible for making decisions about strangers.
>
> When you're by yourself or with your friends, you must follow the rules with *all* strangers.

② *What*—Criterion 2 is met because the article references a detailed description of the program and describes its content.

The rules are taught positively through example, discussion, and extensive role play that allows children to actually experience implementing the rules and teaches them about the various things that might affect their thoughts. Each child has an opportunity to demonstrate mastery and to build his or her sense of competence and confidence in a wide range of possible situations.

Following are the specific rules the children learn to apply when they are without supervision:

> Stay an arm's reach away from someone you don't know. Keep a "Circle of Safety" around yourself.
>
> Don't talk to someone you don't know, including answering questions.
>
> Don't take anything from someone you don't know, not even something that belongs to you or your family.
>
> Don't go with someone you don't know, unless (for children six and up) the individual knows your predetermined family code word.

Through discussion, children visualize the point at which they might begin to feel uncomfortable or afraid with a stranger and plan just where and how to get help immediately and effectively.

FIGURE 9.1
continued

72   CHILD WELFARE / Volume LXVII, Number 1 / January–February 1988

The "What if . . . Game" is used to encourage children to think about the many applications of the rules, to actually walk through the scenarios, to provide a forum for dealing with existing fears and anxieties, and to engage teachers, parents, and even other children, in the process of continuing to build and reinforce their skills [Kraizer 1985].

The program is developmentally appropriate and skills are refined from year to year depending on the needs of the children in that particular age group. It focuses on empowerment and specifically omits all language that implies that children *should* be afraid.

Random Assignment   Number of Subjects ≥ 21

The Evaluation   (6)   (9)

The evaluation took place with kindergarten and first and second graders in a mid-town Denver elementary school in 1986. (Twenty-four children) each were (randomly assigned) to the treatment and (control groups.) A pretest-posttest control group design, the classical experimental design, was employed. Treatment group children participated in an (eight-day block of instruction consisting of 20-minute lessons each day.) Control group children participated in the program in the second phase six months later.   (4) *When*—Eight twenty-minute treatments

(8) Control Group

The simulation was undertaken only after extensive discussions with officials of the school district, parents, and teachers. In designing the simulation, the school setting was chosen because it is a protected and controlled environment were children encounter strangers every day.

(7) *No Random Selection*—This is the only part that discusses subject selection.

In the simulation, each child had an opportunity to leave the school building with a stranger (actually a member of the research team) [Fryer et al. 1987a]. As the child was encountered in the hall, the researcher/stranger requested the child's assistance by saying, "Hello, I'm presenting a puppet show here at the school today. I have some puppets and other neat things outside in my car. Will you come and help me bring them inside?" If the child agreed, he was told that the stranger would come for him later. If the child refused, the stranger responded with "Thanks anyway." After all of the children had participated in the simulation, a member of the research team went to the classrooms to let them know that the stranger had come to the office, as he should have, and had gotten the assistance he needed.

(10) *Face Validity of Outcome Measure*—Whether the child refuses a stranger seems valid.

Each simulated situation was simple, plausible, tightly controlled, and did not create anxiety or upset for the participating children. Because they perceived it to be a real situation, it was an accurate measure of the children's vulnerability to abduction and subsequent abuse. A hidden camera and wireless microphone provided a record of each encounter and enabled scores to

FIGURE 9.1
continued

Sherryll Kerns Kraizer / George E. Fryer / Marilyn Miller   73

be reviewed. A simple pass-fail rating was awarded each child. This indicated simply the child's agreement or nonagreement to accompany the stranger out of the building. Interrater reliability was 1.0 among the four evaluation team members.

The outcome measure was checked for reliability; the reliability coefficient was ≥ .70.

After the simulation, each child spent the next 30 minutes in a one-to-one meeting with a member of the research team. This allowed ample time to express any fear or anxiety and to report the encounter. Logistically, this was time consuming and labor intensive, but this considerable allocation of resources is necessary; one should not be made complacent by the fact that none of these 44 children required the special care for which provision had been made. It was during this time that instruments to measure receptive language ability, self-esteem, and knowledge and attitudes about personal safety were administered to the children.

One-half of the children (the treatment group, n = 23*) participated in the prevention program, which emphasized discovering and clarifying existing misconceptions about strangers; establishing clear, simple concrete rules and guidelines for their application; and intensive role-playing, practice, and discussion.

After the program, the simulations were repeated with another "stranger," making a different request, in another part of the school building. The knowledge-attitude and self-esteem instruments were also readministered. The performance of the group receiving no instruction (control group, n = 21**) remained the same in the second simulation. The children who participated in the prevention program dramatically improved their performance with only five of 23 children agreeing to the stranger's request. (See table 1.)

Outcome was measured after treatment ended.

The following school year, the control group participated in the prevention program and all the children participated in a final simulation [Fryer et al. 1987b]. After the prevention program, all of the control group children successfully refused the stranger's request to leave the school. Four of the treatment group children, who had failed in the previous year, participated in the program a second time and half of them subsequently demonstrated mastery of the program's techniques. The remaining treatment group children, who had received no intervention for six months, were resimulated to assess retention of their skills. All of these children successfully applied the rules and refused to go with the stranger.

In addition to the clear-cut reduction of vulnerability evidenced in the sim-

---

* 1 child from the original treatment group was absent.

**3 children from the original control group were absent.

Follow-up—23/24, or 96%, of the treatment group and 21/24, or 88%, of controls were posttested.

FIGURE 9.1
continued

TABLE 1   Program Participation and Simulation Outcome Sequence

	% Passed First Simulation	*Received the Program*	*% Passed Second Simulation*	*Received the Program*	*% Passed Third Simulation*
Control Group (N = 21)	52.4%	No	52.4%	Yes	100%
Experimental Group (N = 23)	43.5%	No	78.3%	(Previous Failures Only)	86.7%

⑱ $ES2 = P_t - P_c$
$= 78.3\% - 52.4\%$
$= 25.9\%$

$ES2 = P_t - P_c$
$= 86.7\% - 100\%$
$= -13.3\%$

ulation, this evaluation yielded valuable insights about programming and its relationship to other factors in the child's overall profile. These are significant as we strive to improve prevention programming and to make it responsive to the individual needs of all children.

Discussion and Implications

The most important notation that must be made about the evaluation of this approach to prevention is that it worked. The vulnerability of children was reduced and was sustained over time. The knowledge-attitude instrument and the assurance the children manifested in the simulation reflected the children's feeling more able to keep themselves safe, which acts as an antidote to fear. Beyond that, there are a number of related findings that are significant for refining existing and future programming for children.

⑭ *No Test of Statistical Significance*—The unreported X^2 is not statistically significant ($X^2 = 3.27$, $df = 1$, $p < .10 > .05$)

Knowing the "right" answers was not significantly predictive of success. Children's answers to the pencil-and-paper questions about personal safety did not ensure their ability to actually implement those techniques in the simulation. This is of major importance because pencil-and-paper tests have been the main criteria to date for assessing the effectiveness of prevention programs. It is clear that this measure of children's mastery of prevention concepts may be misleading as a predictor of their actual ability to protect themselves. In fact, the guidelines published by the National Committee for the Prevention of Child Abuse, mentioned earlier, suggest that, "Behavioral assessment strategies . . . represent the only means of estimating the strength of the behaviors that are being taught."

Nor is past performance a predictor of future successful resistance in the absence of prevention training. Three of the children who passed the first

FIGURE 9.1
continued

TABLE 9.2
Quality of Study Rating Form

| Client Type(s) |
| Potentially sexually abused school children |

| Treatment Method(s) |
| Role play in interpersonal safety training program |

Outcome Measure to Compute ES1

Outcome Measure to Compute ES2
    Whether child agreed to leave school with a stranger

Source (APA Format)

Criteria for Rating Study

Clear Definition of Treatment					6. Subjects randomly assigned to treatment or control (20 pts)	7. Subjects randomly selected (4 pts)	8. Nontreated control group (4 pts)
1 Who (4 pts)	2 What (4 pts)	3 Where (4 pts)	4 When (4 pts)	5 Why (4 pts)			
0	4	4	4	0	20	0	4

Criteria for Rating Study (cont.)

9. Number of subjects in smallest treatment group exceeds 20 (4 pts)	10. Outcome measure has face validity (4 pts)	11. Treatment outcome measure was checked for reliability (5 pts)	12. Reliability measure has value greater than .70 or percent of rater agreement greater than 70% (5 pts)	13. Outcome of treatment was measured after treatment was completed (4 pts)	14. Test of statistical significance was made and $p < 0.5$ (20 pts)
4	4	5	5	4	0

Criteria for Rating Study (cont.)   Criteria for Rating Effect Size

15. Follow-up greater than 75% (10 pts)	16. Total quality points (TQP)	17. Effect Size (ES1) $$ES1 = \frac{\bar{x}_t - \bar{x}_c}{s_c} = \frac{\text{(mean of treatment)} - \text{(mean of alternate treatment or control)}}{\text{standard deviation of control or alternate treatment}}$$	18. Effect Size (ES2) $ES2 = P_t - P_c$ = (proportion improved in treatment) − (proportion improved in control group or alternate treatment)
10	60		25.9%, −13.3%

Note: From "Quality of Study Rating Form: An Instrument for Synthesizing Evaluation Studies" by L. E. Gibbs, 1989, *Journal of Social Work Education, 25*(1), p. 67. Copyright 1989 by The Council on Social Work Education. Adapted by permission.

TABLE 9.3

Relative merits of intervention method for client type

Reference (Author, Date)	Treatment Method	Client Type	Outcome Measure	TQP	Average TQP for Five Best Studies	Mean ES1	Mean ES2

Directions:
1. Select your five best studies for a particular method and client type (highest TQP).
2. Enter the five studies' values in the table.
3. Make comparisons to see which methods tend to be best supported by good studies and which method produced greatest effect size.

4. For each method, compute the average for TQP, ES1, and ES2.
5. Use the method that scores highest on the averages described.

SOME STRENGTHS OF QSRF

Widely Applicable

An exciting characteristic of meta-analysis is the way effect size can be compared across studies and client types by method. Regardless of the outcomes being compared, if the outcome mean and standard deviation can be computed, then a rough comparison of the magnitude of a treatment's effect in standard deviation units (ES1) can be averaged for particular interventions. Such comparisons have generally been made across methods, including, for example: effects of inquiry methods for teaching science (Lott, 1983); 18 different forms of psychotherapy, including cognitive behavioral therapy, rational emotive therapy, client-centered therapy, reality therapy (Glass & Kliegel, 1983); small groups (Tallant, 1987); and a wide variety of methods used to alleviate behavioral, interpersonal, and medical problems (Dickersin, 1987). Similarly, if the proportion of those who improve in treatment can be determined for each method (ES2), the proportions can be compared across methods. Such proportions have been compared between methods used to help alcoholics (Glass et al., 1981, p. 32) and depressed persons (Janicak et al., 1985).

Basic procedures for meta-analysis are very simple. Fieldwork methods students can use the QSRF to rate study quality and effect size. Generally, students use the QSRF most efficiently in teams of three to search for studies that evaluate a chosen method. For each method and client type, students pool their studies, rate them, compute average ES1 and ES2 for each study, and present results of their review, using Table 9.3.

Rates Both Quality and Effect Size

The QSRF has two kinds of indices. Those doing meta-analyses generally compute indices of treatment effect size, but typically they do not systematically weigh study quality. Critics of meta-analysis are concerned that just computing effect size by itself ignores the quality of studies that underlie effect size (Bryant & Wortman, 1984; Eysenck, 1978; Kazdin, 1984; Wilson & Rachman, 1983). In spite of such warnings, works on meta-analysis still focus almost exclusively on its statistical aspects (Hedges, 1984; Hedges & Olkin, 1985; Wolf, 1986). To address this deficiency, the QSRF contains items for rating study quality.

Produces Reliable Ratings

High agreement among the QSRF's users is desirable. Higher agreement among independent raters implies that greater confidence can be placed in ratings. If practitioners have common referents about what they mean by a "good study" and "treatment effect size," then they can communicate more effectively about what methods are most likely to help clients.

An earlier version of the QSRF was evaluated by two different classes of fieldwork methods students (Gibbs, 1989). Students in both classes received instruction in how to use the QSRF and then rated studies for a graded quiz. On the first trial, 40 students rated an article by Denicola and Sandler (1980) concerning training abusive parents in child management skills. Students also rated an article by Liberman and Eckman (1981) analyzing the relative effectiveness of behavioral versus insight-oriented treatment methods for repeated suicide attempters. For the first article, the average was 96% agreement with the key for the first 14 items of the QSRF; 56% got the exact TQP value on the key, but none were asked to compute an index of effect size. For the second article, students averaged 95% agreement with the key for the first 14 items of the QSRF; 53% got the exact TQP value on the key, and in two trials student agreement with the key's value for ES1 was 53%.

During the second trial a year later, 48 students rated an article by Hefner and Prochaska (1984) regarding relative effectiveness of concurrent versus conjoint marital therapy. For this trial, the average was 81% agreement for the first 14 items of the QSRF; 23% got the exact TQP value on the key, and 94% and 77% of the students computed ES1 correctly in two trials.

Therefore, it seems fair to claim that users can use the QSRF reliably with these reservations: (a) reliability for ES2 was not evaluated; (b) the earlier version of the QSRF did not include item 15 regarding proportion lost to follow-up; and (c) students computed ES1 consistently in one trial but less reliably in another.

INTERPRETING INDICES ON THE QSRF

Total Quality Points

TQP is just a guide. Higher TQP implies greater confidence in a study's causal inference. TQP is only an ordinal scale, that is, a study with 80 points is higher than one with 40 points, but not necessarily twice as credible. Interpreting TQP values could be more meaningful if distributions of TQP values were available for many studies in social work that evaluate particular interventions with particular client types. Then one could compare one value against the appropriate distribution to judge its size. Students in methods classes have developed small distributions of TQP values while computing selection scores, but their reviews are not extensive enough to be reported here.

Computing ES1

ES1 refers to the mean of the treatment group, $\bar{x}_t$, minus the mean of the control group, or second treatment group, $\bar{x}_c$, all divided by the standard deviation of the control group, S_c:

$$ES1 = \frac{\bar{x}_t - \bar{x}_c}{S_c}$$

Variously designated as **d** by Cohen (1988, p. 20), **g** by Hedges (1984, p. 31), and Δ by Glass et al. (1981, p. 29), ES1 is an increasingly common statistic. Rosenthal (1978) lists ES1's formula among eight other formulas for computing effect size.

ES1 may be biased if variances are unequal across treatment, t, and control, c, groups. The denominator in the following formula compensates for such inequality:

$$ES1 = \frac{\bar{x}_t - \bar{x}_c}{\sqrt{[(N_t - 1)(S_t)^2 + (N_c - 1)(S_c)^2]/(N_t + N_c - 2)}}$$

Where

$\bar{x}_t$ and $\bar{x}_c$ = mean of the treatment group and mean of the control or
alternate treatment group, respectively

N_t = number in treatment group

S_t = standard deviation in treatment group

N_c = number in control or alternate treatment group

S_c = standard deviation in control or alternate treatment group

Here we use the shorter formula because: (a) it is simpler to compute; (b) differences in variances between groups are often negligible; (c) it is the one most commonly used; (d) using the control group variance avoids variance introduced by treatment; and (e) the untreated control group's variance may more accurately reflect the population. However, when two treatments are compared, and their standard deviations appear widely different, we use the longer formula.

For studies that include multiple comparisons over several time periods, one way to interpret ES1 for a study is to compute the mean of the multiple ES1s for the study. Another method, one that fieldwork students favor, is to identify the one outcome in a study that seems most valid and then compute that outcome's ES1 over the longest follow-up period.

Interpreting ES1

Cohen's Rule of Thumb

Jacob Cohen (1977) has proposed that, as a rule of thumb, ES1 values be considered "small" if approximately .2, "medium" if approximately .5, and "large" if approximately .8 (p. 24). These three broad levels are only approximate.

The Mean of the Treatment Group as a Percentile of the Control or Alternate Treatment Group

Another way to interpret ES1 assumes that the population values of both groups for some characteristic are normally distributed. In such cases, the first step is to compute ES1. Let us assume that the data in Table 9.4 summarize the number of independent living tasks (e.g., dressing, brushing teeth, combing hair, getting on a bus and arriving at the proper destination) accomplished by developmentally disabled persons in a social skills training group or in a control group (Dunlap & Iceman, 1985). The first column of Table 9.4 for both groups is the pretest, the second column is the posttest, the third column is a difference value—positive if the client has increased the number of independent living tasks during the interval from pretest to posttest, zero for no change, and negative for worse performance at posttest.

For the data in Table 9.4

$$\text{ES1} = \frac{\bar{x}_t - \bar{x}_c}{S_c} = \frac{3.33 - .35}{5.62} = .53$$

To interpret this "medium" effect size value more precisely, look up ES1 = .53 as the Z value in a table of cumulative normal probabilities in a statistics text. In this case, the corresponding cumulative probability is .7019, or almost exactly 70% (Hays, 1981, p. 646). Thus the mean of the social skills training group is above 70% of the values in the control group. Note in Figure 9.2 that the mean of the treatment group lies at the 70th percentile of the control group. If the groups were identical in the amount of change between pretest and posttest, the cumulative normal probability value would be 50%. If those in the social skills group did worse than the control group, indicating possible iatrogenic effects of group treatment, the cumulative normal probability value would be lower than 50%.

Experience with ES1

A third way to interpret ES1 is to look at distributions of ES1 values for studies of methods that have been used to help similar clients with similar problems. For example, a meta-analysis might report mean ES1 values for multiple evaluations of treatments for developmentally disabled persons who are trying to learn independent living tasks. Unfortunately, this problem does not appear to have been addressed by published meta-analyses. However, to illustrate how a summary of effect sizes might be laid out, Table 9.5 shows how ES1 values have been summarized for different forms of psychotherapy. Table 9.5 summarizes the mean and standard deviations for effect sizes from 475 studies for 18 different methods of psychotherapy. Clearly, cognitive therapies appear to be generally most effective among psychotherapies (their average ES1 = 2.38).

TABLE 9.4
Independent living tasks completed for social skills training group versus controls

Social Skills Group			Control Group		
Pretest	Posttest	Difference	Pretest	Posttest	Difference
9	10	1	9	8	−1
8	12	2	8	4	−4
9	15	6	9	2	−7
5	1	−4	5	3	−2
8	17	9	8	1	−7
17	19	2	17	10	−7
2	6	4	2	8	6
11	14	3	11	14	3
5	10	5	5	19	14
3	5	2	3	5	2
4	9	5	4	9	5
2	20	18	2	4	2
3	10	7	3	10	7
4	1	−3	4	10	6
9	5	−4	9	15	6
2	1	−1	2	1	−1
8	4	−4	8	5	−3
1	6	5	10	5	−5
9	15	6	9	8	−1
10	17	7	10	4	−6

Note: $N_t = 20$; $N_c = 20$; $\bar{x}_t = 3.33$; $\bar{x}_c = .35$; $S_t = 5.14$; $S_c = 5.62$; $P_t = (^{15}/_{20})\,100 = 75\%$; $P_c = (^9/_{20})\,100 = 45\%$; $t = 1.688$, 38 df; $x^2 = 3.75$, 1 df.

Interpreting ES2

ES2 is quite simple to interpret. ES2—the difference between the proportion improved in one treatment compared with the proportion improved in another treatment or control group—may be displayed graphically in what Rosenthal and Rubin (1982, p. 167) refer to as a binomial effect size display (BESD). A BESD appears in Table 9.6 for the proportions improved given in Table 9.4.

　　In the BESD in Table 9.6, ES2 = $P_t - P_c$ = 75% − 45% = 30%; that is, there is a 30% difference favoring those who received social skills training over those who did not.

Relationships Between ES1 and ES2

If insufficient information is given to compute ES2, it can sometimes be approximated. If we can assume that groups to be compared have characteristics that are normally distributed, are of approximately equal variance, are of approximately equal size, and individuals change in equal amounts, there are ways to approximate ES2 given ES1 or common tests of statistical significance (Rosenthal, 1984, p. 25; Rosenthal & Rubin, 1982, p. 167). These approximate transfor-

FIGURE 9.2
*For ES1 = .53 the mean of the
treatment group lies at the 70th
percentile of the control group's
distribution.*

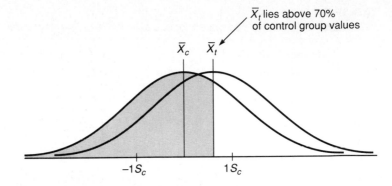

mations might be useful to complete item 18 of the QSRF, or to determine the more interpretable ES2 from ES1 or from statistical tests.

Assuming such conditions, to approximate ES2 from ES1 for data in Table 9.4:

$$ES2 = \frac{ES1}{\sqrt{(ES1)^2 + 4}}$$

$$ES2 = \frac{.53}{\sqrt{.53^2 + 4}}$$

ES2 = .26 (does not equal exactly .30 because continuous values were used to compute ES1 from data in Table 9.4)

To approximate ES2 from a *t* test of statistical significance for data in Table 9.4:

$$ES2 = \sqrt{\frac{t^2}{t^2 + df}}$$

$$ES2 = \sqrt{\frac{1.688^2}{1.688^2 + 38}}$$

ES2 = .26 (does not equal exactly .30 because continuous values were used to compute *t* from data in Table 9.4)

CONCLUSION AND CAUTIONS

The QSRF helps to operationalize an eclectic approach to practice by providing a reliable standard for weighing evidence. A reliable standard implies that practitioners who share a knowledge of the QSRF may come to better agreement about which methods hold the most promise in terms of ways to help clients.

On the other hand, as with any measurement instrument, there are problems with the QSRF. First, although QSRF's criteria numbered 1–16 may be applied

TABLE 9.5

Average effect size, standard deviation, standard error, and number of effects for each therapy type

Type of Therapy	Average Effect Size	SD	SE_m	No. of Effects[a]
1. Other cognitive therapies	2.38	2.05	.27	57
2. Hypnotherapy	1.82	1.15	.26	19
3. Cognitive-behavioral therapy	1.13	.83	.07	127
4. Systematic desensitization	1.05	1.58	.08	373
5. Dynamic-eclectic therapy	.89	.86	.08	103
6. Eclectic-behavioral therapy	.89	.75	.12	37
7. Behavior modification	.73	.67	.05	201
8. Psychodynamic therapy	.69	.50	.05	108
9. Rational-emotive therapy	.68	.54	.08	50
10. Implosion	.68	.70	.09	60
11. Transactional analysis	.67	.91	.17	28
12. Vocational-personal development	.65	.58	.08	59
13. Gestalt therapy	.64	.91	.11	68
14. Client-centered therapy	.62	.87	.07	150
15. Adlerian therapy	.62	.68	.18	15
16. Placebo treatment	.56	.77	.05	200
17. Undifferentiated counseling	.28	.55	.06	97
18. Reality therapy	.14	.38	.13	9
Total	.85	1.25	.03	1,761

[a]The number of effects, not the number of studies; 475 studies produced 1,761 effects, or about 3.7 effects per study.

Note: From "An Apology for Research Integration in the Study of Psychotherapy" by G. V. Glass and R. M. Kliegel, 1983, *Journal of Consulting and Clinical Psychology, 51*(1), p. 31. Copyright 1983 by the American Psychological Association, Inc. Reprinted by permission.

TABLE 9.6
Binomial effect size display for proportions improved in social skills training and control groups

	Improved	Not Improved	Total
Treatment	15 (75%) P_t	5 (25%)	20 (100%)
Control	9 (45%) P_c	11 (55%)	20 (100%)

to single-subject studies, ES3 and ES4 were not added to the form as indices to synthesize single-subject studies. Indices of effect size for single-subject study synthesis are being developed that are analogous to ES1 (Corcoran, 1985; Gingerich, 1984) and ES2 (Scruggs, Mastropieri, & Casto, 1987a), but such indices are too controversial to apply until the dust settles a bit (Salzberg, Strain, & Baer, 1987; Scruggs, Mastropieri, & Casto, 1987b; White, 1987). Second, although ES1 and ES2 are often averaged across studies to arrive at a composite statistic, more refined procedures exist for aggregating indices of effect size (Wolf, 1986, pp. 39–40). And finally, there are numerous problems with meta-analysis as a method, including the "file drawer" problem: Negative findings may be filed away and not get into the literature because journal editors are biased toward accepting articles that demonstrate effective methods (Rosenthal, 1984, p. 125).

SUMMARY

The filter approach to weighing evidence is superior to the sponge approach because it fosters clearer decision making against specific standards. In this chapter we presented the Quality of Study Rating Form, which operationally defines a filter approach for evaluating social work literature.

The QSRF, an instrument for rating the strength of a study's causal inference and magnitude of its treatment effect, was developed because: (a) even professionals, who are highly trained in research methods, can have difficulty rating study quality objectively; (b) busy practitioners need a quick way to weigh study quality and treatment effect size to guide their decision making; and (c) faced with increasing numbers of relevant studies, practitioners need a way to sort through the evidence quickly.

The QSRF as a measurement tool has been applied reliably by social work students to rate study quality and effect size. Indices of effect size can be used to make more precise comparisons across treatments to compare their effects.

EXERCISES

For some practice with the QSRF, obtain one or more of these three studies:

- Denicola, J., & Sandler, J. (1980). Training abusive parents in child management and self-control skills. *Behavior Therapy, 11,* 263–270.
- Hefner, C. W., & Prochaska, J. O. (1984). Concurrent vs. conjoint marital therapy. *Social Work, 29*(3), 287–291.
- Liberman, R. P., & Eckman, T. (1981). Behavior therapy vs. insight-oriented therapy for re-

peated suicide attempters. *Archives of General Psychiatry, 38*(1), 1126–1130.

1. Rate each of the three studies according to the first 16 criteria on the Quality of Study Rating Form; then compare your rating against the answer key in Appendix C.
2. Compute the following effect sizes.
   For the Hefner and Prochaska (1984) article:
   a. What is ES1 for the Index of Marital Satisfaction at posttest for concurrent therapy

as the first treatment? (Use the standard deviation for conjoint therapy.)

b. What is ES1 for the Locke-Wallace Marital Adjustment Test at posttest?

For the Liberman and Eckman (1981) article:

c. What is ES1 at 36-week follow-up on the Reinforcement Survey Schedule for behavior therapy as the first treatment? (Use the standard deviation for insight-oriented psychotherapy.)

d. What is ES2 at 2-year follow-up for success being no suicide attempts across the behavior therapy versus insight-oriented psychotherapy groups?

e. What is ES2 at 2-year follow-up for success being no suicidal plans or vague plans across behavior therapy versus insight-oriented therapy?

REFERENCES

American Psychological Association (1983). *Publication manual of the American Psychological Association* (3rd ed.). Washington, DC: American Psychological Association.

Atherton, C. R., & Klemmak, D. L. (1982). *Research methods in social work*. Lexington, MA: D. C. Heath.

Browne, M. N., & Keeley, S. M. (1981). *Asking the right questions*. Englewood Cliffs, NJ: Prentice-Hall.

Bryant, F. B., & Wortman, P. M. (1984). Methodological issues in the meta-analysis of quasi-experiments. In W. H. Yeaton & P. M. Wortman (Eds.), *New Directions for Program Evaluation: Issues in data synthesis* (pp. 5–24). *Vol. 24*. San Francisco: Jossey-Bass.

Chalmers, T. C., Smith, H., Blackburn, B., Silverman, B., Schroeder, B., Reitman, D., & Ambroz, A. (1981). A method for assessing the quality of a randomized control trial. *Controlled Clinical Trials, 2*, 31–49.

Cohen, J. (1977). *Statistical power analysis for the behavioral sciences.* (rev. ed.). New York: Academic Press.

Cohen, J. (1988). *Statistical power analysis for the behavioral sciences.* Hillsdale, NJ: Lawrence Erlbaum Associates.

Corcoran, K. J. (1985). Aggregating the idiographic data of single-subject research. *Social Work Research & Abstracts, 21*, 9–12.

Davitz, J. R., & Davitz, L. L. (1967). *Evaluating research proposals in the behavioral sciences: A guide* (2nd ed.). New York: Teachers College Press.

Denicola, J., & Sandler, J. (1980). Training abusive parents in child management and self-control skills. *Behavior Therapy, 11*, 263–270.

Dickersin, K. (Ed.). (1987, April). *Publications concerned with methodological issues related to meta-analysis.* (Available from Kay Dickersin, School of Hygiene and Public Health, Johns Hopkins University, 615 N. Wolfe Street, Baltimore, MD 21205.)

Dunlap, W. R., & Iceman, D. J. (1985). The development and validation of a set of instruments to assess the independent living skills of the handicapped. *Educational and Psychological Measurement, 45*, 54–61.

Emery, R. E., & Wyer, M. M. (1987). Child custody mediation and litigation: An experimental evaluation of the experience of parents. *Journal of Consulting and Clinical Psychology, 55*(2), 179–186.

Epstein, W. M. (1989). *Confirmational response bias among social work journals.* Manuscript submitted for publication.

Eysenck, H. J. (1978). An exercise in mega-silliness. *American Psychologist, 33*, 517.

Feinberg, L. (1988, December 17). Panel orders social worker to apologize. *Washington Post*, p. B5.

Fischer, J. (1978). *Effective casework practice: An eclectic approach.* New York: McGraw-Hill.

Fischer, J. (1981). A framework for evaluating empirical research reports. In R. M. Grinnell (Ed.), *Social work research and evaluation.* Itasca, IL: F. E. Peacock.

Gibbs, L. E. (1989). Quality of Study Rating Form: An instrument for synthesizing evaluation studies. *Journal of Social Work Education, 25*(1), 55–67.

Gingerich, W. J. (1984). Meta-analysis of applied time-series data. *Journal of Applied Behavioral Science, 20*(1), 71–79.

Glass, G. V. (1976). Primary, secondary, and meta-analysis of research. *Educational Researcher, 5*(10), 3–8.

Glass, G. V., & Kliegel, R. M. (1983). An apology for research integration in the study of psychotherapy. *Journal of Consulting and Clinical Psychology, 51*(1), 28–41.

Glass, G. V., McGaw, B., & Smith, M. L. (1981). *Meta-analysis in social research*. Beverly Hills, CA: Sage.

Grinnell, R. M. (Ed.). (1988). *Social work research & evaluation*. (3rd ed.). Itasca, IL: F. E. Peacock.

Hays, W. L. (1981). *Statistics* (3rd ed.). New York: Holt, Rinehart & Winston.

Hazelrigg, M. D., Cooper, H. M., & Borduin, C. M. (1987). Evaluating the effectiveness of family therapies: An integrative review and analysis. *Psychological Bulletin, 101*(3), 428–442.

Hedges, L. V. (1984). Advances in statistical methods for meta-analysis. In W. H. Yeaton & P. M. Wortman (Eds.). *New Directions for Program Evaluation. Vol. 24. Issues in data synthesis* (pp. 25–42). San Francisco: Jossey-Bass.

Hedges, L. V., & Olkin, I. (1985). *Statistical methods for meta-analysis*. Orlando: Academic Press.

Hefner, C. W., & Prochaska, J. O. (1984). Concurrent vs. conjoint marital therapy. *Social Work, 29*(3), 287–291.

Herink, R. (1980). *The psychotherapy handbook*. New York: New American Library.

Janicak, P. G., Davis, J. M., Gibbons, R. D., Ericksen, S., Chang, S., & Gallagher, P. (1985). Efficacy of ECT: A meta-analysis. *American Journal of Psychiatry, 142*(3), 297–302.

Katzer, J., Cook, K. H., & Crouch, W. W. (1978). *Evaluating information: A guide for users of social science research*. Reading, MA: Addison-Wesley.

Kazdin, A. E. (1984). The role of meta-analysis in the evaluation of psychotherapy. *Clinical Psychology Review, 5*(1), 49–61.

Kraizer, S. K., Fryer, G. E., & Miller, M. P. (1988). Programming for preventing sexual abuses and abduction: What does it mean when it works? *Child Welfare, 67*(1), 69–78.

Liberman, R. P., & Eckman, T. (1981). Behavior therapy vs. insight-oriented therapy for repeated suicide attempters. *Archives of General Psychiatry, 38*(1), 1126–1130.

Lord, C. G., Ross, L., & Lepper, M. R. (1979). Biased assimilation and attitude polarization: The effects of prior theories on subsequently considered evidence. *Journal of Personality and Social Psychology, 37*(11), 2098–2109.

Lott, G. W. (1983). The effect of inquiry teaching and advance organizers upon student outcomes in science education. *Journal of Research in Science Teaching, 20*(5), 437–451.

Mahoney, M. J. (1977). Publication prejudice: An experimental study of confirmatory bias in the peer review system. *Cognitive Therapy and Research, 1*(2), 161–175.

Meehl, P. E. (1973). *Psychodiagnosis: Selected papers*. Minneapolis: University of Minnesota Press.

Monette, D. R., Sullivan, T. J., & DeJong, C. R. (1986). *Applied social research*. New York: Holt, Rinehart and Winston.

Nurius, P. S. (1984). Utility of data synthesis for social work. *Social Work Research & Abstracts, 20*(3), 23–32.

Pearson, J., & Thoennes, N. (1982). *Divorce mediation: Strengths and weaknesses over time*. Denver, CO: Center for Policy Research and the Divorce Mediation Project.

Rosenthal, R. (1978). Combining results of independent studies. *Psychological Bulletin, 85,* 185–193.

Rosenthal, R. (1982). A simple, general purpose display of magnitude of experimental effect. *Journal of Educational Psychology, 79*(2), 166–169.

Rosenthal, R. (1984). Applied social research series, Vol. 6: *Meta-analytic procedures for social research*. Beverly Hills, CA: Sage.

Rosenthal, R. & Rubin, V. B. (1982). A simple, general purpose display of magnitude of experimental effect. *Journal of Educational Psychology, 74*(2), 166–168.

Salzberg, C. L., Strain, P. S., & Baer, D. M. (1987). Meta-analysis of single-subject research: When does it clarify, When does it obscure? *Remedial and Special Education, 8*(2), 43–48.

Scruggs, T. E., Mastropieri, M. A., & Casto, G. (1987a). Response to Salzberg, Strain, and Baer. *Remedial and Special Education, 8*(2), 49–52.

Scruggs, T. E., Mastropieri, M. A., & Casto, G.

(1987b). Reply to Owen White. *Remedial and Special Education, 8*(2), 40–42.

Scruggs, T. E., Mastropieri, M. A., & Casto, G. (1987). The quantitative synthesis of single-subject research: Methodology and validation. *Remedial and Special Education, 8*(2), 24–33.

Soeken, K. L. (1985). Critiquing research: Steps of complete evaluation of an article. *AORN Journal, 41*(5) 882–893.

Tallant, S. H. (1987). Meta-analysis: Statistical considerations and applications in small group treatment research. *Social Work with Groups, 9*(3), 43–53).

Tripodi, T. (1982). The use of data synthesis of social work [Editorial]. *Social Work Research and Abstracts, 18,* 2.

White, O. R. (1987). Some comments concerning "The Quantitative Synthesis of Single-Subject Research." *Remedial and Special Education, 8*(2), 34–39.

Wilson, G. T., & Rachman, S. J. (1983). Meta-analysis and the evaluation of psychotherapy outcome: Limitations and liabilities. *Journal of Consulting and Clinical Psychology, 51*(1), 54–64.

Wolf, F. M. (1986). *Meta-analysis: Quantitative methods for research synthesis.* Beverly Hills, CA: Sage.

Better Decision Making in Social Work Practice

THE INESCAPABILITY OF DECISION MAKING

Social workers are eminently practical people. They have to be. Although typically overworked and short on time and resources, they must try to solve some of the most complex, resistive, and knotty problems faced by any discipline. To make maximum use of scarce resources, their decision making often involves assessing the probability that clients will behave in particular ways. They also typically decide which interventions will benefit clients in general and which interventions will benefit high-risk clients.

To illustrate how a social worker can grapple with life-affecting decisions Marilynn Carrier, a social worker with a BSW degree and 16 years of experience, agreed to keep a week's log as she worked in the community with her 45 chronically mentally ill clients. Following are some excerpts from Ms. Carrier's diary (terms that imply judgment are italicized):

> Joe is chronically mentally ill and has been in and out of institutions for 33 years; I have had Joe for the last 2. I have placed him everywhere in the world. I placed him 2 weeks ago at L. E. Phillips [chemical dependency treatment facility] for using drugs and alcohol. Joe is also diagnosed as schizophrenic and sociopathic. He was really using heavily. He stayed at L. E. Phillips one week, and suddenly it blew. He called me up and wanted me to get him, "Right now!" I said, "No! You choose to leave there, you walk. I'm not a taxi service. If you can make that judgment, go." At L. E. Phillips, he was also threatening to kill his wife. Well, Joe didn't have anywhere to go and he wound up sleeping in poison ivy. He was extremely miserable by Saturday and he turned himself in to the police. . . . We got him out of jail Monday and placed him. . . . If Joe doesn't make it there in his placement,

he *probably* won't make it anywhere. . . . Joe has been in prison, now he's on probation. When people make threats of suicide or killing someone I *never take them
lightly,* and I am real glad that I haven't. . . . When *they are making threats like that,*
you get them somewhere safe. . . . With Joe I was aware that he had been in prison;
he had been violent; he had shot his own hand off; he broke a police officer's nose;
and I think it was *highly likely* that he could hurt his wife. [Ms. Carrier has assessed
risk of violence in Joe's case.]

We decided to commit Bill [another client]. Bill was severely depressed. He
had a linoleum knife, and he was talking about doing himself in. He met the criteria for admission because he was so depressed and suicidal. With Bill it is hard to
say what he would do. He gets control by using his depression and "poor me" behavior. I think he *could hurt himself* unintentionally. . . . I'm *sure* he would have
gestured [attempted suicide]. . . . His mom and I went up there [to the hospital] last
Thursday at his insistence. Bill would not talk with me. He had his legs up to his
nose and a blanket over his head with a pillow over that. [Ms. Carrier has assessed
suicide risk here.]

Janet is a very middle class gal, very pretty gal, and I have been talking with
her mother trying to find out what is going on with her. I have said all along, listening to her mom, that she did not have emotional problems. . . . Is she chemically
dependent, or is she mentally ill? Anyway, my gut feeling back in April was that
Janet was *probably* chemically dependent, and that her emotional problems were
probably caused by her playing around with pills. [Ms. Carrier judges that it is more
likely that Janet is chemically dependent.]

HOW DECISIONS IMPLY WEIGHING PROBABILITIES

Ms. Carrier's decisions imply a weighing of the likelihood of events, for example:
"If Joe doesn't make it there in his placement, he *probably* won't make it
anywhere."

Any practice-related decision requires a judgment about the underlying
likelihood of an event, a weighing of a probability. For example the statement,
"Innovative strategies are being tested in an attempt to develop more effective
ways to deal with children and families at risk," (Harris, 1988, p. 483) implies
that particular children and families with a higher probability of child abuse and
neglect can be identified. The statement, "Many states are attempting to change
the odds for children in high risk families by moving toward intensive home-based
services," (Harris, 1988, p. 483) implies that the probability of improvement for
such families will be greater in intensive home-based programs. The statement,
"Ideally, programs should be individually tailored to provide the particular skills
and supports each person requires," (Salem, Seidman, & Rappaport, 1988, p.
403) assumes that the probability of improvement is greater when particular
clients are matched with particular support programs.

MAKING PROBABILITIES EXPLICIT

Typically, practitioners use imprecise words—high risk, at risk, probable, chance,
likely, unlikely, possible, impossible, probably, certainly—to describe their judgments about the likelihood of events. These words express an assessment of like-

lihood, but, unfortunately, they can imply a wide range of probabilities to different individuals. For example, when 18 social work fieldwork students were asked to rate the frequency implied by the word *probably,* from 0% (meaning no occurrences) through 50% (meaning exactly as likely as not to occur) to 100% (meaning 100 events of 100 possible), the fieldwork students had a mean rating for *probably* of 69%, *SD* = 12%, with a range from 50% to 90%. Even for the term *certainly,* the students' mean was 92%, *SD* = 8%, with a range from 75% to 100%. Various meanings for quantifying words can confuse decision makers.

Practitioners who learn how to state probabilities explicitly tend to communicate more clearly with each other and consequently make more accurate decisions. Probability refers to a number ranging from 0 to 1 that reflects a judgment about how likely it is that an event will occur (see Figure 10.1). Although probabilities are conventionally expressed as a decimal value between 0 and 1, the familiar percentage seems easier to understand and will be used here. Probabilities expressed as a percentage have these four characteristics: (a) events that are certain to happen have a value of 100%; (b) events that are certain not to happen have a value of 0%; (c) events that are exactly as likely as not to happen have value of 50%; and (d) the probability that an event will not happen plus the probability that it will happen is 100%.

Belief about the relative frequency of an event in the long run underlies judgment about probability. For example, if experience over the past 3 years in a protective service agency has shown that there were 154 cases of reabused children among the 512 initially confirmed cases handled by the agency, the probability of reabuse in that sample is: (154/512)100 = 30%. The figure 30% is the value of the **prior probability**—probability of the problem before any new assessment information is interpreted on new cases. (See Figure 10.2.) This concept is basic to decision making (Sox, Blatt, Higgins, & Marton, 1988, p. 5), although its importance is often ignored or misunderstood by those making decisions (Arkes, 1981; Eddy, 1982). Prior probability will be covered in more detail later, but for now let us consider the prior probability to be the **base rate** or **prevalence rate,** which is the frequency of a problem's occurrence among a group of people.

Judgments about probabilities have powerful implications for action. For example, if a protective service worker, who is knowledgeable about prior probability and additional assessment data, states that the probability is 90% that a child will be abused or neglected during the next 6 months, the practitioner is pretty sure that the child will be abused. In this case, the protective service worker would take action to prevent abuse by petitioning the court to remove the child from the home or would take some other conservative action to prevent abuse/neglect. If the probability were judged to be 10%, the protective service worker would take less drastic action.

FIGURE 10.1
Probability of an event.

0%	50%	100%
Event Certain *Not* to Happen	Event as Likely as Not to Happen	Event Certain to Happen

FIGURE 10.2
Prior probability of an event.

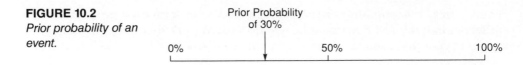

THE NEED TO ASSESS RISK

Social workers are called on to weigh **risk**—the probability of an undesirable event. They cannot escape the need to assess risk in literally every social work setting with literally every type of client. How the social worker weighs risk can have a profound effect on the life of a client and indirectly on the lives of others with whom the client comes in contact. For example, intake workers in mental health facilities can encounter clients who may be suicidal. Assessing risk in such cases requires weighing the probability that a client might commit suicide in the immediate future if not hospitalized, against the costs, inconvenience, and stigma that would result from an unnecessary inpatient stay in a treatment facility if the client is not suicidal. Because suicide is such an irreversible tragedy, it has been the subject of numerous risk-assessment measures (Beck, Kovacs, & Weissman, 1979; Motto, Heilbron, & Juster, 1985; Zung, 1974). Likewise, social workers in corrections, who weigh the risk of recidivism among probationers and parolees, record their impressions in presentence reports or parole plans for a judge's consideration. Such impressions play a major role in determining the client's freedom and substantially affect the lives of potential victims. Consequently, weighing the likelihood of a new offense in corrections has generated risk-assessment tools (Hoffman, 1986). Social workers in child welfare have developed measures to determine which families have greater likelihood of a child being placed in foster care (Magura, Moses, & Jones, 1987) and which foster home placements are more likely to be successful (Stone & Stone, 1983). Family therapists have developed an instrument to predict marital success (Fowers & Olson, 1986). Measures are also being developed to assess the probability of a child being reabused when the initial abuse has been confirmed (Wells, 1986, p. 52).

As these examples show, there seems to be a trend toward developing risk-assessment instruments, especially for decision making in child welfare. Practitioners need to know how to judge whether a risk-assessment measure is likely to be useful. The rest of this chapter clarifies issues in risk assessment and shows how to judge the predictive value of a risk-assessment tool.

DEFINING CLINICAL AND ACTUARIAL METHODS

Before describing literature that compares the efficiency of clinical versus actuarial (statistical) methods for predicting client behavior, a brief definition would be helpful. **Actuarial methods** for prediction involve, in some form, the following steps:

1. Identifying client characteristics that may have predictive value
2. Developing ways to measure those characteristics through interview guides, questionnaires, or rating scales

3. Measuring those characteristics among clients in an at-risk group

4. Determining through statistical means which characteristics were of the greatest predictive value

5. Revising the risk-assessment instrument and classifying at-risk clients into high- and low-risk groups

6. Comparing the predictive accuracy of the classification against the prevalence rate in a new sample of clients

7. Judging the utility of the predictive instrument based on that comparison

Clinical prediction is less systematic. In **clinical prediction** the practitioner looks at salient features of a client's records, examines test results, conducts interviews, and considers whatever information seems salient to classifying subjects into high- and low-risk groups, and then makes a prediction.

One actuarial method, the Michigan Screening Profile of Parenting (MSPP), is a 72-item questionnaire devised to predict child abuse (Schneider, 1982); other abuse prediction instruments are also available (Vietze, O'Connor, Hopkins, Sandler, & Altemeier, 1982). The MSPP measures attributes that are currently believed to be distinguishing characteristics of parents who will later abuse or neglect their child. Parents who score above a particular cutoff score are considered high risk. The MSPP measures four dimensions: (a) the relationship that new parents have had with their own parents, (b) whether new parents have reasonable expectations of a child, (c) the parents' ability to trust others based on their own upbringing, and (d) the parents' ability to cope effectively with stress. To measure each of these dimensions, respondents are asked to rate their degree of disagreement/agreement with each of the 72 test items. Here are four MSPP items, each from one of the four dimensions MSPP measures:

1. No one has ever really listened to me.

2. Children need to be taught, even before the age of 2 years, what parents want them to do.

3. My mother and I have always gotten along well.

4. Sometimes I feel like running away. (Schneider, 1982, pp. 160–161)

If the MSPP has predictive value, it might guide successful prevention efforts; for example, a practitioner who works with children in day care might want to administer the MSPP to the children's parents to identify those who might be in serious need of parenting skills training or to prevent abuse by high-risk parents. Medical social workers associated with prenatal care clinics might also use the MSPP to identify those who might benefit from parenting classes.

EMPIRICAL EVIDENCE REGARDING SUPERIORITY OF ACTUARIAL PREDICTION

Practitioners who have been seasoned by years of assessing, treating, and following-up clients sometimes become confident that they can assess risk effectively, but in virtually every formal comparison, when judgments by clinicians are pitted against judgments based on actuarial methods, the actuarial method has predicted client behavior at least as effectively. Paul Meehl's 1954 review of approximately 16 studies of clinical versus statistical prediction for recidivism, performance in training or schooling, and prognosis among mentally ill persons, found that in all but one study predictions made actuarially were either approximately equal or superior to those made by a clinician (p. 119). Since Meehl's review, there has been a flurry of studies and several reviews. A recent summary of reviews of over 100 studies on the topic concluded: "Research comparing these two approaches shows the actuarial method to be superior" (Dawes, Faust, & Meehl, 1989, p. 1668). Indeed, the superiority of actuarial methods for prediction is one of the major reasons for the increasing interest in how clinicians formulate their judgments (Kleinmuntz, 1984).

HOW TO ASSESS THE PREDICTIVE VALUE OF A RISK-ASSESSMENT INSTRUMENT

The purpose here is not to describe how to develop a risk-assessment instrument, nor is it to describe the statistical techniques used to sift through potential predictors and clusterlike indicators or derive cutoff scores for classifying persons into high- and low-risk groups. Developing such instruments demands a great deal of time and resources from researchers and subjects, and development requires methodology that goes beyond our scope here. This chapter does, however, describe how the average practitioner can rate the utility of a risk-assessment instrument with respect to a few basic principles, regardless of the behavior being predicted. To grasp a few principles that are relevant to prediction, you need only an understanding of grade-school arithmetic, but as is the case with many truly important matters, understanding these essential principles requires a little concentration. As you read this section's definitions, refer often to referenced tables and figures. Doing so will clarify definitions greatly.

To underscore the importance of prediction principles, and to show how these principles can apply to risk assessment in social work, we will relate prediction principles to two problems: assessing risk of child abuse in the general population (lower prevalence) and assessing risk of reabuse among persons referred to a protective service agency because an abuse has already been confirmed on at least one prior occasion (higher prevalence). Much of this discussion will have to be hypothetical because not much is known about risk assessment in these two areas, but whenever possible, results of child protective service research will be integrated into examples.

Key principles for prediction are positive predictive value, negative predictive value, sensitivity, specificity, and prevalence rate. The last term may be used interchangeably—with some caution—with prior probability or base rate (Larson, 1986; Sox, 1986). Those who understand these principles as they apply to an assessment instrument can judge an instrument's likely utility. Ultimately, practitioners will be most concerned about **positive predictive value**—the proportion of clients who test positive who truly do have or will have the problem. Keep in mind that it is more important for practitioners to know, given a prediction test's score, what proportion have or will have the behavior predicted than it is to know, among those who have the problem, what proportion scored positively on the test. This vital distinction is often ignored in prediction literature.

For example, a positive predictive value of 70% for a suicide-prediction interview guide means that among those who score positively (high risk) on the interview, on follow-up, 70% will be found to have committed suicide. Or for an 80% positive predictive value of a test for Alzheimer's disease, among those who scored positively on the test, autopsy results confirmed the disease in 80% of the cases. A positive predictive value of 95% on a screening test to predict which new parents in the general population will eventually abuse or neglect their children means that 95% of those whom the test predicted would abuse or neglect their child actually had on later evaluation.

Statistics based on a normal distribution (i.e., bell-shaped) are not particularly useful in assessing risk (Galen & Gambino, 1975, pp. 2–7). Such statistics are based on how a client's score compares with others in a normal distribution of score values. The client's raw score may be converted to a percentile or to a standard score to show how that score compares with others in the distribution. For example, if the client has a standard, or Z, score of $+2$ on a measure of child abuse/neglect potential, this means that the client's score lies above about 97% of others who took the test, and a score that lies at 2 standard deviations is at the 98th percentile; but knowing how unusual a person's score may be does not necessarily tell anything about what the person is likely to do in the future.

We need a **reference** or **cutoff score** on some risk-assessment test that has actually been checked for its predictive value and we need a clear procedure for evaluating the score's predictive efficiency in a typical at-risk population. For example, the hypothetical child abuse/neglect potential scores presented in Table 10.1 might be compared with actual behavior among parents such as those to be screened for potential abuse/neglect in the future.

To judge the predictive efficiency of the test, we need a **gold standard,** a solidly agreed upon criterion for judging prediction instruments (Department of Clinical Epidemiology and Biostatistics, 1981, p. 704; Larson, 1986). Ideally, there should be some reliable way, possibly a systematic investigation that is blind to the screening test's results and that yields consistent, reliable results, to determine whether child abuse/neglect has occurred. Given such an investigation's results, the predictive value of the abuse/neglect screening instrument could be determined. It is essential that those who administer the gold standard do so independently of those who administer the prediction instrument, so that prediction can be assessed accurately. Let us assume that there is such a gold standard available for the purposes of the following two examples—this may be quite an assumption given vague and inconsistent definitions of child abuse (Besharov, 1981).

Positive Predictive Value of a Risk-Assessment Test in Which Prevalence (Prior Probability) Is Low

Figure 10.3 clarifies essential principles in prediction. When judging a screening test's results, **true positives** are cases in which abuse/neglect has been predicted,

TABLE 10.1
Hypothetical abuse/neglect scores and their predictive value

Abuse/Neglect Score	Investigation Confirms Abuse/ Neglect (Gold Standard)	Predictive Value % (Proportion Abused and/or Neglected)
25	yes	70%
35	yes	80%
45	yes	95%

and the investigation (gold standard) has confirmed the screening test's positive prediction. **True negatives** are cases in which abuse/neglect was predicted not to occur, and true to the screening tests results, the investigation confirmed this negative result. Note that instances in which the instrument makes correct judgments will appear in the upper left/lower right diagonal of Figure 10.3. There are also two off-diagonal situations in which the screening test gives false predictions. **False positives** are situations in which the test says that there will be abuse/neglect, but the investigation finds that the test's prediction is false. **False negatives** are situations in which the test says there will be no abuse/neglect, but the investigation finds that this negative prediction is false: The children are, in fact, abused/neglected. Understanding prediction requires that all four conditions must be considered, not just true positives. There may be a natural tendency for people to remember true positives and true negatives to the exclusion of the other two cells (Fischhoff, 1975; Fischhoff & Beyth, 1975); therefore practitioners should be forewarned of this tendency when evaluating their own predictions.

As already stated, positive predictive value is what matters to practitioners most. Practitioners want to know: if an individual's abuse/neglect test score is 45, what the probability is that they will find on investigation that this child will be abused/neglected. That is, practitioners typically have test scores for assessing risk, not the results of a validation study. Positive predictive value depends on sensitivity, specificity, and the prevalence (base) rate. To clarify how this is so, we first need to define sensitivity and specificity.

Sensitivity is the number of true positives divided by the total number of true positives plus false negatives (see Figure 10.3). In other words, sensitivity refers to the proportion among those known to have the problem—assume we have results of the gold standard or investigation—who test positively. Usually this is not the situation—practitioners will have test results, but not results of the gold standard. In contrast to sensitivity, **positive predictive value** is the proportion that scored in the abused/neglected range of the test (true positives) divided by the total of true positives plus false positives.

Using the investigation as the gold standard again, **specificity** is the proportion obtained by dividing the number of true negatives by the total of false positives plus true negatives—the proportion of those who actually are negative against the gold standard's results. Of greater importance for practice than specificity is **negative predictive value,** the number of true negatives divided by the

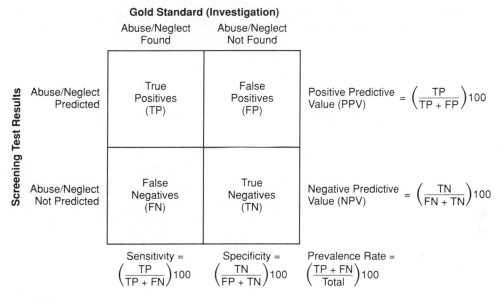

FIGURE 10.3
Elements for judging a prediction instrument's value.

total of false negatives plus true negatives. In this example, negative predictive value is the probability of being truly negative, that is, not being abused/neglected, when the test predicts there will be no abuse/neglect.

Given these principles for measurement, let us take a look at how prediction might take place in protective service work. Assume that an abuse/neglect screening test has been administered to 1,200 families and that independent investigators, who did not know the screening test's results, interviewed subjects to determine whether the child in the family had been abused/neglected. Let us further assume that the prevalence rate of abuse among those studied is about 3%, because the prevalence rate of abuse/neglect in various studies ranges from 1% (Vietze et al., 1982), to 3% (Gill, 1973, p. 69; Straus, 1987, p. 87) to 4% (Straus, 1987, p. 87). Let us also assume that sensitivity and specificity are both incredibly good—94% and 95%, respectively.

Using the hypothetical data for such a situation (34 true positives, 2 false negatives, 58 false positives, and 1106 true negatives), Figure 10.4 shows that if there are 1,200 families for which a prediction is made, sensitivity and specificity both equal almost exactly 95%. Our practical interest is in positive predictive value, however. In the Figure 10.4 example, the test's positive predictive value is only 37%, that is, in only 37% of those families in which a person has taken the test and the test was positive, will there actually be abuse/neglect. If this hypothetical abuse/neglect screening test were used on a wider scale under similar circumstances, perhaps on 5,000 one-child families, there would be 242 false positives and only 142 true positives. This example illustrates that when the prevalence rate is low, the number of false positives may easily overwhelm the

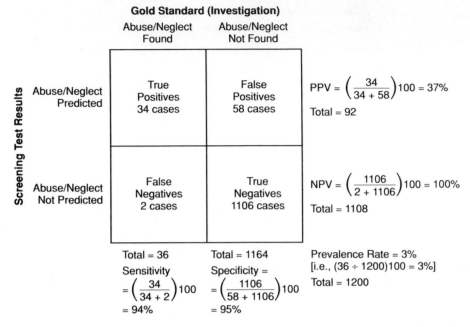

FIGURE 10.4
Predictive value of a hypothetical abuse/neglect screening test where applied to the general population (prevalence = 3%).

predictive effort and therefore overwhelm any preventative program for high-risk persons.

Is it ethical to make decisions based on risk-assessment instruments with such a high rate of false positives? Consider the stigma to persons who have been identified as "high risk" for child abuse when there is a high probability that such identification is in error. The following section describes a situation in which risk assessment, and action based on that assessment, may be more ethically defensible.

POSITIVE PREDICTIVE VALUE OF A RISK-ASSESSMENT TEST IN WHICH PREVALENCE (PRIOR PROBABILITY) IS HIGH

Let us assume that we are confronted with a situation in a county protective service agency where abuse and neglect investigations are performed. In this situation we would like to predict reabuse among cases seen at the protective service agency. Among such cases, in which an abuse has already been confirmed, experience has shown that the probability is often 30%–40% that reabuse will occur (K. Casey, National Committee for Prevention of Child Abuse, personal communication, May 10, 1989). Although instruments have been developed for assessing risk of reabuse (Johnson & L'Esperance, 1984), information is often not available on the sensitivity and specificity of these risk-assessment instruments, so let us assume that a trial of a hypothetical reabuse risk-assessment instrument on 300 protective service subjects found sensitivity and specificity to both be 95%, with a prevalence rate of 40%, as illustrated in Figure 10.5.

Figure 10.5 shows graphically why it is more practical to try to develop instruments to assess risk of reabuse in a group in which prevalence is higher, than in a group in which prevalence is lower, as is the case with trying to predict an initial abuse in the general population (Figure 10.4). In the reabuse example, where prevalence is 40% and sensitivity and specificity are both 95% (almost identical to sensitivity and specificity in the previous example), the positive predictive value is now 93% and negative predictive value is 97%. This shows how a reabuse assessment instrument could be very useful in a protective service agency, because it improves substantially on prevalence rate. That is, if we knew nothing about a particular referral to a protective service agency, our guess would be that referral would have a 40% prior probability of reabuse because all come from a group in which the prevalence rate is 40%. However, by knowing that the instrument's positive predictive value equals 93%, we can be 53% more sure about which families present the greatest risk.

Positive predictive value can be calculated directly from information about a risk-assessment instrument's performance. The formula, based on Bayes's theorem, and using information from the reabuse example, is:

$$\text{PPV} = \frac{(\text{prevalence rate})\,(\text{sensitivity})}{(\text{prevalence})\,(\text{sensitivity}) + (1 - \text{prevalence})\,(1 - \text{sensitivity})}$$

$$= \frac{(.40)\,(.95)}{(.4)\,(.95) + (1 - .40)(1 - .95)}$$

$$= .93$$

Bayes's theorem is particularly useful because it allows the practitioner to take into account prior probability (prevalence, or base, rate) and **posterior probability** (the probability of a problem that takes into account prior probability and new assessment information). The relationship between prior probability and posterior probability for the example in Figure 10.5 is shown in Figure 10.6.

One major lesson of this chapter is that in assessing risk two components should be considered: prior probability (e.g., proportion of those referred to a protective service agency who in the past went on to have a confirmed reabuse) and posterior probability (e.g., high score on a risk-assessment instrument and knowledge of prior probability). As the two examples show, the rate of occurrence of the problem (low rate of abuse, high rate of reabuse) in the risk-assessment samples can have a profound effect on positive predictive value. Another lesson is that we must be careful when using a risk-assessment instrument developed on one group of clients to predict for another group of clients. A risk-assessment instrument that had high positive predictive value where prevalence is higher will most likely not predict as well where the prevalence is lower. Also, personal characteristics of clients of the group for which the risk-assessment instrument was developed may be different from another agency's clients' characteristics, further affecting a risk-assessment measure's generalizability.

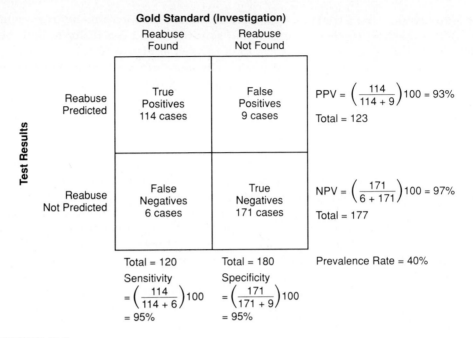

FIGURE 10.5
Predictive value of a hypothetical reabuse risk-assessment instrument in which prevalence is higher (40% reabuse rate).

ASSESSING RISK: SOME USEFUL IDEAS

Understanding intuitively how these concepts apply to practice can be difficult. Even those who are statistically sophisticated sometimes fail to generalize from their statistical knowledge to how it applies to risk assessment (Borak & Veilleux, 1982). The following practitioners' fallacies can help us understand how these concepts apply to practice.

Discriminating practitioners will learn to recognize the common **ignoring prevalence rate fallacy.** Meehl (1973, p. 232) calls this the forgetting Bayes's theorem fallacy, but for those who may never have heard of Bayes, *ignoring prevalence rate, ignoring prior probability fallacy,* or *ignoring base rate fallacy* might be better labels. Here is how the fallacy might be overheard in a child welfare agency's case conference:

- This foster placement risk measure will take the guesswork out of foster home placements! Researchers who developed the measure had 100 subjects in a failed placement group. The researchers administered the risk measure there and found that 90% of the 100 were in the test's high-risk category. If we can predict with 90% accuracy when a placement will fail, we can make much better decisions!

This fallacy involves ignorance of prior probability's effect on judgment. Those who have read this chapter carefully know that risk assessment involves more

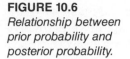

FIGURE 10.6
Relationship between prior probability and posterior probability.

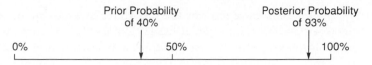

than sensitivity. Specificity and prevalence rate must also be considered to arrive at the positive predictive value of a test. The predictive value of a positive test result may be much lower than 90% if the prevalence rate (base rate, prior probability) is small.

In social work, where assessment and outcome instruments are in early stages of development and may be unreliable, attempts to predict events that have an extremely low prevalence rate (e.g., suicide, murder, child abuse in the general population) will probably be unproductive. Experience with suicide prediction seems to support this contention. Typically, well-planned and well-executed suicide-prediction studies have been overwhelmed with false positives (Murphy, 1972; Pokorny, 1983), and researchers have speculated that suicide-prediction instruments will never exceed a 20% positive predictive efficiency (MacKinnon & Farberow, 1976). On the other hand, predicting events in which the prevalence rate is higher (e.g., reabuse among known abusers, disruption in adoption of older children, disruption in foster home placement for older children) may present better payoffs at this time.

The next practitioners' fallacy is the **everybody's unique fallacy.** Here is an example of this form of thinking:

- I understand fully that your parole risk-assessment instrument's positive predictive value is 97%, and that the instrument has predictive validity for clients other than where it was developed, but in Mr. Cezak's case of assaultive behavior, my experience tells me that he is a low-risk client. His case is unique. I will recommend that he be paroled.

Research cited earlier in this chapter shows that virtually every time a practitioner and actuarial methods meet in the arena, in spite of all the practitioner's dedication and hard-won experience, the practitioner cannot out-predict an actuarially based assessment tool. In the parole example, if the practitioner overrules the instrument often, the practitioner will most likely make more wrong decisions than she would by simply following the instrument.

Next are the **this case disproves the rule fallacy** and the **this case will prove the rule fallacy.** These two fallacies are the reverse of each other. Both fallacies ignore the fact that probabilities speak to long-run expectations, assuming that cases are independent of each other. The this case disproves the rule fallacy might be stated in a case conference as follows:

- The prediction instrument indicated that Joe had a high parole risk for 6 months postparole. I am glad we overruled that darned prediction instrument! When his community corrections agent made an institution visit 6 months after Joe's release to discuss another client in this prison, the agent told us that Joe was still clean. I'm going to ignore the instrument's predictions in the future.

This reasoning ignores the fact that risk assessment should involve experience with a large number of cases. Unless the instrument's positive predictive value is nearly perfect, false positives will appear. Such cases can always be found to disprove the instrument. To disprove the instrument in a methodologically sound way, it would be necessary to keep careful records of predictions made by the instrument and those made by the practitioner over many cases and then compare their accuracy for many clients.

Here is an example of the this case will prove the rule fallacy:

- The instrument failed to predict foster home placement success in the last three cases. Therefore, in this fourth case, the instrument is bound to predict success.

This reasoning, sometimes called the "gambler's fallacy" (Yackulic & Kelly, 1984) ignores the fact that risk assessment involves long-run experience with a large number of cases. Also, since foster home households are generally independent of each other—what happens in one foster family does not affect what happens in another—an instrument's failure to predict in one foster home will not make it more or less likely that the instrument will predict accurately in another home. Again, a fair assessment of an instrument's predictive value requires long-run records.

Finally, there is the **if it saves just one life fallacy.** Here is an example of this fallacy at work in a protective service worker's reasoning:

- I know that predicting suicide in the general population with this risk-assessment instrument is a long shot, but if we can save just one life the effort will be worth it.

If our resources were infinite, this line of reasoning might be tenable, but a realistic policy of risk assessment implies that we look at the cost of administering the instrument, the cost of treating those who do not need treatment (false positives), and the cost of treating those who do need treatment (true positives). Our decision implies that we answer the following questions: What is the cost of administering the risk-assessment instrument? Is there an effective way to treat high-risk persons? Are there ethical and legal implications of identifying high-risk persons? How many false positives would be likely? Such questions should be answered before adopting any risk-assessment instrument.

Please do the risk-assessment exercises at the end of the chapter now. Your comprehension of the next section is dependent on the completion of those exercises.

INTEGRATING PROBABILITIES INTO DECISIONS: USING A DECISION TREE

A risk-assessment instrument may open new doors to helping clients. If high-risk clients can be identified, then they might receive more intensive treatment. If results of studies that evaluate effects of intensive treatment for high-risk persons become available, they could be integrated into decision-making procedures.

To integrate such information, this final section of the chapter demonstrates a technique for decision analysis. (This section is included to illustrate a decision tree and how it might be used in practice, not how to construct one.)

This chapter's exercises describe an experiment (Experiment 2) conducted by a small group of farsighted and innovative protective service workers to test the predictive efficiency of their reabuse-prediction instrument (Johnson, Clancy, Robinson & Wong, 1989). Results of their experiment are given in Figure 10.7. That information, coupled with results of evaluation studies, might be incorporated into a **decision tree**—a diagram that expresses the likely outcome of alternative choices—to help practitioners make life-affecting decisions rationally and systematically.

Figure 10.8 illustrates how a decision tree can be applied to decisions in protective services. Decision trees are useful because: (a) they make decision making more systematic and therefore more effective; (b) they help to resolve differences of opinion regarding decision making; and (c) they encourage the integration of assessment and research findings into the decision-making process through probability statements. Decision trees are essential to a new and useful science, clinical decision analysis (Sox et al., 1988; Weinstein et al., 1980).

All those who construct decision trees follow basically the same steps, which are much more completely described by Sox et al. (1988) and Weinstein et al. (1980). To illustrate how study data can be integrated into steps for constructing

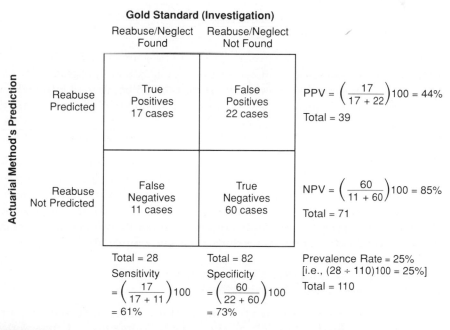

FIGURE 10.7
Predictive value for a real child reabuse study: actuarial method (prevalence rate = 25%).
(*Note: Courtesy of Johnson et al., 1989.*)

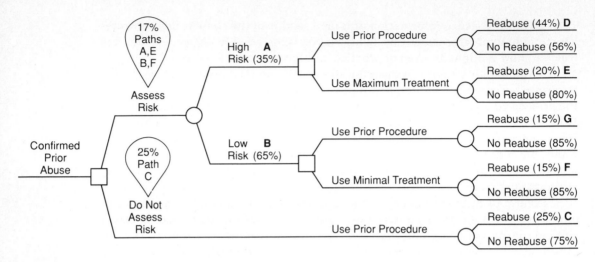

FIGURE 10.8
Decision tree based on a reabuse risk-assessment instrument (probabilities are risk of reabuse).

a decision tree, results of the protective service experiment of Figure 10.7 will be used.

Step 1: Pose a Decision Question That Includes Alternatives and Outcomes

Protective service workers are chronically short of resources. They simply do not have the time and funds to administer an intensive treatment program to all cases in which child abuse has been confirmed. If cases could be divided into high- and low-risk groups, and an intervention could be tailored to meet the needs of high-risk cases, limited resources might be used more effectively. Here is a hypothetical question that lists decision alternatives and potential outcomes:

- Among cases at _____ agency, where an abuse has been confirmed by an investigation, if confirmed cases are divided into high- and low-risk cases, what would be the likelihood of reabuse by parents treated according to their risk category, from _____ (date) to _____ (date), compared with the likelihood of reabuse by parents treated without knowledge of risk assessment to guide treatment decisions during the same interval?

Step 2: Draw a Tree Diagram That Includes a Logical Sequence of Chance and Decision Nodes

The tree diagram in Figure 10.8 is a type of flow chart that is organized temporally from left to right. The diagram follows the sequence of events and choices that a protective service practitioner might go through during case management. In this step, we examine only the trunk and its branches, not the probabilities associated with each branch.

The question in Step 1 stated that the decision process begins with cases in which an investigation has confirmed that child abuse has occurred. Next, the practitioner decides whether or not to use a risk-assessment instrument. The practitioner's decision is marked by a **decision node**—a point in the tree at which a choice can be made.

Moving right, the next node in the decision tree is a chance node regarding whether clients score into high-risk or low-risk categories. **A chance node** (marked by a circle) appears where chance determines what will happen; in this case, chance determines that a client will fall into the high- or low-risk category.

Next, two parallel decisions are made: Low-risk clients get the same procedure that was used in the past or they get a new minimal treatment. High-risk cases are given the same procedure that was used in the past or they are given a maximum treatment designed specifically for high-risk persons. Some who examine the decision tree may think it unconscionable not to use the risk-assessment results to identify high-risk persons and then apply maximum treatment. Agency policy might mandate that high-risk persons all get special treatment. In such cases, in which a particular **path**—a unique chain of decisions and chance events in a decision tree—is impossible, it can be removed from the tree. Removing impossible paths from a decision tree is called **pruning.** (In this case, all decision paths have been included to clarify this illustration's decision making.)

Finally, another chance node, whether clients reabuse or do not reabuse their child, lists the possible outcome at the end of each branch. Notice that at the far right there are eight possible paths (and two for those cases whose risk was not classified and treated).

Step 3: Determine What Probabilities Are Needed and Fill In the Decision Tree

A probability can be stated as a frequency of a problem in some population; that is, as a proportion per 100, a percent. Such proportions can come from observations, as in the experience summarized in Figure 10.7. Now we will move across the decision tree, from left to right, filling in probabilities that come from the information in Figure 10.7.

The note at the far left that the decision tree's decision making will concern only those cases that have been referred to the agency in which an investigation has found that a child in the home has been abused. The first decision node branches in two directions to indicate a decision to assess risk for reabuse or to not use the risk-assessment instrument and follow prior treatment procedures. If we decide to use the risk-assessment instrument, subjects will be divided into high-risk and low-risk groups. Point A of the tree gets a probability of 35% because Figure 10.7 shows that there are 39 high-risk cases (reabuse predicted), or $(39/110)100 = 35\%$. Point B gets a probability of 65% because Figure 10.7 shows the instrument predicted 71 low-risk cases, or $(71/110)100 = 65\%$.

Other probabilities can also be determined from Figure 10.8. Point C of the decision tree is the probability of reabuse among cases in which subjects are not classified and treated according to risk (prior procedure). Point C is the prevalence rate of reabuse, or $(28/110)100 = 25\%$.

High-risk clients (another decision node) can be treated in two ways (branches containing D or E). If high-risk clients get the prior treatment without regard to their high- or low-risk status, the probability of a reabuse, D, given the test result will be what it was in the original reabuse prediction study, or [17/(17 + 22)]100 = 44%. This is the positive predictive value. On the other hand, if high-risk clients get a special maximum treatment, the probability of reabuse might be much lower than 44%. How much lower is critical here. Unfortunately, although there are studies that evaluate treatments for child abusers (Burch & Mohr, 1980; Whiteman, Fanshel, & Grundy, 1987; Wolfe, Sandler, & Kaufman, 1981), no studies seem to include reabuse rates as an outcome measure. Apparently, there is no sound empirical basis for estimating the probability of reabuse among treated high-risk clients.

The absence of empirical evidence on which to base an estimate of probability brings us to a new topic, **subjective probability,** the strength of a belief about the likelihood of an event, expressed as a percent. Since there are no studies that would help estimate the success of a maximum treatment effort for high-risk clients, expected success would have to be estimated. Let us assume that protective service workers have collaborated to design a maximum treatment procedure for high-risk clients. Workers will have extra time to treat high-risk parents in court-mandated parenting skills and stress-management groups. Workers will also have the power to manage high-risk cases very conservatively. Let us further assume that the workers who designed this maximum treatment estimate that reabuse for clients so treated would be 20%. Their estimate appears at point E in the tree diagram (Figure 10.8).

Low-risk clients (another decision node) can be treated in two ways. If low-risk clients get the prior treatment without regard to their high- or low-risk status, the probability of a reabuse will be what it was in the original reabuse prediction study, or $100 - [60/(11 + 60)] 100 = 15\%$, as indicated at point G in the tree diagram. Low-risk clients may also, based on their low-risk status, get minimal treatment, possibly brief counseling, advice, and a referral, where appropriate. If we assume that this minimal treatment will be appropriate to the needs of low-risk clients, the probability of reabuse in this group may be assumed to be the same as it was, or 15%. This estimate, a semisubjective probability, appears at point F of the tree diagram.

It should be noted that risk should be stated over a particular interval of time. The risk-assessment figures in Figure 10.7 were for one year; so assume that all probabilities are for one year in this tree diagram. Ideally, follow-up should continue until children reach age 18, but long follow-up is seldom feasible.

Step 4: Choose the Best Decision

The final step is relatively straightforward. The principal question in Step 1 was whether reabuse would be lower among clients matched with treatment or if reabuse would be lower by just following the prior procedure, which does not involve classification. Thus, we need to compute the probability of reabuse for two paths. For clients who are classified and then treated according to their classification (paths A, E and B, F), the probability of reabuse is 17% [(.20 × .35) + (.65 × .15)]. For clients not classified and treated accordingly (paths A, D and B, G), the probability of reabuse is 25%—[(.35 × .44) + (.65 × .15)], or the prevalence rate among the clients treated without matching (25%), as was noted at point C of the tree diagram. Thus, by matching high- and low-risk clients with treatment we can expect to reduce recidivism from 25% to 17%. Deciding whether this is a great enough difference to initiate the changes necessary is a judgment call that workers, the county board, and interested persons will have to make.

SUMMARY

Senior practitioners often make statements such as: "This type of case needs special attention." "With clients who act like that, I would try this." Implicit in such statements are risk assessment and belief about the probability of success for particular client types with particular treatment methods. In this chapter, we have presented evidence that actuarial methods for assessing such risk have proven more efficient than clinical methods.

Decision analysis is a way to incorporate results of risk assessment and evaluation studies into decision making about client care. Decision trees, whether made explicit or implied by a practitioner's chain of reasoning, are the framework for what we do in practice. Decision trees, with their probabilities based on empirical work or based on the best subjective judgments possible, show great promise as a way to bridge the gap between research findings and practice.

EXERCISES

Following are results from an experiment that tested the ability of a battery of tests given to infants and their mothers to predict the infants' later abuse and/or neglect. The experimenters prospectively (before following-up to test predictions) classified participants into low- or high-risk categories.

Based on the authors' description of their experiment's results below, see if you can fill in a blank Figure 10.3. Fill in as many blank values as you can according to definitions in the text; then look at completed Figure C.1 in Appendix C to check your results. Here is the authors' description of their experiment's results:

> The first question to be asked is how many of the children who were followed were identified as victims of maltreatment. Of the 498 families selected for follow-up, 70 (14 percent) had index children [abused and/or neglected] later identified by our criteria as having suffered some form of maltreatment. The outcomes considered as maltreatment included physical abuse,

nonorganic failure to thrive, and neglect or other forms of maltreatment such as abandonment. Of these 70 children, 53 came from families who had been identified as being high risk for maltreatment. When we compared the incidence of maltreatment in the high risk group with that in the low risk comparison group we found that this was statistically significant ($X^2 = 13.27$, $p < .003$). Thus 76 percent of the maltreated children came from the high-risk group while only 24 percent were found in the low risk group. Another way of looking at these data is in terms of the proportion of each group who were maltreated. In the high risk group of 273 children. . . . (Vietze et al., 1982, pp. 147–148)

The authors, who were concerned enough about child abuse to spend hundreds of hours answering questions about its prediction, have erroneously focused on sensitivity. The true test of their instrument's usefulness, assuming that their study could be replicated elsewhere and that they could teach practitioners to administer their measure reliably, is still positive predictive value (PPV). In this case (see Figure C.1), PPV = 19%. Prevalence rate is 14%; so PPV is not much of an improvement on prior probability (i.e., 5%).

Next are preliminary data from a real recidivism prediction experiment provided by experimenters at the Alameda County Social Service Agency, Oakland, California (Johnson, Clancy, Robinson, & Wong, 1989). Their earlier work (Johnson & L'Esperance) was published in 1984. Their experiment pits the predictions of protective service workers (clinical prediction) against prediction by the actuarial method. The example also illustrates prediction where prevalence rate is higher than in the previous example—note that *reabuse* is being predicted. Their data for predictions by protective service workers are as follows: true positives (TP) = 21; true negatives (TN) = 24; false positives (FP) = 58; false negatives (FN) = 7. The risk-assessment instrument's predictions for the same clients are: TP = 17; TN = 60; FP = 22; FN = 11.

Using this information, answer the following questions.

1. Prevalence of abuse is identical in the prediction experiment for clinicians and for the actuarial method because predictions were made for the same group of 110 clients. What is the prevalence rate for both sets of these data?
2. What are sensitivity and specificity for the clinical prediction experiment?
3. What are sensitivity and specificity for the actuarial prediction experiment?
4. What is the positive predictive value for the protective service workers' predictions?
5. What is the positive predictive value for the actuarial method on these same clients?
6. Do the protective service workers improve much on prevalence rate?
7. Is it clinical prediction or actuarial prediction that does the better job of predicting reabuse among these cases?
8. What is the negative predictive value for the actuarial method?
9. Why is it vital to know both positive predictive value and negative predictive value in this example?

REFERENCES

Arkes, H. R. (1981). Impediments to accurate clinical judgment and possible ways to minimize their impact. *Journal of Consulting and Clinical Psychology, 49*(3), 323–330.

Beck, A. T., Kovacs, M., & Weissman, A. (1979). Assessment of suicidal ideation. *Journal of Consulting and Clinical Psychology, 47*(2), 343–352.

Besharov, J. D. (1981). Toward better research on child abuse and neglect: Making definitional issues an explicit methodological concern. *Child Abuse and Neglect, 5*, 383–390.

Borak, J., & Veilleux, S. (1982). Errors in intuitive logic among physicians. *Social Science & Medicine, 16*, 1939–1947.

Burch, G., & Mohr, V. (1980, February). Evaluation of a child abuse intervention program. *Social Casework, 61*(2), p. 90ff

Dawes, R. M., Faust, D., & Meehl, P. E. (1989). Clinical versus actuarial judgment. *Science, 243*, 1668–1673.

Department of Clinical Epidemiology and Biostatistics, McMaster University Health Sciences Centre. (1981). How to read clinical journals: II. To learn about a diagnostic test. *Canadian Medical Association Journal, 124*, 703–710.

Eddy, D. M. (1982). Probabalistic reasoning in clinical medicine: Problems and opportunities. In D. Kahneman, P. Slovic, & A. Tversky (Eds.), *Judgment under uncertainty: Heuristics and biases* (pp. 249–267). Cambridge: Cambridge University Press.

Fischhoff, B. (1975). Hindsight ≠ foresight: The effect of outcome knowledge on judgment under uncertainty. *Journal of Experimental Psychology, 1*(3), 288–299.

Fischhoff, B., & Beyth, R. (1975). "I knew it would happen." Remembered probabilities of once-future things. *Organizational Behavior and Human Performance, 13*, 1–16.

Fowers, B. J., & Olson, D. H. (1986). Predicting marital success with PREPARE: A predictive validity study. *Journal of Marital and Family Therapy, 12*(1), 403–413.

Galen, R. S., & Gambino, S. R. (1975). *Beyond normality: The predictive value and efficiency of medical diagnoses*. New York: Wiley.

Gil, D. G. (1973). *Violence against children: Physical child abuse in the United States*. Cambridge, MA: Harvard University Press.

Harris, D. (1988). Renewing our commitment to child welfare. *Social Work, 33*(6), 483–484.

Hoffman, P. (1986). *Predicting criminality* (Crime File Study Guide No. NCJ 97228). Rockville, MD: National Institute of Justice.

Johnson, W., Clancy, T., Robinson, E., & Wong, E. (1989, February 14). *Letter to Alameda County Board of Supervisors*. Alameda County Social Service Agency, Oakland, CA.

Johnson, W., & L'Esperance, J. (1984). Predicting the recurrence of child abuse. *Social Work Research and Abstracts, 20*(2), 21–26.

Kleinmuntz, B. (1984). The scientific study of clinical judgment in psychology and medicine. *Clinical Psychology Review, 4*, 111–126.

Larson, E. (1986). Evaluating validity of screening tests. *Nursing Research, 35*, 186–188.

MacKinnon, D. R., & Farberow, N. L. (1976). An assessment of the utility of suicide prediction. *Suicide and Life-Threatening Behavior, 6*(2), 86-91.

Magura, S., Moses, B. S., & Jones, M. A. (1987). *Assessing risk and measuring change in families*. Washington, DC: Child Welfare League of America.

Meehl, P. E. (1954). *Clinical versus statistical prediction: A theoretical analysis and a review of the evidence*. Minneapolis: University of Minnesota Press.

Meehl, P. E. (1973). *Psychodiagnosis: Selected papers*. Minneapolis, MN: University of Minnesota Press.

Motto, J. A., Heilbron, D. C., & Juster, R. P. (1985). Development of a clinical instrument to estimate suicide risk. *American Journal of Psychiatry, 142*(6), 680–686.

Murphy, G. E. (1972). Clinical identification of suicidal risk. *Archives of General Psychiatry, 27*, 356–359.

Pokorny, A. D. (1983). Prediction of suicide in psychiatric patients. *Archives of General Psychiatry, 40*, 249–257.

Salem, D. A., Seidman, E., & Rappaport, J. (1988). Community treatment of the mentally ill: The promise of mutual-help organizations. *Social Work, 33*(5), 403–408.

Schneider, C. J. (1982). The Michigan Screening Profile of Parenting. In R. H. Starr (Ed.), *Child abuse prediction: Policy implications* (pp. 157–174). Cambridge, MA: Ballinger.

Sox, H. C. (1986). Probability theory in the use of diagnostic tests. *Annals of Internal Medicine, 104*(1), 60–66.

Sox, H. C., Blatt, M. A., Higgins, M. C., & Martin, K. I. (1988). *Medical decision making*. Boston: Butterworths.

Stone, N. M., & Stone, S. F. (1983). The prediction of successful foster placement. *Social Casework, 64*(1), 11–17.

Straus, M. A. (1987). Is violence toward children increasing: A comparison of 1975 and 1985 survey rates. In R. J. Gelles (Ed.), *Family violence*. Newbury Park, CA: Sage.

Vietze, P. M., O'Connor, S., Hopkins, J. B., Sandler, H. M., & Altemeier, W. A. (1982). Prospective study of child maltreatment from a transactional perspective. In R. H. Starr (Ed.), *Child abuse prediction: Policy implications* (pp. 135–156). Cambridge, MA: Ballinger.

Weinstein, M. C., Fineberg, H. V., Elstein, A. S., Frazier, H. S., Neuhauser, D., Neutra, R. R., & McNeil, B. J. (1980). *Clinical decision analysis*. Philadelphia: W. B. Saunders.

Wells, S. J. (1986, January). *Decision-making in child protective service intake and investigation, final report*. (Available from National Legal Resource Center for Child Advocacy and Protection, Young Lawyers Division, American Bar Association, 1800 M Street NW, Washington, D. C. 20036)

Whiteman, M., Fanshel, D., & Grundy, J. F. (1987). Cognitive-behavioral interventions aimed at anger of parents at risk of child abuse. *Social Work, 32*(6), 469–474.

Wolfe, D. A., Sandler, J., & Kaufman, K. (1981). A competency-based parent training program for child abusers. *Journal of Consulting and Clinical Psychology, 49*(5), 633–640.

Yackulic, R. A., & Kelly, I. W. (1984). The psychology of the "Gambler's Fallacy" in probabalistic reasoning. *Psychology, 21*(3-4), 55–58.

Zung, W. W. K. (1974). Index of Potential Suicide (IPS): A rating scale for suicide prediction. In A. T. Beck, H. L. P. Resnik & D. J. Lettieri (Eds.). *The prediction of suicide* (pp. 221–249). Bowie, MD: The Charles Press.

The Case Example Fallacy

IDENTIFYING THE CASE EXAMPLE FALLACY

Those deceived by **case example** draw conclusions about many clients based on only a few unrepresentatively chosen ones. Case example, although a weak form of evidence, snares the unwary for the following reasons: (a) because the details of case examples portray cases so vividly, they have far greater emotional appeal than do painstakingly constructed surveys of clients and evaluation studies, which are infinitely more accurate sources of generalizations about clients; (b) by encouraging practitioners to become immersed in the specifics of particular cases—something that any practitioner can easily do—case example encourages practitioners to oversimplify complex issues concerning what is generally true of clients; (c) case example is notoriously open to intentional and unintentional bias because if a large enough pool is available, cases that prove a point can always be chosen.

Case example is only a fallacy if, based on a single case or a few cases, a statement is made about what is generally true of a whole group. Concluding that a rape crisis center's method is effective based on the experience of one woman who went through treatment at the center or generalizing about all children of alcoholics based on a handful of such children are examples of the case example fallacy. Using case examples to illustrate how intervention may be conducted, that is, demonstrating the how-to of practice, is not a fallacy if no generalization is made.

To illustrate the case example fallacy, assume that a newsperson writes a story describing someone who has been arrested and charged with welfare fraud. The story describes how this "welfare queen" used 12 fictitious names, forged several birth certificates, claimed 50 nonexistent children as dependents, remained on the Aid to Families with Dependent Children (AFDC) rolls for 10 years, and defrauded the state of Michigan out of $400,000 in AFDC payments. The story implies that almost all AFDC recipients are black and it describes how the "welfare queen" drives expensive cars, takes vacations in Mexico, and lives in an expensive house. Real news stories, just like this, complete with pictures of "welfare queens," can be found in popular press articles (California Woman Earns 'Welfare Queen' Title, 1981).

The facts of the story are not in question. However, any inference based on this single case, that AFDC recipients generally cheat, would be an example of the case example fallacy. Apparently, such welfare queen stories foster generalizations about welfare recipients and the welfare system in general. A "welfare queen" story that appeared in *U.S. News & World Report* ("She's Known as Chicago's 'Welfare Queen'," 1978), cited a local prosecutor who said, "Atrocious things are going on in the welfare department, and the taxpayer is catching it. . . . If this Otis case [another welfare queen] doesn't prove to the taxpayer that something needs to be done, nothing will" (p. 28).

WHY IS CASE EXAMPLE SO SEDUCTIVE?

The case example fallacy is so seductive that it has generated keen interest among social psychologists and experts in clinical reasoning, who want to understand why clinicians have such difficulty making sound generalizations. Although findings of their studies are only preliminary—and scattered—three common obstacles to making sound generalizations seem to be emerging: (a) vividness of the case example, (b) ignorance of the law of large numbers in **sampling**—taking any portion of a larger population to make generalizations about the entire population and (c) ignorance of the issue of sample representativeness. Let us take a careful look at each problem.

Vividness of Case Example

Hamill, Nisbett, and Wilson (1980) conducted an experiment to examine the influence of a vivid and derogatory case example on attitudes toward welfare recipients. To begin, they randomly assigned 124 psychology students to three groups. The first group read an article that presented a negative image of a welfare recipient. "The article provided a detailed description of a 43-year-old, obese, friendly, irresponsible, ne'er-do-well woman who had lived in New York City for 16 years, the last 13 of which had been spent on welfare" (Hamill et al., 1980, p. 580). Her story encouraged certain stereotypes:

> unhappy teenage marriage that produced three children . . . endless succession of common-law husbands, children at roughly 18-month intervals, and dependence on welfare . . . eating high-priced cuts of meat and playing the numbers on the days immediately after the welfare check arrived . . . dwelling was a decaying, malodorous apartment . . . children attended school as they pleased. (Hamill et al., 1980, p. 580)

In addition to reading this case example, the first group of psychology students read fictitious survey data that confirmed that the stereotype was typical (the authors thoroughly debriefed the students after the experiment to counter this misinformation).

The second group read the same stereotypical case example, but then read survey results that discredited the vivid case example. The third group of psychology students served as controls and did not read the vivid, erroneous stereotype of the welfare recipient.

What do you suppose the relative impact on attitudes toward welfare recipients would be of the vivid, stereotypical, erroneous case example when compared with that of the survey? You guessed it—the psychology students swallowed the vivid case example hook, line, and sinker. Students in both experimental groups had equally more negative attitudes toward welfare recipients than did the controls. That is, it did not matter that students in one group were told that the survey of welfare recipients refuted the case example and those in another were told that a survey supported the case example: In both groups the case example appeared to make the students more prejudiced against welfare recipients. Students ignored the survey; they accepted the case example.

Just think of the damage that stereotypical case examples do to the public's perceptions. Then think of how devastating a vivid case example might be to the mind of a social worker who must make life-affecting decisions every day.

Other investigations show that vivid case examples can overshadow better evidence: Anderson (1983) found that a vivid description of two cases had greater impact on the way in which students judged how firefighters would perform than did a large, well-designed (but fictitious) prediction study; Oskamp (1982) found that among both a group of experienced and a group of less-experienced psychologists confidence in judgments that are based on case material increases as more material about the cases is learned, but the accuracy of judgments does not increase.

Ignorance of the Law of Large Numbers

Another way case example deceives is by encouraging practitioners to ignore the law of large numbers. As a general rule, the **law of large numbers** states that samples that include successively larger proportions of a population will generally represent that population more accurately and the sample mean will approach the population mean as sample mean increases, until finally, the sample mean will equal exactly the population mean when the sample includes the entire population (Hays, 1981, p. 186). Unfortunately many who are snared by the case example fallacy behave as though they believe in the reverse principle, the **law of small numbers** (Abraham & Schultz, 1984; Tversky & Kahneman, 1971), which implies that smaller samples will yield an accurate reflection of the population— possibly because individual cases can be more fully examined than those in a larger sample.

The fact that larger samples from a given population more accurately reflect that population is difficult for people to grasp. Tversky and Kahneman (1974, p.

1125) have demonstrated an "insensitivity to sample size" in a couple of experiments. In the first, they asked people to judge how accurately the mean of a sample of height measures would represent the population mean in samples of 10, 100, or 1,000 men. Respondents assigned the same credibility to all three samples. In another experiment conducted by Tversky and Kahneman, respondents were asked whether the proportion of male to female babies would more likely approximate the population—which as we know is about 50%—in a smaller hospital or larger hospital, even though three times as many children are born in the larger hospital than in the smaller hospital. Respondents' answers indicated that they thought that both hospitals had the same probability of finding the unusual proportion of 60% boys.

The law of small numbers might also be erroneously used in a practice. Social workers who attend a professional conference on how to help those exposed to the trauma of sex abuse might watch with interest videotapes of interviews with three rape victims and accept the presenter's stated or implied conclusion that all rape victims are like the ones in the videotape.

Ignorance of Sample Representativeness

The case example fallacy also thrives on the gullible person's willingness to accept samples that are not likely to be representative of the population. **Representativeness** refers to the extent to which the characteristics of a sample taken from a population is typical of the characteristics of that population. There are many ways to select cases in such a way as to give a biased picture of the whole. The first, violating the law of large numbers, has already been described: select just two or three cases. Their mean characteristics are less likely to reflect the population than those of larger samples. Other sources of unrepresentativeness have been described in earlier chapters. Figure 4.3 contains several, including: self-selection (this refers to the fact that individuals who volunteer for experiments tend to be better educated, of higher social class, more intelligent, higher in need for social approval, and more sociable than nonvolunteers, Rosenthal & Rosnow, 1975, p. 195); purposeful selection by the social worker (the social worker, wanting to show a program or intervention in a positive light, might select successful cases to present at a conference); regression toward the mean (persons who score exceptionally high or low are picked by the social worker, who is unaware that such atypical persons will likely regress toward the mean on a later testing, as diagramed in Figure 4.4). Tversky and Kahneman (1974, p. 1127) also list "availability" of cases as a source of unrepresentativeness. Availability may be determined by retrievability of instances (some cases, possibly the practitioner's most notable successes, may be recalled more readily).

HOW BASIC PRINCIPLES OF SURVEY RESEARCH CAN HELP DISPEL THE CASE EXAMPLE FALLACY

The preceding has explained three sources of the case example's snare, but the question of how to make sound generalizations remains. Fortunately, we have available as a tool one of the greatest contributions to sound reasoning ever devised by social scientists: principles of survey research. Survey research's utility for making sound generalizations has been so widely demonstrated that excellent texts have been written exclusively on this topic (Bainbridge, 1989). We can only introduce briefly three methods from survey research that counter each of the three sources of case example's seductiveness: (a) interviews and questionnaires (the case example bases its generalizations on vivid, emotionally gripping, and haphazardly made observations of clients; survey research relies on measures); (b) larger samples (case example oversimplifies complex issues by presenting small numbers or a single case; survey research seeks larger samples); and (c) random sampling procedures (case example is vulnerable to unintentional and intentional bias that arises due to unrepresentatively chosen cases; random selection helps to assure representatively chosen cases). It is hoped that this chapter's short introduction to survey research measures and issues regarding sampling will motivate the reader to learn more about survey research.

Interviews: Countering Case Example's Vivid Emotional Appeal

By applying sound measurement procedures to their observations, those who apply survey research principles to problems in human services can avoid being taken in by emotion, which is so characteristic of case examples. Recall how the welfare queen story appealed to a sense of outrage and injustice because the recipient bilked the state out of more than $400,000 in payments for 50 nonexistent children. To counter such emotional details based on single individuals, survey researchers rely on structured interview techniques to help them make more-objective observations.

To illustrate that a structured interview is the polar opposite of the case example's vividness, let us examine how quality-control workers apply principles of measurement to objectify their investigations of cases receiving AFDC, the program that was abused by the welfare queen. AFDC, a federal program required in each state under the Social Security Act, is administered and partially funded at the state level. The AFDC Program was established "for the purpose of encouraging the care of dependent children in their own homes or in the homes of relatives by enabling each State to furnish financial assistance" (U.S. Department of Health and Human Services, 1989). The program was primarily intended to aid single parents who might find it difficult or impossible to work outside the home because of their child-care responsibilities.

Federal regulations require that states maintain local quality-control offices to apply prescribed sampling methods to select cases for investigation, conduct field investigations, analyze findings of those investigations, take corrective action where benefits have been given or denied in error, and cooperate with the federal government in the quality-control process (Office of the Federal Register, 1988, 45 CFR Chapter II, 205.40(b)(1)(2)). In each district of each state, quality-control workers review documents from local human service agencies and make home visits. Based on their investigations, quality-control workers record voluminous information on each case and analyze that information to classify each case into one of these four categories: correct, payment to an ineligible person, overpayment, and underpayment (U.S. Department of Health and Human Services, 1988, p. 3030).

Quality-control interviewers fill out a 16-page worksheet according to procedures meticulously described in the 268-page *AFDC Quality Control Manual* (Family Support Administration, 1988). Two pages of this worksheet appear in Figure 11.1. To fill it out, reviewers first conduct a thorough audit, or "desk review," of case records at the local state agency (Family Support Administration, 1988, p. 3100). In the event that the desk review discovers that documentation is missing in the case record, such documentation is secured and recorded on the worksheet. For example, an entry into element 110 of the worksheet might include in column 1 that "The case record reflected no verification of age for the child Henry Jones," and column 3 might contain, "The recipient stated that her son, Henry, was born April 10, 1980. Verified by Anywhere, USA, birth certificate number 11234 (see attached copy)" (Family Support Administration, 1988, p. 3110).

Once the desk review is completed, the reviewer, after thorough preparation, arranges to conduct an interview in the recipient's home. During the home visit the reviewer confirms the recipient's residence, the presence of claimed children, the presence of others in the household, and examines documents that verify income, financial assets, and expenses. The manual is very specific about which evidence is sufficient to meet the need for specific information in each element of the worksheet. For example, "primary evidence" regarding element 110 of the worksheet includes: birth certificate, adoption papers or records, hospital or birth records, church birth records, baptismal records, and so on (Family Support Administration, 1988, p. 3531). Less credible "secondary evidence" concerning element 110 includes: school records, census records, court support order, physician's statement (based on knowledge of date of birth), and juvenile court records (Family Support Administration, 1988, p. 3531).

In addition to the face-to-face interview with the recipient, the reviewer interviews collateral sources to verify information about the recipient, including: residence, income, and number of children. Collateral sources include landlords, neighbors, bank officials, postal service workers, teachers in local schools or day-care centers, and welfare workers in local agencies. Information gained from these sources is also entered on the worksheet.

When the worksheet is complete, its principal information is transferred to an Integrated Review Schedule to classify the recipient's case into one of the following categories: payment correct, overpayment, underpayment, or ineligible. The Integrated Review Schedule also helps determine the amount of error, in the event that there is one. All of these steps are completed on an average of 12 cases a month, at approximately 12 hours per case. The whole process is so complex that it takes approximately 2 years for a reviewer to become proficient (J. Baker, personal communication, August 24, 1989).

Strengths and Weaknesses of Interviews
As sources of information, interviews have the following strengths (Monette, Sullivan, & DeJong, 1986, pp. 160–161): (a) because they involve face-to-face inter-

action, they can motivate a higher proportion of respondents to give information than questionnaires can; (b) interviews can elicit accurate information from respondents because the interviewer can clarify questions and can ask questions directly without relying on the respondent's ability to read; (c) well-trained interviewers can introduce control into the way the respondent answers questions by asking questions in proper sequence and by ensuring that the respondent is not helped by others; (d) interview procedures are more flexible than questionnaires because interviews can be less structured for exploratory purposes and more structured for situations that require fine attention to detail (e.g., quality control data for AFDC); and (e) the interviewer can add observational information to the interview that helps verify the information given.

Interviews also have certain disadvantages compared with questionnaires: (a) because of the expense of training and transporting interviewers, interviews cost more to implement; (b) interviews also take more time because interviewers must be trained and must themselves take time to contact respondents and to conduct their interviews; (c) interviewers, in spite of careful training, may introduce bias due to the way they relate to clients or the way clients perceive them; and (d) interviewers, although well trained, require constant monitoring to keep them asking questions consistently according to instructions.

Questionnaires: Another Antidote to Case Example's Vivid Emotional Appeal

Questionnaires generally consist of a cover letter that explains the study's purpose and solicits the respondent's cooperation, numbered questions that are constructed in such a way that the respondent's answers can be coded and scored for analysis, and directions for responding to the questions. Questionnaires are constructed so they can be mailed or distributed quickly and filled out without assistance.

Needs assessment is one very common type of survey research that often involves questionnaires (Bell, Nguyen, Warheit, & Buhl, 1978). For example, to identify unmet needs among the mentally ill clients in Montgomery County, Pennsylvania, Bell and her associates, with support from the Montgomery County mental health administrator, asked professionals in 30 county mental health agencies to identify persons served by their agency who met the criteria of chronic mental illness. There were 2,389 clients so identified in their county's population. Then they asked the agency people to fill out a questionnaire to define a hierarchy of needs for each of 286 clients who had been selected randomly from among the population. They found that among clients who used the county's mental health services, the following hierarchy of needs was identified, in descending order of need: medication checks, individual therapy, episodic case management, ongoing case management, and partial hospitalization (p. 242).

Questionnaire construction may seem simple, but complexities regarding question order, wording, and interpretation can occupy whole volumes (Labaw, 1980). However, survey researchers have uncovered so much helpful information about question wording that some high points are summarized here:

WORKSHEET FOR INTEGRATED AFDC, FOOD STAMPS AND MEDICAID QUALITY CONTROL REVIEWS

Integrated Review No. _____
Form Approved
OMB No 0960-0176

PRIVACY ACT/PAPERWORK ACT NOTICE: This report is required under provisions of 45CFR 205.40 (AFDC), 7 CFR 275.14 (Food Stamp) and 42 CFR 431.800 (Medicaid). This information is needed for the review of State performance in determining recipient eligibility. The information is used to determine State compliance and failure to report may result in a finding of non-compliance.

A. IDENTIFYING INFORMATION

PROGRAMS UNDER REVIEW

☐ AFDC ☐ FOOD STAMPS ☐ MEDICAID
☐ ADULT ☐ ACTIVE ☐ AFDC ☐ AFDC RELATED NEEDY INDIVIDUAL UNDER 21
          ☐ NEGATIVE ☐ SSI ☐ SSI RELATED

1. LOCAL AGENCY: _____
2. CASE NAME: _____
3. ADDRESS: _____
4. PHONE NUMBER: _____
5. DIRECTIONS TO LOCATE: _____

	AFDC/ADULT	FOOD STAMPS	MEDICAID
6. CASE NUMBER(S)			
7. REVIEW NUMBER(S)			
8. REVIEW DATE/MONTH			
9. DATE OF MOST RECENT OPENING/CERTIFICATION		Date Application Received	
10. MOST RECENT ACTION			
a. Date			
b. Type			
11. CERTIFICATION PERIOD		from: to:	from: to:
12. PARTICIPATED DURING SAMPLE MONTH		☐ YES ☐ NO	
13. REC'D EXPEDITED SERVICE		☐ YES ☐ NO	
14. REVIEWER(S)			
15. DATE(S) ASSIGNED			
16. DATE OF CASE READING(S)			
17. DATE OF HOME VISIT(S)			
18. DATE(S) COMPLETED			
19. SUPERVISOR(S)			
20. DATE(S) CLEARED			

B. PERSONS LIVING IN THE HOME

	NAME	BIRTHDATE	AGE	RELATIONSHIP OR SIGNIFICANCE	SOCIAL SECURITY NUMBER	AFDC/ADULT Recip.	AFDC/ADULT Elig.	FS Recip.	MEDICAID Recip.	MEDICAID Elig.	MEDICAID Serv. Rec.	MEDICAID TPL
1												
2												
3												
4												
5												
6												
7												
8												
9												
10												

C. SIGNIFICANT PERSONS NOT LIVING IN THE HOME

	NAME	RELATIONSHIP OR SIGNIFICANCE	SOCIAL SECURITY NUMBER	ADDRESS	FINANCIAL SUPPORT	TPL RESOURCE
11						
12						
13						
14						
15						

D. REVIEW FINDINGS

AFDC/ADULT

GRANT AMOUNT _____

☐ AMOUNT CORRECT
☐ OVERPAYMENT
☐ UNDERPAYMENT
☐ INELIGIBLE

AMOUNT IN ERROR _____
NUMBER OF ELEMENTS IN ERROR _____

FOOD STAMPS

ALLOTMENT _____

☐ AMOUNT CORRECT
☐ OVERISSUANCE
☐ UNDERISSUANCE
☐ INELIGIBLE
☐ VALID NEGATIVE CASE
☐ INVALID NEGATIVE CASE

AMOUNT IN ERROR _____

MEDICAID

ELIGIBILITY STATUS
☐ ELIGIBLE
☐ LIABILITY UNDERSTATED
☐ LIABILITY OVERSTATED
☐ TOTALLY INELIGIBLE
☐ ELIGIBLE WITH INELIGIBLE MEMBER(S)
☐ LIABILITY UNDERSTATED WITH INELIGIBLE MEMBERS
☐ LIABILITY OVERSTATED WITH INELIGIBLE MEMBERS

INITIAL LIABILITY ERROR _____
NUMBER OF ELEMENTS IN ERROR _____

Form SSA-4340 (4-84)
Form HCFA-316 (4-84)   Prior editions may be used until supply is exhausted
Form FNS-380 (4-84)

FIGURE 11.1

Worksheet for Integrated AFDC, Food Stamps and Medicaid Quality Control Reviews.

Work Sheet   ELEMENTS OF ELIGIBILITY AND PAYMENT DETERMINATION   Review No. _____

(1) ELEMENTS OF ELIGIBILITY AND PAYMENT DETERMINATION	(2) QC ANALYSIS OF CASE RECORD (Pertinent facts, sources of verification, reliability, gaps or deficiencies)	(3) FINDINGS OF FIELD INVESTIGATION (Facts obtained, verification and substantiation, nature of errors)	RESULTS			
			AFDC (4)	FS (5)	MQC (6)	ADUL1 (7)
110 AGE AND SCHOOL ATTENDANCE	BASIC PROGRAM REQUIREMENTS (100)		1 2 3	1 2 3		1 2 3
120 RELATIONSHIP					1 2 3	
130 CITIZENSHIP AND ALIENAGE			1 2 3	1 2 3	1 2 3	1 2 3
140 RESIDENCY			1 2 3	1 2 3	1 2 3	1 2 3

Form SSA-4340 (4-84) Prior Editions May Be Used Until Supply Is Exhausted
Form HCFA-316 (4-84)
Form FNS-380 (4-84)

Page 2

FIGURE 11.1
continued

1. Avoid instances of two questions presented as one (double-barreled, two-headed), because the respondent does not know which to answer, for example (Belson, 1981, p. 24): "Do you think there are enough job opportunities for a person like you in this district or do you think there are better jobs elsewhere?" To avoid this kind of confusion, pose two separate questions.

2. Avoid questions that contain difficult or unfamiliar words, for example, *constituency, excluding, merit, to-date, antiseptic* (Belson, p. 25). Select instead words that are likely to be in the client's vocabulary, for example, *neighbors who vote in the candidate's district, other than, reward for good work, up to today, cleaning agent,* respectively.

3. Avoid questions that contain multiple ideas or subjects (Belson, 1981, p. 25): "Can you give me some idea of the number, makes, and sizes of each that you have sold to date or have in stock at the moment?"

4. Avoid very long questions.

5. Avoid leading or loaded questions that tell the respondent how to answer: "You know that you will not be eligible for alimony don't you?" To avoid this source of bias, pose the question so that any answer would be acceptable: "Do you think you will be eligible for alimony?"

These pointers were based on a comparison of questionnaire responses that were checked for accuracy by a later follow-up interview in order to identify common sources of confusion in question wording (Belson, 1981).

Surveys Are More Credible Than Case Examples Because They Use Larger Samples

As stated earlier, the law of large numbers means that samples that include successively larger proportions of a population will generally represent that population more accurately (Hays, 1981, p. 186). Consequently, survey researchers base their generalizations on samples large enough to represent the population's characteristics within a computable margin of error. To demonstrate the law of large numbers in a practical situation, let us assume that counselors who administer a treatment program for chemically dependent adolescents have kept a record of pretest and posttest scores for all 100 of the program's participants during the past 6 months. Further assume that the counselors have measured, among other outcomes, the Index of Peer Relations (Hudson, 1982). The Index of Peer Relations (IPR) is a 25-item, self-administered measure concerning feelings of acceptance, group belonging, and the clients' perceptions of how others perceive them. IPR scores range from 0, meaning extremely good self-rated relationships with peers, to 100, meaning extremely poor acceptance. Scores greater than 30 imply pathological peer relationships. Reliability figures are not available for the IPR scale (Hudson, 1982, p. 91).

Further assume that to compute a rough index of their program's effect on its 100 participants, the counselors have subtracted each participant's posttest score from the participant's pretest score. Thus, a positive difference score means improvement; a negative score means deterioration. Figure 11.2 shows how means of 5 successively larger samples that include 1, 5, 20, and 50 individuals from the treated population ($N = 100$, IPR mean $= 20$, $SD = 8$) successively more accurately represent the total treated population within successively narrower 68% confidence intervals.

This simulation illustrates how samples of successively larger portions of the population generally represent the population's characteristics more accurately. Note in Figure 11.2 that as the samples increase in size, their means move toward the population mean change score of 20. The mean of their means does likewise. Note also how decreases in variation among the sample means occur with larger sample sizes. This simulation was made using a computer program developed by Frankenberger (1986).

The moral of this example is that, even if we assume that people who present case examples at case conferences intend to select them randomly (a not very tenable assumption given the tendency of many people to want to prove their point), and even if five cases (a relatively large number as case conferences go) were chosen to represent a program's effects, such cases would probably be very unrepresentative of the population served by the agency. Obviously, survey tech-

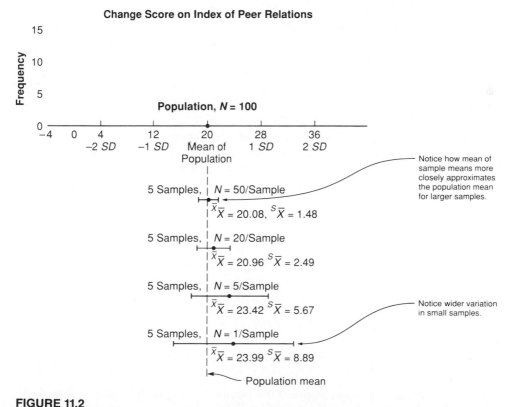

FIGURE 11.2
How means of sample means for successively larger samples better estimate the population mean.

niques that use larger samples are far superior to case examples as sources of accurate generalizations about clients.

A caution is in order here. Even if the chemically dependent adolescents averaged 20 points higher at posttest than they did at pretest, their improvement might be due to confounders; that is, causal factors other than the counselors' intervention (see Figure 4.3 for a list of such confounders).

Surveys Are Superior to Case Examples Because Survey Researchers Draw Samples Representatively

Ideally, samples should be representative. A sample is representative regarding a given characteristic when its aggregate characteristic (e.g., mean difference on Index of Peer Relations) closely approximates that of the population. Representativeness depends on how individuals are chosen for inclusion in the sample. Simple random selection is an excellent way to ensure, within limits due to error in any sample, that a sample is representative of the population from which it was taken. As defined and described in Chapter 5, random selection means that each individual has an equal and independent chance of being selected for study from the population. Samples that are drawn randomly are advantageous because they best represent their population, and they also obey rules of probability that allow us to estimate their accuracy (Kish, 1965).

Nonprobability samples do not rely on random procedures as guides to subject selection, but instead rely on availability or the selector's judgment. Nonprobability samples are notoriously subject to bias. For example, one way to construct a nonprobability sample might be to ask all 100 adolescent participants in the chemical dependency treatment program to volunteer to take a posttest on the Index of Peer Relations. Volunteers, signified by V in the hypothetical data charted in Figure 11.3 might be quite different from nonvolunteers. Nonvolunteers may not be proud of their progress, they may be less communicative, less socially stable, less traceable for questioning, and so on. Therefore, a report of mean change among volunteers might overestimate change for all participants in the chemical dependency program. Note that in Figure 11.3 the mean change score for volunteers is substantially higher than that for nonvolunteers.

Practitioners in charge of the program, who probably would not intentionally try to bias a case presentation at a case conference, might further bias the picture of the program's effectiveness by picking as a case example the one volunteer they recall best, an individual who might also happen to be one of their most successful cases. Such a hypothetical individual is also indicated in Figure 11.3.

AN ILLUSTRATION OF SURVEY RESEARCH: HOW AFDC QUALITY-CONTROL FINDINGS REFUTE THE WELFARE QUEEN CASE EXAMPLE

Recall the welfare queen example at the beginning of this chapter. She was black, had many children, stayed on AFDC forever, and received payments fraudulently. The welfare queen stereotype, an emotion-packed case example, is atyp-

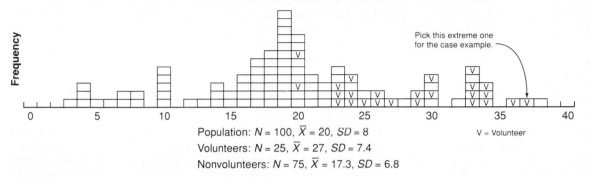

FIGURE 11.3
Hypothetical data showing how volunteers and selected case examples may not represent the treated population.

ical. Survey researchers at both the federal and local level have for many years been exercising good survey research procedures that refute the welfare queen case example. Their excellent survey methodology helps dispel case example's emotional appeal.

Federal and state quality-control's systematic random sampling procedures (Office of Family Assistance, 1984) further illustrate how to avoid the case example fallacy. Recall how case example depends on the user's ignorance of the law of large numbers and ignorance of sample representativeness. The AFDC quality-control program carefully avoids these errors by systematically sampling cases monthly for review. Systematic random sampling means that every kth individual in the total list of individuals (AFDC recipients in a given month in each state) is selected. If the state's proportion of AFDC recipients dictates that among 10,000 AFDC recipients 300 must be sampled annually, then by the end of the year every 33rd case should have been selected for review. Randomness enters into case selection by choosing the first case randomly, then every 33rd case thereafter from the list. Systematic random sampling can become biased if the list is compiled in some way that makes every 33rd case different from others; such periodicity is avoided by listing cases randomly according to eligibility factors, amount of payment, and so on.

National quality-control figures based on interviews of representatively chosen cases refute the welfare queen stereotype (Family Support Administration, 1987). Results of quality-control surveys show the following characteristics of recipients nationally: 88% female; 39.8% black, 38.8% white, 15.5% Hispanic, 2.6% Asian, 1.3% Native American; family size of two children and one adult; median length of time since most recent opening of the case, 27 months; and percent of families on AFDC rolls for 5 or more years, 26%. The national error rate refutes the perception that the typical AFDC recipient is a cheat. The national error rate of overpayments is 13.8%, but of this 13.8%, 8% of errors were traced to the AFDC agency, leaving only 5.8% that could be due to the client

(Family Support Administration, 1984, p. 23). Even among the 5.8% who receive payments in error that can be traced to the client's not reporting information or providing incorrect or incomplete information, the question of intent arises. In many cases, client error may be traced to the recipient not understanding questions about eligibility.

SUMMARY

This chapter has demonstrated the vast superiority of survey research techniques over case example as a way to make generalizations about clients. Although this may seem obvious, if the lessons in this chapter were, in fact, obvious, then case example would be almost unheard of among social workers. If case example were widely understood for the fallacy it is, anyone trying to present one at a case conference or professional meeting would fail to find a receptive audience. The appeal of case example lies in the way it plays on emotions and oversimplifies complex issues. As antidotes to case example's seductiveness, survey research offers interviews, questionnaires, and larger samples of representatively chosen individuals.

EXERCISES

A Case of Role Reversal—The Q Family: A 58-year-old gentle, bright, successful businessman joined the Alzheimer Family Support Group two years ago and has continued active participation to date. His 55-year-old wife whom he loves dearly had been diagnosed several years earlier as having Alzheimer's Disease. He was deeply troubled by her angry denial that she had Alzheimer's, by his inability to please her in any way and by the burden and anger he felt at having to take care of everything, a job previously carried very well by his wife. . . . The husband's participation in the support group over the months has been thoughtful, reflecting the great pain he felt at the turn his life has taken. . . . He was subsequently helped to resolve the following issues. . . . He discussed them with their three sons who lived out of state. . . . Next, he was helped to hire a part-time home health aide. . . . He accepted gradually that as the responsible caretaker, he had to do what he believed was genuinely in her best interest. . . . The Support Group has played a helpful role in his improved functioning. (Bernstein, 1984, pp. 165–166).

The authors conclude: "Over the two-year period several staff members served such clients on their caseloads with positive results" (Bernstein, 1984, p. 167).

1. What kind of evidence is given in this example?
2. How would you proceed, assuming you had the resources and the necessary permission to study group members, to estimate whether clients exposed to the Alzheimer Family Support Group will improve during the next 6 months?
3. Ideally, assuming you had the resources and the necessary permission, how would you determine whether the group is causing its members to change?

REFERENCES

Abraham, I. L., & Schultz, S. (1984). The "law of small numbers": An unexpected and incidental replication. *The Journal of Psychology, 117,* 183–188.

Anderson, C. A. (1983). Abstract and concrete data in the perseverance of social theories: When weak data lead to unshakeable beliefs. *Journal of Experimental Social Psychology, 19,* 93–108.

Bainbridge, W. S. (1989). *Survey research: A computer-assisted introduction.* Belmont, CA: Wadsworth.

Bell, R. A., Nguyen, T. D., Warheit, G. J., & Buhl, J. M. (1978). In C. C. Atkisson, W. A. Hargreaves, M. J. Horowitz, & J. E. Sorensen (Eds.), *Evaluation of human service programs* (pp. 253–300). New York: Academic Press.

Belson, W. A. (1981). *The design and understanding of survey questions*. Aldershot, Hants, England: Gower.

Bernstein, H. (1984). An Alzheimer family support group project. *Journal of Jewish Communal Service, 61*(2), 160–168.

California woman earns 'welfare queen' title. (1981, March 12). *Jet, 59,* p. 8.

Family Support Administration. (1984). *Quality control, Aid to Families with Dependent Children, detailed statistical tables, findings*. Washington, DC: U.S. Department of Health and Human Services.

Family Support Administration. (1987). *Characteristics and financial circumstances of AFDC recipients*. Washington, DC: U.S. Department of Health and Human Services.

Family Support Administration. (1988, February). *AFDC quality control manual; section 3. Case review process*. Washington, DC: U. S. Department of Health and Human Services.

Frankenberger, W. (1986). *Introductory statistics: Software package*. Reading, MA: Addison-Wesley.

Hamill, R., Nisbett, R. E., & Wilson, T. D. (1980). Insensitivity to sample bias: Generalizing from atypical cases. *Journal of Personality and Social Psychology, 39*(4), 578–589.

Hays, W. L. (1981). *Statistics* (3rd ed.). New York: Holt, Rinehart and Winston.

Hudson, W. W. (1982). *The clinical measurement package*. Homewood, IL: Dorsey.

Kish, L. (1965). *Survey sampling*. New York: Wiley.

Labow, P. J. (1980). *Advanced questionnaire design*. Cambridge, MA: Abt Books.

Monette, D. R., Sullivan, T. J., & DeJong, C. R. (1986). *Applied social research,* New York: Holt, Rinehart & Winston.

Office of Family Assistance. (1984). *QC Manual/2000: Quality Control in AFDC, Section 2, Sampling & Statistical Methods*. Washington, DC: U.S. Department of Health and Human Services.

Office of the Federal Register, National Archives and Records Administration. (1988, October 1). *Code of Federal Regulations, Title 45, Part 20, Section 0* (p. 31). Washington, DC: U.S. Government Printing Office.

Oskamp, S. (1982). Overconfidence in case-study judgments. In D. Kahneman, P. Slovic, & A. Tversky (Eds.), *Judgment under uncertainty: Heuristics and biases* (pp. 287–293). Cambridge: Cambridge University Press.

Rosenthal, R., & Rosnow, R. L. (1975). *The volunteer subject*. New York: Wiley.

She's known as Chicago's "welfare queen." (1978, July 3). *U.S. News & World Report, 84,* p. 28.

Tversky, A., & Kahneman, D. (1971). Belief in "the law of small numbers." *Psychological Bulletin, 76,* 105–110.

Tversky, A., & Kahneman, D. (1974). Judgment under uncertainty: Heuristics and biases. *Science, 185,* 1124–1131.

U.S. Department of Health and Human Services, Social Security Administration. (1989). *Compilation of the Social Security Laws: Including the Social Security Act, as amended and related enactments through January 1, 1989* (WMCP: 101–10; p. 236). Washington, DC: U.S. Government Printing Office.

12

Candid Comments
for Scientist-Practitioners

MASTER: [To apprentice who is pacing back and forth across the room in a distracting manner]: Please dear boy, I am trying to think.

APPRENTICE: So am I master; so am I.

MASTER: Then try using your head instead of your heart, and we might make some progress.

APPRENTICE: A book's more important than people to you.

MASTER: Did I say that [it was] they were?

APPRENTICE: You never seem to care about anyone; couldn't you at least show a little pity?

MASTER: Perhaps that is the style of my pity. Pity won't save her from the fire. (Eichinger, 1986)

MOTIVATION FOR THE SCIENTIST-PRACTITIONER

The dialogue between medieval master and apprentice concerns their thinking about how to save a young peasant girl from the forces of dogma, superstition, and unsubstantiated speculation that would have the girl burned to death at the stake as a witch. The apprentice erroneously assumes that because the master tries to be analytical about what to do that his heart is cold. This assumption abounds even today. Bierter's (1977) caution about "The Dangers of Allowing Social Work to Be Invaded by Science" may be the most extreme statement of the ancient soft-hearted therefore soft-headed dichotomy. Yet, just recently, the great voices of social work have been heard debating whether scientific reasoning can guide practice (Brekke, 1986; Ivanoff, Blythe, & Briar, 1987; Heineman, 1981; Robinson, Bronson, & Blythe, 1988; Smith, 1987).

This text has tried to show that it is precisely because practitioners do care about clients that they turn to principles of scientific reasoning. Scientist-practitioners who know that their use of science arises out of love for others will have the motivation that is so essential to persevere in their search for effective methods. Those whose work was described in Chapter 1, who tried to help the frail elderly by relocating them to nursing homes, meant well; but only principles of scientific reasoning, expertly and conscientiously applied, can explain the sad story of higher death rates among those relocated (Blenkner, Bloom, & Nielsen, 1971). It helps to remember that love motivates the desire to help; scientific reasoning shows the way. Those who chronically deny their responsibility to produce measurable change deprive themselves of the chance to learn; they also condemn their clients to endure effects of repeated errors.

EFFECTIVENESS PYRAMID

First Cornerstone: Resolution to Question Effectiveness

The four principal attributes of the scientist-practitioner role may be thought of as the cornerstones at the base of a pyramid—all supporting effective practice at the pyramid's peak (see Figure 12.1). Without any one of the cornerstones, the pyramid is dangerously unstable. The first of the four corners, arising out of a commitment to producing measurable change, is a resolution to ask two questions: Does it work? How do you know?

Resolving to ask these two questions is easy; doing so is quite another task. For over a decade now, whenever I hear that my students are planning to attend a professional conference, I have commended them on being determined to stay current with their discipline and to take the extra time and resources to attend the conference. In addition, I have asked them if while attending the conference they would ask those two questions. The students, who have studied ideas in this text, have consistently promised that they would.

Upon their return from the conference—whether on techniques of family therapy, adoptions, reality therapy, validation therapy, reality orientation therapy, dealing with guilt, or myriad other topics—the students invariably report that they felt uncomfortable posing questions about effectiveness. They reported not wanting to stand out among hundreds who were not asking about the method's effectiveness; they feared others would see them as impertinent; they felt out of step thinking about the issue of effectiveness. Most often they reported having felt so uncomfortable that neither they, nor anyone else at the conference, questioned the effectiveness of methods—to say nothing about the potential good or harm to clients who would be exposed to the method—that hundreds of people had traveled great distances, paid high conference fees, and spent days to learn about. The point is that the resolution to question may place scientist-practitioners in an uncomfortable position. Be prepared for the discomfort; it is a normal feeling and perhaps even a healthy one.

Second Cornerstone: Resolution to Be As Objective As Possible

The second cornerstone of the pyramid is the motivation to be objective while pursuing the issue of effectiveness. Asking questions about effectiveness is a beginning; but the scientist-practitioner must be ready to listen to the answer with an open mind. My students report that evidence presented at professional conferences they have attended, without a single exception, has been one-sided. That is, if the issue of effectiveness arises at all, the evidence presented by the method's proponents only supports the methods' *effectiveness*—never is counterevidence summarized. If we are really to know the truth about what works, we must advocate that *all* the relevant evidence be presented, that which supports and that which refutes the method's effectiveness. How else could we ever know where the truth lies?

Some intriguing research suggests how scientist-practitioners may overcome the bias that clouds attempts to see the issue of effectiveness clearly. One study, by Lord, Ross, and Lepper (1979), suggests that those who read studies will interpret study methodology to be stronger when the study's conclusions support the reader's bias; methodology will be judged weaker where findings refute a favored conclusion. The Quality of Study Rating Form presented in Chapter 9 introduced standards for interpreting studies that can make study interpretation more systematic, and thus foster greater objectivity. This assumes, of course, that studies supporting and refuting a method's effects will be included in the study synthesis. Another procedure is restating as accurately as possible the proponent's argument—resisting any urge to formulate a reaction to the argument until it is fully understood—and only then examining the argument's credibility. Callaway and Esser's (1984, p. 157) study suggests that "groupthink" hobbles objective thinking. Apparently, groups that are highly cohesive may stifle discussions of dissenting opinions and, consequently, the group misses the benefit of hearing a variety of opinions before reaching a conclusion. Perhaps, in addition to using aids such as the QSRF, professional meetings could be structured to encourage examination of supporting and refuting evidence.

FIGURE 12.1
Effective practice pyramid.

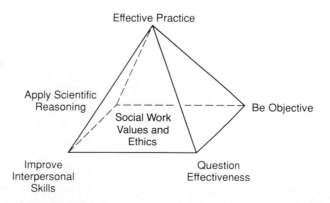

Third Cornerstone: Resolution to Apply Scientific Reasoning

Scientist-practitioners will try to reason scientifically about problems that arise in practice. They resolve to apply research methods to practice including single-subject and group experimental designs, measurement, and the use of probability in risk assessment. Scientist-practitioners believe that no conclusion about a method's effectiveness can be any better than the method by which that conclusion was drawn. They will also resolve to follow ethical guidelines in chapter 6.

The real problem of closing the gap between practice and research may not be so much learning to understand principles of research methods as it is knowing how scientific principles apply to everyday practice. For example, knowing measurement implies an understanding of reliability and validity of outcome measures; application implies knowing how measurement helps to avoid the vagueness and bias inherent in client testimonials. Or, students of research methods may fully understand the principle of representativeness of a sample, but they must also understand how it applies to practice well enough not to get taken in by case examples that violate every principle of survey design. In addition to understanding and avoiding practitioners' fallacies, other principles for bridging the practice-research chasm include: soliciting researchable questions from practitioners; learning how to formulate a specific, answerable question; and applying principles of risk assessment to decision making.

Fourth Cornerstone: Resolution to Improve Interpersonal Skills

At least as important as the preceding ones, the fourth and final cornerstone is knowing how to exercise effective interpersonal skills in relationships with clients, peers, and administrators. Interpersonal skills are essential to surviving in the scientist-practitioner role. It is possible to be dead right but to lose the battle—and the war—by ignoring the simple fact that discussions regarding client care go on in an interpersonal context.

The hypothetical scientist-practitioner whose reasoning follows, has laid the first three cornerstones of the pyramid properly, but lets the whole structure topple by ignoring the fourth.

> Ms. Phillips, a protective service worker herself, has planned and executed a study in her child protective service agency. The study compares 6-month reabuse/no reabuse predictions by her fellow protective service workers against an actuarial prediction device's results for the same cases. She has found that the actuarial method's positive predictive value was 48% against only 28% for the professionals' predictions. Ms. Phillips is excited about the practical implications of the study, and she is now presenting them to her colleagues.

MS. PHILLIPS: So now you have it! This table shows that the prediction instrument outperformed your predictions by 20%! That's a substantial margin. I was astounded myself. What do you think we should do with these findings? (At this point Ms. Phillips is confident that her detailed description shows that she has made a great contribution to her agency and its clients.)

MS. GRAHAM (A CO-WORKER): I know you put a lot of work into this but, well, I'm not so sure what to think of your findings. It puts us all into a kind of bad light, and I'm not sure about making decisions about clients using your instrument— that is where you're headed with this, isn't it?—because it would reduce them all to numbers. I prefer to treat people as individuals in a humane way. You know what I mean?

MS. PHILLIPS: If I can rephrase your position accurately, it sounds as though you're saying that we either use the risk-assessment instrument in this agency or we treat our clients humanely. Your thinking is either-or reasoning.

MS. GRAHAM: Can you pass that one by me one more time in English?

MS. PHILLIPS: We can do both. We can even help our clients *more* humanely, because we can administer the risk-assessment instrument quickly, shorten our lengthy assessment, and use the time saved to work more intensively with the high-risk clients. (Ms. Phillips is feeling a little needled at this point but tries not to show it. She is thinking: "Why don't they see the sense in this? What's bothering them?")

MR. REID (ANOTHER CO-WORKER): I never accepted the way you defined abuse. I think you should have considered abuse to mean emotional abuse when you conducted the study. That was what I was taking into account when I made my predictions.

MS. PHILLIPS: Well, that may be a valid definitional point, but now your concern is a little late. We did

get good interrater reliability for the follow-up determination of reabuse in this
study. Perhaps we could add your criteria
to a replication study. I tried to get your in-
put when we set the criteria for measuring
abuse, but you did not attend the planning
meetings that I scheduled. . . .

SUGGESTIONS FOR SCIENTIST-PRACTITIONERS

This hypothetical example could go on, but the point has been made: Even though
the scientist-practitioner has engaged in effective thinking based on empirical
evidence that has practical implications, it does not necessarily follow that good
reasoners will win the day. Interpersonal factors, the fourth cornerstone of the
pyramid, can profoundly affect acceptance of scientific reasoning in human service agencies.

Following are suggestions for functioning more effectively in the scientist-
practitioner role:

1. Practice Good Social Skills: While thinking scientifically, practice interpersonal skills learned in courses on interviewing, fieldwork methods, and interpersonal relations. The interpersonal skills component in social work
   education is just as important as the research component. In the example,
   Ms. Phillips might have included co-workers more effectively in goal setting,
   established rapport at the beginning of the meeting, and reflected feelings of
   being threatened by the study's findings.

2. Be Mission-Oriented: Keep in mind that ultimately agencies should help clients to achieve specific goals. There is a tendency to get so involved in daily
   routines of *how* that the *why* is forgotten. Others may be more likely to accept
   scientific reasoning if it is prefaced by a restatement of the agency's objectives and how the research applies to them. Perhaps Ms. Phillips could have
   established better rapport with others in the agency by constantly referring
   to the mission of the protective service department—protecting children and
   helping parents to deal with problems that foster abuse.

3. Trust Yourself: At times scientific reasoning can be quite revolutionary and
   seemingly out of step. When you find yourself thinking in an "unusual" way
   based on principles in this text, consider that the unusual may be right.
   Sometimes it helps to have someone who also subscribes to the scientist-
   practitioner role to whom you can turn for support. Ms. Phillips might have
   had supporters in the meeting who were not speaking up. Supporters might
   have been included in the presentation.

4. Be Positive: It is easy to blame others and question their motives when they
   disagree. As a general rule, people do not wake up in the morning and resolve to be difficult, obstinate, and oppositional all day. Being positive does
   not imply accepting a weak argument but it does imply giving others credit

for being motivated to help clients too. Give others credit for being well intentioned and listen carefully to what they have to say. Ms. Phillips might have done so.

5. Choose the Best Time to Present Scientific Thinking: Some situations are hopeless: Nothing done or said will change the thinking of others when they are heavily stressed, angry, or feeling threatened. Wait until the time is right to approach others about how scientific thinking may help. Ms. Phillips might have called the meeting at a less stressful time.

6. Define Your Terms: Sometimes arguments can be avoided by defining specifically what you mean by "improvement" or "reabuse." Defining such concepts operationally can take a lot more time than expected, so allow for it. Consensus takes time to establish. Ms. Phillips did not have the consensus of the group on what to measure to determine reabuse.

7. Avoid Arrogance: There may be a tendency to think that those who commit practitioners' fallacies are inferior somehow and to be short with such persons. Nothing can prevent good teamwork as surely as such an attitude. It is likely that detractors possess great native intelligence, are masters of interpersonal skills and are highly motivated to help clients. Recognize, acknowledge, and respect the strengths of those who may not share your views.

8. Be Patient: Introducing scientific reasoning into agency life is a lifelong calling. Far-reaching and long-lasting gains are not achieved in one day. Haste can only slow efforts to foster scientific thinking.

9. Be Competent: Demands of social work practice can be extreme indeed. It may be all you can do to stay current with literature regarding a few principal questions central to helping your clients. You may be able to implement only a few single-subject studies each month; or you may be able to conduct only one small group study in a year. Still, you can hold yourself accountable and reward yourself for a job well done if you are making a genuine effort toward increasing your skill in scientific thinking.

Although these suggestions are, for the most part, without empirical foundation they may prove helpful to those who are struggling to adopt the scientist-practitioner role. It is hoped that the day will come when the term "scientist-practitioner" will be obsolete, and the reaction to the term might then be: "What else could a practitioner rely on but science? Surely not dogma and speculation!"

SUMMARY

Love motivates us to want to help; scientific reasoning shows us the way. Those who chronically deny their responsibility to produce measurable change deprive themselves of the chance to learn; they also condemn their clients to endure effects of repeated errors. This chapter describes a pyramid with effectiveness at its apex. Supporting effectiveness are the four cornerstones of the scientist-practitioner role: questioning effectiveness, striving for objectivity when weighing evidence about effectiveness, applying scientific reasoning, and employing effective interpersonal skills. Suggestions for facilitating the scientist-practitioner role concluded the chapter.

EXERCISES

1. The Professional Thinking Form presented in Chapter 3 contains practitioners' fallacies that can provide 23 topics for instructive, enjoyable, and brief role plays. Ask groups of students to select *one* practitioners' fallacy to demonstrate before the class (mixing fallacies makes it hard for the audience to guess the fallacy). The role play should be as realistic as possible and therefore role players will need to become thoroughly familiar with how the fallacy works so they can write a brief script. (When students observe a fallacy firsthand in their fieldwork, they can role play the fallacy best while the incident is fresh in their minds.) At the role play's beginning, it helps to have a narrator provide background information about the type of agency, type of clients served, and the problem under discussion. The audience's task is to name the fallacy and to explain how it works. (A similar exercise has been called "Clinical Flaw Catching" by the Clinical Scholars at the University of North Carolina, Michael, Boyce, & Wilcox, 1984, p. xi.)

2. Students can plan a mock case conference that includes a series of practitioners' fallacies. For example, role players might act the parts of a social work practitioner, nurse, psychiatrist, and clinical psychologist who are discussing what treatment may best help a particular mental health client. Ideally, one of the participants present will cite research that strongly supports a particular controversial treatment, for example electroconvulsive shock for depression (Janicak, Davis, Gibbons, Ericksen, Chang, & Gallagher, 1985). Each of the other players might engage in lame thinking to portray various practitioners' fallacies. If the role play is videotaped, it will be possible to stop the videotape after each fallacy so the audience can name the fallacy and explain how it was committed; then go on to the next vignette. (For a sample script, see Stehle-Werner & Gibbs, 1987.)

3. Obtain a videotaped or filmed description of an intervention method that purports to demonstrate, in highly emotional ways, an intervention method's effectiveness. The film should display as many practitioners' fallacies as possible, and it should provide no empirical evidence. Possible selections include: Bell, 1976; Pool, Kasper, and Zitske, undated; Scarpaci and Scarpaci, 1989; Shapiro, 1978; WXYZ Television Station, 1987. Have students view the audiovisual material and ask them the following questions: Based purely on this audiovisual material, would you recommend that (name of the intervention method) be adopted to help clients? Why would you or would you not recommend that the method be adopted?

   To score responses to this exercise, give 5 points for a no answer to the first question. Give 1 point for each practitioners' fallacy named and 1 point for each explanation that describes how the practitioners' fallacy is working in the audiovisual presentation. Videotaped examples of social work students at work doing this exercise are available (Gibbs & Capra, 1985; Gibbs & Schleicher, 1987).

4. Here is an experiment that might be done as an exercise by a research methods class. This experiment evaluates whether there is an association between a measure of knowledge of research principles and ability to see how basic research principles apply to social work practice. In other words, do social workers transfer knowledge of basic research principles to social work practice? To conduct the experiment, administer Chapter 3's Professional Thinking Form to students who have taken at least one research course that does not use this text. Also administer the Research Information Scale portion of the Kirk-Rosenblatt Research Inventory—this form, developed in 1978 measures knowledge of research principles—to the same students. The following research question should accompany the experiment:

   > Among _____(number) of social work students who attended _____(name of course) at _____(college or university), during _____(period of time), who reported having completed at least one research methods course, and who have never read any part of this text, will there be a positive correlation between their score on the Professional Thinking Form and the Research Information Scale of the Kirk-Rosenblatt Re-

search Inventory (Pearson *r, p* < .10) for those who took both measures on ＿＿＿＿＿＿＿ (date)?

5. The Kirk-Rosenblatt Research Inventory's Research Information Scale, the Professional Thinking Form, and the procedure for rating responses to highly emotional videotaped case material in exercise 3 might all serve as outcome measures to evaluate effectiveness of different approaches to teaching research courses in social work. Presently, there do not appear to be published evaluations that compare the effectiveness of one method against another for teaching scientific reasoning to social workers. As an exercise, apply these three measures to classes that have been exposed to different methods for teaching research methods and evaluate their effects.

REFERENCES

Bell, D. (Producer). (1976). *Reality therapy in high school: New approaches to high school learning and discipline* [Film]. Hollywood, CA: Media Five Film Distributors.

Bierter, W. (1977). The dangers of allowing social work to be invaded by science. *International Social Service Journal, 29*(4), 789–794.

Blenkner, M., Bloom, M., & Nielsen, M. (1971). A research and demonstration project of protective services. *Social Casework, 52*(8), 483–499.

Brekke, J. S. (1986). Scientific imperatives in social work research: Pluralism is not skepticism. *Social Service Review, 60*(4), 538–554.

Callaway, M. R., & Esser, J. K. (1984). Groupthink: Effects of cohesiveness and problem-solving procedures on group decision making. *Social Behavior and Personality, 12*(2), 157–164.

Eichinger, B. (Producer), & Annaud, J. (Director). (1986). *The name of the rose* [Film]. Beverly Hills, CA: Twentieth-Century Fox.

Gibbs, L. E. (Speaker), & Capra, L. (Director). (1985). *Critical thinking exercise for professional social workers.* (Cassette Recording No. 666). Eau Claire, WI: Media Development Department, University of Wisconsin—Eau Claire.

Gibbs, L. E. (Speaker), & Schleicher, D. (Director). (1987). *Scared Straight! Classroom discussion.* (Cassette Recording No. 1065). Eau Claire, WI: Media Development Department, University of Wisconsin—Eau Claire.

Ivanoff, A., Blythe, B. J., & Briar, S. (1987). The empirical clinical practice debate. *Social Casework, 68,* 290–298.

Janicak, P. G., Davis, J. M., Gibbons, R. D., Ericksen, S., Chang, S., & Gallagher, P. (1985). Efficacy of ECT: A meta-analysis. *American Journal of Psychiatry, 142*(3), 297–302.

Kirk, S. A., & Rosenblatt, A. (1978). *Kirk-Rosenblatt Research Inventory.* Unpublished test. State University of New York at Albany, NY.

Lord, C. G., Ross, L., & Lepper, M. R. (1979). Biased assimilation and attitude polarization: The effects of prior theories on subsequently considered evidence. *Journal of Personality and Social Psychology, 37*(11), 2098–2109.

Michael, M., Boyce, W. T., & Wilcox, A. J. (1984). *Biomedical bestiary: An epidemiologic guide to flaws and fallacies in the medical literature.* Boston: Little, Brown.

Poole, M. E., Kasper, K. M. (Producers), & Zitske, J. (Technical Assistant). (Undated). *Creating alternative futures: Choice and change through the Community Options Program* [Slide and Audiotape]. Madison, WI: Image Makers. Office of Program Initiatives, Division of Community Service, P.O. Box 7851.

Robinson, E. A. R., Bronson, D. E., & Blythe, B. J. (1988). An analysis of the implementation of single-case evaluation by practitioners. *Social Service Review, 62*(2), 285–301.

Scarpaci, M. (Producer), & Scarpaci, P. (Director). (1989). *Mind power: Winning at losing weight* [Film]. Ojai, CA: Gateways Research Institute.

Shapiro, A. (Producer). (1978). *Scared straight* [Film]. Santa Monica, CA: Pyramid Films.

Smith, D. (1987). The limits of positivism in social work research. *British Journal of Social Work, 17*(4), 401–416.

Stehl-Werner, J., & Gibbs, L. E. (1987). Clinicians' fallacies in psychiatric practice. *Journal of Psychosocial Nursing and Mental Health Services, 25*(8), 14–17.

WXYZ Television Station (Producer) (1976). *Group therapy and the fight to overcome substance abuse.* [Videotape]. Southfield, MI: WXYZ Television Station.

Appendix A

Sample Consent Form

(STUDY TOPIC)

I agree to participate in the study being conducted by (name of university or research group) in cooperation with: (name of human service agency supplying subjects). The study, funded by (source of funding) , concerns characteristics of people related to (study topic) . The information is being gathered to (objective of study) . I understand that the information will be kept *strictly confidential and anonymous*. I understand that I am under no obligation to complete the study and that I may withdraw my participation at any time. I also understand that the responses I give to the *questionnaire will in no way affect my treatment*.

_____
(Signature)

_____
(Date)

Two copies of this page will be made, one for the subject to keep the other for the experimenter's records.

Appendix B

Manual for Conducting an On-Line Search

BACKGROUND

The old "left hind foot and then the right forepaw" method for searching social work literature is yielding to newer technologies. Now it is possible for social workers to take a quick look at the contents of hundreds of journals and thousands of articles to find just the source that fits a particular need. All of the citations and abstracts that have appeared in *Social Work Research and Abstracts* can be quickly accessed using descriptors, key words in the title, and words in the abstract.

These instructions describe in step-by-step fashion how to: (a) set up the equipment; (b) identify yourself to BRS; (c) conduct your search; (d) log off and save your file, and (e) print the file that has been saved.

Please note that all searches must be done *after dark*, that is, on Mondays through Fridays from 6:00 P.M. to 4:00 A.M., Saturdays from 6:00 A.M. to 2:00 A.M., and Sundays 6:00 A.M. to 4:00 P.M.

We need to be accountable to the library for our searches so that they can audit BRS charges to make sure they are legitimate. This accountability requires that we fill in the sections of the BRS log for every search. The last element in every search—assuming that we have connected with BRS and interacted with the SWAB data base—contains the number of minutes of on-line contact. This time total should be included in column 5 of the BRS log. (There is a 3¢ BRS charge for every abstract printed.)

Instructions in the BRS manual are complete. You can get the essence of what goes on in a search by reading pages 1–23 of the BRS manual, by consulting the BRS/After Dark Quick Reference Card, and by taking a look at the example search included here. At our level of sophistication, and given the efficiency of the command, I think searching the *title* for key words is the most efficient method. Also, it is essential to plan a search on paper completely by listing the computer's anticipated statements and the commands you plan to use *before* you begin your search. Doing so will make the search faster and therefore less costly.

Please report any "bugs" you may find in the procedures and program described in this manual so that modifications can be made to future editions.

To Set Up the Equipment

1. You will need a modem, a telephone line receptacle (it is the 3/8″-square hole in the wall directly above the other little square hole in the telephone outlet), a computer with a communications card in it (our portable has one), a TV monitor (our portable has the monitor built into it), communications software (in our case this is the KERMIT floppy disk), the BRS manual with its instructions for doing an "After Dark" search, and a formatted blank disk (marked "Formatted Disk").

2. Plug the computer's black cord into a 110-volt socket.

3. Plug the modem transformer (it is the 2″ × 3″ × 3″ black box) into a 110-volt socket and the other end, which looks like a circle with a period in the middle of it, into the modem in the "adapter" receptacle.

4. Connect the wire that comes out of the back of the telephone to the back of the modem where it is marked "to phone."

5. Connect the "to line" cord from the back of the modem to the telephone jack in the wall (use the top receptacle; first push the little door down).

6. Connect the serial port on the back of the computer (it is the 25-pin connection, second from the right when looking toward the back of the computer) to the 25-pin connection on the back of the modem with a 25-pin male-to-female cable. Tighten both screws on both connections firmly.

7. Open the IBM-PC portable computer by pushing the pins on the top front in and pulling down on the top front of the door.

8. Make sure the two buttons on the left front of the modem are pushed in. The right button, of the three there, should be out.

To Identify Yourself to BRS:

Task	You enter	Screen shows
1. Insert the Kermit Disk into drive A, (lettered side up) into the top slot and close the door.	All keys pressed are marked between the ⟨ ⟩ signs. If a command shows a space or no space between its elements be sure to follow that pattern.	

2. Insert "Formatted Disk" into drive **B**, (lettered side up) and close the door.		
3. Turn the computer on using the large red switch on the back left of the computer.		KERMIT—MS⟩
4.	Push ⟨caps lock⟩ and then ⟨Ret⟩ keys	KERMIT—MS⟩
5.	C ⟨Ret⟩	[Gibberish at bottom of screen]
6. Turn the modem on using the silver lever on the back right of the modem.		
7.	ATDT 98369295 ⟨Ret⟩ (If this number is busy you can connect with Timenet by dialing 98330121, waiting to hear the squeak, and typing A without following with a ⟨Ret⟩, then entering ⟨Ret⟩ after the letters BRS appear.)	
8. Wait for the squeak, then	⟨Ret⟩⟨Ret⟩	Terminal =
9.	⟨Ret⟩	@
10.	C 31520B ⟨Ret⟩	Connected
11.	3A1359 ⟨Ret⟩	Enter BRS Password MMMMM
12.	WALK ⟨Ret⟩	Enter Security Password MMMMM
		Welcome to . . .
13. Save your file	Hold down ⟨CTRL⟩ and then press]	
14.	C	KERMIT—MS⟩

| 15. | LOG enter a file name that you will remember in less than 9 characters ⟨Ret⟩ | KERMIT–MS⟩ |
| 16. | C⟨Ret⟩ | |

17. Conduct your search according to the BRS commands in the left column

N.B.: As your file is saved, the small red light-emitting diode on drive B should go on, off, and on again, as the search is saved. If the light for B drive is not going on and off periodically, your search is not being saved. Also, corrections made after the LOG command must be made by backspacing with ⟨Ctrl⟩ held down and ⟨H⟩.

To Conduct Your Search

1. Having a specific, planned, presearch strategy before turning the computer on always saves time. It is best, if you get stalled about what descriptor to use, to just log off and consult the descriptors in the back of *Social Work Research and Abstracts.*

2. The BRS manual is specific. Read pages 1–42 and keep handy the BRS/After Dark Quick Reference Card. As you read the manual, commands for your search will become evident. Here is a plan for a two-term search:

Commands	Explanation
SOCIAL WORK AND MINORITIES.TI.⟨Ret⟩	This command searches for the words "social work" *and* for the word "minorities" anywhere in the title. Searching titles has been a productive way to locate articles that pertain generally to a particular topic.
AUNT FANNY TALK ⟨Ret⟩	This command will search for the phrase "Aunt Fanny Talk" anywhere in the citation, the descriptors list, or the abstract. Use this general procedure for highly specific topics that have unusual descriptors.

3. Documents are added to the data base with document #1 being the most recent document added; if you want just the most recent sources on a given topic, you can limit the topic search by telling the computer that you only want documents 1–_____ (fill in the blank) for the most recent few documents.

4. You can always push H ⟨Ret⟩ for help at any time during a search.

To Log Off and Save the File

Task	You enter	Screen shows
1. Log off BRS-SWAB	O ⟨Ret⟩ (this is the letter "O")	CONNECT TIME 0:00:00 denoting hours, minutes, seconds; record in this time log.
2. Save your file!!!!!!!!!!! Enter these two commands; hold down ⟨Ctrl⟩ then press ⟨]⟩	⟨Ctrl⟩⟨]⟩	
3.	C ⟨Ret⟩	Kermit–MS⟩
4.	Close ⟨Ret⟩	
5.	Q ⟨Ret⟩	

To Print a File Saved

Task	You enter	Screen shows
1. Insert DOS disk into drive A.		
2. Insert "File Disk" into drive B of the computer. This "File Disk" is the one that was in drive B during your search.		
3. Turn the computer on.		A⟩

4. Turn the printer on. Usually, as in room 250, there are several computers connected to one printer; so you'll need to push the "A" button on the print selector box if you have computer "A," to make the printer connect to your computer.

```
TYPE B:your file name
)PRN:(Ret) (be sure to
leave a space after the
word TYPE and after
your filename just be-
fore the ) sign).
```

5. The printer should print your file until it reaches the end of the information entered during your search. The printing will include all of your commands too, so you can do a postmortem on your search to make future ones smoother. The Department's Volkswriter disk can also be used to print the file by just using Volkswriter to call up the file. The extraneous material can be deleted using Volkswriter commands to save printing time.

Appendix C

Answers to Exercises

CHAPTER 2

1. Manner—The speaker's manner, although entertaining, does not prove that a method is effective.

2. Popularity, Numbers—It does not necessarily follow that because the speaker is popular that the methods are effective.

3. Experience—Years of experience with hundreds of clients do not ensure that methods are effective.

4. *Ad Verecundium,* Authority, Status—The speaker's status does not, in itself, prove that methods are effective.

5. Tradition, Newness—Accepting methods because they are tried and true or because they are new does not assure success.

6. Testimonial—Clients can give useful information about how they are feeling and acting, but because they are subject to pressure and are not trained, objective observers their impressions are likely to be biased. Such bias, and the way unscrupulous presenters may avoid discussing unsuccessful cases, preclude testimonials as reliable evidence.

7. Either-Or Fallacy, False Dilemma, Soft-Hearted Therefore Soft-Headed— Here Dr. Wiley assumes that good intentions and interpersonal skill are sufficient in themselves to produce good results. This ignores the need to weigh evidence about effectiveness.

8. *Ad Hominem*—Dr. Wiley becomes angry when his ideas are examined, as though he himself were under attack. Such a position, when client care is

ultimately what matters more than any person's ego, can block the search for effective methods.

9. Uncritical Documentation—Documentation is desirable, but is not proof by itself. The arguments and evidence in the documentation must be sound.

CHAPTER 3

Key Words to Be Located in Answers	Explanation
1. manner, style, charisma, stage presence	The likeable and endearing way that a speaker presents an idea does not ensure that the idea is valid; only an examination of the speaker's argument can determine that (Allen & Greene, 1975, p. 20).
2. new, newness, tried-and-true, tradition	Accepting a method based on its newness or its traditional use ignores the fundamental issue of whether the method works (Fearnside & Holther, 1959, p. 89).
3. uncritical documentation, relying on citation alone	Just because an idea can be cited does not prove a point. The reference needs to be examined to see if its argument is cogent (Evans, 1958).
4. *ad hominem,* personal attack against the person	Here the co-worker rejects Bill's evidence because of Bill's personal life, not because of the co-worker's examination of the evidence (Johnson, Kurtz, Tomlinson, & Howe, 1986; Weddle, 1978, p. 38).
5. appeal to experience, all evidence is equally good, experience, ignorance of scientific evidence, ignoring evidence	The worker does not discriminate between more credible scientific evidence, with its procedures for controlling for bias, and personal experience, which is more subject to bias (Arkava & Lane, 1983, p. 8; Meehl, 1973, p. 228; Miller & Bogal, 1977).
6. popularity, peer pressure, bandwagon, numbers, because everybody. . . .	Widespread use of a treatment method does not prove its effectiveness (Fischer, 1978, p. 70; Moore & Parker, 1986, p. 134).
7. appeal to authority, status, titles, degrees, *ad verecundium*	Simply because an argument is espoused by someone with status or titles, it does not mean the argument is true or valid (Fischer, 1978, p. 70; Johnson & Blair, 1983, p. 144).
8. *ad hominem,* personal attack against the person	Ms. Hughes argument is rejected because of her personal appearance. Instead, the validity of her argument should be examined (Johnson,

Kurtz, Tomlinson, & Howe, 1986; Weddle, 1978, p. 83).

9. objectivity, objective, honest(ly), bias(ed), vested interest

Why conduct a study if it is only to produce particular results? If this is the purpose, just present the results without doing the study. Consultants should follow scientific principles, without allowing their client's self-interest to influence the findings (Gibbs, 1983; Kerlinger, 1986, p. 6).

10. either-or, only two sides, only two alternatives, false dilemma

Here the agency supervisor limits thinking about the problem by allowing discussion of only one alternative or the other. Both alternatives may be inappropriate. A combination of the two alternatives may be appropriate (Ruggerio, 1984, p. 155).

11. testimonial

Clients who give a testimonial are subject to bias about treatment effectiveness. Full credit may be given for listing any bias, for example, emotional appeal in the case material, subtle demand by therapists that the client give a positive report about therapy, any lack of objectivity in reports by clients, and unrepresentativeness of the client giving the testimonial (Smith, 1969, p. 123–141).

12. hasty generalization, possibly biased sample

Those who called the planners may not have reflected the whole community's sentiments. The callers may have been merely the most vocal. Reference to the need for survey scores 2 points (Atherton & Klemmack, 1982, p. 156; Johnson & Blair, 1983).

13. vagueness, unclear term, undefined term

Before looking for causal relationships, one must first define the related behaviors. What does "depressed" mean? How do we know the death was a "suicide"? What proportion is "most" (Johnson & Blair, 1983, p. 135)?

14. case example

Here it is inappropriate to judge a method's general effectiveness based on experience with a single individual (Hamill, Wilson, & Nisbett, 1980; Nisbett & Ross, 1980, p. 55).

15. two questions, double-barreled, two-headed, ambiguous bipolar

This question is confusing to the client because it poses two questions at once (Stewart & Cash, 1982, p. 79).

16. leading, loaded, biased question

This question strongly implies the answer wanted from the client, thus limiting the client's freedom to give an accurate answer (Cannell, Lawson, & Hausser, 1975, p. 15; Stewart & Cash, 1982, p. 86).

17. sweeping generalization, hasty generalization

This general statement is made without a shred of empirical evidence to support it. Respondents should get full credit on this item for asking any methodological question (Govier, 1985, p. 354; Schuerman, 1983, p. 63), for example, "What does 'conjoint family therapy' imply? Have studies been done to evaluate this treatment method? 'Most effective' relative to what?"

18. tautology, word defines itself, "progress" defines "progress"

By defining "progress" as being "progress," the reader does not know what specific behaviors are required to gauge progress (Fearnside & Holther, 1959, p. 137).

19. *post hoc,* after this, just because treatment precedes outcome

Simply because improvement follows treatment does not mean that treatment caused the improvement. Other factors may have caused the improvement; or improvement may have occurred in spite of the treatment (Cook & Campbell, 1979, p. 99; Govier, 1988, p. 302).

20. jargon

The worker uses professional words that the client cannot readily understand (Belson, 1981, p. 30; Kadushin, 1963).

21. regression, regression fallacy, regression to the mean

Individuals scoring extremely low or high on pretest tend to score closer to the mean on posttest. This is because extreme scores at pretest often have a high error component in them (Michael, Boyce, & Wilcox, 1984, p. 75).

22. ignoring: base rate, prior probability, prevalence rate

The probability (chance rated from 0 to 100) that an abuse has occurred, given that Donohue's test is positive, is 37%. Give 2 points for any value below 50%. Most respondents will not take into account that the base rate is only 3%; so the test, even one with a 95% sensitivity and 95% specificity, has a positive predictive value less than 95% (Eddy, 1982, p. 253; Meehl, 1973, p. 232).

The probability that abuse has occurred, given the Donohue's Family Positive ST score, P(A/POS), is:

$$P(A/POS) = \frac{P(pos/A)P(A)}{P(pos/A)P(A) + P(pos/nonA)P(nonA)}$$

$$= \frac{(.95)(.03)}{(.95)(.03) + (.05)(.97)}$$

$$= .37$$

where

$P(pos/A) =$ the probability that, if an abuse has occurred, the test will correctly detect it (true positive rate)

$P(A) =$ prior probability, or base rate, of abuse in the sample population

$P(nonA) =$ the rate of nonabuse in the sampled population [1 − P(A)] or [1 − .03]

$P(pos/nonA) =$ the probability that, if the client was not abused, the ST score will incorrectly predict abuse (false positive).

23. selection bias, biased selection of clients. RARC's 75% treatment success may be due to the way higher functioning clients selected themselves to be treated at RARC (Grinnell, 1985, p. 241; Michael, Boyce, & Wilcox, 1984, p. 31).

Using the PTF for Research Purposes

Although the instrument was designed as a teaching tool, the PTF may be used to evaluate whether students are learning to apply research concepts to practice. For example, it might be interesting to see if those who score high on the Kirk-Rosenblatt Research Inventory (Kirk, 1985) also score high on PTF. Apparently, measures to evaluate scientific reasoning about practice in social work and in other disciplines have not yet been developed: Reviews of instruments to measure critical thinking (Gibbs, 1985) and ability to reason scientifically (Mayer & Richmond, 1982) uncovered no such measures.

For use as a research instrument, use the scoring key to score responses. Experienced raters can score each PTF in about 6 minutes.

Key

All items are scored from 0 through 5 with the following weights:

0 = the item is not answered, or the item is not questioned in some specific way;

1 = the respondent phrases any specific objection to the validity of the item's statement;

2 = the respondent uses a key word as stated in the "key word" column;

1 = the answer raises approximately the same question as the one raised in the "explanation";

2 = the answer raises the same question that is raised in the "explanation."

Thus, if a respondent questions an item, uses a key word, and raises the same question as the one in the "explanation" column, give the respondent 5 points.

Reliability and Validity of PTF

For items 4–23, two scoring trials (on social work and nursing students) to measure agreement between independent raters (Gibbs & Werner, 1988) yielded a Pearson $r = .89$ for the first trial ($p < .0001$, $N = 21$), and a second trial also yielded $r = .89$ ($p < .0001$, $N = 31$). Spearman rho for independent scoring of each of the 20 items ranged from .46 to .99 ($\bar{x} = .78$, $SD = .13$) on the first trial, and ranged from .65 to .95 ($\bar{x} = .80$, $SD = .08$) for the second trial. John Gibson and Paula Nurius of the University of Washington at Seattle report a .88 Spearman *rho* for their trial.

PTF is based on the format of an instrument developed by Logan (1976). PTF is intended to measure ability to apply principles of research methods to social work practice. PTF's validity is based on case content for each item and literature to document principles of research methods. PTF is *not* expected to correlate with measures of knowledge about research methods. No correlation is expected because students may learn research concepts, but they still need special training to generalize research concepts to practice.

Note: References cited in the PTF Answers are listed at the end of Chapter 3.

CHAPTER 4

1. Contiguity. The key word in this example is "immediately." That is, event A (participation in the Survivor Group) occurred together in time and space concurrently with event B (improved self-esteem). The assumption is made that by occurring together there is a causal relationship between the two.

2. Priority (i.e., post hoc, after this, just because treatment precedes outcome). The key word in this example is "after." Event A (participation in the department's program for noncompliant patients) preceded event B (better compliance), so it is assumed that A caused B.

3. Association. A higher proportion of Triniteam participants were nondelinquent than was the proportion of nondelinquents among nonparticipants. Therefore, it is assumed that participation in Triniteam caused the difference in delinquency rates. This form of reasoning ignores potential confounders that may be the real cause which are associated with participation in the program.

4. Causal Chain Strength. Although it "makes sense" that event A caused event B according to what appears to be a logical relationship between these events, there may not be a causal relationship. Causal relationships that seem plausible need to be demonstrated through experimentation, the subject of following chapters.

5. Client Selection (IIC2)—Purposeful Selection by Social Worker. By selecting clients who have greater socioeconomic resources at the front end of treat-

ment, later posttreatment high success rates may reflect that high potential clients were selected into the program.

6. Client Selection (IIC1)—Self-Selection. Voluntary clients may have higher motivation to improve; thus, posttreatment success may reflect to a large extent initial strengths of volunteers. Be careful when claims of successful intervention concern volunteers.

7. Participation in Other Treatments Concurrently (IB). Because so many interventions occur concurrently, it is impossible to say with confidence which one may have caused the change.

8. Mortality (IID). The 30% lost to follow-up may be strikingly different in their suicidal ideation and behavior. A fair assessment of success rate implies that all who entered the intervention program be considered in success rates.

CHAPTER 6

1. Here is a slight revision of how the student (Shipley, 1989, p. 2) posed the first question and hypothesis:

   - Among UWEC freshmen who are randomly assigned to either of two, 2-hour AIDS prevention programs presented on September 25, or to a control group, will *both* experimental groups report a statistically significantly ($p < .05$) higher proportion of condom use during six months posttreatment on March 25, than control group students?

   - To formulate the hypothesis, merely move the word "will" to between "groups" and "report."

2. Here is how the student (Elmer, 1989, p. 2) posed this question and hypothesis about John:

   - Will John, a learning disabled student at North High School in Eau Claire, Wisconsin, have a higher rate of on-task behavior during the reinforcement of on-task behaviors during his second treatment period, from May 1 to May 16, than during his first baseline, from April 1 to April 16?

   - This question can be transformed to a hypothesis by moving "will" from the beginning to just before "have a higher."

CHAPTER 7

1. Proportion of agreement = .74 or 74%.
2. Kappa = .47
3. This kappa does not exceed .70.
4. It is difficult to imagine judgment where interrater agreement could be as important as this one in any discipline, including medicine. When making judgments in infant adoption, the rest of the child's life will be profoundly affected by the acceptable for placement/not acceptable for placement judg-

ment. Consistency in such judgments is important to be fair to applicants and to judge the accuracy of predictions in a follow-up study.

CHAPTER 9

1. Denicola and Sandler (1980):
   4,4,4,4,4,0,0,0,0,4,5,5,4,0,10,48.
   (Note that this is a single-subject study.)
   Liberman and Eckman (1981):
   4,4,4,4,4,20,0,0,0,4,0,0,4,20,10,78.
   Hefner and Prochaska (1984):
   4,0,4,4,4,20,0,0,4,4,5,5,4,20,0,78.

2. Answers:
   a. ES1 = (67.9 − 65.2)/14.9 = .18
   b. ES1 = (38.2 − 38.2)/11.9 = 0
   c. ES1 = (259 − 226)/110 = .3
   d. ES2 = [(9/12)100] − [(9/12)100] = 0%
   e. ES2 = [(12/12)100] − [(8/12)100] = 33%

CHAPTER 10

Answers to the Experiment 1 exercise are in Figure C.1.

1. 25%

2. Sensitivity = 75%, specificity = 29%

3. Sensitivity = 61%, specificity = 73%

4. 27%

5. 44%

6. Protective service workers predict reabuse only 2% better than the prevalence rate, not much of an improvement (27% − 25% = 2%)

7. The actuarial method wins by a substantial margin over clinical prediction in this sample of 110 cases (44% positive predictive value over 27%)

8. 85%

9. In protective service work it is important to identify by a risk estimate test, those who are most likely to abuse a child (PPV) so they can be helped; it is also vital to know which are less likely to abuse (NPV) so stigma, expense, and family disruption can be avoided where intervention is not called for.

CHAPTER 11

1. This is a case example. The example tells a touching story about a member of the group. (Examining this case example as a form of evidence in no way negates the tragic sadness about the unfortunate victim's pain.) Based on this

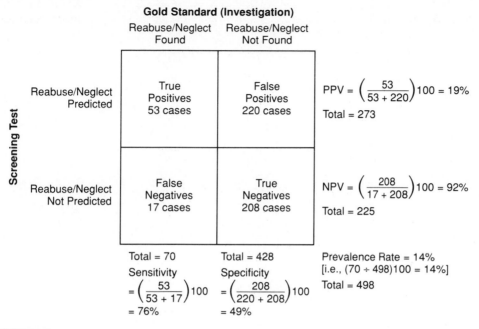

FIGURE C.1
Predictive value based on real data from a child-abuse-prediction study, prevalence rate 14%.

example and two others in the article, the authors conclude that the group effectively helps clients.

2. Ideally, to determine whether the support group affects its members, one would do a randomized trial that meets criteria listed in Chapter 5 for such trials.

INDEX

ABOUT THE AUTHOR

Professor Leonard E. Gibbs, ACSW, Ph.D., earned all of his degrees at the University of Wisconsin—Madison and has been a professor of social work at the University of Wisconsin—Eau Claire since 1977. Early in his career while in the United States Air Force, Professor worked as a clinician at hospitals in San Antonio, Texas, and in the Azores, islands near Portugal.

Dr. Gibbs has published widely in the areas of juvenile justice, substance abuse, clinical decision-making, and the use of computers in social work research and practice. In addition, he has served as principal investigator for many research and evaluation studies, including a randomized evaluation utilized to enhance critical thinking skills among faculty members and a quasi-experimental evaluation of alcoholic type by treatment interaction.

An avid cross-country skier, Dr. Gibbs recently participated in the Birkebeiner, a 55-kilometer race in Northern Wisconsin. His other hobbies include arrowhead crafting and canoeing with his family. He is married and the father of one son.